PLAYHOUSE WILLS, 1558–1642
*An edition of wills by Shakespeare
and his contemporaries in the London theatre*

This edition constitutes a new archive of source materials in the field of Elizabethan and Jacobean theatre. It is a collection of over one hundred wills left by those who participated in the life of the theatre—from actors and dramatists to carpenters and costumiers. The wills not only offer vital historical evidence but are also important human documents, testaments to the social, financial, religious and sentimental lives of Shakespeare's contemporaries.

Of the wills reprinted here, one third are newly discovered, and many of the rest printed for the first time from the original wills, thus preserving the vacillations and abandoned intentions of the testators.

E. A. J. Honigmann was Joseph Cowen Professor of English at the University of Newcastle-upon-Tyne until his retirement, and is a General Editor of *The Revels Plays* series.

Susan Brock is Librarian and Honorary Fellow of the Shakespeare Institute at the University of Birmingham.

The Revels Plays
COMPANION LIBRARY

E. A. J. HONIGMANN, J. R. MULRYNE
R. L. SMALLWOOD and PETER CORBIN general editors

For over thirty years *The Revels Plays* have offered the most authoritative editions of Elizabethan and Jacobean plays by authors other than Shakespeare. The *Companion Library* provides a fuller background to the main series by publishing worthwhile dramatic and non-dramatic material that will be essential for the serious student of the period.

Documents of the Rose Playhouse ed. RUTTER
Three Jacobean witchcraft plays ed. CORBIN, SEDGE
John Weever HONIGMANN*
Rare Sir William Davenant EDMOND*
'Art made tongue-tied by authority' CLARE*
The Oldcastle controversy: Sir John Oldcastle, Part I and The Famous victories of Henry V CORBIN, SEDGE*
Brawl ridiculous: Swordfighting in Shakespeare's plays CHARLES EDELMAN*
A textual companion to Doctor Faustus ERIC RASMUSSEN*

*these titles published in the USA by St. Martin's Press

THE REVELS PLAYS COMPANION LIBRARY

Playhouse wills
1558–1642

*An edition of wills by Shakespeare
and his contemporaries in the London theatre*

E. A. J. HONIGMANN
AND SUSAN BROCK

Manchester University Press

Copyright © E. A. J. Honigmann and Susan Brock 1993

The right of E. A. J. Honigmann and Susan Brock to be identified as the editors of this work has been asserted by them in accordance with the Copyright, Designs and Patents Act 1988.

Published by Manchester University Press
Altrincham Street, Manchester M1 7JA, UK
www.manchesteruniversitypress.co.uk

British Library Cataloguing-in-Publication Data is available

Library of Congress Cataloging-in-Publication Data is available

ISBN 978 0 7190 3017 8 paperback

First published by Manchester University Press 1993

This paperback edition first published 2015

The publisher has no responsibility for the persistence or accuracy of URLs for any external or third-party internet websites referred to in this book, and does not guarantee that any content on such websites is, or will remain, accurate or appropriate.

Printed by Lightning Source

CONTENTS

LIST OF FIGURES	*page* vi
GENERAL EDITORS' PREFACE	vii
PREFACE	viii
ACKNOWLEDGEMENTS	xii
CONVENTIONS AND ABBREVIATIONS	xiii
MAP OF LONDON PARISHES *c.* 1666	xviii
INTRODUCTION	1
Social history	2
The theatrical community	5
Wealth and finance	7
The personal voice	10
Testamentary procedure	11
Wills and the law	11
The making of the will	15
The form of the will	18
Probate	22
Conclusion	26
LIST OF TESTATORS by date of will or administration	31
LIST OF TESTATORS by occupation	33
DOCUMENTS	39
Wills	39
Some administrations of interest	227
Inventories	236
APPENDICES	245
1. Acting companies to 1642	245
2. Printed indexes to wills	248
INDEX OF PERSONS	251

LIST OF FIGURES

1. Parishes of London c.1666 From *A Survey of Documentary Sources for Property Holding in London before the Great Fire* by Derek Keene and Vanessa Harding, London, 1985, by permission of the London Record Society   xviii

Extracts from two holograph wills:

2. Alexander Cooke 1614 (PRO PROB10/311).   16
3. James Shirley 1666 (PRO PROB10/993)   16

4. Will of Richard Burbage written by Ralph Crane 1619 (PRO PROB1/32)   115

GENERAL EDITORS' PREFACE

Since the late 1950s the series known as the Revels Plays has provided for students of the English Renaissance drama carefully edited texts of the major Elizabethan and Jacobean plays. The series now includes some of the best known drama of the period and has continued to expand, both within its original field and, to a lesser extent, beyond it, to include some important plays from the earlier Tudor and from the Restoration periods. The Revels Plays Companion Library is intended to further this expansion and to allow for new developments.

The aim of the Companion Library is to provide students of the Elizabethan and Jacobean drama with a fuller sense of its background and context. The series includes volumes of a variety of kinds. Small collections of plays, by a single author or concerned with a single theme and edited in accordance with the principles of textual modernisation of the Revels Plays, offer a wider range of drama than the main series can include. Together with editions of masques, pageants, and the non-dramatic work of Elizabethan and Jacobean playwrights, these volumes make it possible, within the overall Revels enterprise, to examine the achievement of the major dramatists from a broader perspective. Other volumes provide a fuller context for the plays of the period by offering new collections of documentary evidence on Elizabethan theatrical conditions and on the performance of plays during that period and later. A third aim of the series is to offer modern critical interpretation, in the form of collections of essays or of monographs, of the dramatic achievement of the English Renaissance.

So wide a range of material necessarily precludes the standard format and uniform general editorial control which is possible in the original series of Revels Plays. To a considerable extent, therefore, treatment and approach are determined by the needs and intentions of individual volume editors. Within this rather ampler area, however, we hope that the Companion Library maintains the standards of scholarship which have for so long characterised the Revels Plays, and that it offers a useful enlargement of the work of the series in preserving, illuminating, and celebrating the drama of Elizabethan and Jacobean England.

E. A. J. HONIGMANN
J. R. MULRYNE
R. L. SMALLWOOD
PETER CORBIN

PREFACE

The idea for this collection of wills came to me some ten years ago, when I was working on wills for another project and first realised that a surprising number of published and unpublished playhouse wills had survived and that, brought together in a single volume, they would add significantly to our understanding of the Elizabethan theatre. (The term Elizabethan is here used to refer to the period 1558 to 1642.) It turned out to be a much bigger undertaking than I had imagined, for several reasons: no consolidated list of actors and others connected with the theatre is available; the wills are housed in many different archives, for some of which there are no published indexes; and, even if one knows roughly when an actor died and one finds his name in an index, more often than not one cannot prove that the testator was the actor, or the will discloses that he could not have been the actor. A complicating problem, soon obvious when one peruses this volume, is the unwillingness of the actors to describe themselves by their profession, as other testators did. Many actors were freemen of one of the London guilds, and described themselves as such ('citizen and goldsmith', etc.), or as gentlemen or yeomen; with very few exceptions they preferred not to call themselves 'players'—which, given the social conditions of the time, is understandable but, from a modern point of view, decidedly unhelpful.

After two or three years I began to think that *Playhouse Wills* would never be completed—when, most fortunately, Robert Smallwood suggested that I join forces with Susan Brock, whose expertise as an archivist brought support where it was most needed. The endorsements, sentences and notes attached to our wills are usually in abbreviated legal Latin, and many of the wills are damaged by time and hard to decipher. We agreed that Dr Brock would take charge of all transcriptions and that I would continue to search for more wills. Nevertheless, we have frequently crossed these boundaries, and we have checked each other's work—in short, we have collaborated as fully as we could. In the Introduction Dr Brock wrote the sections on testamentary procedure (pp. 11–25) and I wrote those on social history; here and elsewhere we have not signed our separate contributions but have consulted closely and, again, we accept joint responsibility.

Our original intention was to include actors who performed in the London professional theatre in the period 1558 to 1642. We were aware that some actors' widows left wills that refer to the theatre or to their husbands' colleagues, and that others connected with the theatre might also be included, thus giving a more rounded view of the life of the theatre as a social organism. Our collection has outgrown the original plan, for it now contains the wills of the great variety of men and women who participated in the life of the London theatres, and of some of the former boys of the boys' companies and their masters or managers (professionals in their own way). We have cast our net widely, as far as the Masters of the Revels, the officials who were responsible for the control of the theatre and answered directly to the Lord Chamberlain. We also make room for a few less defensible items—for instance, the will of Edward Pudsey (1612), an enthusiastic theatre-goer whose notebooks contain extracts from plays, even from an unpublished play, *Othello*, first printed in 1622 (he refers to his precious notebooks in his will, and he may well be the father of the minor actor Edward Pudsey).

We have not included the wills of theatrical patrons, as theirs rarely refer, even indirectly, to theatrical affairs. (Lord Hunsdon, the Lord Chamberlain, may have had his players in mind when in July 1596 he recommended his 'poor servants' to his son, some of whom he was 'able to do nothing for', being in financial difficulties when he died.)[1] We have largely—though not entirely—excluded 'gentlemen' dramatists who, we assume, did not think of the theatre as their profession (e.g. Sackville and Norton, authors of *Gorboduc*, Sir John Denham, Sir Jasper Mayne). Our guiding principles have been to concentrate on those who had a continuing or professional relationship with the London theatres at any time between 1558 and 1642 and, as far as possible, to print their wills in entirety, thus illustrating the lifestyle of the rich and the poor; because of pressures of space, some wills of those on the fringes of the theatrical community are, however, presented in abstract. Admittedly we have not been wholly consistent, and for this we blame the wealth and interest of the material available.

Readers should be warned that we are also very conscious of further failings. Although we include many hitherto unpublished wills, we take it for granted that we have missed others. We would, of course, like to hear from anyone who can add to our collection, for we look forward to future editions which may reap the benefit. All such help will be acknowledged.

How did we go about our self-inflicted task, hunting for unknown wills? We started with the lists of actors provided by E. K. Chambers, G. E. Bentley and Edwin Nungezer,[2] supplemented with some later publications, e.g. G. E. Bentley's *The Profession of Player in Shakespeare's Time*, and we looked for these names in the published indexes of wills. One name usually led to another, or to several others. We did not find the will of Aaron Holland, who built the Red Bull playhouse, but administration of the estate of Aaron Holland of Clerkenwell was granted to his widow Elizabeth (A1631), and the will of Elizabeth Holland, widow, of Clerkenwell, survives and contains references to known actors: accordingly, we print her will (1631). Robert Leigh of St James, Clerkenwell, in his will (1629) names his cousin Joan Baxter, wife of Richard Baxter of Clerkenwell; the actor Richard Baxter and his wife Joan seem to have lived in Clerkenwell (Bentley II, 360–2); Leigh also names his loving friend Mr Robert Treat, goldsmith, who had been an overseer and loved friend of the actor Robert Armin (1615)—and this is why we think that Leigh was 'probably' Robert Lee, the actor and joint-lessee of the Fortune playhouse, who lived in Clerkenwell Close in 1623 (Bentley II, 496–7). The more common the name the greater the need for corroborative evidence, such as a connection with known actors or their friends—otherwise the trail goes cold.

Over the years we have examined thousands of wills. We excluded some, even though the name and the date seemed right, because we were not satisfied that they were definitely playhouse wills; and we have included a few where the balance of probability seemed to us to tip the other way. The large majority of those here printed, however, can claim to have playhouse connections that are self-evident and beyond reproach.

Annotation has been kept to the minimum, or, as some will think, below the minimum. Given the space available, we have decided to print as many wills as we could, imposing a self-denying ordinance on annotation. Instead of offering biographical accounts of every testator we simply refer the reader to standard works. We do not attempt to identify all of the hundreds of names cited in the wills (our index helps to draw attention to all that appear several times), nor do we explain every obscurity. We note the 'playhouse' names and, where a person or place is of particular interest in the context of this collection, we add brief explanations or cross-references which are not readily available, but, again, we must stress that much more can be done. Readers will find that our collection is in effect a new archive, one that still awaits systematic study: comparing our brief notes on Shakespeare's will and the more detailed analyses already in print, one sees that this volume offers challenges and opportunities for further research—a form of research that brings many disappointments but also much curious information and, now and then, enlightenment.

E. H.
August 1992

NOTES

1 Will of Henry Carey, Lord Hunsdon, dated 21 July, proved 26 July 1596 (PRO PROB11/88 fo. 14v).
2 For full references see the list of abbreviations.

ACKNOWLEDGEMENTS

We are grateful to the Public Record Office, to the Corporation of London (Guildhall Library and Greater London Record Office) and to the Niedersächsisches Staatsarchiv at Wolfenbüttel, for permission to publish documents in their keeping, as indicated in our notes, and to their officials for help and advice; to the officials at Dulwich College, Lambeth Palace Library, Goldsmiths' Hall and Grocers' Hall for sending photocopies and answering our enquiries; to the British Academy and to the University of Birmingham for grants towards the costs of travel and photocopying. In addition we are greatly indebted to colleagues in the university libraries of Birmingham and Newcastle-upon-Tyne for their friendly service and help.

The following individuals kindly answered our letters and helped in other ways: Mr John Banks, Dr Nigel Bawcutt, Professor Herbert Berry, Professor S. P. Cerasano, Professor Mark Eccles, Miss Mary Edmond, Mr A. P. P. Honigmann, Professor William Ingram, Dr Elmar Neuss, Mr Philip Riden, Professor Willem Schrickx, Mr I. A. Shapiro, Professor Kurt Tetzeli von Rosador, Professor Stanley Wells, Professor Glynne Wickham. We wish to thank particularly Gervase Hood whose willingness to help we exploited shamelessly.

Finally we have to acknowledge our very special gratitude to Dr Robert Smallwood, our general editor, and to Anita Roy of Manchester University Press, for much detailed comment and for their encouragement. And to our spouses, Elsie and Brian, who fortunately did not foresee—any more than we did—that our project would take up so many years.

CONVENTIONS AND ABBREVIATIONS

The wills are arranged chronologically according to the date on which they were signed and witnessed. The wills of significant figures and those of particular interest have been transcribed in full from the originals or office copies where these are extant; in the case of lacunae or illegibility register copies have been consulted and emendations made accordingly. These cases are signalled in the notes. Wills that we judge to be less central to the concerns of this collection are presented as abstracts which preserve all names of persons and places in the original spelling, except for capitalisation. Inventories and administrations will be found in separate sections. References to documents in the introduction and notes are by date printed in bold type (prefix A indicates an administration, In an inventory).

Each document is followed by information about its present location, its status (register entry, office copy or original will), its physical appearance (except for register copies), information about the grant of probate or administration, the existence of the earliest printed transcripts, and a brief biography of the testator drawn from the standard sources. Superior numbers in the text signal textual notes. A commentary keyed by asterisks provides glosses and draws attention to new facts. Dates in headings and notes have been modernised.

Transcripts are in semi-diplomatic form in order to provide for scholars an accurate record of the documents included. They retain the punctuation, paragraphing and spelling of the original, including the use of u/v, i/j, c/t, and ff. I/J is transcribed uniformly as I. All unambiguous abbreviations are expanded (supplied letters being indicated by italic type). Where meaning or form is uncertain abbreviations are retained and indicated with an apostrophe. Exceptions to this practice are as follows: names in signatures, forms currently in use (Mr, St, &c), ordinal numbers (vjto), and currency (l or li: *libra* (pound), s: *solidus* (shilling), d: *denarius* (penny)), where MS forms are retained and superior letters dropped. In case of currency a space is inserted after the number. Unless the marks of witnesses and testators are particularly distinctive they are rendered as X. Page breaks are given in bold type in parentheses. Deletions are indicated by square brackets. Insertions are included in the appropriate place in the text, enclosed in curly brackets. Accidental obliterations are indicated by diamond brackets with conjectural readings supplied inside them.

SUMMARY OF TRANSCRIPTION CONVENTIONS

italic   editorial expansions of abbreviated forms
[. . .]   material deleted in MS
{ . . . }   material inserted in MS
< . . . >   material illegible in MS
(. . .)   parentheses in MS

ABBREVIATIONS

ACL	Archdeaconry Court of London
ACM	Archdeaconry Court of Middlesex
ACS	Archdeaconry Court of Surrey
admon	administration
CCL	Commissary Court of London
co.	county
ConCL	Consistory Court of London
GL	Guildhall Library London
GLRO	Greater London Record Office
OffC	Office Copy
OW	Original Will
pa.	parish
PAB	Probate Act Book
PCC	Prerogative Court of Canterbury
PRO	Public Record Office
RegC	Register Copy

STANDARD WORKS

Baldwin, *Organization*   T. W. Baldwin, *The Organization and Personnel of the Shakespearean Company*, Princeton, 1927

Bentley   G. E. Bentley, *The Jacobean and Caroline Stage*, 7 vols, Oxford, 1941–68

Bentley, *Profession*   G. E. Bentley, *The Profession of Player in Shakespeare's Time*, Princeton, 1984

Berry, *Boar's Head Playhouse*   Herbert Berry, *The Boar's Head Playhouse*, Washington, DC, 1986

Berry, 'Handlist'   Herbert Berry, 'A handlist of documents about the Theatre in Shoreditch' in *The First Public Playhouse: The Theatre in Shoreditch, 1576–1598*, ed. H. Berry, Montreal, 1979, pp. 97–133

Berry, *Playhouses*   Herbert Berry, *Shakespeare's Playhouses*, New York, 1987

Boswell   *The Plays and Poems of William Shakespeare*, ed. J. Boswell, 21 vols, London, 1821

Cerasano, 'New ... wills'   S. P. Cerasano, 'New Renaissance players' wills', *Modern Philology*, LXXXII, 1985, pp. 299–304

Chalmers, *Apology*   George Chalmers, *An Apology for the Believers in the Shakspeare-papers*, London, 1797

Chalmers, *Supplemental Apology*   George Chalmers, *A Supplemental Apology for the Believers in the Shakspeare-papers*, London, 1799

Chambers   E. K. Chambers, *The Elizabethan Stage*, 4 vols, Oxford, 1923

Collier, *Memoirs*   J. P. Collier, *Memoirs of the Principal Actors in the Plays of Shakespeare*, Shakespeare Society, London, 1846

DNB   *Dictionary of National Biography*

Dutton, *Mastering the Revels*   Richard Dutton, *Mastering the Revels: The Regulation and Censorship of English Renaissance Drama*, Basingstoke, 1991

Eccles, 'Actors I'   Mark Eccles, 'Elizabethan actors I: A–D', *Notes and Queries*, CCXXXVI, 1991, pp. 38–49
Eccles, 'Actors II'   Mark Eccles, 'Elizabethan actors II: E–J', *Notes and Queries*, CCXXXVI, 1991, pp. 454–61
Eccles, 'Brief lives'   Mark Eccles, 'Brief lives': Tudor and Stuart authors, *Studies in Philology*, LXXIX, no. 4, 1982
Eccles, *Shakespeare*   Mark Eccles, *Shakespeare in Warwickshire*, Madison, WIS, 1961
Feuillerat   Albert Feuillerat, *Documents Relating to the Office of the Revels in the Time of Queen Elizabeth*, Materialien zur Kunde des älteren englischen Dramas, 21, Louvain, 1908
Greg, *Henslowe's Diary*   *Henslowe's Diary*, ed. W. W. Greg, 2 vols, London, 1904–8
Highfill et al.   Philip H. Highfill, Kalman A. Burnim and Edward A. Langhans, *A Biographical Dictionary of Actors, Actresses, Musicians, Dancers, Managers, and Other Stage Personnel in London, 1660–1800*, Carbondale, IL, 1973–, vol. 1–
Henslowe's Diary   *Henslowe's Diary*, ed. R. A. Foakes and R. T. Rickert, Cambridge, 1961
Hillebrand, *Child Actors*   H. N. Hillebrand, *The Child Actors: A Chapter in Elizabethan Stage History*, Urbana, IL, 1926
Hillebrand, 'Early history'   H. N. Hillebrand, 'The early history of the Chapel Royal', *Modern Philology*, XVIII, 1920, pp. 233–68
Holdsworth   W. S. Holdsworth, *A History of English Law*, 4th ed., 9 vols, London, 1935
Honigmann, 'Lost Years'   E. A. J. Honigmann, *Shakespeare: The 'Lost Years'*, Manchester, 1985
Hotson   Leslie Hotson, *The Commonwealth and Restoration Stage*, Cambridge, MA, 1928
Ingram, *London Life*   William Ingram, *A London Life in the Brazen Age: Francis Langley 1548–1602*, Cambridge, MA, 1978
London Stage   *The London Stage 1660–1800*, ed. W. Van Lennep and others, Part 1 1660–1700, Carbondale, IL, 1965
LPS   *Local Population Studies*
McKerrow, *Dictionary*   *A Dictionary of Printers and Booksellers in England, Scotland and Ireland, and of Foreign Printers of English Books 1557–1640*, ed. R. B. McKerrow, London, 1910
Malone (1790)   *Plays and Poems of William Shakspeare*, ed. Edmond Malone, 10 vols, London, 1790
MLN   *Modern Language Notes*
MLR   *Modern Language Review*
MP   *Modern Philology*
Murray   J. T. Murray, *English Dramatic Companies 1558–1642*, 2 vols, London, 1910
New Grove   *The New Grove Dictionary of Music and Musicians*, ed. S. Sadie, 20 vols, London, 1980
N&Q   *Notes and Queries*
NUS   *Nebraska University Studies*

Nungezer   Edwin Nungezer, *A Dictionary of Actors and of Other Persons Associated with the Public Representation of Plays in England before 1642*, Cornell Studies in English, 13, New Haven, 1929
PBSA   *Papers of the Bibliographical Society of America*
Plomer, *Dictionary*   H. R. Plomer, *A Dictionary of the Booksellers and Printers Who Were at Work in England, Scotland and Ireland from 1641 to 1667*, London, 1907
Plomer, *Dictionary . . . 1668 to 1725*   H. R. Plomer, *A Dictionary of the Printers and Booksellers Who Were at Work in England, Scotland and Ireland from 1668 to 1725*, London, 1922
Records of the Nation   *Records of the Nation: The Public Records Office 1838–1988, the British Record Society 1888–1988*, ed. G. H. Martin and P. Spufford, Woodbridge, 1990
RES   *Review of English Studies*
Schrickx, *Foreign Envoys*   Willem Schrickx, *Foreign Envoys and Travelling Players in the Age of Shakespeare and Jonson*, Wetteren, 1986
'Sharers' Papers'   'Sharers' papers' in 'Dramatic Records: The Lord Chamberlain's Office', *Malone Society Collections II*, London, 1913–31, pp. 321–416 (pp. 362–73)
ShS   *Shakespeare Survey*
Sisson, *Boar's Head*   C. J. Sisson, *The Boar's Head Theatre*, ed. S. W. Wells, London, 1972
Sisson, *Lost Plays*   C. J. Sisson, *Lost Plays of Shakespeare's Age*, Cambridge, 1936
Sisson, 'Notes'   C. J. Sisson, 'Notes on early Stuart stage history', *Modern Language Review*, XXXVII, 1942, pp. 25–36
SP   *Studies in Philology*
SQ   *Shakespeare Quarterly*
Stopes, *Burbage*   C. C. Stopes, *Burbage and Shakespeare's Stage*, London, 1913
Swinburne   Henry Swinburne, *A Briefe Treatise of Testaments and Last Willes Newly Corrected and Augmented*, London, 1611
Wallace, *Evolution*   C. W. Wallace, *The Evolution of the English Drama up to Shakespeare*, Berlin, 1912
Wallace   C. W. Wallace, *The First London Theatre: Materials for a History*, University of Nebraska Studies, 13, Lincoln, NEB, 1913
Warner   G. F. Warner, *Catalogue of the Manuscripts and Muniments of Alleyn's College of God's Gift at Dulwich*, London, 1881
West   William West, *The First Part of Simboleography*, London, 1610
Young, *Dulwich*   William Young, *The History of Dulwich College*, 2 vols, London, 1889

MAP OF LONDON PARISHES c.1666

(Figure 1 *overleaf*)

The numbers represent parishes: only those marked * in the list are shown. Numbers in parentheses represent parishes, or parts of parishes, which had been suppressed, and their approximate location. The letters represent extra-parochial precincts or liberties as follows: A, Furnival's Inn; B, Barnard's Inn; C, Thavie's Inn; D, Serjeants' Inn; E, Temple; F, Whitefriars; G, Bridewell (formerly part of 46); H, St Katharine's Hospital. Southwark parishes, St George the Martyr, St Olave, St Saviour and St Thomas, are not listed or shown.

  1 St Agnes (alias 23, 24)
*2 St Alban Wood Street
  3 All Hallows (unspecified)
*4 All Hallows Barking (by the Tower; alias 102)
*5 All Hallows Bread Street (Watling Street)
  6 All Hallows Colemanchurch (alias 50, 77)
  7 All Hallows Cornhill (probably identical with 9)
  8 All Hallows Fenchurch (alias 60, 106, 107)
*9 All Hallows Gracechurch (Lombard Street; probably identical with 7)
*10 All Hallows the Great (*ad fenum*, at the Hay Wharf, in the Ropery; earlier *Semannescyrce*)
*11 All Hallows Honey Lane
*12 All Hallows the Less (on the Cellars, on the Solars)
*13 All Hallows Staining
*14 All Hallows on the Wall (London Wall; 29 added, 1442)
*15 St Alphage
 16 St Amand (alias 159, 160)
 17 St Andrew (unspecified)
*18 St Andrew Castle Baynard (by the Wardrobe)
*19 St Andrew Cornhill (*atte Knappe*, Undershaft; 101 added, 1565)
*20 St Andrew Holborn
*21 St Andrew Hubbard (Eastcheap, towards the Tower)
 22 St Anne (unspecified)
*23 St Anne & St Agnes (alias 1, 24)
 24 St Anne Aldersgate (alias 1, 23)
*25 St Anne Blackfriars (created after the Dissolution from Blackfriars precinct)
*26 St Antonin (later St Antholin)
(*27) St Audoen (alias St Ewen, St Owen; taken into 47, 1547)
 28 St Augustine (unspecified)
(*29) St Augustine Papey (on the Wall; joined to 14, 1442)
*30 St Augustine by St Paul (*parvus*, Watling Street)
 31 St Bartholomew (unspecified)

xviii   Map of London parishes

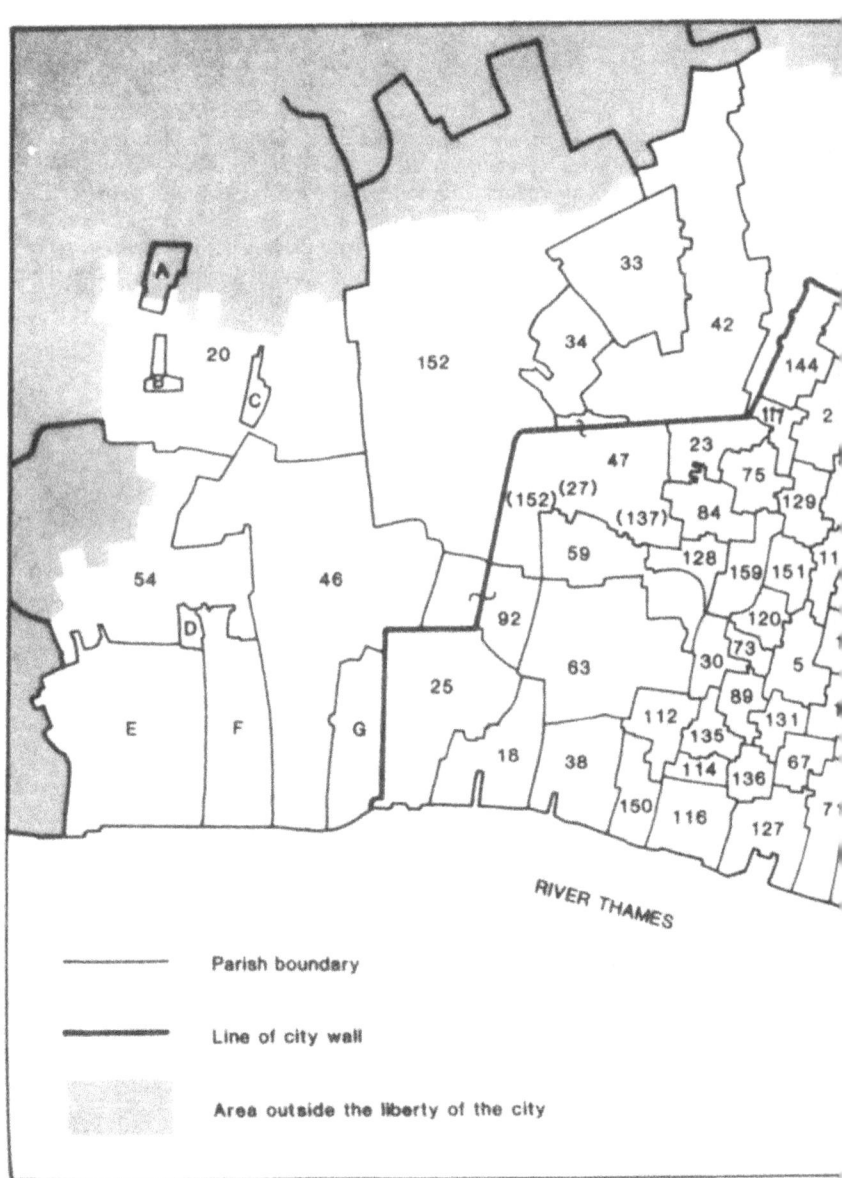

Map of London parishes xix

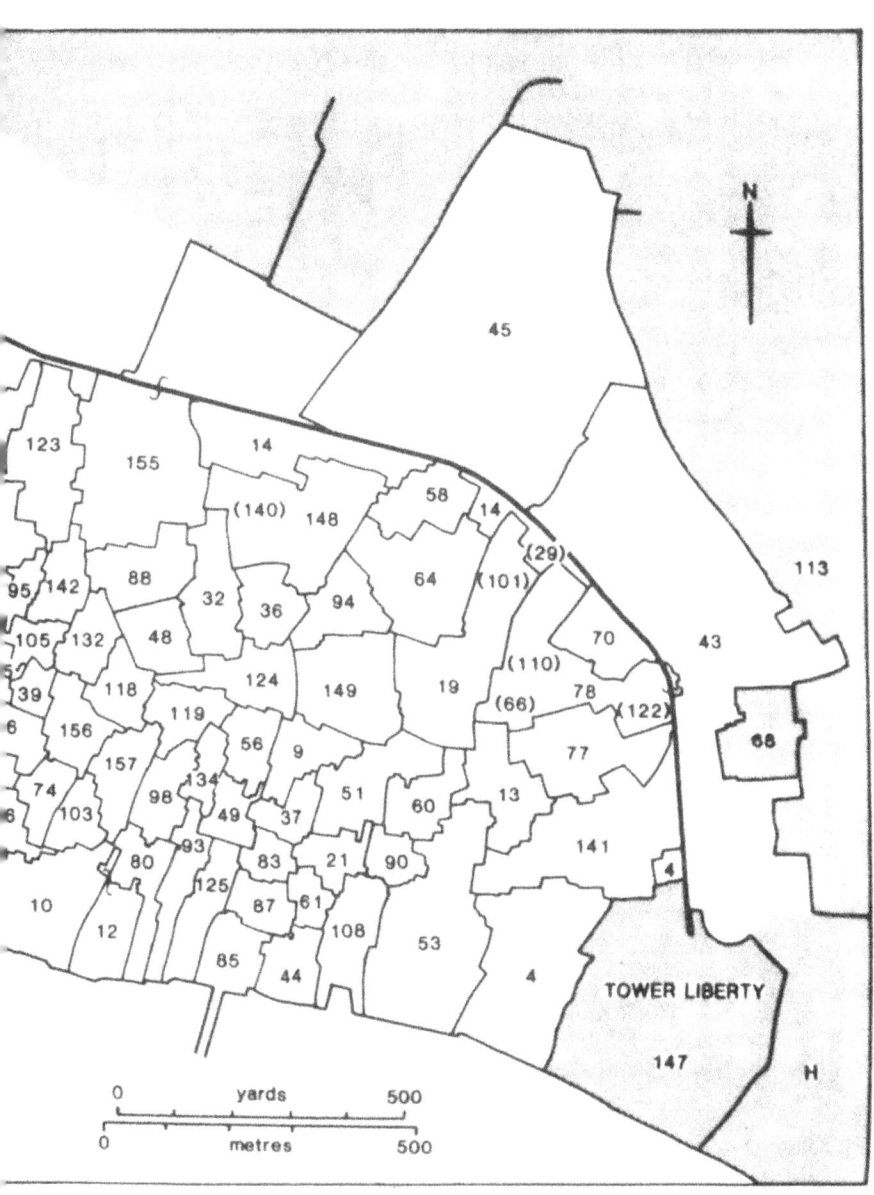

*32 St Bartholomew the Little (by the Exchange)
*33 St Bartholomew the Great (created after Dissolution from precinct of St Bartholomew's Priory)
*34 St Bartholomew the Less (created after Dissolution from precinct of St Bartholomew's Hospital)
 35 St Benet (unspecified)
*36 St Benet Fink
*37 St Benet Gracechurch
*38 St Benet Paul's Wharf (Hithe, Woodwharf)
*39 St Benet Sherehog (alias 40, 153)
 40 St Benet & St Sithe (alias 39, 153)
 41 St Botolph (unspecified)
*42 St Botolph without Aldersgate
*43 St Botolph without Aldgate
*44 St Botolph Billingsgate
*45 St Botolph without Bishopsgate
*46 St Bride (Fleet Street)
*47 Christ Church Newgate Street (created 1547 from Grey Friars precinct, 27, 137, intramural part of 152)
*48 St Christopher (le Stocks)
*49 St Clement (Candlewick Street, Eastcheap)
 50 Colemanchurch (alias 6, 77)
*51 St Dionis Backchurch
 52 St Dunstan (unspecified)
*53 St Dunstan in the East (towards the Tower)
*54 St Dunstan in the West (Fleet Street)
 55 St Edmund (unspecified)
*56 St Edmund Lombard Street (King and Martyr)
 57 St Edmund without Newgate (alias 152)
*58 St Ethelburga
*59 St Faith (by St Paul's)
*60 St Gabriel (Fenchurch; alias 8, 106, 107)
*61 St George (Botolph Lane, Eastcheap)
*62 St Giles Cripplegate
*63 St Gregory (by St Paul's)
*64 St Helen (Bishopsgate)
 65 Holy Trinity (unspecified)
(*66) Holy Trinity Aldgate (absorbed by 78 or precinct of Holy Trinity Priory)
*67 Holy Trinity the Less
*68 Holy Trinity Minories (created after the Dissolution from the Minoresses' precinct)
 69 St James (unspecified)
*70 St James Duke's Place (created 17c from former precinct of Holy Trinity Priory)
*71 St James Garlickhithe (Vintry)
 72 St John (unspecified)
*73 St John the Evangelist (Watling Street; earlier 162)
*74 St John Walbrook

Map of London parishes

- *75 St John Zachary
- 76 St Katharine (unspecified)
- *77 St Katharine Coleman (alias 6, 50)
- *78 St Katharine Cree (Christ Church)
- 79 St Lawrence (unspecified)
- *80 St Lawrence Candlewick Street (Pountney)
- *81 St Lawrence Jewry
- 82 St Leonard (unspecified)
- *83 St Leonard Eastcheap
- *84 St Leonard Foster Lane
- *85 St Magnus (Bridge, the Martyr)
- 86 St Margaret (unspecified)
- *87 St Margaret Bridge Street (New Fish Street)
- *88 St Margaret Lothbury
- *89 St Margaret Moses (Friday Street)
- *90 St Margaret Pattens
- 91 St Martin (unspecified)
- *92 St Martin Ludgate
- *93 St Martin Orgar (Candlewick Street)
- *94 St Martin Outwich
- *95 St Martin Pomary (Ironmonger Lane)
- *96 St Martin Vintry (Bermanchurch)
- 97 St Mary (unspecified)
- *98 St Mary Abchurch
- *99 St Mary Aldermanbury
- *100 St Mary Aldermary
- (*101) St Mary Axe (joined to 19, 1565)
- 102 St Mary de Berkyngcherch (alias 4)
- *103 St Mary Bothaw
- *104 St Mary le Bow (de Arcubus)
- *105 St Mary Colechurch
- 106 St Mary Fenchurch (alias 8, 60, 107)
- 107 St Mary & St Gabriel Fenchurch (alias 8, 60, 106)
- *108 St Mary at Hill
- 109 St Mary Magdalen (unspecified)
- (*110) St Mary Magdalen Aldgate (absorbed by 78 or precinct of Holy Trinity Priory)
- *111 St Mary Magdalen Milk Street
- *112 St Mary Magdalen Old Fish Street (in (nova) piscaria, Westpiscaria; earlier 161)
- *113 St Mary Matfellon (Whitechapel)
- *114 St Mary Mounthaw
- 115 St Mary Olaf (alias 144)
- *116 St Mary Somerset
- *117 St Mary Staining
- *118 St Mary Woolchurch (Newchurch)
- *119 St Mary Woolnoth
- *120 St Matthew Friday Street

Map of London parishes

- 121 St Michael (unspecified)
- (*122) St Michael Aldgate (absorbed by 78 or precinct of Holy Trinity Priory)
- *123 St Michael Bassishaw
- *124 St Michael Cornhill
- *125 St Michael Crooked Lane (Candlewick Street)
- *126 St Michael Paternoster (Paternoster Royal, in the Riole)
- *127 St Michael Queenhithe (*Ripa Regine*)
- *128 St Michael le Querne (*ad bladum, ubi bladum venditur*, atte Corne, *in foro*)
- *129 St Michael Wood Street (Huggin Lane)
- 130 St Mildred (unspecified)
- *131 St Mildred Bread Street
- *132 St Mildred Poultry (Walbrook)
- 133 St Nicholas (unspecified)
- *134 St Nicholas Acon (Hakon)
- *135 St Nicholas Cole Abbey (Old Fish Street, *in piscaria, Westpiscaria*)
- *136 St Nicholas Olave (Bernard, ? *in piscaria*; alias *139*)
- (*137) St Nicholas in the Shambles (alias *143*; taken into *47*, 1547)
- 138 St Olave (unspecified)
- 139 St Olave Bread Street (alias *136*)
- (*140) St Olave Broad Street (absorbed by Austin Friars precinct and later *148*)
- *141 St Olave Hart Street (Crutched Friars, Mark Lane, by the Tower)
- *142 St Olave Old Jewry
- 143 St Olave in the Shambles (alias *137*)
- *144 St Olave Silver Street (Cripplegate, Monkwell Street; alias *115*)
- *145 St Pancras (Soper Lane)
- *146 St Peter (unspecified)
- *147 St Peter in the Bailey (in the Tower, *ad Vincula*)
- *148 St Peter Broad Street (the Poor; incl. former Austin Friars precinct and *140* from 16c)
- *149 St Peter Cornhill
- *150 St Peter Paul's Wharf (the Less)
- *151 St Peter Westcheap (Wood Street)
- *152 St Sepulchre (without Newgate; alias *57*; part taken into *47*, 1547)
- 153 St Sithe (alias *39, 40*)
- 154 St Stephen (unspecified)
- *155 St Stephen Coleman Street
- *156 St Stephen Walbrook
- *157 St Swithin (Candlewick Street, London Stone)
- *158 St Thomas the Apostle
- *159 St Vedast (Foster Lane; alias *16, 160*)
- 160 St Vedast & St Amand (alias *16, 159*)
- 161 St Wandrille (later *112*)
- 162 St Werburga (later *73*)

Map of London parishes c. 1666 (from *A Survey of Documentary Sources for Property Holding in London before the Great Fire* by Derek Keene and Vanessa Harding, London, 1985), by permission of London Record Society. (A street map of the City of London c. 1600 can be found in John Stow, *Survey of London*, ed. C. L. Kingsford, 2 vols, Oxford, 1908.)

Introduction

Edmond Malone in the eighteenth century recognised the importance of actors' wills, publishing several in his edition of Shakespeare (1790). Over the years, more wills were discovered and published; G. E. Bentley printed eighteen 'wills of theatrical interest' (twenty-one pages in Volume II of *The Jacobean and Caroline Stage*, 1941), and others continued the search.[1] Malone and Bentley, however, and many of their successors, usually printed their versions from the 'register copy', the official record of every will retained by the ecclesiastical authorities. Here, as in other contemporary copies, the clerks edited out deletions and irregularities, omitted endorsements, mistranscribed, changed spellings (especially of proper names) in order to produce a fair copy of the testator's final dispensations, for the testator's abandoned intentions were of no significance after probate was granted. Biographers can therefore learn much more from the original wills, as may be seen from Shirley's (**1666**) or Shakespeare's (**1616**). The signature of the testator and of witnesses, only found in original wills, can also clinch an identification; and of course some original wills are in the hand of the testator or of an identifiable individual—so there are many reasons for our decision to print from the original wills, even though register copies are much easier to find. Not all of the originals have survived, and some of those officially classed with original wills are actually contemporary copies; nevertheless we—and the archivists in some of the record offices—were pleasantly surprised by the large proportion of originals that we were able to track down, and that are now published for the first time.

Taken as a collection, these wills tell us much about the personality of the testators, about the relationships of actors and others concerned with theatrical matters, about individual transactions, and about the social history of the theatre. The new light they throw on social history is particularly valuable, since the professional theatre developed so rapidly in the period 1558–1642, as did society at large, advancing from the

Tudor settlement towards civil war, the closing of all theatres, and the Commonwealth. The wills bear the claw-marks of religion and the rise of capitalism, to borrow a famous phrase, reflecting the preoccupations of their period, and they also show that the Church and the theatre were by no means as hostile to one another as is sometimes alleged (cf. p. 5).

SOCIAL HISTORY

We begin with wills as reflectors of social history. Each testator usually identified himself or herself by name, parish, and by profession or rank (if a man) or by marital status (if a woman). Actors tended to be yeomen or gentlemen, or something lower; Edward Alleyn was the only former actor who had the right to call himself esquire. What did these labels mean?

Social boundaries change as society changes. In our period there are many observations on the social classes that testators claimed for themselves—not entirely consistent with one another, yet welcome as general indicators. William Harrison wrote in the middle years of Queen Elizabeth's reign that 'we in England divide our people commonly into four sorts, as gentlemen, citizens or burgesses, yeomen, and artificers or labourers'.[2] The gentlemen included the nobility down to knights, esquires and plain gentlemen. Citizens 'have next place to gentlemen', are 'free within the cities' and rich enough to 'bear office'. Yeomen are 'freemen born English', who 'may dispend of their own free land' £6 or more annually. The fourth class included labourers, poor husbandmen and all poor tradesmen.

No man could be a knight by succession: knights 'be not borne but made'. On the other hand, esquires 'be all those which beare armes [i.e. have a coat of arms] . . . which to beare is a testimonie of the nobilitie or race from whence they do come'.[3] Thomas Wilson reckoned in 1600 that England contained about five hundred knights, each worth £1,000 to £2,000 per annum, and about sixteen thousand esquires, each worth £500 to £1,000 per annum.[4] The younger brothers of armorial families would be gentlemen, and others could achieve this rank and a coat of arms by bettering themselves (e.g. by becoming university graduates or holding civic offices). Nicholas Brend (**1601**), Philip Henslowe (**1616**) and Edward Alleyn (**1626**) were esquires because each was the 'lord' of a manor. For our purposes the following divisions are significant: the Master of the Revels was always a knight or esquire; leading sharers in the acting companies usually described themselves as gentlemen or citizens; other actors were yeomen or citizens, or nothing at all.

Introduction 3

The London guilds, of course, allowed members who had become freemen in one company to practise in another, and not a few actors or former actors described themselves as 'citizen and vintner', or the like. Several guilds seem to have had close contacts with the theatre: the goldsmiths, as actors (e.g. Robert Armin (**1615**), John Lowin, Andrew Cane) and investors; grocers and watermen, many of whom lived in Southwark. The acting companies, however, had no guild of their own, even though some testators refer to other actors as their former masters or apprentices (e.g. Phillips (**1605**), Cooke (**1614**), Hovell (**1615**)). Precisely what was involved when a young actor was 'apprenticed' is not known, but some at least of the apprentices were formally registered with their master's guild. We learn from Elizabeth Holland's will (**1631**) that she left forty shillings to 'Arthur Savill Apprentize vnto Mr Cayne Gooldsmyth'. Arthur Savill and Andrew Cane both had parts in Marmion's *Holland's Leaguer* in December 1631, Savill as a gentlewoman; another female part in the same play was taken by John Wright—and Wright and Savill were apprenticed to Cane in 1629 and on 1 August 1631.[5] Similarly Alexander Cooke became free of the Grocers' Company in 1608, having served his time as an apprentice of John Heminges.[6] Some actors and their apprentices, it seems, led double lives.

Unless they acquired the protection of a master, strolling players were classed as 'rogues and vagabonds'. Queen Elizabeth, King James and his queen and children all had their own companies of players, as had a number of noblemen and others of lower degree, for example Alexander Hoghton (cf. p. 27). Yet being a player was not, apparently, a career to be proud of. In the golden years of the Elizabethan theatre very few testators described themselves as players, though this is what they were called in church and legal records written by others.[7] And of the few who referred in their wills to their companies, all were members of the premier company of their day. John Bentley (**1585**) and Tarlton (**1588**) called themselves 'servaunt to our sou*e*raigne ladie the Quenes ma*ie*stie' and 'one of the Groomes of the Queenes maiesties chamber', without naming their profession; John Shank senior (**1635**) and John Honyman (**1636**) were less coy, and used precisely the same words, 'one of his Maiesties servants the players'. While the standing of those at the top of the profession had improved by the 1630s, the great majority wanted to be known as gentlemen, citizens or yeomen rather than as players when they identified themselves in their wills' opening sentences. In the body of the will, however, several left bequests to their 'fellows' or asked other players to act as witnesses. Sometimes a known legatee or witness is vital in establishing a testator's 'playhouse' credentials.

The higher a man was placed on the social ladder the more probable is it that he would leave a will—hence the wills we print tell us more about the upper than the lower levels of the profession. Poorer actors, then as now, had little or nothing to bequeath. Every Master of the Revels from 1558 to 1642 made a will, except Sir George Buck, who died insane; many of the sharers of the adult companies did so (particularly of the most successful company, the Chamberlain's/King's Men), as did several of the managers of the boy companies. We have in addition traced some more elusive testators: minor actors, the widows of actors, former boy actors, musicians,[8] and carpenters who worked in or for the theatres, a gatherer (a money-collector in the theatre), a theatrical supplier, owners or part owners of theatres, and some dramatists. Not all can be identified with absolute certainty—in cases of doubt we warn the reader.

A word about the women, who are strongly represented both as testators and executors: Margaret Brayne, Mary Bird, Mary Bryan, Elizabeth Condell, Elizabeth Holland, Joan Hovell and others seem to have been just as forceful as their menfolk (as was Susan Browne-Greene-Baskervile, who figures in several wills), even though their legal rights as testators were restricted (see p. 12). Women did not perform on the stage, but they had other roles in the theatre, as gatherers, as sharers (when widows inherited shares from their husbands), as investors, and, no doubt, as vendors, sempstresses and cleaners. Indeed, several important theatrical patrons were women (Queen Elizabeth, Queen Anne, Princess Elizabeth, Queen Henrietta): we can be confident that a female point of view would make itself heard from within the profession, as it does from the audience in, for example, *The Knight of the Burning Pestle*.

The profession of player really begins in England in the period we have chosen, with the building of the first theatres and, we assume, with full-time actors forming professional companies that will have developed from earlier Tudor models. 'Elizabethan' actors, like their predecessors, were all-purpose entertainers. They danced, they tumbled, fenced, made music—and their musical talents, at least, leave traces in their wills (notably Augustine Phillips 1605). They also commissioned plays, and a surprising number wrote plays.[9] This does not show in the wills, though the 'bookishness' of the profession is visible: quite a few actors and one widow, Elizabeth Condell, bequeathed books. It would have been more visible if more inventories had survived with the wills. Unfortunately these lists, which assessed the value of the contents of the house or business premises of the deceased room by room, item by item, sometimes identifying, for example, individual books, rarely survive in Prerogative Court of Canterbury records or in those of the other courts relating to what was formerly Greater London for the period before 1670. Many were lost during the upheavals of the Interregnum or in the Great Fire of

1666, and those that survived these catastrophes are, for the most part, not calendared or available for inspection. We should have liked to find an actor's will that bequeaths plays as did that of Richard Langhorne, citizen and apothecary of London, in 1635: 'And also I giue & bequeath vnto my vnckle Mr Thomas Eaton my greate guilte bible in folio, Item, I giue & bequeath to mr. Iohn Legatt My book of mr. Shakespeare's wor*kes*'.[10] We did find references to unidentified plays as in Theophilus Bird's (**1663**): 'I doe giue to my Sone Theophilus Bird and to my Sonne George Bird all my right tytle in all the playes and playbookes that are mine by payment and Survivourshipp'. In fact the only identifiable plays in an inventory in our collection prior to 1642, Ben Jonson's *Workes* (1616), occur in a list of books of Thomas Sackville (**In1638**), a former actor turned merchant who traded and died in Germany. Another former actor, who ended his life as a vintner, Thomas Downton, referred in his will (**1625**) to 'all my librarie of books both of Devinitie and humainitie'. A library suggests a considerable number. Later in the century William Cartwright (**1686, In1687**), also a former actor, bequeathed two hundred and thirty-nine pictures and a valuable collection of plays to Dulwich College; he, however, having been a bookseller in the Commonwealth period, cannot be considered a typical actor–collector.[11] Downton's 'library', like Ben Jonson's before it was destroyed by fire, may also have been exceptional, and Sackville's may have been closer to the norm.

From Downton's books of divinity and Sackville's book-list we deduce that the theatre was less antagonistic to the Church than some churchmen, particularly Puritans, were to the theatre; bequests to ministers, churchwardens, etc. confirm this impression, as does other evidence.[12] Downton and Sackville also remind us of the social mobility of the acting profession: many actors, as already mentioned, started in other professions, and others left the theatre and settled down in less risky careers. This has made identification more problematic in some instances.

The theatrical community

Despite the coming and going, not a few actors remained in the profession for life, or until the closing of the theatres in 1642. Inevitably they married into each other's families. John Heminges's wife Rebecca is thought to have been the widow of the actor William Knell (**A1587**); their daughter Thomasine married the actor William Ostler (**A1614**), and their son William, inheriting his father's shares in 1630, later sold them to John Shank (Nungezer, pp. 179–86). Richard Burbage was the son of James Burbage, an actor and the builder of the Theatre who died in 1597 (**A1597**); after Richard's death in 1619, his widow Winifred married the actor Richard Robinson; Richard Burbage's brother, Cuthbert (**A1636**), though not an actor, appears in several of our wills. Christopher Beeston's son William followed his father as an actor, and was later known as 'the chronicle of the stage' (Nungezer, p. 41); William's sister Anne married Theophilus Bird, son of William Bird, actor with the Palsgrave's company. Their daughter Anne married Michael Mohun who acted at Beeston's Cockpit.[13] The actor Robert Beeston, one assumes, was related to them. Edward Alleyn married the stepdaughter of Philip Henslowe; his older brother, John Alleyn, was 'closely engaged in theatrical affairs' (**A1596**) (Nungezer, p. 11). All of these men and women must have been familiar with the history of the theatre from the inside, over several generations. They were the leaders of their profession—more important, in the eyes of their fellows, than the dramatists who worked for them.

One fact that emerges in its full significance from this collection of playhouse wills is that the leading theatrical families intermarried repeatedly and thus retained their financial and professional dominance. The same family names reappear again and again. Surnames used as Christian names indicate other close relationships: for instance, Beaumont Ostler, baptised in 1612 (Nungezer, p. 262), Burbage Underwood (Underwood **1624**), Swanston Namecott (Islip **1639**). One wonders therefore whether the baptism in 1588 of Lowin Allen (Nungezer, p. 3), son of John Allen, player, implies that the actor John Lowin, born 1576, belonged to a family connected with the Allens or Alleyns before Lowin began his career. Again, Richard Bower (**1561**), Master of the Chapel Royal, was the father-in-law of Richard Farrant (**1580**), who likewise had charge of boy actors, as had Samuel Daniel (**1619**), who licensed plays for the Children of the Queen's Revels from 1604; here one wonders whether family influence helped Daniel to secure the appointment, since several members of the 'Bowre' family were left bequests in his will. Equally, one would like to know more about the interconnections of the Burbage and Turner families. Administration of the estate of Edmund Turner[14] was granted in 1622 to his daughter Winifred Burbage, alias Turner,[15] who must have been the widow of Richard Burbage, before her second marriage to Richard Robinson. Does this throw light on the careers of the actors Anthony and Drew Turner, and, perhaps, on the shadowy dramatist Cyril Tourneur? These and similar questions will, we hope, intrigue students of our playhouse wills.

Since the family history of players is likely to lead to other discoveries it should be noted that their friends and relations also left testamentary records that are worth investigating. Edward Alleyn's father, another Edward, made his will in 1570 (proved 22 Sept. 1570 PRO PROB11/52 fo. 194r); he was a citizen and innholder, and as such could have hired out his yard for theatrical performances (but we do not know, and we have not printed his will). Inigo Jones, clothworker, the father of Jonson's unloved collaborator, made his will in 1597 (proved 4 Apr. 1597 PRO PROB11/89 fo. 275v). We encounter Ellis Guest, butcher, father of the actor of the same name, in a grant of administration of his goods in 1604[16] and Nicholas Tooley of Surrey, yeoman, namesake of the actor, in 1601.[17] Henry Knell, who made his will in 1585 (proved 17 Sept. 1585 PRO PROB11/68 fos 331r–332r) was born in Bremen—might that help us to track down the celebrated Knell, who acted with Tarlton in the 1580s?

The legatees named in a will probably give us a good idea of the testator's circle of trusted friends. Not always: Tarlton (**1588**) appointed Robert Adams and another, 'my very loving and trustie friend*es*', as guardians of his young son on 3 September 1588. Administration was granted to Adams on 6 September, yet between these dates Tarlton, on his death-bed, petitioned Walsingham not to allow 'a sly fellow, one Mr Adams' to defraud his son, and we now know that the grant to Adams was dissolved (cf. p. 58 and Nungezer, pp. 351–2). John Brayne (**1578**) asked 'my welbeloued frend*es*' Robert Miles and another to be his overseers, his widow Margaret Brayne (**1593**) named Robert Miles as her executor—we learn from another source, however, that Brayne, suffering from 'stripes' administered by Miles, charged this well beloved friend with being the cause of his death (Chambers II, 390). Shakespeare (**1616**) remembered many friends in his will, even adding a few as afterthoughts: if they were the ones closest to him, his inner circle, it is strange that he left no bequests to female friends apart from his immediate family. Other testators not infrequently left rings or keepsakes to both a husband and wife, when they had been on friendly terms with both, and several of Shakespeare's male legatees had wives in 1616, including Burbage, Condell, and his overseers Thomas Russell and Francis Collins: their wives, it seems, received nothing.

Wealth and finance

Our knowledge of the social background of the Elizabethan theatre, though considerable, could still benefit greatly from a more systematic study of the testamentary records. What of the financial background? And first, what was the value of money at this time? It was a period of gradual inflation,[18] which makes comparison difficult. Many sums of money are mentioned in the wills, yet not often illuminatingly. An inventory may give us a valuation (Beeston **In1683**), without commenting on the condition of the items valued. William Hovell (**1615**) thought that £15 would buy his sister a house in Northamptonshire. John Shank (1635) valued his 'share' in the company's 'stocke bookes apparrell and other thinges' at £50, and two gowns at £16 12s. The high cost of apparel and more normal prices can also be checked in Philip Henslowe's pawn accounts (a man's gown faced with fur and an embroidered waistcoat, thirty shillings; a gold ring with a death's head, fifteen shillings; a pair of black silk stockings, ten shillings).[19] We know from other sources that in 1588 skilled workmen were paid various rates by the year, with meat and drink: pewterers, glovers, draymen, £3 6s 8d; drapers, shoemakers, saddlers, £4; blacksmiths, millers, £6; brewers, £10.[20] Some prices and wages rose, some remained the same. The cheapest gold rings in our wills are always ten shillings, over a long period of time; payments to actors for court performances remained the same for many years (Chambers IV, 150ff.), as did the cost (one penny) of watching a play from the yard.

The actors of course locked up much of their capital in their profession, as 'sharers' in their company and as 'housekeepers'.[21] The wills show, however, that a surprising number had funds to spare and invested in property, mostly in the London area.[22] For their own convenience the actors bought houses or lived in lodgings close to the theatres.[23] Thomas Downton lived in the parish of St Saviour's in Southwark while he acted at the Rose and the Swan, then in St Giles Cripplegate when the Admiral's Men moved to the Fortune.[24] Richard Gunnell also lived near the Fortune, in which he was a sharer, but moved to the parish of St Bride's Fleet Street after he built the Salisbury Court theatre there. His widow, Elizabeth, subsequently married to the actor John Robinson who was buried at St Giles's, moved back to St Bride's after her second husband's death. Kept at arm's length by the city authorities, both public and private theatres were erected on the borders of their jurisdiction: the Theatre and the Curtain in Shoreditch, the Fortune in Cripplegate, the Boar's Head in Whitechapel, the Red Bull in Clerkenwell, the Cockpit or Phoenix in Drury Lane, the Salisbury Court off Fleet Street, all in the county of Middlesex, and south of the river on Bankside in Surrey, the Rose, the Globe, the Hope and the Swan.

Here, as in other things, Shakespeare stands out as different, and deserves a short digression. He bought houses and land in or near Stratford, and waited until 1613 before acquiring his first London property. It is sometimes said that he had already retired, and that he purchased the Blackfriars gatehouse purely as an investment. 'There is no evidence that he ever contemplated using his tenement as a lodging. Indeed, shortly after the purchase, Shakespeare installed a tenant . . . .'[25] We think otherwise: in 1613 he was still in his forties, the gatehouse was conveniently close to the Blackfriars theatre, and had he not pledged in

1608 to pay his share of this theatre's rent for twenty-one years? Had he not once installed a tenant in New Place? He could not foresee in 1613 that he had only three more years to live; he might reasonably hope to continue his London career. He referred in his will to his 'fellows' (which suggests present rather than former fellows)—and, even if he failed to refer to his 'shares' in his will, unlike some of his colleagues, we assume, as others have done, that his shares passed to his daughter Susanna with the rest of his estate and were disposed of after his death.

On its own an actor's will rarely gives us an accurate account of the testator's wealth. It gives us an impression—and now and then probably a misleading impression. Tarlton's will (1588), made for the benefit of a natural son who was to be brought up 'in the feare of god and good le*tt*res', mentions plate, jewels, bonds, etc., yet who would have guessed that Tarlton was worth £700 in property, as his mother later alleged (Nungezer, p. 352)? The laws relating to the devise of land can produce misleading bequests (see p. 13) and it cannot be assumed that the testator always had sufficient assets to cover the bequests in his will or that all the legatees survived the testator, especially if some time separates the drawing up of a will and probate.

Notwithstanding the bequests in his will a testator had the right to give away during his lifetime any part of his estate unencumbered by the laws of inheritance. Even in circumstances where land and goods could be bequeathed by will without restriction it was common practice to distribute property before death in the form of marriage settlements or to advance children or, less admirably, to defraud creditors. After his death James Burbage was accused by Giles Allen of having distributed his property to his sons Cuthbert and Richard for this purpose:

> the sayd James had in his lyefe time made A deede of guift of all his goodes to the sayd Cuthbert Burbage and Richard Burbage his sonnes, whoe after the death of the sayd James Burbage procured Ellen Burbage his widdowe being a verye poore woman to take the Administracion vppon her which was done, to defraude your Subiect and other Creditors of the sayd James Burbage[26]

In order to save property from the claims of creditors it was common practice to make it over by deed of gift to a third person. During his financial embarrassments in 1576 occasioned by the expense of building the Theatre John Brayne had recourse to this ruse, and he did the same when he got into debt over the building of the George Inn in Whitechapel in the year of his death (Wallace, pp. 8–9, 14). In his will, dated July 1578 (proved 1586), Brayne makes no mention of the Theatre although he might reasonably have done so in the expectation of Burbage's performance of the obligation of a bond signed only two months before, in May

1578, to make over to Brayne half of the lease, an assignment which seems never to have been made (Wallace, p. 7). The will does, however, include a number of properties which Brayne had earlier put into the hands of others. Such circumstances explain the disappointing absence in some of these playhouse wills of property known to be in the possession of a testator at his death (e.g. Nicholas Brend and the Globe site).

We cannot tell from his will how rich Shakespeare was, though we may guess that his plays earned him more than Henslowe's hacks were paid, and all the other evidence suggests that he died a wealthy man. Wills offer glimpses of the testator's assets and lifestyle, not certified accounts. Other documents arising from and required by the probate process can provide additional information. Executors' and administrators' accounts give details of settlements made during the lifetime of the deceased which might explain the absence of a bequest to a particular member of the family or of a property known to have belonged to the testator. Inventories provide information about domestic arrangements and material wealth in goods and chattels. Sometimes lawsuits or deeds of sale help to complete the picture, but much remains unknown and then we are tempted to read between the lines. 'To mr Thomas Combe my Sword', said Shakespeare, and we guess that he had only one sword; to his granddaughter he gave 'All my Plate except my brod silver & gilt bole', and the three particulars suggest that he owned other bowls of precious metal. Nuncupative wills, dictated rather than written, often from the death-bed, in the nature of things are bound to be less revealing: no one could guess from Richard Burbage's (**1619**) that he too must have been a wealthy man.

The personal voice

A testator's personality can break through the set phrases, as when a will transmits what sounds like an authentic voice from the death-bed. If he or she denounces a member of the family, or bequeaths a disproportionately small sum, we can be fairly certain that an individual voice addresses us. Jacob Meade (**1624**) disliked his son-in-law, 'whom I wyll shall have nothing to doe or meddlle therwyth' (a bequest to his daughter); Elizabeth Condell (**1635**) restricted a bequest to her daughter, for reasons 'which I hold fitt herein not to mencion', 'yet soe I doe intend the same as that my said sonne in lawe Mr Herbert ffynch shall neuer have possession of the same'. Sir Henry Herbert (**1673**) gave a nephew twenty guineas and mourning, his daughter fifty guineas and mourning, and his son-in-law one guinea and mourning: as Gibbon might have said, a son-in-law's tears are soon dried. Shakespeare's treatment of his younger son-in-law, Thomas Quiney, should be compared: it is hard to decide whether his not actually naming Quiney was meant to be considerate or a gesture of contempt; the anxieties of the father-in-law are unmistakable.

It has been argued that the lawyer or scrivener prepared the will according to the wishes expressed by the testator but not in his actual words.[27] It may have been so at times. 'Draft' wills, not yet formalised by the scrivener, probably give us the testator's words as spoken. The curious ramble of Mary Bird's will (1625), with its zig-zag thinking and confusing pronouns, is pure 'stream of consciousness', somewhat like Molly Bloom's monologue, and certainly represents the 'draft' phase of composition. In short we think that we often hear the living voice of the testator, particularly when we are aware of any deviation from standard practice.

TESTAMENTARY PROCEDURE

Wills and the law

Wills are referred to in classical literature[28] and English wills survive from the medieval period. In sixteenth- and early seventeenth-century England the administering of wills was normally, although not exclusively, a matter for the Church. The Elizabethan Book of Common Prayer instructed both the sick man and and the one still in health to make a will and declare his debts 'for discharging of his conscience and quietness of his executours'.[29] 'Weake in bodie' Robert Armin drew up his will in 1614, a year before his death,

> ffor the preventing of all controversies and contentions, which many tymes doe arise amongest deare ffreendes for the goodes and possessions of such as leave theire estates vndisposed of, being either prevented by sudden deathe or by protracting of tyme vntill such feeblenes and Debillitie of bodie and memorie overtake them, that they cannot sett any certeyne course or order therein.

It was the Church's teaching that a person about to meet his or her maker should have earthly affairs in good order and it was the Church courts which authenticated and recorded the deceased's final dispensations of his or her property.

It has been calculated that in the 1560s at least 18 per cent of all adults made wills, rising to 19 per cent in the 1620s.[30] When some irregularity invalidated a will or no will was made the Church courts might grant the right to administer the estate of the deceased. It is estimated that in the

Prerogative Court of Canterbury (PCC) one administration was granted for every two wills proved between 1558 and 1660.[31] In the majority of cases, however, the property of the deceased was distributed by family or friends without recourse to any authority and leaving no formal record. There was no legal requirement to make a will, but all persons were deemed capable of making a valid will unless specifically disabled by law, as were male children under fourteen and female children under twelve,[32] convicted criminals (which included traitors, suicides, recusants and the excommunicated), imbeciles and married women.[33]

When a woman married, she became *covert baron*, under the protection and influence of her *baron* or lord, and by law any property she owned became her husband's. She was therefore unqualified to make a will as she had no property to bequeath or, in testamentary terminology, devise. With her husband's permission she might bequeath money given to her as an allowance during marriage or items purchased with such an allowance, or credits and legacies due to her which were in her possession on marriage.[34] These circumstances were exceptional. In the period 1558 to 1639 less than a half per cent of testators[35] were wives and of these many were widows who had remarried. Widows remarrying sometimes made freedom of testation a provision of the marriage contract, especially when they had inherited from a former husband and wished to make bequests to the children of that marriage. All the female testators in our collection are widows.[36]

The many laws, passed in the reigns of Henry VIII and Elizabeth I to control the devise of property by will, are laid down in the Statutes of the Realm,[37] while explication of testamentary procedure is provided by contemporary legal handbooks, such as Henry Swinburne's *A Briefe Treatise of Testaments and Last Wills* (1590)[38] and Thomas Wentworth's *The Office and Duty of Executors* (1641), and formularies like William West's *Symbolaeographia . . . ; Or, The Notarie and Scrivener* (1590).[39] For a testator's last wishes to have legal force it was necessary that they be authenticated by witnesses or by writing (Swinburne, sig. Ee8v) and that an executor be named to perform them by arranging probate and the distribution of the estate (West, sect. 639). Theoretically witnesses were not required when a will was written or signed by the testator (Swinburne, sig. Ff5r) although, in practice, a minimum of two was advised (Swinburne, sig. Ee8v) and three or four were required for the devise of real estate (Statute of Wills 1540, 32 Hen. VIII, c. 1).

Testators (Shakespeare **1616**, Condell **1627**) would occasionally sign each sheet of a will as well as the last page but there was no requirement to do so; indeed, the absence of the seal or signature of the testator or witnesses in no way invalidated a written document provided there were two or three witnesses and its authenticity was unquestioned (Swinburne, sig. Ff3r). The use of a mark instead of a signature by testators and witnesses was common and, although a mark normally indicated illiteracy, the unusual and extreme circumstances in which wills were often signed make it dangerous to assume that a testator who made only a mark could, in his or her prime, neither read nor write.[40] Thomas Campion's nuncupative will (**1620**) has no named witnesses but states merely that there were 'then and there present divers Credible Witnesses'. It failed probate because no executor was appointed.

Technically the will and the testament were distinct, the will disposing of real estate, that is land,[41] and the testament dealing with personal estate, that is goods and chattels. Although we use the term 'will' to describe a single document containing the last will *and* testament, which was the norm in our period, these separate functions radically affect the value of wills used in isolation as evidence of the property and wealth of an individual. There is a fundamental distinction in English law between real and personal property, between land on the one hand, and goods and chattels on the other, somewhat blurred by the fact that some interests in land, tenancies 'at will' and leases for years, were regarded in common law as personal estate.

The freedom of the testator to distribute his or her estate after death was limited by law and custom. Before the 1540 Statute of Wills real property could not be devised by will at all, originally because it was forbidden by common law and, after 1535, because it was specifically prohibited by the Statute of Uses (27 Hen. VIII, c. 10), except in special cases where ancient custom obtained.[42] Land was subject to the rules of inheritance, the essential features of which were that lineal descendants of the deceased were preferred to collaterals, males were preferred to females of the same degree, and the first-born male was preferred to the exclusion of all others.[43] Henry VIII's Statute of Wills granted to the majority of landowners the right to devise their freehold land as they wished without regard to inheritance laws. Only those who held lands by knight's service (mostly in the upper strata of society) and were therefore liable to feudal dues to the Crown, continued to suffer restraint, being permitted to dispose freely of only two-thirds of that part of their estates which they held by knight's service, in order to safeguard a proportion of the Crown's feudal revenues. These controls were rendered meaningless by the passing of the Military Tenures Abolition Act in 1660 (12 Car. II, c. 24). The necessity to provide for spouses, daughters and younger sons drove testators to circumvent the laws of inheritance which governed the transfer of such land by making provision in the form of gifts and settlements in advance of death, if the terms of tenure allowed it. Land held by copyhold (according to the custom of the manor), for example Shakespeare's tenement in the manor of Rowington, could not be devised by will until 1815, without the succession being approved by the lord of the manor and recorded by enrolment in the manorial court. There was no need to specify in a will the passing of copyhold property from father to eldest son as the inheritance was by custom.

A few wills in the present collection (Giles **1583**, Savage **1611**, Leveson **1621**, Shank **1635**) refer to the Custom of London which applied to the freemen of the City. Although the City and liberties of London held land from the King in conditions which allowed the inhabitants free devise of land as chattels, other limitations, laid down by custom, applied. Half of a married man's property, after the payment of debts, was reserved to his widow or, if there were children, a third to the widow and a third to the children who had not received an advancement from their father in his lifetime, only one third, the dead man's part, being available for distribution according to the wishes of the testator. These rights were established in common law by the fourteenth century and were not abolished in London until 1724 (Holdsworth, III, 552). The division of an estate on this basis is fairly common in the predominantly London wills brought together in this collection but there are many more where it is not invoked and it is clear that although customary in the City it was frequently ignored. In 1584 the anonymous author of *A Breefe Discourse Declaring and Approving the Necessarie and Inviolable Maintenance of the Laudable Customes of London* defended its practice, which was 'yet by the wiser and better sort religiously regarded' (p. 23 (STC 16747)). Similar arrangements for the provision for widows and children were in use in the Province of York until 1692 and in Wales until 1696, but it is by no means clear how far this custom prevailed in other parts of the country. Apparent disregard for a wife in seventeenth-century wills from these areas might conceal a tacit reliance on custom. The sins of omission in Shakespeare's will with respect to his wife have been explained away by the conjecture that he expected a third of his property to have passed to Anne by such custom. There is, inconveniently, no evidence that it was observed in Warwickshire.[44] Before about 1600 freedom of testation was allowed in the Province of Canterbury with the above exceptions. In the regions where they obtained these customs formed the basis for distribution of property in case of intestacy until the Act for the Better Settling of Intestates' Estates of 1670–1 (22 & 23 Car. II, c. 10) regularised such matters for the country as a whole, retaining the thirds rule (Holdsworth III, 552).

The claims of a widow to her husband's property were further complicated by rights of dower or jointure, property settled on the wife at marriage in order to entitle her to some part of the estate if her husband predeceased her.[45] These arrangements were predominantly a matter for the wealthy. Sir John Astley (**1640**), Master of the Revels, referred to his wife's jointure among his bequests to her, and Sir Henry Herbert (**1673**), his successor at the Revels, made elaborate arrangements for the safeguarding of his daughter's jointure against a wastrel of a son-in-law. Further down the social scale Thomas Downton (**1625**), a member of the Palsgrave's Men and in later life a vintner, made his wife executrix of his estate and 'whattsoever I have inloyed or possessed for hir & to her vse since my marriadge to her freing my selfe of [i.e. fulfilling] my promise that I have not Altered Any Estate of hers since my marriadge to her'.[46] Nevertheless Swinburne points out (sig. F3r) that it was quite within the law for a testator, enjoying freedom of testation, to dispose of his goods and chattels (but not land) as he pleased, and that his dependants, wife or children, could claim only what had been specifically devised to them.

Until the Court of Probate Act in 1857 the Church courts had jurisdiction over succession to goods and chattels but, even after the system of feudal tenure was abolished in 1660, land and its inheritance were the province of the secular courts. A will which included personal estate had to be proved in the Church courts but, though that same last will and testament might also include bequests of land, the Church courts had no power to enforce those bequests. The growing disputes in the sixteenth and seventeenth centuries over jurisdiction between common law courts, equity courts and ecclesiastical courts affect both the contents of wills and their legal consequences. Despite the formal supervisory procedures of the ecclesiastical courts, supported by an elaborate system of bonds, inventories and accounts, those courts were prohibited by common law courts from acting in cases of default or malpractice which might be construed as concerning temporal matters and thereby falling within the jurisdiction of the King's courts. So unenforceable was the Church's control over the proper administration of testamentary affairs after the initial grant of probate or commission of administration, that as early as 1530 it was advised that property should be dispersed before death to avoid the possibility of fraud after it.[47]

The making of the will

A study of some extant wills from this period suggests that the will was usually drafted shortly before death, the normal interval being less than a week.[48] Swinburne recounts the belief, common then as now, that 'if a man should chance to be so wise, as to make his will in his good health,

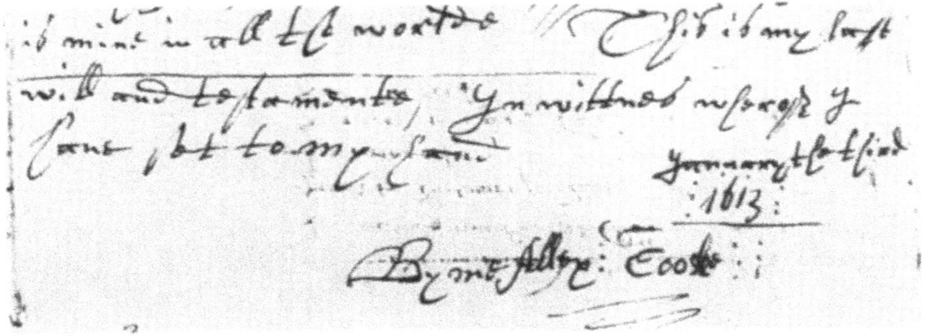

Figure 2 Alexander Cooke 1614

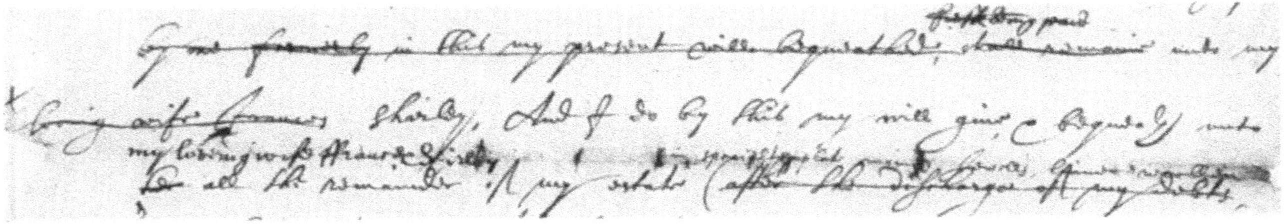

Figure 3 James Shirley 1666

... that then surely he should not liue long after' (sig. F3r). The average time elapsing between the making of a will and the day of burial (where this is known) in our collection is two weeks, a triumph of superstition over good sense. In several cases where a number of years separate the preparation of a will and its implementation it was illness which drove the testator to premature action: Sir Thomas Benger (**1572**), John Brayne (**1578**) and Thomas Gilbourne (**1627**) were 'sick in body' when they made their wills but they cheated death for another five, eight and fifteeen years respectively. Shakespeare, signing his will a month before his death, was more far-sighted, or more fortunate, than most of his playhouse contemporaries, even those of comparable financial substance. Henslowe died the same day that he signed his will (**1616**), Burbage (**1619**) the day after, Alleyn (**1626**) twelve days later.[49]

A will was normally made in writing, but if death came quickly and unexpectedly, word of mouth was sufficient for devise of goods and chattels (but not of land).[50] In January 1618 Richard Cowley, supposing himself near to death, dictated his last wishes but survived for another fifteen months without bothering to put anything more formal on paper. Usually the testator employed a second person, often a notary public or professional scrivener, to draft the will on his or her behalf. Humphrey Dyson, the notary public who witnessed the wills of Thomas Savage (**1611**), Nicholas Tooley (**1623**), and Henry Condell (**1627**), was presumably responsible for their drafting and passed them on for copying to scribes in his employ, Savage's to John Grome, the other two to Robert Dickens. Ralph Crane, a scrivener now better known as copyist of play texts for the King's Men, wrote out Richard Burbage's will (**1619**) (see p. 115 for facsimile). Although custom demands that a will is written in the first person it is dangerous to assume that a will is holograph even in those exceptional cases when the testator clearly states that he has written the will himself and appears to have signed it.[51] Edmund Tylney, Master of the Revels, made his will in 1610 'Written with my owne hand' but the document among the original wills at PRO is a scribal copy.[52] Holograph wills in this collection are those of Alexander Cooke (**1614**, see Figure 2), Thomas Gilbourne (**1627**), Arthur Wilson (**1652**), James Shirley (**1666**, see Figure 3), and, perhaps, Sir John Astley (**1640**).

The normal procedure seems to have been to make a first rough draft of the bequests and special requirements of the testator from which the scribe prepared a fair copy, leaving space for the signatures or marks of the testator and witnesses and sometimes for the date (e.g. Astley **1640**, Beeston **1682**).[53] The wills of Mary Bird (**1625**) and Francis Grace (**1624**) seem to be such first drafts rather than nuncupative wills, which were normally expressed in the third person. Death overtook them before fair copies, with the formal preambles and the naming of executors, were ready and witnesses signed the draft which was all that was to hand.[54] William Sly (**1608**) had no time to have his will drawn up formally before he died but he signed the rudimentary statement of his intentions which had been copied out and added a nuncupative codicil. John Underwood (**1624**) also added to his written bequests on his death-bed a few days after he had signed the fair copy and Edmund Tylney (**1610**) made provision in his will for 'What other legacies I shall give vppon my Death Bedd by Word of mouth'.

Robert Armin's will (**1614**) gives us a first-hand account of this last stage in a statement, headed 'in the hall of mr Armyns howse', that the will was 'Published ... & the same reade to the Testator by me Iohn Warnar scrivenor, and the same sealled & subscribed by the saide Testator ...'. Before signing and dating the final draft, scribal errors and omissions[55] might be corrected or ambiguities clarified by making deletions and insertions as necessary in the text, with the more cautious adding a memorandum authenticating those changes (e.g. Savage **1611**, Rowley **1624**, Holland **1631**, Herbert **1673**). A formal codicil might be annexed to the same end. Nicholas Tooley alias Wilkinson (**1623**) used a codicil to avoid potential confusion arising from his two surnames; he seems to have been of a particularly anxious disposition, signing each sheet of his will and enlisting no fewer than nine witnesses. Nathaniel Giles (**1633**) made good the omission of a forgotten son, six years away from England. Christopher Beeston (**1638**) and Arthur Wilson (**1652**) changed their minds about the distribution of their property. Codicils might also be added at any time after the signing of the original (e.g. Meade **1624**, Pudsey **1612**).

The form of the will

Swinburne stated that words and sentences were 'not required for the forme of a testament, but for the expressing of the will and meaning of the testator' (sig. Ff4v). The wills of the period, like most legal documents, are constructed and worded to unchanging formulae. It seems likely that common forms for wills circulated widely both in manuscript and in print. An early example is printed in the legal formulary *A Newe Boke of Presidentes*, published in 1543 (STC 3327).[56] They were probably included in the many almanacs which were so popular in all levels of society.[57] The publication in 1590 of Swinburne's and West's handbooks and their frequent reprintings in the decades following argue for an acknowledgement, in both the legal profession and the lay community, of the need for standardisation. Such standard forms doubtless explain the similarity in phraseology between Shakespeare's will, drawn up in Stratford in 1616 by a local lawyer (Stratford's Clerk, Francis Collins or his servant) and that of Jacob Meade written in London in 1624.

The will was in the first person whether it was composed, or indeed written, by the testator or, as was most frequently the case, by a second person, a notary public, a professional scrivener or merely a helpful and literate neighbour. The will begins with a formal invocation 'In the name of God Amen', and a declaration of the identity of the testator. A religious preamble frequently commends the testator's soul to God and his body to the earth. Such a statement of religious commitment was not a required part of a will: Swinburne does not discuss it; Adam Islip's will of 1639 has none and Elizabeth Condell's of 1635 has only a cursory reference, but it is the norm in this period. The view that these preambles offer evidence of the religious leanings of the testator (to Roman Catholicism, signalled by references to the Virgin Mary and the company of angels, or to Calvinism, by statements that the testator expected salvation through Christ's death and passion, or inclusion among the elect) finds no corroboration in this collection.[58] Christopher Beeston had Catholic connections but the wording of his will (**1638**), commending his soul to Jesus Christ 'my only sauior and redeemer, by the merrit*es* of whose most bitter death and bloody passion I doe assuredlie trust to bee saued and haue remission for all my sinnes' does not differ from that of his non-Catholic contemporaries.[59] It is dangerous to read too much into an unusually elaborate expression of faith; Robert Armin's long preamble is copied almost verbatim from West's *Simboleography* (Bk III, sect. 404).

Then follow instructions concerning burial. Normally these arrangements were left to the discretion of the executor but special conditions can give evidence both of the social and financial status or aspirations and of the sentimental connections of the testator. Burial in the church with which the testator had particular links was the norm, most commonly his or her own parish church, but Thomas Giles (**1583**), citizen and haberdasher, specified the chapel of his guild at Mercers' Hall, and John Marston (**1634**) was buried in the Inn of Court of which he had been a member. A frequent request was to be buried near a spouse (Downton **1625**, Hovell **1620**) or a parent (Browne **1634**, Honyman **1636**). The concept of purgatory and thus the opportunity for the living to intercede for the dead with prayer was rejected at the Reformation but many testators in our period provided in their wills for some equivalent measure to keep their memory alive. The most common bequest of this sort was a dole of money or bread to the poor of the parish of the testator's birth or residence, often to be paid on the day of the funeral, a guarantee of an impressive number of mourners (Bower **1561**, Kendall **1608**, Hovell

1615, and his widow in 1620, Meade 1624, Rowley 1624). Another relic of pre-Reformation practice was a bequest of money to the parson of the church in which the testator wished to be buried, the equivalent of the mortuary fee. Other spiritual dues were paid by bequests for funeral sermons[60] (Towne 1612, Greene 1612, Hovell 1620, Tooley 1623), to the poor in return for attendance at church (Herbert 1673) and to prisons and hospitals (Westcott 1582, Giles 1583, Savage 1611).

The more substantial testators specified funeral monuments (Pope 1603, Tylney 1610, Benfield 1639, Astley 1640), and dinners for colleagues (Giles 1583, Savage 1611, Towne 1612, Hovell 1615). Philip Henslowe (1616) asked for a stylish funeral in the church of St Saviour's Southwark, to include a sermon and the attendance of 'fortie poore men of the Libertie of the Clyncke' to swell the number of mourners, while his wife, making her will a month later, was adamant that she wished only to 'be decently buryed without anye vayne pompe or shewe'.[61] Such directions were unenforceable by law and executors tended to provide more rather than less lavishly for funeral ceremonies. The more elaborate the funeral and the larger the number of mourners the greater the evidence of the material prosperity of the deceased and of the family surviving him. Despite Puritan disapproval of ostentation and 'superstitious' practices, for example the wearing of mourning, Thomas Pope (1603) set aside £20 for his funeral and Richard Benfield (1639) reserved £100. Only the prosperous could afford a memorial monument or burial inside the parish church rather than in the crowded churchyard. The burial arrangements for Brian Ellam (1593), a carpenter who worked on the Theatre, and for his wife, called for 'the knyll with the greate Bell and the Pytt in the Churche' of St Alban Wood Street which cost 29s 4d[62] while the inventory value of his estate was only £6 9s 7d.[63]

In the first half of the seventeenth century it became fashionable to be buried at night, a practice begun by the aristocracy (to avoid the elaborate heraldic funerals required by the College of Arms) and aped by the middle classes. Both John Heminges (1630) and Henry Condell (1627) chose this arrangement and were buried in the parish of St Mary Aldermanbury rather than in the parishes where they were living at the time of death, Heminges in St Saviour's Southwark (although he held parish offices in St Mary's), Condell in Fulham. Such irregularities were costly: fees for burial at night could be twice the normal and to be buried outside one's own parish incurred fees payable to two parishes.[64]

The executor was obliged to cover the costs of the funeral and to discharge the testator's outstanding debts before any legacies could be paid and statements to this effect were included in many wills to ensure the liability of the executors. Provided creditors could produce written evidence, debts were to be paid in a specified order, from those owing to the Crown down to simple bills and servants' wages (Swinburne, sigs Nn1v–Nn3r). In this period real estate could not be sold to pay debts although in order to circumvent this restriction testators could charge income from specific lands for this purpose depending on their terms of tenure. The sale of chattels to cover debts (Heminges 1630) and the sale of land for the payment of legacies (Tylney 1610) was not so forbidden. The extent of debts owed by the testator no less than those payable to him or her can provide evidence of standing in the community, as a good credit risk and as a man or woman of substance.

As well as money, property and goods, personal items are often bequeathed, clothing and bedding being the most unusual to modern eyes but illustrative of their relative value in the period. Unlike modern testators, many actors thought of their 'apparel' as an important bequest. A gentleman's clothes could be very expensive; when Pope (**1603**) leaves 'all my wering aparrell' to two playhouse colleagues one assumes that he meant apparel worn in the theatre. Yet apparel was also bequeathed to and by non-actors, and we know from Henslowe's diary that some special garments were bought by the company, not by individuals (pp. 99, 102, etc.). It would make sense, however, if the leading actors each kept a good stock of clothes for performances, and this is probably confirmed by William Hovell (**1615**) who bequeathed to Nathaniel Clay and John Podger 'my fyfte parte of my stock of app*a*rell and other thing*es* w*hi*ch I haue in the companie wherein they playe'. The two legatees must have been actors; Clay is first recorded as an actor in 1618, and Podger is known only from Hovell's will, hitherto unpublished.

Apart from apparel, actors also bequeathed to their friends many kinds of keepsake, most of which were traditional at the time: rings, gloves (Greene **1612**), black ribbons (Browne **1634**). A number bequeathed their swords (Phillips **1605**, Sly **1608**, Shakespeare **1616**), or other weapons ('all my armes', Pope **1603**; 'my Muskett', Downton **1625**).

After specific legacies had been settled the residue of the testator's property was normally granted to the wife, or to the executors as compensation for the duties devolving upon them. The appointment of executors was the most important part of the testamentary process. Normally more than one executor might be chosen from among those involved in the business and domestic affairs of the testator, most often his wife, otherwise a relative, friend or business partner. Christopher Beeston (**1638**) made his wife executor because of his debts and contracts 'for greate som*m*es of money, w*h*ich noe one but my wife vnderstand*es*, where or how to receaue pay or take in'. Sir Thomas Benger (**1572**) appointed as one of the executors of his estate his chaplain Thomas Fugall 'for that he knoweth best how I haue alwaies determined to bestowe the benefitt thereof'. Frequently overseers were also appointed to offer counsel and advice to the executors and to monitor the proper execution of the will.

As a rule the will ends with the dating of the document, normally recording the occasion on which the document was signed and witnessed rather than drawn up, and the signature or mark of the testator and witnesses. The disqualification of a beneficiary as a witness did not then apply.[65] Generally witnesses seem to have been chosen for their credibility and social standing. The multiple occurrences of John Shank in this role speak for his status in the London theatrical community, as does the frequency with which John Heminges and Henry Condell acted as executors. Others were no doubt asked to act as witnesses simply because they happened to be at hand: the notary public who drew up the will, the women who were attending the sickbed (Tooley **1623**), members of the family and neighbours.

Probate

In this collection we are primarily interested in the contents of wills as evidence of the status, wealth and personal predilections of the testators during their lifetimes. No less informative for the unravelling of the network which bound together the theatrical community of Shakespeare's time are the procedures which followed their deaths, the actions of the executors and the actual rather than intended distribution of property. Nor can the final resting places of these documents be discovered without some knowledge of probate jurisdiction.

To prove a will the executor, who had normally already arranged for the burial of the deceased, took the document to the appropriate Church court; the archdeaconry court if the testator had goods and chattels exceeding £5 in value (*bona notabilia*) in a single archdeaconry, the diocesan (consistory) or, where one existed, the commissary court if the goods were held within more than one archdeaconry in the same diocese, the provincial court (York or Canterbury as appropriate) if within more than one diocese, and to the Prerogative Court of Canterbury (PCC) if *bona notabilia* were held within more than one province.[66] Estates of testators dying overseas belonged to the PCC although, in practice, many of their wills were proved in other courts. The Church courts which dealt with wills of testators holding property in what was formerly Greater London were the Consistory Court of London (the superior court of the Diocese of London), the Commissary Court of London, and the courts of the archdeaconries of Middlesex and London in that diocese, the

Consistory Court of Winchester (the superior court of the Diocese of Winchester which included Southwark), the Archdeaconry Court of Surrey which was also part of the Diocese of Winchester, and the peculiars of St Katharine by the Tower, the Dean and Chapter of St Paul's and of the Dean and Chapter of Westminster.[67] The Court of Husting, the court of the Corporation of the City of London, had jurisdiction over the wills of the freemen of the City concurrent with the Church courts. The will (**1611**) of Thomas Savage, citizen and goldsmith of London, was proved in the PCC on 26 October 1611 and enrolled in the Court of Husting on 20 November. The PCC records would normally be expected to yield only wills of the most prosperous but a surprising number of wills of minor figures have been found there. During the Commonwealth (1653–60), renamed and reformed, it had sole testamentary jurisdiction over the whole of England, functioning as a Court of Civil Commission.

The courts protected their jurisdiction jealously, poaching business where possible for the sake of the fees involved, especially in London where jurisdictions overlapped both geographically and hierarchically. In 1529 an Act Concerning Fines and Sums of Money ... for the Probate of Testaments (21 Hen. VIII, c. 5) specified that there should be no charge for probate of an estate worth less than £5, but there was substantial revenue to be had from wealthier testators, up to 5s for probate and 2s 6d for administrations where clear goods exceeded £40.[68] With several courts close at hand executors often elected to prove a will in the highest court for greater publicity and security of record. Occasionally wills were proved successively in separate courts for this reason (William Browne's will (**1634**) was proved first in PCC then in the Archdeaconry of London court) or were referred to a higher court for procedural reasons. The procedure varied slightly from court to court but generally followed the same stages, that in the PCC being most elaborate, as might be expected in the court of highest authority.

If the court approved the will, probate was granted to the executor, who was required in most courts, although not in the PCC, to take out a bond to administer the estate faithfully. The grant of probate was entered into an act book. Normally a copy of the will was made, which, with the certificate of probate attached, was given to the executor, the original will, with the probate clause subscribed or endorsed, being filed among the court records and a copy enrolled in the court registers. Practice was not always consistent, however, and until the 1620s, especially in the PCC, the original will was often returned and a copy filed. In the PCC, if it was expected that the provisions of the will were likely to be contested, the executor could apply for probate in solemn form which involved the summoning to court of all those likely to make objections and the promulgating of a sentence by the court upholding the validity of a will not yet proved or confirming a will where probate had already been granted, which usually could not then be further disputed. The procedure in this case was for the promoter (plaintiff), usually the executor or heir, to bring a case against the ministrants (defendants), usually those most likely to challenge the will. The lack of accompanying documentation for the period before 1660 makes it difficult to distinguish between cases where real conflict existed and those where the sentence was merely a legal device to ensure a smooth passage for the executor.[69] At this period, unless there were disputes or other complications, probate could be granted very quickly; normally within a few days of death or burial in minor courts, a few weeks in the PCC, although there are examples in our collection where wills were proved in the PCC before the testator had been buried (Towne **1612**, Philip Henslowe **1616**, Grace **1624**, Heminges **1630**).

Anyone could act as executor, except those deemed unfit to receive a legacy, that is those outside the law for civil or religious reasons, traitors, felons, heretics, excommunicates and, after 1605, Catholic recusants.[70] Children could be appointed although they were unable to act before reaching the age of seventeen, until which time an administrator was appointed *durante minore aetate* (Swinburne, sigs Gg3r-Gg4v). Women played an active and responsible role as executors and administrators of their husbands' and, sometimes, sons' wills (Browne **1623**, Browne **1634**, Honyman **1636**). A study of probate accounts from late sixteenth- to mid eighteenth-century England finds that most married men named their wife as executrix.[71] It seems that a woman could not be another's executor without her husband's permission,[72] no doubt because the assumption of these duties carried with it the right to make a will, generally denied to married women (Swinburne, sig. I3v; West, sect. 634).

The duties and rights of executors were carefully delineated.[73] An executor need not accept the responsibility placed upon him by the testator but once he had done so he could not retire until formally acquitted by the court. If the executor died before completing his duties, the responsibility to do so passed to his executors if he left a will. If the executor died intestate the original testator was deemed to have done the same and it became necessary to appoint an administrator. Henry Condell's account in his will (**1627**) of the duties he had carried out as executor to John Underwood, his fellow in the King's Men who had died more than two years earlier, and which he passed on to his wife as his executor, gives some indication of how onerous such a responsibility might be. In certain circumstances executors could be liable for wrongs done by the deceased, if these resulted in an enrichment of the estate

(Holdsworth III, 579), and had greater liability for the payment of debts incurred by the deceased than the heir. This liability was a common reason for renouncing the duty if the estate was known to be encumbered with debts which might exceed assets.

If a will existed, however, even if it was invalid on a technicality, for example when no executors were named, or if executors renounced responsibility or died before the testator, its provisions had to be followed. In such cases the appropriate court with probate jurisdiction[74] granted letters of administration *cum testamento annexo* (with will annexed) normally to the next-of-kin or to the residuary legatee, allowing the person or persons appointed to act with the same powers as executors.

If there was no will, the right to distribute the testator's goods belonged to the widow or next-of-kin by statute (21 Hen. VIII, c. 5) providing they were granted letters of administration, or could be applied for by interested parties, often the testator's creditors. Administrators had the same powers and duties as executors but fewer liabilities.[75] Their responsibility died with them. Agnes Farrant, for example, renounced the executorship of her husband's will (Farrant **1580**) but took out letters of administration, thereby ensuring that his debts would not be passed on. Until the passing of the Act for the Better Settling of Intestates' Estates in 1670 an administrator, having settled outstanding debts, could claim the residue of the estate without regard to the needs of widow or children. Administration could be a reasonable proposition for a creditor who could thus arrange for his own claims to be settled as a priority and gamble on the residue covering his costs and providing a profit. Opportunities for fraud by setting up a third party as administrator to avoid liability were curtailed in 1601 by the Act against Fraudulent Administration of Intestates' Goods (43 Eliz. I, c. 8) although the practice continued. Sir William Davenant's widow was accused of such a subterfuge by her stepsons (Davenant **A1668**).

Before acting on the instructions of the will, the executor or administrator was expected to exhibit to the court an inventory of the moveable property of the testator within a reasonable period (between two to six months from the date of probate). The date set was generally entered in the probate act book, where the final valuation was also sometimes noted, and frequently marked, as a memorandum, on the copy of the will filed in court. Once accounts of the expenses incurred in the disposal of the estate had been submitted, the executor or administrator was finally acquitted of any further responsibility, the whole process from death to acquittance taking about twelve months.[76]

CONCLUSION

This collection records the testamentary arrangements of one hundred and thirty-five persons connected with the London theatre in Shakespeare's time. More than a third of these documents will be new to theatre historians. One fifth of the wills are published in full for the first time, and many of the rest are printed for the first time from the original will, rather than from a register copy. These are important historical documents; as we have already made clear, we have not attempted to draw attention to all the new material that they contain. In addition, they are also human documents: we believe that they still speak home to us today, bringing us very close to the social, financial, religious and sentimental lives of the men and women of the Elizabethan theatre. We have pointed out some of the limitations of these documents and the legal processes that governed them. To those who will use these raw materials we offer a reminder and warning from William West:

> many times it is doubtfull in what sence the Testator would haue his words taken, insomuch that his will therein may rather by probable argument be ghessed then rightly gathered. (sect. 632)

NOTES

1 The notes on each document indicate where it was first printed.
2 William Harrison, *The Description of England*, ed. G. Edelen, Ithaca, NY, 1968, pp. 94, 115, 117.
3 Thomas Smith, *De Republica Anglorum*, ed. Mary Dewar, Cambridge, 1982, pp. 67, 70.
4 Thomas Wilson, 'The state of England, *anno dom.* 1600', ed. F. J. Fisher, *Camden Miscellany 16*, Camden Society Publications 3rd ser., 52, London, 1936, p. 23.
5 From the records of the Worshipful Company of Goldsmiths at Goldsmiths' Hall.
6 Private communication from D. A. J. Taylor, Grocers' Hall.
7 See the records of christenings, marriages and burials in Bentley II, 343 ff.
8 As Bentley pointed out, musicians, stagekeepers, tiremen, gatherers and other employees of the theatre 'could be called upon to act minor roles in performances, especially in crowd scenes' (*Profession*, p. 66).
9 Actors who were also dramatists include Tarlton, Christopher Beeston, Nathan Field, John Honyman, William Bird, John Shank senior, William Rowley. Sir George Buck, Master of the Revels, also wrote plays (Bentley III, 93), as did several of the masters of the boy companies (Farrant, Westcott, etc.).
10 GL MS 9052/5 fo. 60r, ACL Original Wills (probate 24 Mar. 1635).
11 See Warner, p. 202.

Introduction 27

12 For example Alleyn's College (n. 11 above), or the fact that Heminges 'filled various parochial posts from 1608 to 1619 in St. Mary's, Aldermanbury' (Chambers II, 321).
13 The wills of the two Beestons (**1638, 1682**), of Theophilus Bird (**1663**) and his parents, William (**1624**) and Mary (**1625**), are printed in this collection. Anne Mohun's will is PRO PROB10/1347.
14 GL MS 9050/5 fo. 153v, ACL Probate and Administration Act Book.
15 This seems to have been a marital alias, but a surprising number of male testators in our period also had an alias, including Nicholas Tooley (**1623**) and Christopher Beeston (**1638**).
16 GL MS 9050/4 fo. 267r, ACL Probate and Administration Act Book.
17 Ipswich and East Suffolk Record Office MSS R39/429, W37/91, listed in *Union Index of Surrey Probate Records which Survive from before the Year 1650*, ed. Cliff Webb, London, 1990, p. 506.
18 See R. B. Outhwaite, *Inflation in Tudor and Early Stuart England*, Studies in Economic History, 2nd ed., London, 1982.
19 *Henslowe's Diary*, pp. 143, 146, 151 (all later references are to this edition unless otherwise indicated).
20 P. L. Hughes and J. F. Larkin, ed., *Tudor Royal Proclamations*, 3 vols, New Haven, 1964–9, III, 22–5.
21 For sharers and housekeepers see Andrew Gurr, *The Shakespearean Stage*, 3rd ed., Cambridge, 1992, pp. 69–70.
22 Before 1858 Church courts had no jurisdiction over bequests of real property except leases, and freehold land would not necessarily be mentioned in a will (Jane Cox, *The Records of the Prerogative Court of Canterbury and the Death Duty Registers*, London, 1980, p. 1); see pp. 13–15 below.
23 Baldwin, *Organization*, Chapt. V draws on Collier's *Memoirs* to reconstruct communities of actors on Bankside, in St Andrew's Blackfriars, and St Mary's Aldermanbury. For wills relating to actors working and/or dying in the provinces see the Records of Early English Drama series and elsewhere; e.g. Honigmann (*'Lost Years'*, pp. 135–8) reprints the will, dated 3 Aug. 1581, of Alexander Hoghton of Lea, co. Lancs., who bequeaths to his brother 'all my instruments belonging to musics, & all manner of play clothes if he be minded to keep and do keep players' (p. 136).
24 Mark Eccles, 'Actors I', p. 46.
25 Samuel Schoenbaum, *William Shakespeare: Records and Images*, London, 1981, p. 47.
26 PRO A. 12/35, Star Chamber Proceedings, 44 Eliz. I (1601–2), Allen v. Burbage, reprinted in Wallace, pp. 276–83 (p. 278).
27 Christopher Marsh, 'In the name of God? Willmaking and faith in early modern England', in *Records of the Nation*, pp. 215–48 (p. 228).
28 Livy mentions a will made in the seventh century B.C. (*Annales*, I. xxxiv), and Cicero often refers to wills in his *Epistulae ad Familiares*, including wills made by women e.g. VII, xxi.
29 *The Book of Common Prayer 1559: The Elizabethan Prayer Book*, ed. J. E. Booty, Washington, 1976, p. 303 ('Visitation of the sick').
30 Motoyasu Takahashi, 'The number of wills proved in the sixteenth and

seventeenth centuries: Graphs with tables and commentary' in *Records of the Nation*, pp. 187–213 (p. 212).
31 J. S. W. Gibson estimates 178,000 wills were proved and 85,000 letters of administration granted (*Wills and Where to Find Them*, Chichester, 1974, p. 2).
32 The Act for the Explanation of the Statute of Wills (34 & 35 Hen. VIII, c. 5) specified that a testator must be over twenty-one to devise land.
33 Swinburne, Part II 'Wherein is declared what persons may make a Testament and who may not so doe', sigs G3r–L8r.
34 See T. E., ed., *The Lawes Resolutions of Womens Rights*, London, 1632 p. 143 (sig. K8r) for circumstances in which a wife might make a will. Abigail Babham made a nuncupative will in 1621 (proved 8 Oct. 1622 PRO PROB11/ 140 fos 220r–v)with the consent of her husband, Christopher Babham, gent., probably the Christopher Babham who was connected with the Blackfriars playhouse (see Nungezer, p. 26).
35 Mary Prior, 'Wives and wills 1558–1700', in *English Rural Society, 1500–1800: Essays in Honour of Joan Thirsk*, ed. J. Chartres and D. Hey, Cambridge, 1990, pp. 201–25 (p. 208). Prior provides a useful summary of women's rights in testamentary matters in this period.
36 Brayne **1593**, Poley **1601**, Agnes Henslowe **1616**, Hovell **1620**, Dambrooke **1624**, Bird **1625**, Bryan **1625**, Holland **1631**, Condell **1635**, Robinson **1641**.
37 Collected in Alison Reppy and Leslie J. Tompkins, *Historical and Statutory Background of the Law of Wills, Descent and Distribution, Probate and Administration*, Chicago, 1928.
38 New editions in 1611, 1635 and 1640. All subsequent references are to the 1611 edition.
39 There were thirteen editions before 1632. All subsequent references are to the edition of 1610, *The First Part of Simboleography*.
40 David Cressy, *Literacy and the Social Order: Reading and Writing in Tudor and Stuart England*, Cambridge, 1980, pp. 106–7; e.g. Hugh Davis (**1608**) and Jaques Jones (**1628**) who made their marks on their wills but whose connections with the literary world of the theatre presuppose a reasonable level of literacy.
41 For an example see the 'voluntas' of Richard Tarlton (**1588**).
42 For example, in London and Oxford; see Swinburne, 'Certaine cases approved by custom, wherein it is lawfull to deuise lands, tenements or hereditaments', sigs M3v–N2v (sig. M4r).
43 J. H. Baker, *An Introduction to English Legal History*, London, 1971, pp. 144–5.
44 B. Roland Lewis, *The Shakespeare Documents*, 2 vols, Stanford, 1940, II, 502–6, argues persuasively against such an explanation.
45 T. E., ed., *The Lawes Resolutions*, pp. 90 (sig. G5v), 93 (sig. G7r).
46 This may refer to his wife's property at their marriage. Widow of Oliver Easton, a vintner, she may have set up Downton in the trade (Bentley II, 426). On Downton's death she refused to act as executrix and administration was granted to his creditors.
47 John Perkins, *A Profitable Book*, London, 1530, quoted in translation in Holdsworth III, 557.

Introduction 29

48 Stephen Coppel, 'Willmaking on the deathbed', *LPS*, XL, spring 1988, pp. 37–40 (p. 38).
49 Marsh, 'In the name of God?', p. 288, warns of the danger of 'comparing the date of the will with that of burial or probate and concluding that most wills were *composed* very shortly before death' (our italics).
50 See Swinburne, sigs F2v–F3r, for a definition, and sigs Ff6v–Ff7v, for the form of a nuncupative will.
51 See Hilary Jenkinson's caveat in 'Elizabethan handwritings: A preliminary sketch', *The Library*, 4th ser. III, 1922–3, pp. 1–34 (p. 31).
52 W. R. Streitberger, 'On Edmond Tyllney's biography', *RES*, n.s. XXIX, 1978, pp. 11–35 (p. 33 fn. 2).
53 See Marsh, 'In the name of God?', pp. 228–30 for a discussion of procedure.
54 See Swinburne, sig. E8v, for this eventuality.
55 Names of legatees were sometimes left incomplete in first draft and spaces left for later insertions: cf. Shakespeare **1616**.
56 Sigs Ee3v–Ff1v. The same formula is included in later editions to 1639 and reprinted in William West's *Symbolaeographia* (1590); see J. D. Alsop, 'Religious preambles in early modern English wills as formulae', *Journal of Ecclesiastical History*, XL, 1989, pp. 19–27 (pp. 20–1).
57 Although the earliest example in an almanac yet found dates from 1658, *Fly: An Almanacke*; see Bernard Capp, 'Will formularies', *LPS*, XIV, 1973, pp. 49–50.
58 See J. D. Alsop, 'Religious preambles' for a review of the debate.
59 For example John Shank (**1635**). Beeston's first wife was a known recusant and his son William was suspected of being one (Chambers II, 302). Cf. similar wording of William Beeston's will (**1682**).
60 The usual fee for a burial sermon before the Restoration was 10s; see Clare Gittings, *Death, Burial and the Individual in Early Modern England*, London, 1984, p. 138.
61 Gittings (p. 54) suggests that requests for 'decent' burial, especially during the Commonwealth, may represent tacit objection to plain Puritan funerals.
62 GL MS 7673/1 fo. 20r, St Alban's Churchwardens' Accounts 1592–3.
63 GL MS 9168/15 fo. 12r, CCL Probate Act Bk.
64 For a representative table of fees see those for St Botolph Bishopsgate in 1620 (Lambeth Palace Library, Court of Arches Proceedings, section F, Muniment Book 1635–1663, fos 169r–173v).
65 Swinburne, sig. Ff1v; see sigs Ee7r–Ff2r for the necessary qualifications of witnesses.
66 See Swinburne, 'Of the probation and approbation of testaments, and namely before whom they are to be proved', sigs Ll5v–Mm1r. There are cases of wills being proved in both the York and Canterbury courts due to testators holding property in both provinces.
67 J. S. W. Gibson, *A Simplified Guide to Probate Jurisdictions: Where to Look for Wills*, 3rd ed., London, 1986, provides useful lists of the parishes included in each jurisdiction.
68 See Swinburne, 'What fees are due for and about the probation and approbation of testaments', sigs Mm6v–Nn1r.
69 There are sentences connected with the following wills: Westcott **1582**, Pope

1603, Sly **1608**, Agnes Henslowe **1616**, Bryan **1625**, Giles **1633**, Elizabeth Condell **1635**, Christopher Beeston **1638**, Cartwright **1686**.
70 An Act to Prevent and Avoid Dangers which May Grow by Popish Recusants (3 Jac. I, c. 5).
71 Amy Louise Erickson, 'An introduction to probate accounts' in *Records of the Nation*, pp. 273–86 (p. 276).
72 T. E., ed., *The Lawes Resolution*, p. 144 (sig. K8v).
73 See Swinburne, 'Of the office of the executor', sigs Hh7r–Oo4v.
74 Not all courts were empowered to grant administrations, e.g. the court of the Archdeaconry of Surrey (A. J. Camp, *Wills and their Whereabouts*, Chichester, 1963, p. 44).
75 See Swinburne, sigs P3r–P3v on the differences between administrators and executors.
76 Amy Louise Erickson, 'An introduction to probate accounts', p. 273.

List of testators by date of will or administration

(A) indicates administration; (In) inventory

1559 Aug. 24 Sir Thomas Cawerden
1561 June 18 Richard Bower
1572 June 25 Sir Thomas Benger
1578 July 1 John Brayne
1580 Nov. 30 Richard Farrant
1582 Apr. 3 Sebastian Westcott
1583 June 19 Thomas Giles
1585 Feb. 9 Richard Hickes (A)
1585 Aug. 12 John Bentley
1587 Dec. 12 William Knell (A)
1588 Sept. 3 Richard Tarlton
1592 Aug. 19 Simon Jewell
1593 Apr. 8 Margaret Brayne
1593 Oct. 20 Brian Ellam
1594 Dec. 30 Thomas Kyd (A)
1596 May 5 John Alleyn (A)
1597 Feb. 3 James Burbage (A)
1597 June 15 Thomas Brend
1598 July 21 George Attwell (A)
1599 Dec. 8 James Tunstall
1601 Apr. 16 Jane Poley
1601 Oct. 10 Nicholas Brend
1602 July 24 Francis Langley (A)
1603 July 22 Thomas Pope
1604 Jan. 9 Robert Browne (A)
1605 May 4 Augustine Phillips
1605 June 6 William Haughton
1606 Mar. 3 Henry Lanman (A)
1608 Apr. 6 Hugh Davis
1608 Apr. 21 Giles Allen (A)
1608 Apr. 22 Edward Sharpham
1608 June 8 Thomas Kendall

1608 Aug. 14 William Sly
1609 Mar. 31 William Pavye (A)
1610 July 1 Edmund Tylney
1610 Sept. 2 Henry Johnson
[c.1611 May] George Pulham
1611 Oct. 3 Thomas Savage
1612 Apr. 16 George Bryan (A)
1612 May 6 (or 5 Oct.) John Mason (A)
1612 July 4 Thomas Towne
1612 July 25 Thomas Greene
1612 Sept. 13 Edward Pudsey
1613 June 1 John Duke (A)
1614 Jan. 3 Alexander Cooke
1614 May 7 John Dutton (A)
1614 Dec. 5 Robert Armin
1614 Dec. 22 William Ostler (A)
1615 Dec. 16 William Hovell
1616 Jan. 6 Philip Henslowe
1616 Feb. 15 Agnes Henslowe
1616 Mar. 25 William Shakespeare
1617 Mar. 3 Ralph Reeve
1617 Sept. 1 Thomas Giles
1618 Jan. 13 Richard Cowley
1618 Oct. 14 George Wilkins (A)
[1618 c.Nov.] Edward Juby
1619 Mar. 12 Richard Burbage
1619 May 22 Gilbert Katherens
1619 June 26 Francis Beaumont (A)
1619 Sept. 4 Samuel Daniel
1620 Jan. 9 Joan Hovell
1620 Mar. 1 Thomas Campion
1620 Aug. 2 Nathan Field (A)

1620 Aug. 21 Rowland Rubbish
1621 Jan. 8 William Leveson
1622 Feb. 8 Nicholas Long (A)
1622 Sept. 23 Robert Payne
1623 Mar. 28 William Jaggard
1623 May 5 Philip Rosseter
1623 June 3 Nicholas Tooley
1623 [c.Dec] Robert Browne
[1624 c.Jan.] Francis Grace
1624 Jan. 17 William Bird
1624 June 21 John Clarke
1624 July 4 Jacob Meade
1624 July 23 Samuel Rowley
1624 Sept. 8 Sarah Dambrooke
1624 Sept. 10 John Garland
1624 Oct. 20 John Underwood
[1625 c.Jan.] Robert Yarington
1625 Aug. 5 Thomas Downton
[1625 c.Sept.] Mary Bird
1625 Sept. 10 William Carpenter (A)
1625 Oct. 12 Thomas Lodge (A)
1625 Dec. 22 Mary Bryan
1626 Feb. 15 William Rowley (A)
1626 Nov. 13 Edward Alleyn
1627 [c.June] Henry Eveseed
1627 Aug. 12 Thomas Gilbourne
1627 Dec. 13 Henry Condell
1628 June 7 Jaques Jones
1629 Jan. 30 Robert Lee
[1629 c.July] Thomas Goffe
1630 Oct. 9 John Heminges
1631 Apr. 2 Aaron Holland (A)
1631 Nov. 12 Elizabeth Holland
1632 Sept. 4 Thomas Dekker (A)
1633 Nov. 15 Nathaniel Giles
1634 Jan. 31 William Fidge

1634 June 17 John Marston
1634 Sept. 11 Thomas Basse
1634 Oct. 18 Richard Gunnell (A)
1634 Oct. 23 William Browne
1635 Sept. 1 Elizabeth Condell
1635 Dec. 31 John Shank
1636 Apr. 7 John Honyman
1636 Oct. 25 Cuthbert Burbage (A)
1637 Aug. 22 Ben Jonson (A)
1638 Jan. 17 Thomas Sackville (In)
1638 Oct. 7 Christopher Beeston
1639 Aug. 26 Richard Benfield
1639 Sept. 4 Adam Islip
1640 Jan. 3 Sir John Astley
1640 May 12 Thomas Hobbes (A)
1641 Apr. 18 John Robinson
1641 Nov. 27 Elizabeth Robinson
1645 Sept. 26 Michael Bowyer
1649 July 20 Roger Nore (A)
1650 July 22 Inigo Jones
1651 June 24 Eyllaerdt Swanston
1652 Jan. 17 Samuel Thompson (A)
1652 Sept. 28 Arthur Wilson
1653 Sept. 28 Thomas Pollard (A)
1655 Dec. 1 John Shank Jr
1659 Apr. 9 Ellis Worth
1663 Mar. 20 Theophilus Bird
1666 July – James Shirley
1668 May 6 Sir William Davenant (A)
1673 Apr. 9 Sir Henry Herbert
1675 July 26 Lodowick Carlell
1682 Aug. 23 William Beeston
1683 July 10 Charles Hart
1684 Nov. 3 Robert Shatterell (A)
1686 Dec. 12 William Cartwright

List of testators by occupation

(Testators are listed in only one category although some may have had more than one occupation)

ACTORS AND MANAGERS

Alleyn, Edward 1626
Armin, Robert 1614
Attwell, George A1598
Basse, Thomas 1634
Beeston, Christopher 1638
Beeston, William 1682
Bentley, John 1585
Bird, Theophilus 1663
Bird, William 1624
Bowyer, Michael 1645
Browne, Robert A1604
Browne, William 1634
Bryan, George A1612
Burbage, James A1597
Burbage, Richard 1619
Carpenter, William A1625
Cartwright, William 1686
Condell, Henry 1627
Cooke, Alexander 1614
Cowley, Richard 1618
Downton, Thomas 1625
Duke, John A1613
Dutton, John A1614
Field, Nathan A1620
Garland, John 1624
Grace, Francis 1624
Greene, Thomas 1612
Gunnell, Richard A1634
Hart, Charles 1683
Heminges, John 1630
Hobbes, Thomas A1640
Honyman, John 1636
Jewell, Simon 1592
Jones, Jaques 1628
Juby, Edward 1618
Knell, William A1587
Lee, Robert 1629
Long, Nicholas A1622
Nore, Roger A1649
Ostler, William A1614
Pavye, William A1609
Phillips, Augustine 1605
Pollard, Thomas A1653
Pope, Thomas 1603
Pulham, George c.1611
Reeve, Ralph 1617
Robinson, John 1641
Rowley, William A1626
Sackville, Thomas In1638
Shank, John 1635
Shank, John Jr 1655
Shatterell, Robert A1684
Sly, William 1608
Swanston, Eyllaerdt 1651
Tarlton, Richard 1588
Thompson, Samuel A1652

Tooley, Nicholas 1623
Towne, Thomas 1612
Tunstall, James 1599

Underwood, John 1624
Worth, Ellis 1659

BOYS' COMPANY ACTORS AND MANAGERS

Bower, Richard 1561
Clarke, John 1624
Daniel, Samuel 1619
Eveseed, Henry 1627
Farrant, Richard 1580
Giles, Nathaniel 1633

Hovell, William 1615
Kendall, Thomas 1608
Mason, John A1612
Payne, Robert 1622
Rosseter, Philip 1623
Westcott, Sebastian 1582

DRAMATISTS

Beaumont, Francis A1619
Campion, Thomas 1620
Carlell, Lodowick 1675
Davenant, Sir William A1668
Dekker, Thomas A1632
Goffe, Thomas 1629
Haughton, William 1605
Jonson, Ben A1637
Kyd, Thomas A1594

Lodge, Thomas A1625
Marston, John 1634
Rowley, Samuel 1624
Shakespeare, William 1616
Sharpham, Edward 1608
Shirley, James 1666
Wilkins, George A1618
Wilson, Arthur 1652

MUSICIANS

Giles, Thomas 1617

Rubbish, Rowland 1620

THEATRE OWNERS/INVESTORS

Allen, Giles A1608
Bird, Mary 1625
Brayne, John 1578
Brayne, Margaret 1593
Brend, Nicholas 1601
Brend, Thomas 1597
Bryan, Mary 1625
Burbage, Cuthbert A1636
Condell, Elizabeth 1635
Gilbourne, Thomas 1627
Henslowe, Agnes 1616

Henslowe, Philip 1616
Hickes, Richard A1585
Holland, Aaron A1631
Islip, Adam 1639
Langley, Francis A1602
Lanman, Henry A1606
Leveson, William 1621
Meade, Jacob 1624
Poley, Jane 1601
Robinson, Elizabeth 1641
Savage, Thomas 1611

MASTERS OF THE REVELS

Astley, Sir John   1640
Benger, Sir Thomas   1572
Cawerden, Sir Thomas   1559

Herbert, Sir Henry   1673
Tylney, Edmund   1610

MISCELLANEOUS

Alleyn, John (engaged in theatrical affairs)   A1596
Benfield, Richard (friend of actors)   1639
Browne, Robert (son and friend of actors)   1623
Dambrooke, Sarah (widow and friend of actors)   1624
Davis, Hugh (connected with the playhouse)   1608
Ellam, Brian (carpenter)   1593
Fidge, William (purchaser of playbooks)   1634
Giles, Thomas (costume supplier)   1583
Holland, Elizabeth (widow of theatre owner and friend of actors)   1631
Hovell, Joan (widow and friend of actors)   1620
Jaggard, William (printer of plays and playbills)   1623
Johnson, Henry (gatherer)   1610
Jones, Inigo (theatre designer and architect)   1650
Katherens, Gilbert (carpenter)   1619
Pudsey, Edward (theatre-goer)   1612
Yarington, Robert (theatre scrivener)   1625

The documents

Wills

1559 Aug. 24 Sir Thomas CAWERDEN (abstract)

Kt. of parish of Blechinglygh co. Surrey. Soul 'vnto almightie god my maker and redemer'. Burial in church of Blechinglighe. To John Brown gent., his servant, Alis, his wife, and their heirs manor of Wylley alias Wyllye, co. Surrey, with rents, etc. from Michaelmas next. Remainder of same manor to John Cawerden, late servant with Mr Beale of London, fishmonger, and to his heirs for ever. To Bryan Dodmer*, son of late Thomas Dodmer gent., annuity of 20 marks from lands within precinct of late black friars* in London from Michaelmas next for life. To Rycharde Leye* of London £20 p.a. from annuity out of said late black friars from Michaelmas next for life. To same Richard Leye 'all suche offall stuff and lumber of tent*es* and other olde howses, and tymber as is now remayninge within the place of office of the tent*es*'.* To each of his servants, men and women, one year's wages with duties due to them at time of death. To such gentlemen of co. Surrey whose names listed on a docket annexed (Thomas Browne esq., Edwarde Slighfelde, William Herne, Thomas Jones, John Agmansam, Rycharde Beden, Edwarde Tylle); to each four almain-rivets, one corselet, or brigandine or shirt of mail. To poor of parishes of Blechinglighe and Hoorne £15, and to pa. Katheram £5, to be distributed at discretion of his executors. To each of his servants Barthilmew Scott, [1] Scotte his brother, Thomas Boothe, Davy ,[2] Thomas Vawghan,* and Otto Willicke one gelding. To same Otto Wyllike one dagger[3] and one hand gun. To [4] Duffelde his servant one gelding if he is alive at time of testator's death. To William Moore esq.* three stoned colts and three geldings, one of the best corselets, two gilt partisans, one rankhorn, two corselets for his men, four pikes, six almain-rivets, six black bills, twelve bows and twelve sheaves of arrows, a fair sword. To Thomas Hawes, his late servant, three corselets, six almain-rivets, six black bills, six bows, twelve sheaves of arrows, two geldings, one colt. To Thomas Blagrave,* his late servant, three corselets, six almain-rivets, six bows, twelve sheaves of arrows, and six black bills, two geldings and a colt. Residue of goods and chattels to Elizabeth, wife,* whom apppoints, with William Moore esq. of Losley, co. Surrey, executor. Appoints Thomas Blagrave and Thomas Hawe overseers. Executors, with consent of overseers, to have power to sell all his lands etc. in precinct of late black friars or friars preachers near Ludgate in London for performance of will, provided any surplus be distributed to such good uses as seem good to executors and overseers. If any ambiguity in meaning of will Anthony Broune, one of the Justices of Common Pleas, Gilbarte Gerrade, the Queen's Majesty's Attorney General, and Richarde Goodridge, esquires, have authority to reform defects. For their pains, to Anthony Browne his 'yonge donn amblinge geldinge' and to Gerrarde and Richarde Goodridges and to each of them one gold ring of 4 marks value. To honorable Lord Clinton* a cup of £10 value as remembrance and testimony of his good will and to his wife a gold ring with a turquoise. To Misteris Wade a gown of black damask and a hood finished 'accordinge to a wydowes estate'. Wit. Thomas Hawe, Richarde Leye, James Calfehill, Bartholmewe Scott, Otto Wylly.

1. Blank in MS.   2. Blank in MS.   3. dagger: MS has *dagg'e*; ?or otiose mark of abbreviation, recte *dogge*.   4. Blank in MS.

PRO PROB11/43 fos 19v-20r. RegC with prob. clause. Marginal note (fo. 19v) records confirmation by sentence.

Noted: Chalmers, *Apology*, p. 480, fn. o.

Prob. PCC, 19 Dec. 1559, to Elizabeth, relict, and William Moore (More), executors. Sentence (PRO PROB11/43 fos 246r–246v) promulgated PCC, 25 May 1560 (William More, promoter, v. John Cawerden, next-of-kin, and other interested parties) upholding the validity of will and confirming Moore as executor after the death of Dame Elizabeth.

fl. 1545–59. Master of Tents and first Master of the Revels, 1545–59. (Feuillerat, passim; Chambers I, 73–4, etc.)

Dodmer] involved in affairs of Revels Office 1571–5 (Chambers I, 81–2, 86); later deputy to T. Blagrave (see below) (Feuillerat, p. 413).
black friars] leased part in 1548; Cawerden received grant 12 Mar. 1550 of all property remaining unalienated since Dissolution (see Chambers II, 485–93).
Leye] Richard Leys appointed Clerk-Controller of Revels 1551 (Feuillerat, pp. 56–7).
office of the tentes] based at Blackfriars under Cawerden (Chambers I, 76; II, 491).
Vawghan] possibly the tailor mentioned in Revels accounts 1558–9 (Feuillerat, pp. 84, 97, 105).
Moore] later Sir William More; acquired papers of Revels during Cawerden's

mastership (Loseley MSS) and Blackfriars estate where let rooms to R. Farrant (1580) used as first Blackfriars theatre.
Blagrave] deputy Clerk of Revels under Cawerden; appointed Clerk 1560 (Feuillerat, p. 68).
wife] died 20 Feb. 1560 (Chambers II, 480); will dated 17 Feb., proved 21 Oct. 1560 (PRO PROB11/43 fo. 381v).
Clinton] Edward Clinton, later Earl of Lincoln, Lord Admiral 1550–3, 1558; had company of players from 1566 (Chambers II, 96–7).

1561 June 18 Richard BOWER

In the name of God amen. This ys the Last will and Testamente of me Richarde Bower made the xviijth daye of Iune in the yere of our Lorde A Thowsande fyve hundrede threscore and one ffyrst I Commende my Sowlle into the handes of Allmauyghty godd and my bodye to be browaught to Christian bwryall with prestes and Clarkes of the paryshe where I shall ende my Lyffe/ Item I Bequethe to Ione my wyffe my howsse with thappurtinaunces in Easte Grenewiche* withe in the Countey of kente, to have to her dwringe her naturall lyffe/ And after her decease I will that Steven Bower my eldeste Sonne, shall have the Same to him dwring his naturall Lyffe/ And after his decease the same to Remayne to his Eldiste Issve malle of his bodye begotten, and to the heyres males of the bodye of the same Eldeste Issue malle, And for Lacke of suche Issue malle, of that Eldeste Issue malle begotten Then I will my Sonne Raffe bower haue yt to him and to his heyers malles of his Body Lawfullye begotten/ And yf yt forttune hime to haue no Suche heire/ Then I will and bequethe the Same to my dawaughter Annes ffarrant* and to her heires males of her bodye lawfullye begotten And yf she have no Suche heire/ Then I will that my dawghter Katherine Bower have yt to her and to her heyers malles of her bodye Lawffully begotten/ And for Lacke of Suche heire male/ Then I will the Same (**p. 2**) to my dawghter Elizabethe Bower and her heiers males of her body Lawfully begotten/ And for lacke of suche heire malle/ Then I will that Blase Latton of ware berebruer have the Same to him and his heyris for euer Item I Bequethe to my Eldeste Sonne Steven Bower a bedsted/ A ffether bede, a bolstar, a pillowe a peare of shettes a peare of Blanckettes and a couerlet Item I bequethe to Raffe Bower A kerued bestede that was his Auntes A fether bedd A bolster A pillowe a peare of Blanckettes a peare of Shettes, and a couerlet Item I Bequethe to my dawghter Katheren Bower a bedstede a fetherbedd A bolster a pillowe a peare of of blanckettes a peare of Shettes and a coverlyte/ Item I Bequethe to my dawghter Elizabeth a Bedsted a ffether-bed a Bolstar a pillowe a peare of Shettes a peare of blancketes and a cou*er*let prouided alwaye that my wiffe shall appoint eche of their Sayd Stwffe here Rehersed according to her discressyon Item I Bequethe to kateren Bower my daw*au*ghter ij gilt pott*es* of Siluer/ and to my dawghter Elizabethe my gilt Salt of Siluer and my syxt syluier Spones w*ith* Apostells at the ende gylt Item I Bequeth to Ionne my wiffe the yerely Rent of xxxiij li vj s viij d by yere, whiche I have of a leas for tearme of yeres yet contynvynge w*ith* in the Isle of Tenet* in the Cowntey of kent she paying yerly after (p. 3) my decease to Steuen Bower v li to Raffe bower v li To katheren Bower v li And to Elizabeth bower v li vntill eche of them have Recevid the full Sum/ of xx li and yf yt fortune that any of them my childerne to dye before they be payde their Seyde seu*er*all Somes of xx li Then that which shall Remay*n* to be payed to every of them as is aforesayde shalbe devided equally amongest them that forttune to ou*er*lyue Item I will that my wyffe shalle have of ye xxxiij li vi s viij d xiij li vj s viij d dwring the tearme of yeres yet to come yf she so Longe shall fortune to lyve and the reste of the rente that shall Remayne of the Same xxxiij li vj s viij d After that my fowre Chidrene aforsaid have eu*ery* of them Recevide their before bequethyd xx li as is aforesayde Then I will that my Seyde wyffe shall yerely paye to my fiue Children here after expressed the Resedewe of the sayde xxxiij li vj s viij d that shall Remaine ouer and above the sayde xiij li vj s viij d to my seyde wyffe before bequethed equally to be devided amongest the Same my fyve Children That is to Saye Steven Bower Raffe Bower, Agnes farrant katherine Bower and Elizabethe Bower, and yf yt fortune my Seyde wyffe to dye before the Leas expyred Then I will that all my seyde children (p. 4) Then Living shall dwring the Seyde terme have equally emongest them all the sayed rent of xxxiij li vj s viij d The Resedew of all my goods and Cattells I bequeth to Ione my wyffe/ whom I make solle executrix Charging her first to se all my debtes payed/ Item I will here be geven in allmes to pore folkes at the daye of my Bwryall   [1] And of this p*res*ent will I make oversears william Ropar of Eltham in the count*ie* of kente Esquyer/ And Thomas Tallis on of {the} gentillme*n* of the Quenes maiestes Chappell/ In wyttnes wher of I have to this my present will put my hand the daye and yere above wrytten By me Richard Bower Robert paternoster* Thomas Tallis* by me william mihell'

1. Blank in MS.

PRO PROB10/47. OffC, prob. clause subscribed (p. 4). Single sheet folded in half to make four pages, unnumbered and unsealed. Text in mid Tudor secretary with displayed matter in chancery style legal hand; otiose abbreviation marks frequent and not noted.

Prob. PCC 25 Aug. 1561 to Richard Farrant, proctor for Joan, relict and executor. PAB (PRO PROB8/4 fo. unnumbered (Aug. 1561)) notes exhibition of inventory and gives pa. of origin as 'Grenewich'.

Noted: Wallace, *Evolution,* p. 106 fn. 3; discussed: Hillebrand, *Child Actors,* p. 65 fn. 89.

fl. 1545–61. Master of Chapel Royal, ?dramatist. Died 26 July 1561, buried Old Greenwich Church. (Chambers II, 31–3, 303; Hillebrand, op. cit., pp. 64–73; Nungezer, p. 53.)

Grenewiche] colony of Chapel Masters and Gentlemen based there (Hillebrand, op. cit., p. 65).
ffarrant] wife of R. Farrant (1580) Gentleman of Chapel, later Master, who acted as proctor for Bower's widow.
Tenet] manor of Minster on Isle of Thanet granted in 1557 by Mary I to Bower and Tallis (Hillebrand, op. cit., p. 64).
paternoster] Gentleman of Chapel Royal from 1561 (Hillebrand, 'Early history', p. 251).
Tallis] musician and composer, associated with Chapel until death in 1585 (*New Grove*).

1572 June 25 Sir Thomas BENGER (abstract)

Kt. Sick. 'thanckes be to allmightie god whom I knowledge to be my onelie trust of saluacion and by the merit*es* of his most bitter passion to haue saued so manie as be his electe and chosen to enherite the kingdom of Heaven of w*hi*ch number I trust to be one And by that faithe in hym to be saved And vtterlie renownce all vaine hope of any good work by my self or any other to be any whitt proffitable towardes Saluacion doo Comitt my Sowle to my said Savio*ur*s tuicion . . . And conceninge the disposinge of my gooddes w*hi*ch are verye litle and my debtes greate havinge nothinge certayne for the payment hereof/ for the chardges in serchinge Record*es* taking owte Copies and notes of matter necessarie for the furtheraunce of her Maiesties graunte of ffynes* for Alienacions &c Takinge Com*m*issions travaylinge in the execucion thereof in hope to haue receyved som*m* benefitt of the saide graunte/ haue ben so greate that for the Mainetena*u*nce thereof I haue ben enforced to sell and Morgage all my Gooddes and howshold stuff So that now remayneth onelie the benefite and com*m*odities of the saide graunte and the surplusage of my saide gooddes in pawne aswell towardes the satisfying of my wieff as also other my Credito*u*rs Wherfore my humble sute and peticion to her highnes ys that the greate Clemencie and bounteo*u*s Liberalitie alwaies by her Ma*i*estie shewed during lief may after death (yf occasion shalbe ministred) be also extended in the furtherance of the execuc*i*on of her highnes saide graunt And that Thomas Benger her olde servant and one of the last of the poore flock of Hatfeilde may reape and enioye the saide profitt*es* to the vses aforesaide acordinge to the true entente and meaninge of the saide graunt.' Assigns grant to Anthonye Winkefelde* esq., gentleman usher to the Queen, cousin Andrewe Vavisour esq., brother William Benger* and Thomas Fugall*, testator's chaplain, to prosecute same and employ benefits as follows: to wife, Dame Dorothie, to be recompensed for money which he had from her; to Margaret Benger £100 and Susan Benger £40 toward their marriages being his brother's daughters. All persons holding bonds or assignments as assurance of money received by him either quietly to enjoy same or be compensated. Whereas he is indebted to Thomas Fugall, both for long and faithful service and money supplied to him, etc., he is to be recompensed from benefits and appoints him 'as one of speciall {trust} to Deale in the saide graunte and all other thinges for that he knoweth best how I haue alwaies determined to bestowe the benefitt thereof And as touchinge the Arrerages demaunded of Barkehampstede He knoweth best what Som*m*es of Moneye was bestowed in buyldinge twoo water mill*es* and other nec*c*essarye thinges to her Ma*ies*ties vse W*h*ich beinge alowed as they are founde by com*m*ission reto*u*rned into thexchequir I trust wilbe little or Nothing at all and that her highnes will not refuse to allowe all thing*es* that by reason and Conscience oughte to be allowed'. To cousin Vavasour and Thomas Fugall residue of goods and appoints them executors. Some of profits of said grant, after debts discharged, to be distributed among his servants. Wit. John Canis, William Marsh, John Andrewes, and ¹ Dansey*

1. Blank in MS.

PRO PROB11/59 fos 84r–84v. RegC with prob. clause.

Prob. PCC 26 Mar. 1577 to Thomas Fugall, chaplain and executor, the second executor, Andrew Vavesour, cousin, having died. PAB (PRO PROB8/6 fo. unnumbered (Mar. 1576/7)) gives pa. of origin as 'Milton magna' (Great Milton), co. Oxon.

fl. 1553–72. Master of the Revels 1560–72; may have had own company of players (Chambers I, 318 fn. 3). Died between July 1572 and June 1573. (Feuillerat (pp. 427–9, etc.) corrects Chalmers (*Apology*, p. 482) on date of Benger's death and amplifies Chalmers's account of his life in reign of Mary (*Supplemental Apology*, pp. 195–6); Chambers I, 75, 80.)

graunte of ffynes] dated 25 June 1569 (*Calendar of Patent Rolls, Elizabeth I*, vol. 4, *1566–1569*, London, 1964, p. 439).

Winkefelde] son of Sir Anthony Wingfield, Controller of the Household to Henry VIII and Edward VI (Feuillerat, p. 437).

William Benger] listed among 'Taylers and Attendantes' in Revels accounts 1571–2 (Feuillerat, pp. 133, 147).

Fugall] listed with W. Benger in Revels accounts 1571–2 (Feuillerat, p. 133).
Dansey] John Dauncy was porter of St John's Gate, Clerkenwell, 1571–89, where Revels Office was housed (Feuillerat, p. 47).

1578 July 1 John BRAYNE

In the name of god Amen The ffirste daye of the moneth of July in the yere of our lord god <one> thowsand ffyve hunderith thre skore and eightene And in the Twentith yere of the Reigne of our Souer*eig*ne <Lady> Elizabeth by the grace of god Quene of Englond ffrance and Irelond defendor of the faithe &c I Iohn Brayne citizen and grocer of London beinge syck in body But of good and p*er*fect memory and remembrans lawde and prayse be geven vnto almightye god make and ordeyne this my testament conteyneng therein my Last will in manner and forme followinge that ys to saye ffirste and principally I gyve and bequeath my sowle into the hand*es* of almightye god my maker savyo*ur* and redemer throwgh whose deathe passion and resurrection I Interly and wholy truste to be saved and be an Inherito*ur* of the kyngdome of heaven, And my body to be buryed w*i*thin the p*a*rishe churche of Saynt Lenord*es* whereof I am a p*ar*ishoner Item my will and mynde ys that all suche debt*es* and dewties wh*i*ch of right I ow to any p*er*son or p*er*sons shalbe well and trewly paied by my executrix herevnder named {Item I gyve to the poore of the said p*a*rishe of St leonard*es* twenty shilling*es*} Item I gyve will and bequeathe to margaret* my welbeloued wyef All that my howse or tene*men*te set lyenge and beinge in Trumpington in the Countye of Cambridge w*i*th all land*es* meadowes buylding*es* and app*ur*tena*un*ces whatso̩eu*er* to the said howse or tene*men*te belonginge or in any wise apperteynenge now in the teno*ur* or occupac*i*on of one Robert Walker or his assignes/ To haue and to holde the said howse or tene*men*te with all land*es* buylding*es* and app*ur*tena*un*ces to the same belonginge vnto the said Margaret my wyef, and to the heires of her body lawfully begotten for eu*er*/ Item I gyve will and bequeath to my brother Edward Stowers of Aver<stow> in the Countye of Essex Smythe All that my howse mesuage or tene*men*te w*i*th all land*es* howses <yard*es*> and appurtena*un*ces whatsoeu*er* to the same belonginge wh*i*ch I sometymes purchased and bought of Ales Rapers of london wydow, scituate lyenge and beinge in Bewers St mary in the Countye of Essex now <in> the teno*ur* or occupac*i*on of Iohn' Clay brickler or his assignes/ To haue and to holde the said howse mesuage or tene*men*te w*i*th all land*es* yard*es* and app*ur*tena*un*ces to the same belonginge vnto the said Edward St<owers> and to the heires of his body lawfully begotten for eu*er*/ Item my will and mynde ys that my <said> brother Edward Stowers shall paye and allow vnto the said margaret my wyef the some of Tenne pound*es* of lawfull money of Englond, for suche cost*es* chardg*es* and expenc*es* w*hich* I haue laide <owte and> expended in sut*es* of law towchinge the said howse or mesuage/ The rest and residew of <all and> singuler my good*es* cattell*es* chattell*es* redy money debt*es* leases plate Iuell*es* and substance whatsoeu*er* my debt*es* paied and my funerall*es* dischardged I wholy gyve will and bequeathe vnto my said welbeloued <wy>ef Margaret whome I ordeyne and make my full and sole executrix of this my testament and last will/ And I make overseers thereof my welbeloued frend*es* Henry watson* and Robert myles* goldesmythes desyering them to see this my testament faithefully fulfilled accordinge to the trew meaneng hereof/ And I gyve to either of them for their paynes herein to be taken fforty shilling*es* lawfull money of Engl<ande> a pece/ In witnes whereof to this my present testament and last will I the said Iohn' Brayne haue set my seale the daye and yere firste aboue wrytten/ [Also I gyve and bequeath and my will ys that [Iohn'] Ioan watson the doughter of the said henry watson shall haue Tenne pound*es* lawfull money of Englond at the day of her mariage, So that she wilbe gouerned and ruled by my said wyef/]

                                                                      By me Iohn Brayne g'[1]

Sealed subscribed and deliu*e*red by the said Iohn' Brayne the daye and yere aboue wrytten in the presens of Thomas Cobhead clerke And of me Roger Bouche[2] notary publicque p*er* me thomam cobhed[3]

1. *g'*: ?generosus. 2. *Bouche*: *Bouth* in RegC. 3. *Sealed . . . cobhed*: endorsed.

GL MS 9172/12c no. 125. OW, prob. clause endorsed. Parchment; single sheet, seal and tag lost. Text in set secretary with displayed matter in hybrid secretary. Staining along right margin with some loss of legibility. Doubtful readings inserted from RegC (GL MS 9171/17 fo. 29v).

Prob. CCL 10 Aug. 1586 to Margaret, relict and executor. PAB (GL MS 9168/14 fo. 101r) gives pa. of origin as St Mary Matfellon alias Whitechapel and notes prob. granted on oath of Robert Ordyner, proctor for Margaret Brayne.

Noted: Wallace, adding 'as he had disposed of most of his property by deeds of gift, and the will makes no mention of his theatrical interests, no further notice need be taken of it' (p. 153).

fl. 1576–86. Theatrical speculator. Red Lion Inn 1567; brother-in-law and partner of James Burbage (**A1597**) in building of Theatre 1576. For disputes and litigation over Theatre after Brayne's death see Wallace, and Berry, 'Handlist'. Burbage alleged that Brayne acquired interest in Theatre by promising to leave it to Burbage's children (Wallace, p. 40). Berry states that new will never drawn up (p. 117) but this will postdates building of Theatre by two years. (Chambers II, 380, 387–9.)

margaret] 1593; with Robert Miles continued action against Burbage after husband's death.
watson] will dated 20 Aug., proved 27 Oct. 1590 (PRO PROB11/ 76 fo. 151r).
myles] charged by Brayne's widow with being cause of husband's death (Wallace, p. 14). For Miles's relationship with Brayne and his widow see C. J. Sisson 'Brayne, Burbage and Miles' in his *Boar's Head*, pp. 84–94.

1580 Nov. 30 Richard FARRANT

In dei nomine Amen. I Richard ffarrante one of the gentlemenne of the Queenes Maiesties Chappell beinge sicke in bodye, but whole and of a perfecte memorye, doe make this my last will and Testamente in manner and fforme followinge. ffirst I bequeathe my soule to Allmightie God, And my bodye to be buried and interred at the discrecion of my Executoure. Item I geve and bequeathe to my wieff Anne* ffarrante the Leaze* of my howse in the blacke ffriers in London, whiche Lease is in a Cheste at my howse in Grenewiche,* To haue and enioye the same for and duringe her naturall lieffe, if she lyve so longe, as the yeres yet vnexpired doe contynewe, And if not, then I geve and bequeathe the Residewe of the sayde yeres, vnto whiche of my Childrenne* she shall thincke mete and conveniente. Also I geve and bequeath to my wieffe my howse whiche I firste purchazed in Greenewiche till suche tyme as my sonne Richarde comme to the full age of one and Twentie yeres, condicionallie that shee mayntayne and keepe him vntill the saide yeres Moreover I geve and bequeathe to my wieffe the litle howse in the Gardeyne ende at Grenewich Together withe the litle Gardeine impaled belonginge to the same, for and duringe her naturall lieff. And after her decease, the same to remayne to whiche of my Children she shall thincke meete. All the Reste of my gooddes movable and vnmovable whatsoever I geve and bequeathe to my wieffe, whome I make my sole Executrix. In witnes wherof I haue hereunto putte my hande the Thirtithe daie off November in the three and twentithe yere of the Reigne of *our* sou*e*reigne Ladye Elizabeth by the grace of god of England ffraunce and Irelande Queene Defender of the faithe &c*etera*. (Richard ffarrante). Witnesses hereof Bartholomewe Mason Clarke Nicholas Beighton* Richard Granwall.* William Rodenhurste* Iohn Skeate Clark.

PRO PROB11/63 fo. 67v. RegC with admon clause.

Admon [with will annexed]. PCC 1 Mar. 1581 to Anne Farrant, relict, the said Anne in person of Edward Barker, notary public, proctor, having renounced executorship. PAB (PRO PROB8/7 fo. 8r) gives pa. of origin as 'Grenewich' co. Kent.

Printed: Wallace, *Evolution*, pp. 152–3 fn. 3; discussed: Hillebrand, *Child Actors*, pp. 90–1 fn. 57.

fl. 1553–80. Musician; Gentleman of the Chapel 1553–64, 1570–80; Master (acting) of Children of Chapel 1576–80; Master of Children of Windsor 1564–80; set up first Blackfriars theatre 1576. Died 30 Nov. 1580. (Chambers II, 36, 315; Hillebrand, op. cit., pp. 93–8; Nungezer, p. 133; *New Grove*.)

wieff Anne] daughter of R. Bower (**1561**).
Leaze] dated 20 Dec. 1576 from Sir William More to Farrant, printed by Wallace (op. cit., pp. 132–6 fn. 3) who documents Anne Farrant's controversies over lease following husband's death (pp. 152–68, 174–7).
Grenewiche] Farrant was member of colony of Masters and Gentlemen of Chapel Royal based there (Hillebrand, op. cit., p. 90 fn. 57).
Childrenne] Farrant left ten children (Wallace, op. cit., p. 153 fn. 2).
Beighton] as Brighton sworn as member of Chapel Royal from 1570 (Hillebrand, 'Early history', p. 253).
Granwall] Gentleman of Chapel Royal from 1571 (ibid.).
Rodenhurste] member of Chapel Royal from 1576 (ibid.).

1582 Apr. 3 Sebastian WESTCOTT

In the name of the moste glorious and blessed trynitie, the father, the sone, and the holie ghost so be yt./ I Sebastian westcote Almener* of the Cathedrall Churche of St Pawle in London being greved with syckness, being yet =of} perfect [of] mynde and memorye (to god I geve praise therefore) this third daye of Aprill in the yere of our lord god 1582:/ And in the xxiiijth yere of the raigne of oure most gracious soueraigne Ladye Quene Elizabeth &c. make my last will and testament in manner & fourme ensewing hereby revokyng all other wylls and testament*es* whatsoeuer by me heretofore made/ ffirst and before all thing*es* Commending my soule vnto the mercie of my saviour Ihesus Christ asking pardon for all my synnes and offencs in his bytter death and passion hoping in the last Iudgement daye to ryse and rest with this my wretched bodie in his blessed kyngdome amonge his elect Comytting my earthlie bodye vnto the earth to be buried at the (**fo. 2**) discrecion of my executour of this my said last will & testament hereafter named/ my worldlie goods I giue and dispose as followeth/. vi*delicet*./ ffirst I giue and bequeath to & amongest the Petycannons of the said Cathedrall churche of St Pawle to bryng my bodie to the Churche ffyve powndes./ And to & amongest the vycars of the same Churche to bring my bodye lykewyse to churche fower powndes/ And to the ten Chorasters of the same Churche ffyve powndes/ Item I giue to gyles* Clothier and Iohn Boult* vi*delicet*./ Gyles iij li vi s viij d/ And Boulte I giue fower powndes./ To everye of the vergers of the same churche x s apece to bring me to Churche/ To the keper of the Vestrye iij s iiij d/ To everie of the bellryngers there iij s iiij d/ To the poore of the parishe of Chimley where I was borne in the Cowntie of Devon' iij li. To the poore within the towne of Tawnton in the cowntye of Somerset xl s./ To the poore of Kyrton in Devon L s/ (**fo. 3**) To the poore of Kyngstone nere Taunton aforesaid v s/ To the poore of the pareshe of St gregorie nere Pawles churche in London xx s./ To the poore prysoners within the severall howses and prysons called the fflete, the marshalsey, the Kynges benche, the white Lyon' in Southwark, the twoe Cownters Newgate, Ludgate, Bethelem, and the gatehowse in westmynster, to everie pryson vj s viij d apece/ Item I giue & bequeath to the vse of the Almenerye howse* of the said Cathedrall Churche of St Pawle where I nowe dwell to be & remayne vnto the {same} [said] Almenery howse to the vse of the Almener there for the tyme beyng for ever towards the furnishing of the same house, my chest of vyalyns and vyalls to exercise and Learne the children & Choristers there/ And also one table in the hall with the frame A settle of ioyned worke, a paire of great Iron Aundyrons there, the table, frame & settells, hanginges, Waynscot and Coubourd in the parlour there/ The hanginges in myne owne (**fo. 4**) Chamber, the hangynges in the chamber over the kytchen The great Chest, and great presse ther/ the Coubourd & the great chest at the staires hed, fyve bedsteds, fyve mattresses, fyve parr of blankets, fyve bolsters of floxe fyve Coverleds suche as are acustomablie vsed for the tenne Choresters, together with all suche wood and Coales as shalbe left in the house, excepting some necessarye fewell for my executour for the tyme beyng there vntill suche tyme as the rest of the stuff be ryd oute of the house, A pestle and morter, the third brasse panne, the worser kettle, the second & third brasse pott, a water Chafer, the worser chaffingdishe, fyve latten Candlestickes, the second & third spytt, the second parr of Aundyrons, one parr of tonges & a fyershovell of the worser sorte a dripping panne, twoe parr of hangers, a trevet, three of the worser platters fowre of the worser dishes, the worst skommer, fowre porryngers vj of the worst sawcers of pewter, one of the worser basons A pottle & a quarte pott of pewter, twoe pynte pottes, the (**fo. 5**) worst chamberpotte/ More I giue to the said Almenerye house to remayne for ever as aforesaid, twoe mazers bownd abowte with sylver, one bygger, and the other lesser vj sylver spoones of the smaller sorte with slyps/ All which said plate & househouldstuff so by me as aforesaid given to the said Almenery house (necessarye Waste onlie excepted) I will that an Inventarie Indentyd thereof to be made, one parte whereof I will shalbe & remayne in the safe custodie of the worshipfull Deane and Chapter of the said Cathedrall churche & their successours, And the other parte thereof to be delyveryd vnto the Almener of the said Cathedrall churche for the tyme beyng, to thentent the said Deane and Chapter maye at their pleasures call the Almener for the tyme beyng to an Accompte/ And for the sure delyverie of the same to his successours for ever/ Item I giue & bequeath to my brother george Westcote xl s/ And to everye of his children xxvj s viij d/ Item I giue and bequeath vnto my syster Jaqnet Goodinow x li: And (fo. 6) forgeve all suche debt as she oweth me./ Item I giue & bequeath vnto Elizabeth westcote wydowe my syster in Lawe twentie pownds, together with the Lease of westgrene which I nowe have, and all the householdstuff, and kyene & Cattell there./ Item I giue & bequeath vnto my brother Robert westcote xiij l vj s viij d/ And I forgeve him all suche debts as he oweth me/ To Andrew westcote his sone x li/ And to everye of his other children xxx s Item I giue vnto Roger westcote, Sebastian, and ffrawnces[1] westcote sonnes of my late brother william westcote, to everye of them x li, allowyng suche thinges or somes of money I owe them/ Item I giue to the daughters of my syster Jaqnet Goodinow iij li apece, beyng fowre of them/ Item I giue & bequethe to my systers daughter which was [married of late] marryed of late, towards the buylding of her howse which was bvrnt vj li xiij s iiij d/ And to her twoe children' xx s apece/ Item I giue & bequeath vnto ffrydiswide Clunye widowe nowe being in howse with me, the some of x li. and (fo. 7) the fourth featherbed perfourmed./ Item I giue to Margarett Riche my syster in lawe xl s in money./ Item I giue to Iohn Thornley & his syster ffrauncs xxx s apece/ Item I giue to Henry Redford,* & to Elizabeth ffarthing dwelling att Bierton in the Countie of Buck if they be living at the tyme of my decease xx s apece/ Item I giue to bartholomew Redford xxx s/ Item I giue to Richard my man xxx s./ Item I giue to Katheryn my mayde servaunt iij li/ Item I giue to Thomas Bluet, Thomas Barsey, Robert, and Iohn Aundersone nowe remaynyng in my howse to everye of them v li apece/ Item I giue to peter Phillips* likewise remaynyng with me vj li xiij s iiij d/ Item I giue to Thomas Venge iij li'./ Item I giue to bromeham, Richard Huse,* Robert Knight,* Nicholas Carleton.*   [2] Baylie   [3] Nasyon,* & gregorye Bowryng* sometymes children of the said Almenerye howse, to everie of them xxs apece/ Item I giue & bequeath to the right worshipfull mr Iustice Southcott* (fo. 8) my especiall good frend, my gilt Cupp With the covers having on the Cover St Sebastian/ Item to my lovyng frend Mr Henry Evans* vj li xiij s iiij d/ and a lytle Cuppe of sylver & a cover with ij lytle rynges on the cover/ Item I giue to Westcote that ys blynde iij li/ Item to my frend Iustynian Kydd gentleman a square sault gilted wroughte./ And Whereas I the said Sebastian westcote haue in this my last will and testament given & bequeathed vnto dyvers of the Children of my brothers & systers & to other my frends children all or the most part of them nowe beyng verye yonge and so by lawe not hable to dischardge my executour of the receight of suche legacies as I haue given vnto them/ my will and meanyng is, that if it shall happen anye of the said children to be putt fourthe apprentyces, that the master & parents of everie suche childe puttyng in sufficient assuraunce to my executour to dischardge him against them. & everie of them for the same shall haue the Legacie of everie suche childe as by s⁴ good discrecion of my executour shalbe thought best (**fo. 9**) for the benefytt of suche childe or children/ Item I giue & bequeathe to Mystres Good wydowe, latelye the wief of doctour Good Physicion a ryng of gold with a blew stone, and to her dawghter Kynborowghe a ryng with three Iemmowes small/ To Mystres Sowthcote a gold ryng of some pretye fasshion to be made for her to the value of xl s/ To mr Iohn Sowthcotes wief the yonger a lyke ryng of gold of xl s price/ The resydew of all my goods, Cattells, money, plate, Iewells, with my debts to me owyng not heretofore given & bequeathed (my debts paid & this my testament acomplished and perfourmed, and all other necessarye expencs and Charges from tyme to tyme that my executour shalbe at satisfied allowed and paid) I whollie geue & bequeath porcion & porcion lyke amongest the children of my brethren and systers/ And thexecutour of this my last will & testament I make & ordayne my lovyng frend Iustinian Kydd* gentleman to whome for his frendlie paynes herein to be taken I giue Tenne pownds/ And overseer of the same I make my foresaid deare frend mr Henry Evans prayeng him to be assisting (**fo. 10**) to my executour with his good Councell, and lykewise to be Carefull for my syster Elizabeth westcote wydowe in her affayres and busynes as tyme shall serve/ In wytnes whereof I the said Sebastian westcote to this my last will & testament have putto my hand & seale the daye & yere aboue wrytten/ wytnesses at the sealyng & delyvering hereof/ Signed sealed & delyveryd as his last will & testament the daye & yere abouesaid as his deed in the presence of mr Creake, Robert Nycholles, Iohn ore, and Raphe Parys gentleman, by me Thomas Creake,/

Legacies given by the said Mr Sebastian westcote after the sealyng subscrybing and delyvering aforesaid the sayd third of Aprill/ To Iohn Ore, more then is conteyned afore tenne shillinges/ To Edward Cooper the Innocent in my howse Six pownds thirtene shillinges fowre pence To William Gafford fyve shillinges/ To mother Alyce Tenne shillynges/ To mother Smaley tenne shillinges/ To mother walker tenne shillinges./ To Pole the keper of (**fo. 11**) the gate* tenne shillinges/ By me Thomas Creake: Ro: Nicolles Radul' Paris/ Iohn Ores mark./

Tercio Aprilis Anno predicto/ More he gave after, theis Legacies aforesaid/ To everie of Mr Raphe Paris Children Tenne shillinges apece/ To Shepard that kepeth the dore at Playes* tenne shillinges/ More to

george Paris tenne shilling*es* to make yt vp twentye shilling*es*/ Ro*bert* Nicolles./
The said testator after the making of his said will gaue to Catheryne his maid for that shee tooke greate paines w*i*th him in his sicknes more then he gave her in his former will fforty shilling*es*./[5]

1. *ffrawnces*: otiose special sign for *es*. 2. Blank in MS. 3. Blank in MS. 4. *s*: scribal slip. 5. *The said . . . shillinges* subscribed in a second hand.

PRO PROB10/105. OffC with two codicils of same date, prob. clause and note of collation with OW subscribed (fo. 11) (latter undated, signed by Anthony Lawes), note of registration marginated (fo. 1). Eleven sheets all numbered except the last, unsealed, unsigned. Text in set secretary with displayed matter in bastard secretary; final codicil in smaller facile secretary.

Prob. PCC 14 Apr. 1582 to Justinian Kidd, friend and executor. Sentence (PROB11/64 fos 235v-236r) promulgated PCC 3 July 1582 (Justinian Kidd, promoter, v. Robert Westcote, brother of deceased) upholding validity of will and confirming Kidd as executor. PAB (PRO PROB8/7 fo. 55v) notes exhibition of inventory.

Noted: Wallace, *Evolution*, p. 171 fn. 2; printed: by G. E. P. Arkwright, *The Musical Antiquary*, IV, 1912–13, pp. 187–9 (abstract), Hillebrand, *Child Actors*, pp. 327–30 (RegC); Trevor Lennam (*Sebastian Westcott, the Children of Paul's and 'The Marriage of Wit and Science'*, Toronto, 1975, pp. 8–9) includes genealogy of Westcott's relatives etc. mentioned in will, identifying many individuals.

c.1515–82. Master of Paul's 1557–82. Imprisoned for recusancy 1577–8, many of legatees of same persuasion. (Chambers II, 12–15, 348; Hillebrand, *Child Actors*, pp. 117–24; Lennam, op. cit.)

Almener] appointed 28 Nov. 1556; no specific appointment as Master of Choristers (R. Gair, 'The conditions of appointment for Masters of Choristers at St Paul's (1553–1613)', *N&Q*, CCXXV, 1980, pp. 116–24 (pp. 116–17)).
gyles] Thomas Giles, haberdasher (**1583**).
Boult] court musician, secular priest at Douai (Lennam, p. 24; *Grove's Dictionary of Music and Musicians*, ed. E. Blom, 5th ed., London, 1954, I, 799–800).
Almenerye howse] granted in 1559 in exchange for maintenance of choristers (R. Gair, 'Conditions of appointment', pp. 117–18).
Henry Redford] possibly a relation of John Redford, Westcott's predecessor as Master, who named him as executor and sole legatee in will, dated 7 Oct., proved 29 Nov. 1547 (PRO PROB11/31 fo. 50r); see also Bartholomew Redford (below).
Phillips] former Paul's chorister, composer, possibly assistant music master to Westcott, left England in Aug. 1582 because of his Catholicism (Lennam, p. 39; *New Grove*).
Huse] Paul's chorister in 1554 (Lennam, p. 39).

Knight] Paul's chorister in 1574 (ibid.).
Carleton] later a composer (ibid.; *New Grove*).
Nasyon] Paul's chorister in 1574 (Lennam, p.39).
Bowryng] Paul's chorister in 1574 (ibid.).
Southcott] Justice of Queen's Bench, also from Devon, neighbour in Essex; Catholic (Lennam p. 24 fn. 21).
Evans] lessee of first Blackfriars 1583, and second 1600–8, associated with management of Children of Chapel (later Queen's Revels) (Chambers II, 315; Nungezer, p. 132).
Kydd] refers to duties as executor in will, dated 28 June 1598, proved 22 Jan. 1599 (PRO PROB11/93 fo. 1r).
gate] evidence of theatre in Paul's precincts (Reavley Gair, *The Children of Paul's: The Story of a Theatre Company, 1553–1608*, Cambridge, 1982, p. 56).
dore at Playes] see note on *gate* above.

1583 June 19 Thomas GILES (abstract)

(Gyles) Citizen and haberdasher of London. Sick. Soul 'vnto the Allmightie God my onelye maker Savioure and Redemer'. Burial in parish church where he lives or in church of Saincte Thomas Acon commonly called Mercers' Chapel. To hospital of the poor fatherless children £3 6s 8d, children to be at his burial. To poor people where most need is in City, to be distributed either in money or bread £3 6s 8d. To poorest prisoners in City prisons £3 6s 8d in money or bread. 40s to pay fees of such poor prisoners who are in debt for their delivery. To poorest people in town of Kythermynster co. Worcester 40s and, if he has any poor kindred there, to them another 40s. To poorest of his kindred wherever they live £3 6s 8d. To poorest people in county of Worecester, where he was born, 40s where most need is. To poor people in almshouse of Stowe of the foundation of Mr William Chester 40s. To all his poor tenants who pay less than 20s p.a. rent, a quarter's rent, and to come to his burial. To certain preachers who shall preach a sermon every Sunday for one year after his death, 5s for every sermon preached, that is £13. To eldest son and his heirs, all freehold land in London and suburbs on condition that he and they shall allow his other brothers to enjoy all copyhold lands in Middlesex and Surrey: and if eldest son or his heirs are not willing to release moiety of copyhold, to his other sons and their heirs as much of his freehold as that moiety of copyhold amounts to. Whereas he had bought from Anthonye Longe of Lambeth a tenement and three acres of land in pa. Lambeth co. Surrey, being freehold and leased back to him, if Longe pays to executors for use of his children sum named in covenant made between said Longe and testator, then wife or heirs to release right in same; if they refuse to do this, if said Longe and his heirs pay said sum of money, Longe to have rent out of his freehold land, and all legacies to wife and to eldest heir of his freehold land to stand void. To each of his children living at time of his death, £40 over and above their children's parts, to be paid them at the time of their reaching full age or marriage, provided those which are unmarried marry with assent of executors and overseers; if any die before reaching full age or marriage, their portions to be equally divided among rest of his children that survive. Wife to have convenient place of his in which to live as long as she is unmarried. To brother John Gyles, if he is alive, gold ring to value of 40s and black gown of cloth. To children of eldest brother, John Gyles deceased, £6 to be divided among them. To brother Robert Gyles £10 and good gown of his and to each of his children 20s. To sister Dolytell a gown cloth and 20s to her daughter. To brother Sympson and testator's sister, his wife, £6 13s 4d and to each a gown cloth, and to each of their children 20s. To all brothers and sisters on mother's side by Thomas Thrope 20s each. To brother Chester and wife gown cloth and likewise to brother Howson and wife. To wellbeloved friends Gregorye Charlett, Lawrence Higgens, John England, Roberte England, to each a gown cloth if they are alive. Twenty poor men's gowns to be given for him at his burial, of which Robert Ringsted, Nicholas Gressopp, and other of his poor tenants to have part at discretion of executors. To Richarde Wood, servant, 40s, and to all rest of servants 20s each. To such of his friends as shall take pains with him in the time of his sickness, either gown cloths or rings of some reasonable value at discretion of executors. To brothers of Company of Haberdashers £6 to be spent on dinner on day of burial, or if they refuse it, then money to be distributed to poor people where most need is. One of sons who follows his trade to have house and shop in which testator now lives if wife happens to marry again. £10 to be bestowed in charitable deeds as executors choose. If friends to whom he has bequeathed legacies are not living at time of death, said legacies to be given to certain other friends to 'whome I beare lyke good will vnto aswell as yf I had named theme by name'. Residue of goods and chattels to be bestowed according to custom of the City of London to wife and children. Appoints as executors brother John Gyles, Gregorye Charlett, son Thomas and son Hughe Dyghtonn, to whom gold rings of reasonable value for their pains. Appoints as overseers wellbeloved wife, cousin Trott, Mr William Cob, brother Robert Gyles; to have gowns. To a herald at arms within three months of death £6 13s 4d. Wit. Baldwynn Castelton scrivener, and Rycharde Lambertonn.

PRO PROB11/65 fos 300v-301v. RegC with prob. clause.

Prob. PCC 21 Aug. 1583 to executors, Thomas Giles, his son, and Hugh Dighton, his son-in-law, reserving power to John Giles, his brother, George (rightly Gregory) Charlett, his friend, renouncing. PAB (PRO PROB8/7 fo. 119r) notes exhibition of inventory and gives pa. of origin as All Hallows Honey Lane.

fl. 1571-7. Perhaps haberdasher who supplied Revels Office with vizards and hired out costumes c.1572. Legatee of Sebastian Westcott (1582). (Feuillerat, pp. 409-10, etc.; Chambers I, 79-80.)

1585 Aug. 12 John BENTLEY

In the name of God amen' the Twelveth' daie of Auguste 1585. And in the seaven' and twentith yere of the reigne' of our soueraigne Ladie Elizabeth' by the grace of god Quene of England ffraunce & Irelande defendour of the faith &c. I Iohn Bentley servaunt to our soueraigne ladie the Quenes maiestie beinge sick in body but whole in mynde & of good & perfect remembraunce laude & praise be therefore given to Almightie god do make ordeyne & dispose this my present testament conteyninge herin my last will In manner and fourme following that is to saie first and principally I commende my soule to Almightie god my only Creatour and to Iesus Christe his only son' my saviour & redemer in whome & by the merittes of whose most precious death' and resurrection' I hope & beleve to haue full' & free remission' & forgivenes of my synnes & life everlastinge And my bodie to be buried whereas god shall' ordeyne for the same. Item' I will that all' suche debtes and duties as I do owe of right or in conscience to any person' or persons shalbe well' & truly paid within convenient tyme after my deceas by my executrice vndernamed/ Item I give and bequeth' vnto my sonne Thomas Bentley ffifty Poundes of lawfull' mony of Englande to be paid vnto him at his lawfull' age of twenty and one yeres. Item I give & bequeth vnto Elizabeth Bentley my daughter other ffifty Poundes of Laufull' mony of England to be paid vnto hi<r> at hir laufull age of twentie & one yeres or daie of mariage whether of the two cases first happen'/ Item I will & my minde is & I do devise that if my said sonne Thomas happen to deceas before he shall' accomplishe his saide age of xxj yeres that then as nowe & nowe as then I give and bequeth the said fifty poundes by me before bequeth to the said Thomas vnto & amongest My sisters Matilde Hindes, katherne knocke & vnto my brothers Steven {Richard & Edward} Bentley equally amongest them' part & part like to be devidid. Item I will & my minde is & I do devise that if my said daughter Elizabeth happen to deceas before hir laufull age

of twentie & one yeres or daie of mariage that then' I will the said fifty poundes so before to hir bequethid shall' remayne' & be paid vnto & amongest my said two sisters Matilde & katheren' & my three brothers Steven, Richard & Edwarde equally amongest them' five to be devidid/ And whereas there is the som*m*e of one hundreth poundes owing vnto me by william' waspe of Saxon' strete, Thomas Bently of newmarket, & George knocke of Brinckly. I will there shalbe no allowaunce taken' for the vse thereof. during the tyme that they shall' haue the occupyinge of the same/ Item I will & my minde' is that Johan my welbelovid wife shall' haue the vse & occupyinge of the said one hundreth pound*es* after that it shalbe recyvid vntill the said Legaces bequethid to my sad two children' shalbe due & payable by this my last will & testament. So that she do put in sufficient suerties to my Overseers to be bounde {wit*h* hir} for the payment thereof accordinge to this my last will Item' I do relees & forgive vnto my brother Steven Bently the five pound*es* he oweth me/ Item' I give and bequeth to my loving mother Elizabeth Bentley one gold Ringe in value at the discretion' of my executrice/ The whole (fo. 2) residewes of all' & singuler my goodd*es* chattell*es* Iewells reddy mony and debt*es* whatsoeu*er* they be and wheresoeu*er* they may be founde after my debt*es* paid & my funerall*es* & legacies don*n* and p*er*fourmed I wholly give will & bequeth vnto the saide Johan my wife she therewi*th* to do & dispose hir owne free will & pleasure. w*h*ich said Johan my wife of this my p*re*sent testament & last will I make name ordayne & appoint my sole Execatrice. And of the execuc*i*on of the same I make name & appoint my trustie frend*es*[1] Robert Scotte of Shordiche in the Countie of midd*le*sex yeoman'. and my brother in lawe Henry Haughton' Citizen' & Sadler of london' my overseers. Providid alwaies & my will & minde is that the said Johan' my wife shall' haue the Educac*i*on & bringing vp of my said two children', or the placinge of them' to be vertuously brought vp in respect that I haue appointid hir to haue the vse of their porcions', And I vtterly revoke all' form*er* will*es* executou*r*s & ou*er*seers and I will this. to stand for my very last will & testament & no*n*e other or otherwise/ In witnes whereof I the said John' Bentley to this my p*re*sent testament & last will haue set my [hand] hande & seale/ datid the daie & yeres first aboue written'/   Iohn Bentley
Witnesses at the readinge sealinge subscribinge and deliu*er*ye hereof Richard Gall: notarie Publique & John' lan'eham* & Elizabeth Maye X

1. *ffrendes*: originally *frende*, *es* overwritten.

PRO PROB10/114. OW, note of registration marginated (fo. 1) and prob. clause subscribed (fo. 2). Two numbered sheets joined at the top, sealed (fo. 2). Secretary hand; many otiose marks of abbreviation.

Prob. PCC 19 Aug. 1585 to Peter Johnson, notary public, proctor for Joan, relict and executrix. PAB (PRO PROB8/7 fo. 229r) gives pa. of origin as All Hallows Lombard St.

Printed: G. E. Bentley 'The wills of two Elizabethan actors', MP, XXIX, 1931–2, pp. 110–14 (pp. 111–12) (RegC).

c.1553–85. Actor; Queen Elizabeth's Men 1583. Buried 19 Aug. 1585 St Peter's Cornhill. (Chambers II, 105–7, 303; Nungezer, pp. 44–5.)

lan'eham] actor, Queen Elizabeth's Men 1583, 1588–91 (Chambers II, 328).

1588 Sept. 3 Richard TARLTON

To all christen[1] people to whome this presente Writing shall come Richard Tarlton one of the Groomes of the Queenes maiesties chamber greetinge in our Lord Euerlasting. Knowe Ye that I the said Richard for the naturall love and fatherlie affeccion that I doe beare vnto my naturall and welbeloued sonne Phillip* Tarlton and to the intent that he maie be the better maintained and brought vppe in the feare of god and good lettres haue giuen graunted confirmed assigned and sett over and by theis presentes doe give graunt {confirme} assigne and sett over vnto my said sonne all such goodes cattalles chattelles plate readie money Iewelles bondes obligatorie and specialties whatsoeuer that I nowe haue or am possessed of or hereafter by any meanes shalbe or in whose handes custodie or possession the same nowe bee or hereafter [at] att anye time shalbe together with all suche debtes and sommes of money as nowe or or any tyme hereafter shalbe due or groweinge dewe or owinge vnto me by any person or persons whatsoeuer To haue hold possesse enioye perceive and receave all my said goodes cattelles chattelles plate readie money Iuelles bondes obligatorie speciallties and debtes whatsoever as afore said vnto my said sonne Phillipp Tarlton and to the proper vse and behoufe of the same Phillip his executors and assignes from the daie of the date hereof for ever Prouided alwaies and I do hereby assigne authorise and appointe my most loving mother katherine Tarlton widowe and my very loving and trustie friendes Robert Adams* of the parish of saincte Bridgett alias Bride in the suburbes of London' gentleman and my fellowe William Iohnson* one also of the Groomes of her maiesties chamber to haue the use government custodie and disposicion of my said sonne together with all my said goodes and cattelles to the entent and purpose[2] (p. 2) aforesaid vntill he shall attaine and accomplish his full age of twentie and one yeares and they and every of them that shall take vppon them to deale in this behaulf to yeald a iuste and true accompte vnto my said sonne. In witnes of all and singuler the premisses I the said Richard Tarlton haue at thensealing and deliverie hereof delivered one penny of lawfull money of England to the said Robert Adams to the vse of the said Phillipp Tarlton by waye of possession and seison of all my said good*es* and cattell*es* and herevnto haue sett my hand and sealle with[t] the said penny therein fixed yeouen the third daie of September 1588 and in the xxxth yeare of the Raigne of our soveraigne Ladie Elizabeth by the grace of god of England ffraunce and Ireland Queene defendor of the faith &c. Richard Tarlton. Signed sealled and deliuered vnto the aboue named Robert Adams to the vse of the said Phillipp Tarlton in the presence of theis pe*r*sons vnderwritten Stephen Wassell his marke X Leonard Hodges his marke X Charles Barnard/

1. *christen*: MS has *xp'en*.   2. Catchword *aforesaid*.

PRO PROB10/124. OffC, with grant of admon subscribed (p. 2) and note of registration, describing document as 'Voluntas Rich*ar*di Tarlton de*functi*', marginated (p. 1). Single sheet folded in half to make four pages, unsealed.

Admon [with will annexed]. PCC 6 Sept. 1588 to Robert Adams, one of trustees of Philip Tarlton, his son, in his minority. Admon Act Book (PROB6/4 fo. 89v) records grant of admon 21 Feb. 1589 to Helen Barnard alias Tarleton, sister of deceased, in person of Christopher Smith, notary public, her proctor, admon of Adams having been revoked, and that letters were introduced 18 Jan. 1595.

Printed: J. O. Halliwell, ed., *'Tarlton's Jests' and 'News Out of Purgatory'*, Shakespeare Society, London, 1844, pp. xii–xv (RegC).

fl. 1570–88. Actor and author; Queen Elizabeth's Men 1583. Buried St Leonard's Shoreditch 3 Sept. 1588. See J. O. Halliwell, *Papers Respecting Disputes which Arose from Incidents at the Death-Bed of Richard Tarlton, the Actor, in . . . 1588*, London, 1866. (Chambers II, 342–5; Nungezer, pp. 347–65.)

Phillip] godson of Sir Philip Sidney.
Adams] immediately after signing will Tarlton petitioned Walsingham for protection for his son against Adams (*Calendar of State Papers, Domestic Series of the Reign of Elizabeth, 1581–1590*, ed. R. Lemon, London, 1865, p. 541).
Iohnson] fellow actor with Queen's Men 1583, 1587–8 (Chambers II, 324; Nungezer, p. 206).

1592 Aug. 19 Simon JEWELL

In the name of god amen The ninetenth daie of Auguste one thousand fiue hundrethe ninetie [one] twoe, and in the thirtie fourth yeere of the raigne of our soueraigne Ladie Elizabeth the Queenes ma*ies*tie that nowe is &c I Simon Iewell beinge of good and p*erfe*cte memorie have sett downe heere in writinge as well suche seuerall sommes of moneie as are due to me as also suche seuerall sommes of money w*hi*ch I doe give in forme followinge that is to saie. Inprimis due vnto me the said Simon Iewell from my fellowes for my share of apparrell the somm of thirteene pounde six shillinges eighte pence. Item more due vnto me from my fellowes the sixth parte of thirtie seaven pounde w*hi*ch amounteth to six pounde three shilling*es* fouer pence, and haue paide my share for horses waggen and apparrell newe boughte. Item more due to me from my fellowes xiiij li out of w*hi*ch my share is to be abated w*hi*ch commeth to fortie six shillinges eighte pence, and the residewe (**fo. 131r**) {Remayinge} w*hi*ch is due to me w*hi*ch amountethe to eleven pounde thirteene shillinges fouer pence w*hi*ch xj li xiij s iiij d my fellowes muste paie to mr Brookes at Chrismas nexte only Item my will is that mr Brookes shall vppon the paimente of xj li xiij s iiij d or p*res*entlie after for me to my vse paie or cause to be paide vnto my Land lorde Roberte Scott the said eleven pounde thirteene shillinges fouer pence. Item more due vnto me from my fellowes for plates suger and banquetinge stuf Thirtie shillinges. Item more due vnto me from mr Cooke the somm of eighte shillinges. Somm totall of money due vnto me commeth to thirtie three pounde one shillinge fower pence. Item I doe owe to mr Matthewes five pounde. Item I doe owe to mr Welshe mercer in Cheapeside Three pounde thirteene shillinges fouer pence. Item I doe owe to Richarde ffletcher fouer pounde. Item I doe owe to william Belchen[1] twentie shillinges. Item I doe owe to Thomas Vincente* fortie five shillinges. Item I doe owe to mr Brookes for a paire of veluett hose thirtie shillinges. Item I doe owe to mr Iohnson* the sixte share out of thirteene pounde six shillinge eighte pence w*hi*ch is my parte w*hi*ch share commeth to fortie fouer shillinges five pence w*hi*ch muste be paide to him with my fellowes shares, w*hi*ch is the whole xiij li vj s viij d: Somm totall of the debtes owinge by me cometh to nyneteene pounde twelve shillinges nine pence Soe remaines due to me Thirteene pounde tenn shillinges pennie. Item I giue to mr Brookes a murninge cloak. Item I giue to Roberte Scott my blacke cloke lined with taffatie. Item I giue to Eme Scott my livery coate and to his daughter Harris Scott five pounde. Item I giue vnto mr Smithe* a black veluet purse imbrodered with golde and siluer. Item I giue to Roberte Nicholls* all my playenge things in a box and my veluet shewes, And as for my horse and all the reste of my goodes are p*res*entelie to be solde for my buriall. I doe requeste vppon curtesie the saide Mr Smithe and Roberte Scott to see euerie thinge p*er*formed when they haue receaued in my debt*es* as my trust is in them. In witnes wheareof I haue heervnto sett my hande the daie and yeere abouesaide. Item my share of suche money as shalbe givenn by my ladie Pembrooke or by her meanes I will shalbe distributed and paide towardes my buriall and other charges by mr Scott and the saide mr Smithe Simon Ivell. Teste me Iohanne Browne Scri*uener*./

1. *Belchen*: Edmond reads *Belcher*.

PRO PROB11/80 fo. 130v-131r. RegC with grant of admon and note of execution.

Admon [with will annexed]. PCC 23 Aug. 1592 to Richard Gooddall, notary public, proctor for William Smith of pa. St Leonard in Shoreditch co. Middlesex, gent., and Robert Scott of pa. Stepney (Stebinheth) co. Middlesex, yeoman, trustees. PAB (PRO PROB8/9 fo. 103r) notes exhibition of inventory.

Printed: Mary Edmond, 'Pembroke's Men', *RES* n.s., XXV, 1974, pp. 129–36 (pp. 129–30) (with commentary).

fl. pre-1592. Actor; Earl of Pembroke's Men. Buried 21 Aug. 1592 St Leonard Shoreditch.

Vincente] possibly the prompter at Globe (Bentley II, 612).
Iohnson] Edmond speculates on identification with Ben Jonson (pp. 133–6).
Smithe] actor in Pembroke's (Edmond, p. 131).
Nicholls] actor in Pembroke's (Edmond, pp. 131, 133).

1593 Apr. 8 Margaret BRAYNE

In the name of god Amen, the Eighte daie of Apryll, anno *1593*. and in the xxxvth yeare of the reigne of oure soue*r*eigne ladie Elizabeth by the grace of god Queene of Englande, fraunce and Irelande defendor of the ffaithe &c' I Margarett Brayne of the p*a*rishe of st Marye Matfellon' al*ias* whitechappell in the County of Midd*lesex* widdowe beinge wholle in minde sick of boddye but of a p*er*fecte memory and remembraunce laude and prayse bee gyven' to Allmightie god therefore doe make and ordaine this my p*rese*nte wrytinge conteyninge herein my laste will and Testament in mann*er* and forme followinge that is to saye. Fyrste and principally and aboue all thing*es* I Com*m*end my Sowle to Almightie god my maker and to Ihesus Christ his sonne my Savioure & redeemer trustinge in and by his meritt*es* & p*re*cious bloodsheddinge to bee saued and to attaine lyfe euerlastinge And as concerninge the disposition of all & singuler such my good*es* Chattells, ymplement*es* and howseholdstuffe and other good*es* whatsoeuer mooveable or vnmooveable wh*i*ch I am nowe invested or wh*i*ch to mee is or shalbee by any mann*er* of waies or meanes howsoeuer appertayninge or belonginge. I freelye and whollye gyve & bequeath the same in manner & forme followinge that is to saye. Item I gyve & bequeath vnto Robarte Myles* cittezen & goldsmithe of london in consideracion that I am greately indebted vnto him in such greate somme and sommes of money as that all the goodes I haue in the wholle worlde will nothinge countervaile the same. All such interest right, propertie Clayme and demaund whatsoeu{er} which I the saide Margarett Braine haue sholde or oughte to haue of in or to the one moyetie or half<e> parte of the Playe howse commonly called the Theater nere Hollywell in the Countye of Middlesex And alsoe my minde & will is that the said Robarte Myles shall haue all the benefitt proffytte, an<d> Commodytie thereof arrysinge cominge or growinge or which by any meanes may descend or comme by vir<tue> of the saide moyetie or half parte of the Theater to me in right belonging as aforesaide. I<tem> I gyve & bequeath vnto the saide Robarte Myles All & al manner of bondes bills, specialtyes de<btes> somme & sommes of money whatsoeuer as I nowe haue, or which by virtue of any such bondes or specialties may bee gotten wonne or obtained, or which nowe & hereafter shall growe due and payable. And las<tly> I gyve & bequeath vnto the saide Robarte Myles all & singuler my goodes, Chattells, howsehold<stuffe> and other of my goodes whatsoeuer. Item my will is in consideracion partely of the premisses that the saide Robarte[1] Myles shall keepe, educate & bringe vpp Katherine* Brayne my husbandes daughter of whome I hoape he wilbee good vnto, and haue an honest care for her preferment And I make & ordaine the saide Robarte Myles sole Executour of this my saide Testament and laste will In Wetnes whereof [hereunto] I the saide Margarett Brayne haue hereunto sett my hande & seale. The daye & yeares ffyrste abouewritten   signum dicte Margaret B[2] Brayne Sigillat et delibat pro facto in presencia mei Georgij Harryson Scriuener Nicholas Byshopp* Ihon pattesonn Witnesses Barbary Byshopp & Elizabeth Hunte

1. *Robarte*: R written over T in the same hand. 2. *B*: her mark.

GL MS 9172/16a no. 96. OW, prob. clause and note of registration endorsed. Single sheet, with remnant of applied seal, mark of testator and signatures of witnesses. Text in facile secretary with displayed matter in italic. Right margin crumbling with some loss of legibility, readings supplied from RegC (GL MS 9171/18 fo. 26v–27r).

Prob. CCL 3 May 1593 to Jacob Ireland, notary public, proctor for Robert Miles, executor. PAB (GL MS 9168/14 fo. 260v) gives value of inventory as 48s 4d.

Printed: Wallace, pp. 153–4 (RegC).

fl. 1578–83. Gatherer at Theatre after 1586. Claimed half interest in Theatre as heir of husband John Brayne (1578). For disputes and litigation with J. Burbage (A1597) over Theatre see Wallace, and Berry, 'Handlist'.

Myles] executor of John Brayne; accused by Margaret of causing husband's death but subsequently joined her in dispute with Burbages which he continued after her death. Sisson ('Brayne, Burbage and Miles' in his *Boar's Head*, pp. 84–94) argues that will 'bears all the signs of dictation by Miles' (p. 91). Miles died 1614 (will dated 22 Mar., proved 8 Apr. 1614, PRO PROB11/123 fos 255r–255v).

Katherine] not mentioned in father's will; in 1588 Burbage alleged that Brayne was childless (Wallace, p. 42).

Byshopp] appointed by Margaret in 1590 as collector at Theatre (Chambers II, 392); acted as her witness 1592 in dispute with Burbage; had been Miles's employee and was in business with Miles's son (Sisson, op. cit. pp. 91–2).

1593 Oct. 20 Brian ELLAM (abstract)

Of pa. St Albons in Woodstreete, citizen and carpenter of London. Soul 'into the handes of Allmighty god my heavenly father and to Ihesus christe his only sonne my onlye Saviour and Redemer by whose deathe and resurrection I hope to be made partaker of his heavenly kingdome'. Burial in parish church of St Albons as near as possible to body of late wife. To son John Ellam* one half of all household stuff and utensils; other half to Richard Hudson,* late wife's son, to be equally divided between them. Forgives cousin Raphe Haughton 40s which he owes him by bond. To said son John Ellam and heirs, house in Silverstreete in which testator lives; if he dies without heirs same tenement to Richard Hudson, son-in-law, and heirs for ever. Appoints John Ellam executor. Revokes all former wills. Wit. Gregory Pyford, Christopher Dyson.

GL MS 9172/16d fo. 68r. OffC, grant of admon and note of exhibition of inventory, valued at £6 9s 7d, subscribed, note of registration endorsed. Single sheet, parchment, bound into volume.

Admon [with will annexed]. CCL 24 Nov. 1593 to Richard Hudson, one of legatees, John Ellam, executor, having died.

c.1534–93. Carpenter employed by James Burbage (A1597) to build Theatre; gave evidence for Burbages in disputes with Margaret Brayne (1593) and Giles Allen (A1608). Buried St Alban's Wood Street. (Wallace, p. 76; Berry, 'Handlist', p. 122.)

John Ellam] nuncupative will dated 24 Oct. 1593 (GL MS 9172/16d fo. 69r) refers to death of father which must have taken place between 20 and 24 Oct.

Hudson] bricklayer and carpenter who worked on Theatre; gave evidence for Burbages 1592–1602 (Wallace, pp. 77, 226–9, 289–90; Berry, 'Handlist', pp. 122, 128–9, 131).

1597 June 15 Thomas BREND (abstract)

Of West Moulsey co. Surrey gent. Soul 'to Allmightie God my onely Sauiour, maker, and Redeemer and by whose onely death and passion I hope to be saued'. To son Nicholas his great salt with a cover all gilt, twelve silver spoons with 'wreedendes acorne fashion', two cushions of gold with gold tassels, and his gold ring which he wears with his name engraved. To daughter Anne and her heirs, messuage in pa. Wansworthe co. Surrey, in tenure and occupation of Sence Casellman or her assigns, and house in Kingston upon Thames co. Surrey, now in the tenure and occupation of John Foxe, butcher, or his assigns. To daughter Judith* and her heirs, tenement in Newe Fishestreete now in tenure of Charles Hillton, fishmonger, or his assigns. To nephew Frauncis Brend, son of his brother Thomas Brend, and his heirs for ever, house in Fridaye Streete near Ould Fyshestreete in London now in tenure and occupation of Martyn Crane or his assigns. To nephew Raphe Bowldwin, and to his male heirs, house in town of Greenewiche co. Kent now in tenure and occupation of said Raphe or his assigns. To said Frances Brend £10. To Jone Peirson his late servant 40s. To brother Thomas Brend £10. To either of his daughters Marye Maylard and Katheren Seares 40s in gold to make them two gold rings each. To Jone Pierson tenement with garden adjoining, in which John Henrye lately dwelled, for her life without rent, in consideration of great pains taken with him and his late wife and children during her time of service. Not more than £40 to be spent on his funeral. All his goods, plate, jewels, ready money, chattels and debts to be valued 'to the vttermost value they are worthe of whatsoeuer quality they be of, and that is to the value [of] ffourepence whatsoeuer they be, and not in lumps, as they vse to be praysed, but particulerly by euerie parcell it self', four appraisers to be chosen by overseers and given 40s each, and appraisal to be carried out within one month of his decease. Executors and overseers charged not to keep anything back over value of 4d. To daughter Anne for ever, house at Wanswourth with all lands belonging to it, in which John Casellman lately dwelled, or else £100. To poor of pa. Westmoulsey £4 to be given them quarterly as they have need by his executors. To said daughter Anne, and to her heirs for ever, seven cottages in pa. Saincte Andrewes Undershafte or Saincte Mary Axe near Lymestreate, or Leaden hall in London, or Saincte Mary Axe, now in tenure of a number of tenants. Residue to daughters Anne,* Mercye and Judith, divided equally among them. Appoints daughter Anne executor and two sons-in-law George Seares and John Bodley,* and cousin John Collett his overseers, to whom £5 each. Revokes all other wills. 'I haue stryken out my sonne* to be one of my Executours in consideracion that he [had] {did} marry without my knowledge or consent.'

PRO PROB11/93 fos. 270v–271v. RegC with grant of admon, marginal notes recording two further grants.

Admon [with will annexed]. PCC 8 May 1599 to Edward Saye, notary public, proctor for Nicholas Brend, son, Anne, daughter and executor renouncing; 21 May 1606 to Sir Sigismond Zinzan and to Margaret Zinzan, his wife, widow of Nicholas Brend, brother (rightly son) and administrator of the testator, during minority of Matthew, John, Jane, Mary (rightly Mercy) and Frances Brend, children of Nicholas and Margaret; 26 July 1621 to Jane Brend, having reached her full age. PAB (PRO PROB8/11 fo. unnumbered (May 1599)) notes undated exhibition of inventory.

c.1516–98. Landowner. Acquired site of Globe in 1554; inquisition *post mortem* of estate, taken c.16 May 1599, included interest 'de et in vna Domo de novo edificata . . . in parochia *Sancti* Salvatoris praedicta in Comitatu Surria praedicta in occupacione Willielmi Shakespeare et aliorum', not mentioned in will. Buried St Peter's West Molesey, 21 Sept. 1598. (C. W. Wallace, 'Further new documents', *The Times*, 1 May 1914, p. 4; see Berry, *Playhouses*, pp. 75–119, for account of Brend family and its involvement with Globe.)

Judith] died 1599; will dated 20 Apr., proved 15 May 1599 (PRO PROB11/93 fos 298v–299r).
Anne] died 1599 (Berry, op. cit., p. 87) but appears to have renounced administration before death.
Bodley] Brend's stepson by second wife Mercy's first marriage (Berry, op. cit., p. 83); see index.
sonne] Nicholas (**1601**) married Margaret Strelly in 1595, later wife of Sir Sigismond Zinzan, who, through her interest, owned Globe site from 1624 until her death in 1627 (Berry, op. cit., pp. 89–104).

1599 Dec. 8 James TUNSTALL

Testamentum Iacobi Tunstall[1]

In the name of God Amen the eight daie of December[2] in the yeare of our Lord [God] one thowsand five hundred ninety {and} nine Iames Tunstall of the parish of St Catherin Coleman of the Citty of London Sadler and Cittizen of the same Citty being sick in bodye but of sownde and perfect remembraunce made and declared his last will and Testament nuncupatiue in manner and forme following ffirst he {gave and} bequeathed his soule vnto Iesus Christe his Redeemer, and his body to the earth to be buried at the discrecion of his Executrix hereafter named Item he gave and bequeathed all and singuler his goodes Cattelles Chattells mony debtes and whatsoeuer he was possessed of vnto Iane his wife and made her his whole and only Executrix and overseer of this his last will and Testament nuncupative in the presence of Ellen Euor[3] the wife of Oliver Euor and Margaret Engleton the wife of davie Engleton of the parish of

St Katherin Colman afforesaid signum Ellene Euor signum Margarete Engleton.//

1. T: . . . *Tunstall*: marginated. 2. *December*: written over *September* in same hand. 3. *Euor*: possibly *Euer* throughout.

GL MS 9051/5 fo. 145v. RegC (nuncupative will) with prob. clause.

Prob. ACL 15 Dec. 1599 to Jane Tunstall, relict and executor. PAB (GL MS 9050/3 fo. 121r) records exhibition of inventory on 22 Jan. 1600, valued at £17 17s.

fl. 1583–99. Possibly the actor; Worcester's 1583; Admiral's 1590–1, 1594–7. (Chambers II, 347; Nungezer, p. 381).

1601 Apr. 16 Jane POLEY (abstract)

(Pooley) Of pa. Saint Marie Matefellon alias Whit Chappell co. Middlesex, widow. Revokes all former wills. Soul 'vnto the handes of god Almightie, trustinge to be saved by the deathe And merittes of Iesus Christ his onely sonne my Saviour and Redemer'/ And by no other meanes'. Burial in White Chappell church. To son Sir John Pooley* kt., lease held from William Glascocke gent. deceased, of parcel of ground called Wodlandes in pa. Sainte Marie Matefellon alias White Chappell abutting on Northe Hoge Lane, for several years yet to come, and all her interest and term of years in same both in possession and in reversion, together with rents. Except one little tenement in which Richard Wright, carman, lives, part of her said lease, which he holds at a yearly rent of 40s, said rent to be distributed during term of lease to poor living in pa. White Chappell by her executors and churchwardens of parish half yearly, 20s to be paid at time of her burial. And except rent of one garden being £3 p.a., part of her aforesaid lease, in tenure of John Grynkyn or his assigns, and the garden to her son-in-law Henrie Gibbes gent., during term of lease, towards education and bringing up of the children he now has. To Frauncis Wibard, daughter, £40 to be paid as necessary by her executors for the maintenance of her and her poor children and the bringing up of them, provided that, if she dies before sum is fully paid, the remainder be distributed equally among her children then living, each to be the others' heir; if they all die before they have their portions, the rest to her son Sir John Poolie kt.; or otherwise, if her executors prefer to use the money to bind them as apprentices, or to some other good use. To Henry Wibard, Fabian Wibard, Edmond Wibard and Jane Wibard 50s each, each to be the others' heir, at twenty-one or to bind them to a trade or otherwise, as thought suitable. To Marie Gibbes, grandchild, £10 to be paid at age twenty-one or on marriage whichever happens first; if she dies before, to be divided equally among the present children of son, Henrie Gibbes, and daughter Anne, on marriage or at age twenty-one whichever happens first, each to be the others' heir. To brother John Grove 40s. To sister White's children 40s equally between them. To William Trige,* sister Trige's son, 40s. To Albyn Bond, sister of said William Trige, 20s to be paid within one year of her death. 20s to be distributed among poor of pa. White Walton co. Berks. where she was born, at discretion of executors. To William Pigot 40s. To Mrs Harris 20s. To each of godchildren 5s. To John Bradelei's two children 5s each. To son Sir John Pooley kt. her bracelet of angels, her best gold wedding ring which his father gave her, and a gold ring with a diamond. To daughter Elizabeth Miller a hope ring in gold, five gold buttons, one featherbed and one bolster now on the bed on which she lies, a pair of blankets and a pillow; and to her husband a little ring of gold with a turquoise. To said daughter Fraunces a little hope ringe of gold, a little gold ring with a ruby, a kirtle of camlet, her worsted gown and holiday petticoat. To daughter Anne Gibbes a hope ring of gold and one gold ring with a pearl, a black silk kirtle, her best petticoat guarded with velvet, her cloth gown welted with velvet, a featherbed, one bolster which belongs to her bed, one pair of blankets and a pillow. To nephew John Grove 40s to be paid within one year of her death. To wife of Mr Davis in Gracious Street, daughter of Mrs Skynner, a gold ring with a death's head. To Mistress Palmer her black kirtle guarded with velvet. To old Mother Britton her workday gown and petticoat. To Goodwife Reignoldes, testator's former servant, 20s. Residue to Sir John Pooley her son whom, with nephew Edmond Pooley of Badeley esq., she appoints executor. To said cousin Poolie 40s to make him a small ring as a remembrance and entreats him to be friendly to her children as he has been. To old and loving good friend George Clarcke for a remembrance a gold ring. Wit. John Rogers, W. Pigete, Roger Saunders.

PRO PROB10/204. OffC, prob. clause subscribed (fo. 3), note of registration marginated (fo. 1). Three sheets sewn at the top, second fo. numbered 2. Text in facile secretary with many otiose marks of abbreviation and punctuation.

Prob. PCC 8 July 1601 to Richard Stubbes, notary public, proctor for Sir John Pooley, son and executor, reserving power to Edmund Pooley, nephew and executor.

Noted: Sisson, *Boar's Head*, pp. 25–6.

fl. 1561–1601. Owner of Boar's Head Inn and resident there while in use as theatre. Inn not mentioned in will as sublet from 1595 to, among others, Robert Browne (**A1604**) and Francis Langley (**A1602**). (Sisson, op. cit.; Berry, *Boar's Head Playhouse*, passim.)

John Pooley] for history of Boar's Head under his ownership, see Berry, op. cit., pp. 76–9.

William Trige] possibly actor; with King's Men from c.1626 (Nungezer, p. 380; Bentley II, 604–6); see index.

1601 Oct. 10 Nicholas BREND (abstract)

Of West Mowlsey co. Surrey, esq. Sick. Soul 'into the handes of Almighty God'. Burial at discretion of executrix and overseers. All debts in writing owing to him at death be used toward payment of such debts owed by him. Six tenements in East-grenewich co. Kent, manor or farm called the man in pa. of Cudham co. Kent, in tenure of William Blake or his assigns, seven messuages or tenements in St Mary Actes in pa. St Andrewe Undershaft near Limestreete in London, two messuages or tenements in Candleweekstreete in pa. St Mary Abchurch in London in tenure of William Clarke and William Treherne, messuage or tenement in which he dwells on St Peters Hill London, and one other tenement there in tenure of Thomas Halse, dyer, to be sold by his friends Sir Mathewe Browne of the Castle of West Belchworth co. Surrey kt. and John Bodley* of Stretham in the said county gent., as soon after his decease as possible. Of money thus raised, to his three daughters Jane,* Mercie and Fraunces £1000, i.e. to Jane £400, to Mercy £300, and to Frauncis £300, to be paid at age of twenty-one or day of marriage whichever first happens. If any of his said daughters dies before this, portion of each so dying to be shared among survivors; if two die, survivor to have whole £1000. Rest of money raised, to his wife and son John* equally between them. Daughters to be allowed out of the profits of their portions, from age of sixteen until their portions become due, £30 p.a. each towards their maintenance, and in the meantime to have some reasonable allowance. To loving friends, Sir Mathewe Browne and John Bodley his overseers, and to Mr John Rosse and to cousin Raph Baldwine 40s each to make each a ring. To Katherine Saiers, Mary Maylard widow, Samuel Seares, Mercy Saiers, Raph Baldwine, son of Raph Baldwine, his godson, 20s each to make each a ring. To his servants, both men and maidservants, 13s 4d each. To Joan Martyn, wife of Nicholas Martyn, acre of ground in occupation of the said Nicholas and Joane for her life without rent. To said Mary Maylard widow, sister, £100 to be paid at £20 p.a., first payment to be made at end of ten years after his decease (if she be living) and then every year until the sum be paid. To Edmond Godfrey and his now wife, for their lives and the life of longer liver of them, house or tenement at Brooke End, lately erected by said Edmond on a parcel of ground of the testator's, and, after their deaths, said tenement to Edward Godfrey, his godson, and his heirs to hold the same for the rent due in respect of it to lord of fee. To servant Carpenter 4 nobles more and to his daughter Joane 20s. To Mr George Saers, brother-in-law, and to Mr Doctor Lister and Mr Harlam 40s each to make them rings. Residue to wife Margaret* whom he makes sole executrix. Appoints as overseers the said Sir Mathewe Browne and John Bodley. Wit. John Bodley, Rose Mottershedd, Maudley Hammon, John Smith servant to Roberte Banckworth scrivener.

PRO PROB10/205. OffC, prob. clause endorsed, note of registration superscribed. Single sheet. Secretary hand, displayed matter in italic.

Prob. PCC 6 Nov. 1601 to Edward Say, notary public, proctor for Margaret, relict and executor. PAB (PRO PROB8/11 fo. unnumbered (Nov. 1601)) notes undated exhibition of inventory.

c.1561–1601. Landowner, son of Thomas Brend (1597). In 1599 leased site of Globe (not mentioned in will) to Burbages and others. Died 12 Oct. 1601. See Berry, *Playhouses*, pp. 75–119, for account of Brend family and its involvement with Globe.

Bodley] son of Brend's stepmother, executor of T. Brend; from death of testator 'effectively owned the Globe' (Berry, op. cit., p. 88).
Jane] eldest child; see index.
son John] Brend's second son; elder son Matthew (not mentioned in will) came of age 6 Feb. 1621; regained rights in father's property including Globe 1622 (Berry, op. cit., pp. 94–5).
Margaret] subsequently married Sir Sigismond Zinzan c.1605; see p. 64.

1603 July 22. Thomas POPE

(fo. 2) in the name of god Amen the too and twenti of Iulye in the year of our lord god 16{0}3[1] and in the first year of the raine of our soueraine lord kinge Iames: I thomas pope of the parish of sainte sauiors in southwerk in the county of surrey gentellman being at this present in good and perfect health laud and prais be geuen to the allmighty god therfore do make ordaine an declare this my present testament and last will in maner an forme following, that is to saye first and principally I commend my soule into the handes of allmighty god my maker sauior and redemer, hoping and assuredly bel*i*euing to be saued through the me*rr*its death and passion of my sauiour Iesus christ an to in Ioy eternall' blessednes in the kingdome of heaue<n> And my body I commit to the earth to be buried in cristian buriall in the church caled saint sauiours wher now I dwell and I geue towards the setting up of sume monument on me in the said church and my funerall xx l' Item I geue and bequeath to the pore of the liberty wher now I [well] dwell iij [ll]l' Item I geue and bequeath unto susan gasqune whom I haue brought up euer since she was borne the sume of on hunderd pound of lawfull money of England and all my houshold stuf my plate only excepted: Item I will that the said susan gasqune shall haue the youse and occupacion of all that house or teniment wherin I now dwell in the parish of saint sauiours a forsaid during her naturall life yf the lease and terme of yeres which I haue in the same shall so longe contyneu and indure so as the said susan or her assines do paye the one halfe of the rent reserued by the lease to me ther of from time to time and at such time as is limited in and by the same lease[2] (amongest others) made by frances langley* draper deseased and do all so parforme such couenants tuching the said teniment as ar to be dune by force of the saide lease and yf the said susan shall ha[pne]ppen to die before the expiracion[3] of the saide terme then I will that my brother Iohn pope shall haue the use and occupacion of the said teniment during the residue which at the time of the decease of the sade susan [should] shall be to come and unexpir{e}d of the said tirme he doinge for the same and painge from thence [from thence] forth as the said susan shuld or ought to haue dune yf she had liued to the full end of the said tirme Item I will and bequeath unto my brother Iohn pope the teniment adioyning to the east side of my said dwelling house wher in Iohn moden now dwelleth and duringe all such terme of years as I haue to come and unexpired of and in the same by uertue of the lease a foresaid so as the saide Iohn pope and his assines duringe the contynuance of the said terme do paye the one halfe of the [said] rent reserued by the sayd lease from time to time and at such daies and times as is limited by the same lease and do performe such couenants touching {only} the said teneme<nt> to him my saide brother bequeathed as ar to be dune by force of the saide lease and all so that my saide brother do with in one month next after my desecese enter in to bond of a reasonable sume of money to my executers for paiment of the said moity or one halfe of the sayd rent and performance of the couennts touching the same tenement as a fore said according to my trewe meaning and in tent in that be halfe Item I will and deuise unto mary Clarke* alias wood all that teniment adioyning to the west side of my saide dwelling hous: wher in Iohn holand* now dwelleth for and duringe the contynuaunc of the terme of years which [I] I haue in the same (**fo. 3**) (Amongest others as a foresaid) by force or uertue of the saide lease to me mad by the said franncs langley to be by her houlden and in Ioid from time to time free of ani rent to be paid for the same so longe as she liues and after her decese I geue and bequeath my intrest and terme of years then to come and unexpired of and in the said teniment un to thomas bromley who was her to fore baptised in the parrich of saint Andrews undershaft in lundone: Item I geue and bequeth to the said mary Clarke alias wood and to the said thomas bromley as well all my part right titele and intrest which I haue or ought to haue of in and to all that playhouse with the apurtenances called the curten situated and being in hallywell in the parrish of saint lennards in shordich in the counti of middllsecxt as all so {all} my part estate and intrest which I haue or ought to haue of in and to all that playhouse with the appurteincs caled the globe in the parrish of saint sauiors in the county of surrye Item I geue and bequeth to [the] the said thomas bromley the sume[4] of l l' and my chaine of gould beinge in valew xxx l' x s to be paid and delyuered unto him at such time as he shall haue accomplished his full age of [x] xxjty yeres, prouided in the mene time his mother shall reseue thes legases in regard the yous ther of may bringe up the boy puting in good security [t] for the deliuring in the for said legesis at his full yeres of xxjty and yf the said thomas shall happen to die and depart this mortall liffe before he shall haue acumplished his said age of xxjty yeres then I will geue and bequeth the said sume of l l' and the said chaine of gould unto the said mary clarke alias wood to her oune use: Item I geue and bequeth to the said mary Clarke alias wood the sume of l l' mor prouided all waies and my will and mind is that yf the said mary shall hapen to die and depart this mortall life be fore the said thomas bromley then the said l l' shall remaine to the said [to] thomas bromley to be paid to him at such time as he shall accompish the full age of xxjty yeres Item I geue and bequeth to agnis weebb mi mother the sume of xx l' of lafull mony of Ingland and to my brother Iohn pope the sume of xx l' And to my brother william pope other xx [l] l' Item I geue and bequeth to the children of my said brethren of Iohn and william pope the sume of [ten] x l' to be paid and distrebuted equall amongst the same childre<n> part and part licke Item I geue and bequeth to robart gough* and Iohn edmans* all my wering aparrell and all my armes to be equally deuided betwene them. Item I geue and bequeth to my cussune thomas euen v l' Item I geue and bequeth to my louing freind Iohn Iacsun* on ringe with a square dimont in it Item I geue and bequeth to mary clarke alias wood halfe my plate and to susand gasking the other halfe being equally deuided betwen them Item I geue and bequeth to dority Clarke sister to mary Clarke alias wood on gould ringe with fiue opalls in it all the rest of my ringes I geue to good wife willingesun who[w] is now the keper of my house Item I geue and bequeth to my louing frind [l] basell nicoll scryuanor the sune[5] of v l' and to my neighbour and frind Iohn wrench* the sume of v l' the residew of all my goods rightes and chattels not be fore bequethed my debtes and funarall charges being first satesfied [I wholy geve and bequeath to < . . . . > the children being

equally deuided] (fo. 4) I wholly geue and bequeth to my mother my brothers and their children to be equalye deuided betwene them: and I do ordaine and a point my well beloued frindes basell nicoll and Iohn wrinch to be the executrs of this my last will and testament earnestly praying and desiring them to se the same performed in all things according to my trew mening therin and for be case much of this mony is out upon bonds I do limit for the performanc of this my will sixe munthes and thus not doubting but they will [se the same] performed the trust in this behalff by me in them reposed In witnes wher of I haue sete my hand and [sell] seale   Thomas pope
Seled in the presenc of [. .] Iohn wrench Iohn edmans

1. 16{0}3: insertion in darker ink.   2. *lease*: originally written *leese*.   3. *expiracion*: originally written *experacion*.   4. *sume*: originally written *some*.   5. *sune*: rightly *sume*.

PRO PROB10/224. OW, sentence annexed, prob. clause and note of exhibition of inventory endorsed (fo. 4). Note of registration marginated on sentence. Four sheets joined at top with remnants of seal tag; will written on fos 2–4, with signatures of testator and witnesses. Right margin dirt-stained and crumbling with some loss of text, first page torn at bottom. Text of will in italic. Sentence on separate sheet (parchment).

Prob. PCC 13 Feb. 1604 to Francis Wallis, proctor for Basil Nichols, executor, John Wrench, second executor, having died. Confirmed by sentence promulgated on same date (Mary Clerke alias Wood, promoter, v. Basil Nichols, executor, Laurence Litler, guardian of Susan Gasquine during her minority, and Thomas Ewen). Inventory exhibited 9 Dec. 1603.

Noted: Chalmers, *Apology*, pp. 387–8 fn. y; printed: Chalmers, *Supplemental Apology*, pp. 162–8 fn. s.

fl. 1586–1603. Actor; in Denmark and Germany 1586–7; Strange's from 1590; Chamberlain's from 1594. Held fifth share of moiety of Globe in 1599, increased to fourth on Kempe's retirement in same year, and share in Curtain. 1598 in litigation with William Bird alias Borne (**1624**). (Chambers II, 334–5; Nungezer, pp. 285–7.)

langley] builder of Swan theatre (**A1602**); a Mr Pope had four new houses on Langley's land in St Saviour's 1595 (Ingram, *London Life*, p. 110).
mary Clarke] probably married John Edmonds by 1612 (Chambers II, 418).
holand] Collier suggests identification with actor in Strange's (*Memoirs*, p. 124 fn. 1).
gough] apprentice to Pope; actor in Strange's 1590–1, after 1603 with King's Men (Chambers II, 319; Nungezer, pp. 157–8; Bentley II, 447–8); see index.
edmans] John Edmonds; apprentice to Pope; actor with Queen Anne's (Chambers II, 315; Nungezer, p. 128; Bentley II, 431).

Iacsun] possibly the Jackson who was trustee for Shakespeare in purchase of Blackfriars gatehouse 1613; see index.
wrench] in 1595 Pope was recorded as living in Wrench's rents, Southwark (Collier, *Memoirs*, p. 123).

1605 May 4 Augustine PHILLIPS

In the name of God Amen the ffourthe daie of May Anno domini 1605 And in the Yeres of the Reigne of our soueraigne Lorde Iames by the grace of god Kinge of England Scotland ffraunce and Ireland defendour of the ffaithe &c That is to say of England ffraunce and Ireland the Thirde, and of Scotland the Eighte and Thirtith I Augustyne Phillipps of Mourtlack in the County of Surrey gent beinge at this presente sick and weake in body, but of good and perfecte mynde and Remembraunce thankes be given vnto allmighty god, do make ordeyne and dispose this {my} presente testament and Laste will in manner and forme followinge, That is to say ffirste and principally I Commende my soule into thandes of Allmighty god my maker Saviour and Reedeemer in whome and by the merittes of the second person Iesus Christe I truste and beleave assuredly to be saved, and to have full and Cleire Remission and forgivenes of my sinnes, And I Committ my body to be buried in the Chauncell of the parishe Churche of Mourtelack aforesaid, And after my body buryed and funerall Charges paide, Then I will' that all suche debtes and duetyes as I owe to any person or persons of Righte or in Conscience shalbe truely paide, And that done then I will that all and singuler my goodes Chattells plate houshold stuffe Iewells reedy mony and debtes. shalbe devided by my Executrix and ouerseers of this my Laste will' and testament into Three equall' and indifferente partes and porcions whereof one equall' parte I geve and bequeathe to Anne Phillipps my Loueinge wife* to her owne proper vse and behowfe, one other parte thereof to and amongeste my three eldeste daughters Maudlyne Phillipps Rebecca Phillipps and Anne Phillipps equally amongeste them to be devided porcion and porcion Like, and to be paide and deliuered vnto them as they and euery of them shall' accomplishe and Com{m}e to theire {lawfull}[1] ages of Twenty and one yeres or at theire daies of marriage, and euery of them to be others heyre of theire said partes and porcions yf any of them shall fortune to dye, before theire said seuerall ages of Twenty and one yeres or daies of marriage, And thother parte thereof I reserrve {to}[2] my selfe and to my Executrix to performe my Legaces hereafter followinge, Item I geve and bequeathe to the poore of the parishe of Mourtlack a foresaid, ffyve Poundes of Lawfull money of England, to be distributed by the

Churchewardens of the same parishe within Twelve monethes after my decease Item' I geve and bequeathe to Agnys Bennett* my Loueinge mother duringe her naturall life, euery yere yerely the somme of ffyve Poundes of Lawfull' money of England, To be paid her At the ffoure vsuall' feastes or termes in the yere [out of any] by my Executrix out of any parte and porcion reserrved by this my presente will', Item I geve to my brothers william webb and Iames webb,* yf they shalbe Lyveinge at my decease to eyther of them the somme of Tenne poundes a peece of Lawfull money of England, To be paid vnto them {within}³ Three yeres after my decease, Item I geve and bequeathe to my sister Elizabeth Govghe* the some of Tenne poundes of Lawfull' money of England To be paid her within one yere after my decease, Item I will' and bequeathe vnto Myles Borne and Phillipps Borne two sonnes of my sister Margery Borne* to eyther of them Tenne Poundes a peece of Lawfull' money of England To be paid vnto them when they shall accomplishe the full' age of Twenty and one yeres, Item I geve and bequeathe vnto Tymothy whithorne the some of Twentye poundes of Lawfull' money of England To be paide vnto him within one yere after my decease, Item I geve and bequeathe vnto and amongeste the hyred men' of the [s.tt] Company, which I am of, which shalbe at the tyme of my decease the some of ffyve Poundes of Lawfull' money of England To be {equally}⁴ distributed amongeste them, Item I geve and bequeathe to my ffellowe william Shakespeare a Thirty shillinges peece in gould, To my fellowe Henry Condell' one other Thirty shillinge peece in gould, To my servaunte Christopher Beeson Thirty shillinges in gould, To my fellow Lawrence ffletcher* Twenty shillinges in gould, To my fellowe Robert Armyne Twenty shillinges in gould To my fellowe Richard Coweley Twenty shill<inges>⁵ in gould, To my fellow Alexsander Cook Twenty shillinges in gould, To my fellowe Nicholas Tooley, Twenty shillinges in gould, Item I geve to the Preacher which shall preache at my funerall' the some of Twenty shillinges (fo. 2) Item I giue [vn]to Samuell Gilborne* my Late Aprentice the some of ffortye shillinges and my mouse Colloured veluit hose and a white Taffety dublet A blacke Taffety sute my purple Cloke sword and dagger And my base viall Item I giue to Iames Sandes* my Aprentice the some of ffortye shillinges and a Citterne a Bandore and a Lute, To be paid and deliuered vnto him at thexpiracon of his {terme of} yeares in his Indentur or Aprenticehood Item my will is that Elizabeth Phillips my youngest daughter shall haue and quietly enioye for terme of hir naturall lyfe my howse and Land in Mortelacke which I lately purchased to me Anne my wyfe, and to the said Elizabeth for Terme of our Liues in full Recompence and satisfaction of hir parte and porcion which shee may in any wise Chalenge or demaund of in and to any of my

goodes and Chattells whatsoeuer. And I ordeyne and make the said Anne Phillips my Louing wyfe sole executrix of this my present Testament and laste will provided all waies that yf the said Anne my wyfe doe at any tyme marrye after my decease,* That then and from thenceforth shee shall Cease to be any more or Longer [my] executrix, of this my laste will [and Testament] or any waies intermedle with the same, And the said Anne to haue no parte or porcion' of Goodes [and] {or} Chattells to me or my executours Reserued or Apointed by this my laste will and Testament, And that then and from thenceforth Iohn Heminges Richard Burbage William slye and Tymothie Whithorne shalbe ffully and whollie my executours of this my laste will and Testament, as though the said Anne had neuer bin named, And of thexecution of this my present Testament and laste will I ordayne and make the said Iohn Heminges Richard Burbage William Slye and Tymothie Whithorne ouerseers of this my present Testament and laste will And I bqueathe {vn}to the said Iohn Heminges Richard Burbage and william Slye to either of them my said ouerseers for theire paines heerin to be Taken a boule of siluer of the valew of ffyue poundes apeece In witnes wherof to this my present [will and Laste] Testament and laste will I the said Augustin<e>[6] Phillipes haue put my hand and seale the day and yeare aboue written'   A. Phillips./
Sealed and deliuered by the said Augustine Phillipes as his last will and Testament in the presence of vs Robert Goffe* William shepherd*

1. *Lawfull*: insertion in second hand. 2. *to*: as note 1. 3. *within*: as note 1.
4. *equally*: as note 1. 5. Document torn. 6. Document torn.

PRO PROB10/232. OffC, prob clause subscribed (fo. 2), notes of registration marginated (fo. 1) and of exhibition of inventory endorsed (fo. 2). Two sheets, joined at the top, unsealed. Text in two hands: 1. small and unusually angular form of secretary with frequent otiose abbreviation marks on *ll* (fo. 1); 2. facile Elizabethan secretary (insertions fo. 1, text fo. 2, names of witnesses) (Phillips's 'signature' in italic).

Prob. PCC 13 May 1605 to Anne Phillips, relict and executor. Prob. 16 May 1607 to John Heminges, reserving power to Richard Burbage, William Sly, Timothy Whitehorne, executors, Anne Phillips's executorship having been nullified by her remarriage (PRO PROB11/105 fo. 242r).

Printed: Chalmers, *Apology*, pp. 431–5 fn. e (RegC).

fl. 1590–1605. Actor; Strange's c.1590–3; Chamberlain's/King's Men from 1594. Shareholder in Globe. Bequests to fellow actors with King's Men: Shakespeare (**1616**), Henry Condell (**1627**), Lawrence Fletcher, Robert Armin (**1614**), Richard Cowley (**1618**), Alexander Cooke (**1614**), Nicholas Tooley (**1623**), and to other actors Christopher Beeston (**1638**), Samuel Gilburne, James Sands; names as overseers John Heminges (**1630**), Richard Burbage (**1619**), William Sly (**1608**). (Chambers II, 333–4; Nungezer, pp. 280–2.)

wife] see W. Ingram, 'The wife of Augustine Phillips', *N&Q*, CCXXVIII, 1983, p. 157.

Agnys Bennett] if William and James Webb were her sons, is there a link with the Agnes Webb, mother of Thomas Pope (**1603**), who had sons William and John?

webb] Chambers (II, 334) suggests William and James were Phillips's brothers-in-law.

Govghe] wife of Robert Gough, actor (see Goffe below).

Margery Borne] conjectured by Chambers (II, 333–4) to be wife of William Bird alias Borne (**1624**) but his sons named William, Thomas and Theophilus (**1663**).

ffletcher] although named in patent for King's Men 1603, both Chambers (II, 318) and Nungezer (p. 143) argue that he did not act with company. Phillips makes careful distinction between fellow actors, hired men, apprentices and servants including Fletcher in first category.

Gilborne] member of King's Men (Chambers II, 319; Nungezer, p. 153; Bentley II, 443).

Sand*es*] member of King's Men (Chambers II, 337; Nungezer, pp. 310–11; Bentley II, 559–60); see index.

marrye after my decease] she married John Witter within two years of Phillips's death. See C. W. Wallace, 'Shakespeare and his London associates as revealed in recently discovered documents', *NUS*, X, 1910, pp. 261–360 (pp. 305–336), for litigation between Heminges and Witter over Phillips's share in Globe.

Goffe] member of King's Men, Phillips's brother-in-law (see Elizabeth Govghe above) (Chambers II, 319; Nungezer, pp. 157–8; Bentley II, 447–8); see index.

shepherd] thought by Collier to be scrivener or clerk who drew up will (*Memoirs*, p. 88); possibly Sheppard a 'player' (Chambers II, 339).

1605 June 6 William HAUGHTON

Houghton[1]

Memorandum that on the vjth daie of Iune 1605 William Houghton of the parish of Allhallowes Stayning*es* London made his last will nuncupatiue in manner and forme {or in effect} following {Thatt is to saye} The said William Houghton being Demaunded to whom he would giue his goodes, He awnswered {in theis wordes or like in effect (v*idelice*t)} I Doe giue all my good*es* chattells & debt*es*, whatsoeuer vnto Alice Houghton* my wyffe toward*es* the payment of my debt*es* and the bringing vp of my Children And I doe nominate & appointe the said Alice my wyffe my sole executrix Theis being witnesses wentworth Smith* [and] Elizabeth Lewes and diu*ers* others/

1. *Houghton*: marginated.

GL MS 9172/22d no. 43. OW (nuncupative), prob. clause subscribed. Single sheet unsealed. Text in facile secretary; insertions probably in same hand as text.

Prob. CCL 20 July 1605 to Alice Haughton (Houghton), relict and executor. PAB (GL MS 9168/16 fo. 10v) spells name Hawghton and gives valuation of inventory at £19 1s.

Printed: A. C. Baugh, ed., William Haughton, *Englishmen for My Money; or, A Woman Will Have Her Will*, Philadelphia, 1917, p. 22 (RegC).

c.1575–1605. Dramatist for Admiral's Men 1597–1602. (Chambers III, 334–6; Henslowe's *Diary*.)

Alice] probably not the Alice Houghton whose will was proved in ACS 11 Sept. 1619 (GLRO DW/PA/5/1619/56).
Smith] playwright for Henslowe's companies 1601–3 (Chambers III, 493–4).

1608 Apr. 6 Hugh DAVIS

In the name of god Amen the sixt day of Aprill' Anno domini 1608 in the yeres of the Raigne of our Soueraigne lord Iames, by the grace of god kinge of England Scotland ffraunce and Irlande defendor of the ffaithe &c that is to saye of England ffravnc & Irland the ffift yere. & of Scotland the too and ffortye/ I heughe davis of the parishe of St Saviour in Sowthe warke In The covntie of Surrey waterman beinge of A whole and perfecte Rememberaunce laudes & prayes begeven to alnightie[1] god Therfore do Ordaine & make this my presente testament contayinge[2] herin my very last wyll: In manner and fforme followinge that is to saye ffirst & princepally I commend my sovle vnto almightye god my Creator, to Iesus christ his sonn my Redemer & to the holye ghost my sanctifier, And my bodie to be buryed In Christian// buryale At the discretion' of myne Executrice here vndernamed And Concerninge my worldlye goodes I do bestowe dispose, & I give in this sort, ffirst I bequeathe and {geue} vnto my landlord* Phillip hinchlowe Esquir my best Covnter table. Item I geue & bequeathe to my loveinge ffrind Iames Peningtone my Clooke & my hate, which of my Clokes & hates my Executrice shall thinke good/ Item the Residewe of all my goodes movable & vnmovable boates oares and all that belonge to them, And all my houshould stufe, not before geven & beqwethed & all my other goodes & chattels as well Reale as personall of what nature condition or qualitie so ever the be, I [ge] give & bequeathe vnto my lovinge wiffe Anne davis she payinge my debtes discharginge my ffvneralles & legaces, & I do Constitute Ordayn & make, her to be my

sole & onlye Executrice of this my present will & Testament & I do ordayne & make my oversears for the execution of this my last will & testament my loveinge frendes master Phillip hinchlowe Esquire, and Raphe Trote, vnto which Raphe Trote I do geve hym for his paynes therin A dager to be geven vnto hym by my Executrice & I have desired them hervnto to subscribe there names, Testefiinge This to be my last will & testament: In wytnes herof I have hervnto put my {hande}[3] & seale one the daye & yere first above written. In the presentes of these whose names are hervnder[4] wrytten my hande by me george Tayllor wryter herof
the marcke X of hew Davesse
wittnes Phillippe Henslow Ralfe Trotte the mark of Ross<e[5] X T>rotte

1. *alnightie*: rightly *almightie*. 2. *contayinge*: rightly *contayninge*. 3. *hande*: inserted in different hand from text. 4. *hervnder*: otiose superscript *r*. 5. *Rosse*: Rose in RegC (GLRO DW/PA/17/8/fo. 56v).

GLRO DW/PA/5/1609/39. OW, prob. clause endorsed, note of registration marginated. Single sheet folded in half, with seal and mark of testator and signatures of witnesses; lower margin damaged with some loss of text. Text in fluent secretary, hand of George Taylor.

Prob. ACS 17 Nov. 1609, to Ann, relict and executor.

fl. 1593–1608. Perhaps a hired man with Lord Admiral's 1601. Appears frequently as witness 1593–1603 in diary of Philip Henslowe (**1616**), his landlord and employer; 'in some way connected with the playhouse . . . not, however, known to have been an actor himself' (Greg, *Henslowe's Diary* II, 255). (Chambers II, 176, 313; Nungezer, p. 114.)

landlord] Henslowe records expenditure on Davis's house 1595 and rent paid for same in 1602 (*Diary*, pp. 14–16, 248).

1608 Apr. 22 Edward SHARPHAM

In the name of God amen. the twoe and twentyeth daye of Aprill 1608 And in the yeares of the Raigne or our soueraigne Lorde [g] Iames by the grace of God kinge of England Scotland ffraunce and Ireland defendour of the fayth &c. that is to saye)[1] of England ffraunce and Ireland the sixth and of Scotland the one and ffortyeth I Edwarde Sharpeham of Allington in the Countye of Devon' gent beinge sicke in bodye but of good & perfecte memorye lawde and prayse be therefore given vnto Allmightye God; Doe make and ordeyne this my laste {will} and Testament in manner and forme followeinge (that is to saye) ffirste and pryncypallye I gyve and Commend my soule into the handes of Allmightye God my Creatour and maker trusteinge and moste assuredly beleevinge in his mercye that throughe the merryttes death and passyon of his onely sonne my savyour and Redeemer Iesus Christe I haue and shall haue full and free remyssyon' of all my synnes, And after this transytorye lyfe ended euerlastinge ioye in the kingdome of heaven which neuer shall haue ende Amen, Item I gyve and bequeath [vnt] my bodye to the earth of whence yt came. to be buryed in Christian² buryall att the discrecion of my Executour and Ouerseers hereafter named, Item I gyve devise and bequeath vnto William Gayton* of westminster in the Countye of Middlesex [y] Taylour All and singuler my Apparell goodes Chattles debtes sommes of money due and oweinge vnto me by any person[s] or persons whatsoeuer by specyaltye Composycion or otherwyse; Item I doe gyve devise and bequeath vnto my brother George Heckste my damson Colloured Cloake lyned throughe with blacke veluett and my Rapyer beinge hatched with syluer, and a girdle and hangers³ trymed with syluer belonginge to the same. Item I (fo. 2) gyve devise and bequeath vnto my Cosen Bridgett ffortescue my Cheyne of smalle pearle and my goulde ringe with the Dyamond therein, Item I gyue devise and bequeath vnto my brother in lawe Richard Goteham my rydinge Cloth Cloake and one girdle and hangers³ of leather playne and vnwrought And I gyve devise and bequeath vnto my Cosen William Langeworthye my palle Carnacion sylke stockinges; And of this my laste wyll and testament I make nominate and appoynte my welbelloued the saide William Gayton my full and wholle Executour; And I make and ordeyne Robert Browne of Westminster in the said Countye of Middlesex Notarye publique and Thomas Rowpe of Mylton in the Countye of Devon gent Overseers of the same, Desyreinge them to see the execucion thereof performed; And I vtterly revoke adnihillatte and make voyde all and euerye other former willes testamentes legacyes and bequestes in any wise by me heretofore made, In wytness whereof I haue to this my laste wyll and testament conteyninge twoe sheetes of paper seuerally putt my hande and sealle the daye and yeare firste of all wrytten./ the marke of Edward Edwrde Sharpham⁴ Sharpham

Signed sealled published and declared by the said Edward Sharpeham to be his laste will and testament in the presence of Iohn Owen* Roberte Browne Notary publique Robert Askew

1. Opening parenthesis missing.   2. *Christian*: MS has *Xpian*.   3. *hangers*: otiose superscript *rs*.   4. Testator signed in the space left by scribe between *Edward* and *Sharpham*.

PRO PROB10/256. OW, prob. clause subscribed (fo. 2) and note of registration marginated (fo. 1). Two unnumbered sheets, each with signature of testator, second sheet sealed, with signatures of witnesses. Text in rapid secretary with displayed matter in italic.

Prob. PCC 9 May 1608 to William Gayton, executor. PAB (PRO PROB8/13 p. 328) notes exhibition of inventory.

Printed: G. C. Moore Smith, 'Edward Sharpham and Robert Hayman', N&Q 10th ser., X, 1908, pp. 21–4 (p. 22) (RegC); C. G. Petter, *A Critical Old Spelling Edition of the Works of Edward Sharpham*, New York, 1986, pp. 40–3 (OW, includes facsimile of signatures of testator and witnesses).

1576–1608. Dramatist; plays acted by Children of Revels and Children of King's Revels. May have gained theatrical entrée via Devon neighbour Samuel Daniel (**1619**), who licensed plays for Children of Revels, or fellow member of Middle Temple, John Marston (**1634**), shareholder in Blackfriars company. Died of plague; buried 23 Apr. 1608 St Margaret's Westminster. (Chambers III, 490–1; C. G. Petter, op. cit., pp. 3–56.)

Gayton] Sharpham was apparently in debt to his tailor. Petter speculates that Sharpham used own wardrobe in plays (p. 44).

Owen] possibly the epigrammatist, fellow member of Inns of Court, translator of Sharpham's friend Robert Hayman.

1608 June 8 Thomas KENDALL (abstract)

Citizen and haberdasher of London. Weak. Soul 'to allmighty God my creatour and to Iesus Christe my only saviour and redeemer by whose merrites death and passion I trust assuredly to have everlasting life'. Burial in church of St Andrew in Holborn, London. To two daughters of brother Edmond £20 each at seventeen; if one or both die before, same to said Edmond Kendall at the aforesaid time. Money due to him from brother Christopher Kendall to one of Christopher's sons to apprentice him in London, and to same son 20 nobles to be paid at the end of apprenticeship towards setting up in trade; if he dies in meantime his father to have same sum to give to any other of his sons at his discretion. To Margaret Taylour, sister's daughter, £5 to be paid within one year of her marriage. To kinswoman, now wife of William Felles, £10 to be paid within seven years of his death. To wife's grandchild Anthony Tipsly, son of late Edward Tipsly, £5 towards binding as apprentice. To cousin Christopher Kendall his black grogram gown laid with lace. To cousin John Kendall, parson of Acton, his best black wearing cloak. To cousin Edward Kendall of the strond gold ring worth 20s. To his father, cousin Marmaduke Kendall, gold ring worth 10s. To friend Mr Persivall Golding gold ring worth 20s. To Mr William Hancocke gold ring worth 20s. To poor of pa. St Andrew in Holborn where he now lives 20s to be paid at time of his funeral. Remainder to wife* Anne whom makes sole executrix. Appoints Edward Kirkham* of the strond gent. and Thomas Leedame of Southwarke co. Surrey yeoman as overseers; to either ring of gold worth 10s. Renounces earlier wills including that dated 26 May 1608. Wit. Persivall Golding, John Kennett, Thomas Leedam, Rich Hardye (mark).

GL ACL MS 9052/3b. OW, prob. clause subscribed. Single sheet with remains of seal and original signatures of testator and witnesses. Right margin of document crumbling causing some loss of text. Text in facile secretary; Kendall's signature very shaky and incomplete.

Prob. ACL 27 June 1608 to Anne Kendall, relict and executor. PAB (GL MS 9050/4 fo. 340r) notes exhibition of inventory 23 Jan. 1609, valuation at £362 3< . . . > (damaged margin), besides debt of deceased being 18s.

fl. 1602–8. One of managers of second Blackfriars in 1602, base for Chapel Children under Nathaniel Giles (1633); Children of the Queen's Revels patentee 1604. (Chambers II, 327; Nungezer, p. 223; Hillebrand, *Child Actors*, pp. 186–9, 197–8; 332–4.)

wife] joint plaintiff with Edward Kirkham in suit against Samuel Daniel (1619) (Hillebrand, *Child Actors*, pp. 177–8, 334–8); see index.
Kirkham] Yeoman of Revels, partner with Kendall, Henry Evans and others in management of Blackfriars; from 1605 had financial interest in Children of Paul's (Chambers II, 327; Nungezer, pp. 227–8).

1608 Aug. 14 William SLY

Iane Browne* the daughter of Robert Browne* and Sisley his wife* the howse where he now dwelles to her &c. for ever To Robert Browne his parte of the globe. To Iames Sandes* fourtye pound*es* The rest to Sisley Browne makinge her executrix'. The marke of Willi*a*m Slye. Signu*m* Petr*i* Leather signu*m* Elizabeth Leather. The marke of ffraunces Goodhand The marke of Harte M*r* Goodhand. The marke of Mary Williams. The marke of dorothie Hublethorne./ M*emorandum* that the foresayd Willi*a*m Slye did farther by word of mouth after the making of the will above written v*idelicet* on the fourtenth day of August Anno do*mi*ni 1608 or therabowtes being of p*er*fecte mynde and memory give and bequeathe vnto the poore of the parishe of St Leonard*es* in Shorditche in the County of Midd*lesex* fourty shilling*es* And to Cuthbert Burbaige* his sworde and his hatt. In the presence and hearing of the witnesses afore named./

PRO PROB10/258. OffC (nuncupative) with codicil of same date, prob. clause subscribed, note of registration marginated. Single sheet folded in half to make four pages, unsealed. Text in a facile secretary.

Prob. PCC 24 Aug. 1608 to Cicely Browne, executor. Confirmed by sentence (PRO PROB11/112 fos 345r–345v), promulgated PCC 14 Nov. 1608 (Cicely

Browne, promoter, v. William Sly, testator's kinsman, and any others with claim), Browne having exhibited the will before the court 15 Oct. 1608. Marginal notes in RegC (PRO PROB11/112 fo. 140r) and PAB (PRO PROB8/13 p. 377) give date of confirmation as 2 Mar. 1609. PAB gives pa. of origin as St Leonard's Shoreditch.

Printed: Chalmers, *Apology*, pp. 441–3 (extracts from RegC) and Boswell III, 476–8 (in full).

fl. 1590–1608. Actor; Strange's c.1590, Chamberlain's/King's Men from 1598. Acquired share in Globe after death of Augustine Phillips, who named him as one of overseers/executors and legatee (**1605**), and lease of seventh share in Blackfriars in Aug. 1608. Buried 16 Aug. 1608 St Leonard's Shoreditch. (Chambers II, 340–1; Nungezer, pp. 331–2.)

Iane Browne] married actor Robert Reynolds; see index, also under Renaldes. For account of family of Robert Browne see Schrickx, *Foreign Envoys*, pp. 222–3.

Robert Browne] actor, mostly in Germany 1590–1607, 1618–20; possibly patentee for Queen's Revels company 1608–12. Neighbour of Sly's in St Leonard's. (See Berry, *Boar's Head Playhouse*, pp. 191–7, who disentangles various Robert Brownes conflated in Chambers II, 304.)

Sisley his wife] née Sands, married actor William Robins 1622; see index under Robins.

Sandes] actor in King's Men (Chambers II, 337; Nungezer, pp. 310–11; Bentley II, 559–60); see index.

Burbaige] fellow shareholder in Globe and Blackfriars (**A1636**).

1610 July 1 Edmund TYLNEY (abstract)

Of Leatherhead co. Surry esq., Master of the Revels. Perfect health. 'Written with my owne hand.' Soul to 'allmightie god my Creatour with assured hope by his grace to be saved through ye death and passion of my Savio*u*r Iesus Christe onlye as regenerate by his holie spirritte vnto everlastinge liefe accordinge vnto his promise vnto all such as trewlie and vnfeignedlie beleeve in him . . . in hope and full beleefe to rise againe in ye Resurrecc*i*on at ye latter daie When Christ shall come in his glorye to iudge both ye quicke and ye Dead'. Burial in church of Streateham co. Surrey near monument of his father, without any funeral pomp, except a sermon with 40*s* to preacher, and 40*s* to church. Monument to be erected in same church in place he has appointed, within six months of his decease if he does not finish the same within his lifetime, at cost of 20 marks as agreed with the stone cutter near Charinge Crosse. All his apparel 'wherein I haue spent much money verye vainelie that might haue bynne otherwise better ymployed' to be sold, money to be divided between poor inhabitants of parishes of

Leatherhead and Streateham. To thirteen poor old men and women, inhabitants of Leatherhead, who receive weekly relief from him in bread, to each a black frieze gown and 5s to be paid within six months of his decease. To Margarett Cartwright widow, to whom he is bound in £100 for an annuity of £10 to be paid to her quarterly for her life, if she survives him, £50 upon cancellation of bond, but, if she predeceases him, said £50 to Anne Hassard, wife of Robert Hassard junior, for pains taken in his sickness. To said cousin Robert Hassard* and his wife £100 and to her all the furniture of the chamber 'Where she ordinarilie lyeth for beddinge and hangeinge together With such allowance of brasse Pewter and Lynnen*n* towardes their howskeepeinge' at discretion of executor. To their son Edmond Hassard, godson, £60, and £20 to their daughter Anne Hassard. £100 towards repair of Leatherhead's stone bridge provided means be found from other sources to finish the work within one year after his decease, otherwise not. To Fredericke Tylney, godson, second son of Thomas Tylney, £200 to be employed to his use by his mother until he comes of age. To Mr Ralbett,* parson of Streateham, and to Mr Griffith Vaughan, parson of Ashted, his overseers, for their pains, all his books to be divided between them and to either of them a great silver bowl with the cover. To each of his old servants, one year's wages. To Roger Chambers who waits on him in his chamber £5. For discharge of all which legacies his house at Leatherhead with furniture and the grounds belonging to it to be sold, the remainder, his legacies and debts discharged together with any other legacies he might give upon his deathbed by word of mouth witnessed by two sufficient witnesses, to Thomas Tylney* of Shellie co. Suffolke esq. with all other plate and money remaining to him at his death. Appoints him executor together with Thomas Goddmann of Leatherhead gent. as his assistant, giving to said Thomas Godmann forty ounces of plate. Witnessed by testator's own hand and seal.

PRO PROB10/277. OffC, prob. clause endorsed (fo. 2), and note of registration marginated (fo. 1). Two sheets, unnumbered, joined at top. Text in set secretary hand with displayed matter in italics, not Tylney's hand.

Prob. PCC 17 Oct. 1610 to Thomas Tylney, executor, reserving power to Thomas Godman, second executor. PAB (PRO PROB8/14 fo. 119r) has marginal note 'per decre*tum*'.

Printed: Ethel Stokes, 'Surrey wills proved in the Prerogative Court of Canterbury in 1610', *Surrey Archaeological Collections*, XXIV, 1911, pp. 56–69 (pp. 66–7) (abstract).

c.1536–1610. Master of the Revels 1578–1610; founded Queen's Men 1583. Died 20 Aug., buried St Leonard's Streatham 6 Oct. 1610. (W. R. Streitberger, 'On Edmond Tyllney's biography', *RES* n.s., XXIX, 1978, pp. 11–35, discusses will pp. 33–4 and, in his *Edmond Tyllney Master of the Revels and Censor of Plays*, New York, 1986, pp. 67 ff., his handwriting.)

Robert Hassard] servant of Revels Office, received payment in 1601 on behalf of Tylney from Philip Henslowe (**1616**) (*Diary*, pp. 164, 194).

Ralbett] Michael Rabbett, Vicar of Streatham and St Vedast Foster Lane, London, one of translators of King James Bible (Olga S. Opfell, *The King James Bible Translators*, Jefferson, NC, 1982, pp. 96, 137).

Thomas Tylney] as executor rendered Revels accounts to Exchequer 1609–10.

1610 Sept. 2 Henry JOHNSON

In the name of God Amen The Second daye of September Anno domini 1610 And in the Eight yere of the raigne of our Soueraigne Lord Iames by the grace of god King of England ffraunce & Ireland defendour of the ffaith &c. And of Scotland the ffowre and fforteth I Henry Iohnson Cittizen and Clothworker of London fynding my self to be sicke in body (yet of good & perfect remembraunce praysed be god[1] therefore doe make and ordayne this my last Will and Testament in manner and forme following that is to saye, ffirst I Comitt my self both body & soule to the proteccion of Allmightie god And I will my body to be buried in comely and decent manner referring the charges thereof to my Executour herevnder named and I will that my said Executour shall paie and discharge all such debtes as I doe iustly owe vnto any person or persons and that within convenient tyme next after my decease which debtes and my funerall being ffirst paid & discharged [thereaft] out of my goodes & chattells The residue and remaynder thereof whatsoeuer I doe fully and freely giue and bequeathe to my welbeloued brother Thomas Iohnson Cittizen and Haberdasher of London whome I doe make and ordayne to be my full & sole Executour of this my last Will and Testament And I doe by theis presentes revooke and dissanull all other former Wills heretofore by me made and that this shall stand for my very last will and Testament and none other or otherwyse In witnes whereof I haue herevnto sett my hand and seale yeoven the daye and yeres ffirst aboue written   Henry Iohnson

Sealed and delivered in the presence of vs Iohn Manser Willyam garton Cowper the mark of Joane X Renolds the mark X of margerett Bund

1. Closing parenthesis omitted.

PRO PROB10/276. OW, prob. clause subscribed, note of registration marginated. Single sheet folded to make four pages, sealed, with signatures. Text in facile secretary.

Prob. PCC 6 Sept. 1610 to Thomas Johnson, brother and executor. Note subscribed on will gives pa. of origin as St Dunstan in the East. PAB (PRO PROB8/ 14 fo. 115v) notes exhibition of inventory.

1550–1610. Perhaps this 'clothworker' was gatherer at Theatre under John Brayne (1578) and James Burbage (A1597). Henry Johnson, 'silkweaver' of St Leonard Shoreditch and 'gatherer', gave evidence in 1600 in lawsuit between Giles Allen (A1608) and Cuthbert Burbage (A1636). (Wallace, pp. 218–23; Nungezer, p. 205.)

[c.1611 May] undated George PULHAM

In the Name of God amen I George Poollam sicke in bode and hole in mynd do heere bequeth my sole into the handes of my redemar Iesus christ whensoeuar it shall please him to call me oute of this vale of miserie and my bode to the earth from whence it cane[1] to be buried after my death [at] in the parishe of Saint Leonards shordich. And farther more for all my worldlie possecions. I do giue and bequethe vnto my Godchilde Robert bestone* the somne[2] of ten powndes of lawfull mone of England. and farther I beque<th> to Ieane Browne* the daughter of Sislie browne [daughter] the some of tenn powndes. and to her daughter Elizabeth* broune tenn powndes of lawful monie of england. And I giue vnto Expofer[3] Bestone Sonn* of Mr Expofer Bestone* five poundes {of ye x li which I gaue to Robert Bescon}[4] and if [Expofer] [{Robert}] {Expofer} Bistone shalle die then to be paied to his brother William Biston.* And the other five poindes[5] to be paied to my brother Iohn poollam in Wisfarstone in suffoke. but my meaninge is that if {my} Godchild Robert bestone die that then that tenn powndes is ye tenn powndes which I bequethed to my brother [and] Expofer bestone ye yonger. And I bequeth and giue to my brothe Timothie poollam three powndes vj s viij d and I giue to my brother ffrancis poollame three pownds vj s viij d. to be paid after my death. and I giue vnto my brother Timothe a Iurken and hose of Russat kersie and to my brother ffrancis a black saie sute and a lased lether dooblat and I giue vnto my father Timothie poollam my [6] cloke of mingle coler cloth, and I giue vnto my brother Iohn poollam a gerdell imbrodered with pearle a paier of hangars of silk gold and sillvar. And I do here acknolege and maike my trustie frinde mr Expofer bistone my fooll executor to se all this in my will performed and allthinges els that I shalbeque[7] and giue by word of mouthe in the presence of these witnesses   Georg Pullam witnesses William Sheffarde Esquier William Bedcher

1. *cane*: rightly *came*.   2. *somne*: rightly *somme*.   3. *Expofer* for *Christopher* throughout.   4. *of . . . li* inserted at end of line; *w'ch . . . Bescon* marginated

at beginning of next line. 5. *poindes*: rightly *poundes*. 6. Blank in MS. 7. *shalbeque*: rightly *shal bequeth*.

GL MS 9052/3d. OW, prob. clause endorsed. Single sheet folded to make four pages, unsealed, with signatures of testator and witnesses. Text in mixed hand, likely that of Sheffarde; interlineations and alterations in different ink and possibly in different hand.

Prob. ACL 25 May 1611 to Christopher Beeston, friend and executor. PAB (GL MS 9050/5 fo. 2r) gives pa. of origin as St Leonard's Shoreditch and notes exhibition of inventory.

d. 1611. Actor and sharer, Queen Anne's. (Chambers II, 237, 335; Nungezer, p. 289.)

Robert bestone] fellow member of Queen Anne's (Nungezer, pp. 38–9) or, more likely, infant son of Christopher Beeston b. 1609 (Nungezer, p. 38).
Ieane Browne] Jane, daughter of actor Robert Browne; see index.
Elizabeth] daughter of actor Robert Browne; see index.
Expofer Bestone Sonn] only son of Christopher Beeston of this name, born 1 Dec. 1605, buried 15 July 1610 (Nungezer, p. 38). Pulham may have made his will before 1610.
Expofer Bestone] (**1638**) fellow member of Queen Anne's, succeeded Thomas Greene as manager 1612; see index.
William Biston] born c.1606 (**1682**); see index.

1611 Oct. 3 Thomas SAVAGE (abstract)

(Savadge) Citizen and goldsmith of London. Sick. Soul 'into thy hand*es* O God ffather Sonne and Holie Ghost thou hast first made me and thou hast giuen thy sonne to become man Who dyed for my sinnes and for the sinnes of the people O ffather, for this thy sonnes sake haue mercie vpon me, O Lord Iesus Christ thou sonne of God W*h*ich hast bought me W*i*th thy pretious bloud by one oblac*i*on suffitientlie for all I beleeue in thee, O Christ God and man haue mercie vpon me and be thou my mercifull mediato*ur* for me to God thy father that I maie be saued O Holie Ghost Coequall W*i*th the ffather and the sonne haue mercie vpon me Worke thy dyvine poW*er* in me through thy grace in Sanctificac*i*on, drawe me vnto Iesu Christ that I may find fauo*ur* and be saved Amen'. All goods and chattels to be divided into three equal parts according to custom of the City of London. Third to Alice, loving wife. Third to any of his children as had not been advanced by him at time of his death; eldest son Richard to have no share as he had already advanced him in his lifetime. Third to executor for payment of legacies. Devises messuages, lands etc. as follows: to said son Richard and heirs, messuage in pa. St Olaves in

Silverstreet* in London, in which Mr William Peirson, goldsmith, lives; in default of such issue, to Thomas, second son, and heirs; in default of such issue, to other two sons George and John and heirs; in default of such issue, to heirs of testator for ever. To wife Alice, messuage where he now lives in Great Woodstreet pa. St Albane in Great Woodstreet in London for her life according to a former conveyance; reversion to younger sons Thomas and George and to heirs; if either die without issue, portion to survivor and his heirs; in default of such issue, to remain to said sons Richard and John and heirs; in default of such issue, to heirs of testator for ever. To John, youngest son, and heirs, house and messuage in Adlestreet* pa. St Marie in Aldermanburie in London, in which Mr John Hemynges, grocer, lives; in default of such issue, remainder to rest of sons, Richard, Thomas and George, and heirs; in default of such issue, to heirs of testator for ever. To daughter Elizabeth Savadge and heirs, house and messuage in Adlestreet pa. St Albane in Woodstreet in London, in which Mr John Wotton gent. lives; in default of such issue, to four sons, Richard, Thomas, George and John, and heirs for ever. Whereas Thomas Chappell of London, stationer, John Rowden of London, weaver, William Adderley of London, merchant tailor, and William Tribbeck of London, plumber, by indenture dated 30 May last past, sold to testator messuage called the George with all shops, cellars, etc. in pa. St Sepulchres London, in tenure or occupation of Arthur Strangwayes, with four other messuages or shops adjoining, said property to parson and church-wardens of parish church of St Albane in Great Woodstreet in London and successors for ever, towards repair of said church and provision and repair of goods and ornaments belonging to same. To children of Christes Hospitall in London £4 to be paid within one month of death. To poor in pa. St Albane in Woodstreet 40s to be distributed at discretion of parson and churchwardens of same within one month of death. To poor of town of Rufforth pa. Croston co. Lancaster, where he was born, 40s to be distributed at discretion of brother-in-law John Palmer, Thomas Spencer, Thomas Awty and Hugh Watkinson, or, if all are dead, then to be distributed at discretion of churchwardens of said parish church within two months of death. To Worshipfull Company of Goldsmiths in London, of which he is free member, one spout pot of silver white to weigh thirty ounces and £8 for a supper to be paid on day of burial. To mother Jenet Savadge £10 to be paid within two months of death. To two sisters, Cicelie Peacock and Katherine Palmer, £5 each to be paid within six months of death. To brothers-in-law John Palmer and Ambrose Peacocke 20s each to make each a gold ring, if their wives be living, to be paid within six months of death. To Thomas Peacocke, sister Cicelie's son, £3, and to each of his brothers and sisters 20s to be paid within six months of death. To cousin Fraunicis Savadge of Rufforth 40s to be paid within six months of death and to each of his children 20s to be paid within six months of death or to their father for their use. To cousin Hesketh, widow of Thomas Hesketh* of Rufforth, 20s to be paid within six months of death. To mother-in-law Mistress Wotton widow £3 to make her a gold ring to wear for his sake. To sister Sara Flint £3 to make her a ring, to be paid within one month of death. To fellows, seacoalmeters of City of London, at time of his death £3 for a dinner to be paid immediately after death. To cousin Ann Leland £3 and mourning gown. To servant Marie Partridge, mourning gown. Appoints trusty friend Robert Hill, citizen and merchant tailor of London, sole executor and for his pains £10. Appoints very loving friends Mr Doctor Lister and Mr John Jackson* overseers and to each £3 to make each a gold ring to wear in remembrance of him. Rest among children equally (with exception of son Richard). If said son Richard, within seven days of testator's death, delivers to executor release of all claims to his goods, chattels, etc. either by custom of the City of London or otherwise, then acquits said son Richard of all debt he owes him. Revokes all former wills. 'The Hand Writing of 34h8 G9472.'* Wit. John Grome, Hum. Dyson* notary public.

PRO PROB10/286. OW, note of registration marginated (fo. 1), prob. clause subscribed (fo. 3). Three sheets (fo. 2 numbered 2) joined at top, remnants of seal. Text in facile secretary with displayed matter in italic and engrossing secretary, possibly hand of John Grome.

Prob. PCC 26 Oct. 1611 to Robert Hill, executor. Admon. PCC 23 Nov. 1626 to Peter Fantrat, husband of Elizabeth Fantrat, daughter of Savage, after death of Hill (PRO PROB11/118 fo. 157r). Note endorsed on will (fo. 3) records enrolment of will in Court of Husting on Monday after feast of St Edmund, 9 James I (20 Nov. 1611) (see *Calendar of Wills Proved and Enrolled in the Court of Husting, London, A.D. 1258–A.D. 1688*, ed. R. Sharpe, 2 pts, London, 1889–90, II, 734). PAB (PRO PROB8/14 fo. 195v) gives pa. of origin as St Alban Wood Street.

Noted: Leslie Hotson, *Shakespeare's Sonnets Dated and Other Essays*, London, 1949, p. 127; printed: Honigmann, *'Lost Years'*, pp. 143–4 (RegC extracts).

c.1552–1611. Financier; trustee with William Leveson (**1621**) for division of Globe shares in 1599 on behalf of Shakespeare and others. (Leslie Hotson, 'John Jackson and Thomas Savage' in his *Shakespeare's Sonnets Dated*, pp. 125–40; E. A. J. Honigmann, 'Thomas Savage of Rufford' in *'Lost Years'*, pp. 84–9; Eccles, 'Actors II', p. 458.)

Silverstreet] later purchased from Richard Savage by Heminges (Hotson, op. cit., p. 127).

Adlestreet] purchased from Heminges and leased back to him (Hotson, op. cit., p. 127).

Thomas Hesketh] a William Shakeshafte was commended in will of Alexander Hoghton (1581) to Sir Thomas Hesketh of Rufford, likely to be connected to this Hesketh. Oliver Baker first identified Shakeshafte with Shakespeare (*In Shakespeare's Warwickshire and the Unknown Years*, London, 1937, p. 298).

Jackson] acted as trustee for Shakespeare in purchase of Blackfriars gatehouse 1613; see index.

34h8 G9472] cipher of John Grome.

Dyson] see index.

1612 July 4 Thomas TOWNE

In the name of God Aimen this fowerthe daie of Iulye 1612: And in the yeres of the Raigne of our soveraigne Lorde Iames by the grace of God kinge of England ffraunce and Ireland the Tenth And of Scotland the fyve and fforteithe, &c. defender of the faithe/ I Thomas Towne of the parishe of St Saviour in sowthwerke within the Countie of Surrey gentleman. beinge sicke in bodie, but of good and perfect Remembraunce (thankes be given to the Almightie god) do ordaine and make this my laste Will and Testament in manner and forme followinge (That is to saie) ffirste I <g>ive[1] and bequeathe my soule to Almightie God And to his sonne Iesus christe my onlye saviour and Redemer by whose mercies passion and blood sheedinge I hope and looke for the Remission and full satisfacion for all my sinnes And at the last generall daie of Iudgment to enioye that heavenly kingdome prepared for me and all his elect/ ffirst Concerninge my goods And chattells I give and bequeathe to my Cozen Dorathie ffeeldhowse the somme of ffive Pounds of lawfull mony of England,/ Item I give and bequeathe to my Cozen p phillis Norgatte the somme of six Pounds thirteene shillinges and ffower pence of lawffull mony of England/ Item I give and bequeathe to my Cozen Daniell Norgate for the educacion and vse of his Childeren the somme of ffyve Pounds of like lawffull monye of England Item I give and bequeath vnto my brother Iohn Towne of Dunwiche in suffolke (if he be now livinge) the somme of Tenn Pounds of lawffull monye of Englande/ Item I give and bequeathe vnto my very good frends and [frends] {fellowes}* videlicet William Borne,* Thomas Dowton,* Edward Iubye,* Samuell Rowley,* Charels Mercie* & Humfrye Ieffes,* three pounds to make them a supper when it shall please them to call for it/ Item I give and bequeathe vnto my Cozen John Towne of hackney ffive Pounds of lawffull mony of England// Item I give and bequeathe, to Mr William simons the preacher of this parishe to make a sermon at my buriall (if it shall please god to Call me from this liffe and he Remaine in this parishe, the somme of Twentie shillinges of lawffull mony of England to be paid at my buriall/ Item I give and bequeath vnto Ann Towne my wiffe* the lease and terme of yeres whiche I haue Yett to come and vnexpired of the Woodwharff howse and appertenaunces[2] in St Saviours Close [w] now in the tennure of Mr Champion', Item I give and bequeathe vnto katheren Clarke my late servaumtt[3] Tenn shillinges to be paide at my buriall/ Item I give vnto Ann [4] my now servaunt ffive shillinges to be paide at my funerall/ Item All the Rest of my lands goods Cattells Chattells plate Ieuells ymplementes and howshold stuffe my debtes beinge paide and my funerall expences discharged, I give and bequeath vnto my saide Wiffe Ann Towne/ Item my will is that my said wiffe shall haue one Yere after my descease, to paie the legaseyes before mentioned to be given to my brother and Cozens' vnlesse she Will paie them before, at her pleasure/ Item, I doe ordaine and make my saide wiffe Ann Towne my full and sole executrix to see this my last will and testament performed accordinge to my mynde, And I doe renounce all former wills, giftes, and grauntes, heretofore made or ordained In witnes whereof I haue herevnto sett my hande and seale the daie and Yere ffirste above Written/ Thomas Towne Sealed in the presence of vs William Corden* Edwarde Griffin*

1. *give*: ink blot obscures *g*. 2. *app'tennces*: mark of abbreviation for *au* misplaced over *pp*. 3. *serva'mtt*: rightly *servaunt*. 4. Blank in MS.

PRO PROB10/294. OW, prob. clause and note of exhibition of inventory subscribed, note of registration marginated. Single sheet, with remnants of seal and signatures of testator and witnesses. Text in rapid secretary.

Prob. PCC 1 Aug. 1612 to Ann Towne, relict and executor. PAB (PRO PROB8/15 fo. 7r) notes exhibition of inventory in second year of Abbot's archbishopric (Apr. 1612–Apr. 1613).

Printed: G. E. Bentley 'The wills of two Elizabethan actors', *MP*, XXIX, 1931/2, pp. 110–14 (pp. 113–14) (RegC).

fl. 1594–1610. Actor; Admiral's/Prince Henry's 1594, 1604–10; mentioned passim in Henslowe's diary and 1605–11 in papers of Edward Alleyn (**1626**), who granted Towne and wife annuity of £12 for thirty-one years in 1608 (Warner, pp. 236–7); leaves bequests to actors. Thomas Towne 'a man' buried St Saviour's Southwark, 9 Aug. 1612; if this is testator his will was proved eight days before burial. (Chambers II, 347; Nungezer, pp. 377–8.)

fellowes] all members of Prince's for at least eight years, most earlier associated with Henslowe's companies.
Borne] also known as Bird alias Borne (**1624**).
Dowton] Downton (**1625**).
Iubye] Juby (**1618**).

Rowley] (1624).
Mercie] Massey, actor, Admiral's/Prince Henry's/Palsgrave's 1597–1625 (Nungezer, pp. 247–8; Bentley II, 507–8).
Ieffes] actor, Admiral's/Prince Henry's/Palsgrave's 1598–1616 (Nungezer, pp. 204–5; Bentley II, 483).
wiffe] widow received £50 from Prince's company on death of husband (Warner, p. 36).
Corden] tenant of Henslowe, signatory with Griffin to letter to Alleyn from Churchwardens and others of Liberty of Clink c.1616 (Warner, p. 102); see index.
Griffin] scrivener, acted as witness etc. for Henslowe 1599–1613 (Greg, *Henslowe's Diary*, II, 268); see index.

1612 July 25 Thomas GREENE

In Dei nomine amen I Thomas Greene of the parishe of St Iames Clarkenwell vppon the twenty five daye of Iuly 1612 beinge sicke of body but of perfect sence and memorey doe constitute and make my last will and testament not beinge constrayned thervnto by any but of my owne accord Inprimis I give and bequeath my soule to almighty god my Creator and to his only begotton sonne my gratious redeemer, and to the holy ghost my comforter and sanctifyer, and I give my body (after it shall please god to call me) to be buryed in the churche of St Iames Clarkenwell after the order of Christian buryall Item I give to mr Iohn Andrewes preacher for a sermon at my funerall forty shillinges to be payd by my Executor Item I give and bequeath to my daughter Honnor Green lawfully of my body begotton an hundred powndes vsual money of England to be payd within eyghteen monethes after my decease Item I give and bequeath my sonne in law Robert* Browne forty powndes to be payd¹ (fo. 130r) by my Executor out of my goodes when he shall come to the perfect age of twenty and one yeares and vntill the foresayd tyme of one and twenty yeares my executor shall give the sayd Robert Browne fowr poundes yearly Item I give and bequeath to my sonne in lawe Willyam Brown* forty powndes vsuall money of England to be payd by my executor when he shall come to the age of twenty and one yeares and duringe the space of the sayd Willyams nonage my Executor to give him yearly fowr poundes vsuall money of England Item I give and bequeath to my daughter in lawe* Susanna Browne the some of thirty powndes vsuall money of England to be payd by my executor when shee is fivetene² yeares of age and soe likewise I give and bequeath to my Daughter Elizabeth Browne thirty powndes vsuall money of England to be payd at her age of fivetene² yeares Item I give and bequeath to my daughter in lawe* Anne

Browne thirty powndes vsuall money of England to be payd to her when shee shall come to the age of fivetene yeares Item I give and bequeath to my fore sayd three daughters Susanna Elizabeth and Anne three powndes to each of them yearly to be payd by my executor vntill they come to the foresayd age of fifteen yeares. Item I will and bequeath that if any of my two sonnes Robert and William Brownes or any of my foresayd three daughters Susanna Elizabeth or Anne Brownes shall dye before they come to the full age [of] when I will they should receive their severall legacies that then the legacy of the party deceased shall equally be devided amongest them that survive Item I give and bequeath to my Sister Elizabeth Barrett to be receaved by my brother Iohn Greene* and disposed of by him for hir vse tenn powndes to be payd by my Executor within three moneths after my decease Item I give to my brother Iohn Greene the three lummes³ which he hath in present possession already Item I give to mr Gautres my baker tenn shillinges to be made a ringe as memoriall of me Item I give to mr Standley my brewer tenn shillinges to a memoriall ringe Item I give and bequeath to Iohn Cumbere*   ⁴ powndes to be payd by my Executor within one yeare after my decease Item I give and bequeath to my freind Alexander Pratt twenty shillinges to be payd by my Executor after my funerall imedyatly Item I [giue] give & bequeath to my fellowes* of the house of the redd Bull* forty shillinges to buy gloves for them Item I give and bequeath to my two brothers Iafferey and Iohn Greenes thirty shillinges to each of them to make them seale⁵ (fo. [130v]) Ringes Item I make and ordayne Susann* my very well beloved wife full executrix of this my last will and testament giveing her all my goodes and chattells to the performance hereof and doe make and ordayne Ieafferey Greene my brother Christopher Beeston* and Richard Parkines* overseers to this my last will and Testament In witnes wher<of> I have sett my hand and seale Before theis witnesses Alexander Pratt Christopher Beeston Richard Parkines, Thomas Heyward* and Ieafferey Greene with others. Thomas Greene witnesses Alexander Pratt presbyter Christopher Beeston

1. Catchword *payd*.   2. *fivetene*] originally *fourtene*; corrected in same hand.
3. *lummes*] misreading of *summes*?   4. Blank in MS.   5. Catchword *Ringes*.

GLRO DL/C/360 fos 129v-130v. RegC with prob. clause.

Prob. ConCL 10 Oct. 1612 to Susan Greene, widow and executor.

Printed: James Greenstreet, 'Drury Lane Theatre in the reign of James I', *Athenaeum*, no. 3018, 29. Aug. 1885, p. 282.

c.1572–1612. Actor and sharer in Queen Anne's 1604–12; held Curtain playhouse 1611. Buried St James Clerkenwell 7 Aug. 1612. (Chambers II, 236–7, 320;

Nungezer, pp. 161–5; Bentley II, 451; Eccles, 'Actors II', pp. 456–7.) On lawsuit arising from inheritance by widow of share in Queen Anne's Men see C. J. Sisson, 'The Red Bull company and the importunate widow', *ShS*, VII, 1954, pp. 57–68); on children of Susan Greene see Berry, *Boar's Head Playhouse*, pp. 71, 209 fn. 18.

sonne in lawe Robert] stepson, son of Susan Greene by first husband, Robert Browne; see index.
Willyam Brown] (**1634**) stepson; actor with Queen Anne's by 1617.
daughter in lawe] stepdaughter; see also below.
Iohn Greene] possibly touring actor on Continent (Schrickx, *Foreign Envoys*, p. 204).
Cumbere] actor with Queen Anne's from 1612 (Bentley II, 417–18).
fellowes] included, as well as those mentioned by name, Robert Lee (**1629**), Ellis Worth (**1659**), Thomas Basse (**1634**), John Duke (**A1613**).
redd Bull] built c.1606; home of Queen Anne's to 1617.
Susann] widow of Robert Browne (**A1604**) of Boar's Head where Queen Anne's Men based 1603–4; married James Baskervile 1613; see index.
Beeston] (**1638**) actor with Worcester's/Queen Anne's to 1619; succeeded Greene as business manager; see index.
Parkines] Perkins, actor with Worcester's/Queen Anne's to 1619, particular friend of Thomas Heywood (Chambers II, 332; Nungezer, pp. 274–8; Bentley II, 525–8); see index.
Heyward] Heywood, actor and dramatist, with Worcester's/Queen Anne's 1602–19 (Chambers III, 338–48).

1612 Sept. 13 (codicil) (1610 Jan. 8) Edward PUDSEY (abstract)

Of Tewxburye co. Gloster gent. Health. Soul 'I doe wholy betake & Commytte vnto the infinitt mercye of Almightye god, meekly acknowledginge both by originall corruption & by my many actuall transgressions (in his Iustice) damnation to bee my due, yet assuredly beleevinge by taking hold with ye hand of faith vppon the gracious promisses of our mercifull father to all repentant sinners in his holy writt deliuered, And vppon the merittes bitter death, & earnest mediation of our sweet saviour Christ Iesus, That I am one of the elect before all worldes, ffor the holy & blessed spiritt doth assure my spirit, That I am freed from all my infinit sinnes, & transgressions and the punishment therevnto due, And so beeing Iustifyed by the mercifull Imputation of Christes righteousnes, rest assured to bee glorifyed both in soule & bodye'. A divine to preach at funeral and to have 20s. To poor of parish in which he is buried 20s; if at Tewxbury £3 to be distributed by churchwardens. To dear and well beloved wife £300 and lease of house where he lives and all goods, plate and household stuff belonging to it except hereafter bequeathed. To son

Edward Pudsey* and his heirs for ever all lands, tenements and annuities and £300 to be used by executors for his maintenance until reaches age of nineteen. All his books to be kept for him, especially notebooks,* or at least such as executors think fit, rest to be sold. Wife to have six books of divinity which she chooses, and during her widowhood and children's minority shall have the education of them and allowance for same; but upon her marriage children to be disposed at discretion of executors, entreating them to be careful in giving them religious education and to train son in the university, persuading him to study divinity 'yf the Lordes spirit do worke in him as I trust yt will therto'. To daughter Amye £200 payable at her marriage, in meantime to be employed to her use. If son dies before he reaches nineteen, wife to have all lands and tenements with annuities during her life, and daughter Amy to have said £300 with profits; and after death of her mother all lands etc. to her and heirs for ever; if she dies without issue, said lands to testator's brother Nicholas and heirs for ever. Seal ring to son Edward to be delivered at aforesaid age, in meantime to be in mother's custody. Charges wife to see children brought up in fear of God and learning and entreats brother Nicholas to assist her. To said brother Nicholas £10, his gelding and furniture, all apparel except hereafter bequeathed, sword and dagger, girdles and hangers, and his privy coat. To two brothers Thomas and Samuell £30 each, payable when either be freemen of London and keep trades in open shop, or otherwise follow course of life approved by executors. All that recovered by annuity of 20 marks p.a. on land in Newton Solney in Derby Shyre and arrears arising to 400 marks or thereabouts, to three sisters Elener, Martha and Margery to be equally divided among them, and to each £30 to be paid within one year of death. To fatherly friend Mr Blount of Arlaston esq. 20s to be given as a ring, and the like to honourable and worthy Mrs Blount and whatever books that he has there, which she is pleased to accept. To long approved good friend Mr Phillip Kinge velvet jerkin, carnation silk stockings and garters and 20s to be given as a ring. To other good friend Mr John Daighton of Gloster gold-coloured silk stockings, black garters, scarlet waistcoat and 20s to be given as a ring. Debts to be paid; 'I may forget but now sure I remember not any, except what I stand engaged in for others, wherof all I trust I am well secured' and £50 for which is bound to Mr Spencer of Lincolns In with Mr Beawsoe and cousin Richard Pudsey M.A., who brought him in to it, the money having been paid to tailors and other tradesmen in London, due to them from Sir Thomas Branfor, and not a penny coming to him. Remainder to wife, son and daughter equally, unless she be with child at his death, then child to have £200 as set down for Edwarde and Amye. Appoints as executors friends Mr Phillip King and Mr John

Daighton to whom £5 more each 'intreatinge them to conclude their loue in ye religious education of my children'.
Codicil: To uncle Helyard 20s to be given as a ring, same to his aunt. To Mr Peeter Weekes the same and black doublet in his trunk in London. 10s to Mrs Poulton to be given as a ring all with death's head.

PRO PROB10/307. OW, prob. clause endorsed (fo. 3), note of registration marginated (fo. 1). Three sheets joined at top, each with signature and seal of testator. Text in facile secretary, marginated codicil and endorsed notes in mixed hand sharing some characteristics of main text, both possibly hand of testator; signatures in italic.

Admon [with will annexed]. PCC 17 Nov. 1613 to Edith Pudsey, relict, Philip King and John Daighton, executors, renouncing. PAB (PRO PROB8/15 fo. 142r) notes exhibition of inventory in fifth year of archbishopric of George Abbot (Apr. 1615–Apr. 1616).

1573–1613. Theatre-goer. Notebooks include extracts from quarto editions of several Shakespeare plays and from *Othello*, not published until 1622. (Juliet Mary Gowan, 'An Edition of Edward Pudsey's Commonplace Book (c.1600–1615) from the Manuscript in the Bodleian Library', unpublished M.Phil. thesis, University of London, 1967.)

Edward Pudsey] possibly actor in Germany 1628 and 1640 (Chambers II, 335; Nungezer, p. 289; Bentley II, 537).
notebooks] extracts printed in Richard Savage, comp., *Shakespearean Extracts from 'Edward Pudsey's Booke'*, Stratford-upon-Avon Note Books 1, Stratford-upon-Avon, 1888 (now Bodleian MS Eng. poet.d.3 and Shakespeare Birthplace Trust Record Office ER 82).

1614 Jan. 3 Alexander COOKE

In the name of the father, ye sonne, & the holy ghoste
I Allexander Cooke, Sick of body, but in perfect minde, doe with mine owne hand write my last will & testament
first, I bequeath[e] my Soule into ye hands of god my deere Saviour Iesus Christe who bought it & payd for it deerly with his {bloud} on ye crosse
next my body to ye earthe to be buryed after the manner of Christian buryall
Item I doe giue and bequeathe vnto my sonne Francis the some of fifty powndes, to be deliuerd to him at ye age of one an twenty yeeres
Item I doe giue and bequeathe vnto my daughter rebecca, the some of fiftye pownds allso [which somes are] to be deliuerd to hir at the age of seuenteene yeeres, or at hir day of mariage, which it shall please god to

bring first, which somes of money are bothe in one purse in my Cuberd
Item I doe giue and bequeathe vnto ye childe which my my wife now goeth with the some of fiftye pownds allso, which is in the hand of my fellowes* as my share of ye stock To be deliuerd if it be a boy, at one & twenty yeres, if a girle, at seventeene, or day of maryage, as before. All whiche somes of moneyes, I doe Intreate, my master hennings[1]* mr Cundell,* and mr Frances Caper, (for gods cause) to take into there hands, & see it saflye put into grocers hall,* for <t>he vse and bringinge vp of my poore or<pha>nts (fo. 2)[2]
Item I doe further giue and bequeathe vnto my daughte[3] rebecca, the window-cushens made of needle worke, together withe ye window=cloathe Court cuberd-cloathe, and chimney=cloathe, being all bordered about with needleworke sutable, and greene Silke fringe
If any of my chilldren, dye ere they come to[e] age, my will is yat the survivers shall haue there parte, equallye devided to ye {last}
If all my chilldren dye ere they come to age, my will is that my brother Ellis (or his chilldren) {shall haue} one halfe of all, the other halfe to be thus devided, to my fiue sisters, or there children tenn pownds a peece amongst them, my brother Iohns daughter other tenne pownds, ye rest to my wife if she liue then, if not to Ellis and his, If my brother {Ellis} [ell] dye ere this, and leaue no childe of his body, my will is, it shall all be equally distribute[d]d amongst my sisters <.> and the chilldren of there bodys, only my wives parte recervd If she liue: – – my wife {paying all charges of my buriall} performing my will in euery poynte as I haue set downe my will is she shall Inioy & {be my full and lawfull Executris} all my goods, chattells, movables, debbts, or whatsoeuer is mine in all the worlde /// This is my last will and testamente, In wittnes wherof I haue set to my hand Ianuary the third :<u>1613</u>: By me Allex: Cooke:

1. *hennings*: rightly *Hemings*.   2. Page numbered 112 (top left) and 2 (bottom left).   3. *daughte*: rightly *daughter*.

PRO PROB10/311. OW, prob. clause and note of exhibition of inventory endorsed (fo. 2), note of registration marginated (fo. 1). Two sheets, sewn along left margin, with signature but unsealed. Text in hand of testator; secretary, using y for thorn throughout, each clause separated by a horizontal line (see Figure 2, p. 16).

Prob. PCC 4 May 1614 to relict and executor. Blank left for widow's name; name not given in PAB (PRO PROB8/15 fo. 184v) or in RegC (PROB11/123 fo. 385r–385v). PAB notes exhibition of inventory and gives pa. of origin as St Saviour's Southwark.

Printed: Chalmers, *Apology*, pp. 447–9 fn. v (RegC).

fl. 1590–1614. Actor, Admiral's or Strange's 1590–1, King's Men 1603–13, in which he was sharer; legatee of Augustine Phillips (1605). Buried St Saviour's Southwark 25 Feb. 1614. (Chambers II, 311–12; Nungezer, pp. 102–3.)

fellowes] King's Men.
my master hennings] John Heminges (1630), member of King's Men, 'to whom he had presumably been apprenticed' (Chambers II, 312) but see introduction p. 3; mentioned in wills of other members of company; see index.
Cundell] Henry Condell (1627), member of King's Men; mentioned in wills of other members of company; see index.
grocers hall] Cooke was a freeman of the company.

1614 Dec. 5 Robert ARMIN

20 Armyn[1]

In the name of God Amen, the ffifte Daie of December Anno Domini (1614) And in the yeares of the Raigne of oure Soveraigne Lorde Iames by the grace of god kinge of Englande Scotlande ffraunce and Irelande defender of the faithe &c. (That is to saye) of Englande ffraunce and Irelande the Twelveth, And of Scotlande the Eighte and fforteth, I Roberte Armyn Cittizen and Goldsmithe of London, the vnprofittable servante of Almightie god, weake in bodie, but stronge in minde, doe willingly and with a free harte render and give againe into the handes of my Lorde god and glorious Creator, my spirit, which hee of his moste mercifull and fatherly goodnes gave vnto mee, when hee fashioned mee my[2] [Mothes] Mothers wombe, makeing mee a lyving and a reasonable Creature, nothing doubting but that for his infinite Mercies, sett forthe in the moste pretious bloode of his moste Dearely beloved sonne Iesus Christe, oure only Savioure and moste glorious Redeemer, hee will receave my soule into his glorye, and place it in the Company of the heavenly Angells, and blessed saintes, And as concerning my bodie even with a good will and free harte I give it over, commending it to the earthe whereof it came, Nothing [dob] doubting but that According to the Article of my faithe, Att the greate Daie of the genneral resurrection when wee shall all Appeare before the Iudgment seate of oure blessed Redeemer Iesus Christe, I shall receave the same againe by the Mightie power of God, wherewith hee is Able to subdue all thinges to himself, not a Corruptible Mortall, weake and vile bodie as nowe it is, But an vncorruptible, immortall, stronge, and perfecte bodie, like vnto the [get] glorious {bodye} of my Lorde and Savioure Iesus Christe, And as twoching the worldlie substance which god of his grace hathe given mee, and made mee Steward of, in this mortallitie; ffor the preventing of all controversies and

[coten] contentions, which many tymes doe arise amongest deare ffreendes for the goodes and possessions [as such] of such as leave theire estates vndisposed of, being either prevented by sudden deathe or by protracting of tyme vntill (fo. 2) vntill such feeblenes and [debll] Debillitie of bodie and memorie overtake them, that they cannot sett any certeyne course or order therein, I being as aforesaide weake in bodie but of perfecte memory I hartilie thanke Almightie {God} for the same, for the prevention' of all controversies and contentions {as aforesaide} which mighte Arise betweene my loving wife and f³ kindered for my saide worldly substance doe therefore Advisedly and with good Deliberacion, will and dispose of my saide worldly substance as followeth, first I give and bequeathe vnto my brother Iohn Armyne Cittizen and Marchantaylor of London' my seale ringe of golde with my Armes on it, Item' I give and bequeathe vnto my saide brothers sonne Roberte Armyn a peece of golde or Iacobus of Twentie & two shillinges Item' I give and bequeathe vnto my Sister Tabitha my olde Cloake, Item I give and bequeathe vnto Roberte Treate* Cittizen and gouldsmithe of London, and to George Blundevell Cittizen' and vpholster of London', Eleaven' shillinges a peece in remembraunce of love vnto them, Item' all the rest of my saide worldly substance whatsoever it be, my debtes being paide and funerall discharged I fully & wholly give and bequeathe vnto my saide loving wife Alice Armyn whome I doe make & ordeyne my full and sole Executrix of this my last will and Testament, Item' I earnestly request and desier the saide Roberte Treate and George Blundevell to bee the supervisors of this my last will and Testament, requesting them Also to Aide and Assist my saide Executrix towching this my last will & Testament yf need shall requier, In witnes whereof I have herevnto putt my hande and seale the saide ffifte Daye of December Anno Domini (1614) my saide last will & Testament conteyning two sheetes of paper   Robart Armyn
in the hall of mr Armyns howse⁴
Published the Daye and yeare aboue written & the same reade to the Testator by me Iohn Warnar scrivenor, and the same sealled & subscribed by the saide Testator in the presence of Simon Warren signum Willielmi WB Brice and of mee Iohn' Warnar London scrivener

1. 20 *Armyn*: superscribed. 2. *my*: rightly *in my*. 3. *f*: scribal slip. 4. *in . . . house* marginated.

GL MS 9052/4. OW, prob. clause endorsed (fo. 2). Two sheets, originally secured together at top, each bearing testator's signature, unsealed, with witnesses' marks and signatures. Text in engrossing secretary, hand of John Warnar, scrivener.

Prob. ACL 12 Dec. 1615 to Alice Armin, relict and executor. Notes endorsed on will (fo. 2) give pa. of origin as St Botolph without Aldgate, exhibition and valuation of inventory at £160 13s 2d.

Printed: Leslie Hotson, 'Robert Armin, Shakespeare's fool' in his *Shakespeare's Motley*, London, 1952, pp. 84–128 (pp. 108–9 fn. 1).

c.1568–1615. Actor, dramatist and pamphleteer; Lord Chandos's then Chamberlain's/King's Men from 1599; legatee of Augustine Phillips (**1605**). Buried St Botolph Aldgate 30 Nov. 1615. (Chambers II, 299–300; Nungezer, pp. 15–20.)

Treate] see index.

1615 Dec. 16 William HOVELL

In the name of God Amen, This sixteinth daie of december Anno do*mi*ni 1615/ I William Hovell of the p*a*rishe of St Saviour in sowth Worke wi*t*hin the Countie of Surr*ey* gentleman beinge sicke in bodie, but of good and p*e*rfitt remembraunce, Thankes¹ be given to almightie God) doe ordaine and make this my last will and Testament in manner and forme followinge ffirste I give and bequeath my soule to Almightie God hopinge that of his great mercie, and for the love of his deare sonne Ihesus Christ, (who suffered and dyed for my sinnes,) That he will not onlie pardon and forgive me all my sinnes, but will at my departure out of this vale of misery, receave me into his most blessed and heavenlie kingdome, Item my will and mynde is That my executor and overseers hereafter named shall see my bodie buryed in the Chancell or in one of the {vpp*e*r} Iles of the p*a*rishe Church of St Saviour in Sowth Worke aforesaide, And to bestowe vppon my ffunerall Tenn Poundes of lawfull monie of England, And to give to the poore of the libertie of the Clinke xx s in breade at my funerall, Item whereas I haue a lease of the howse wherein I now dwell, And all the Tenementes in Vnicorne Ally vppon the Bankside in the saide p*a*rishe of St Saviou*r* whiche lease I holde from one master Phillipe Henslow* Esquire for Twentie yeres yetto come at the leaste, And also one other lease, whiche I holde from one Mr Blinco felmonger of Certaine howses in fyve foote lane in Barmonsey street, for sixteene yeres yetto Come at the least whiche saide severall leases after the death of Ione my wiffe* or p*re*sently after her marryage I give and bequeath vnto my brother Nicholas Hovell of Winden in the Countie of Essex Carpenter, his executors administrators or assignes, Item my will and mynde is That my trustie and lovinge ffrende, Mr Roger Cole* of the saide p*a*rishe of St Saviou*r* gent*leman*, whome I do ordaine and make my full and sole executor, shall haue the saide Two leases in his possession and custodie, vntill the death of my saide wife or daie of her marryage, whiche of them shall first happen, And my saide wiffe duringe her widdowhood, shall Receave Take and gather all suche rentes (**p. 2**) proffitt*es* and comodities as shall growe due or issue out or from the saide howses and tenement*es*, from tyme to tyme soe longe as my saide wiffe shall live or vntill the daie of her saide marryadge, And she shall therew*i*th paie vnto the saide Mr Phillip Henslow, and Mr Blinko and to all other p*er*sons all such rentes somme or sommes of monie, Church Duties and other paymentes as shalbe due or payable out, for or from the same houses or tenement*es* from tyme to tyme, And shall also kepe and maintaine the same in good and sufficient rep*a*racio*n*s/ Item my will and mynde is that before my saide wife shall take or receave any benifitt or p*r*ofitt out of my saide howses or tenement*es*, that she shall enter into a bonde or obligac*i*on of a hundereth pounds {to my executor and overseers} to paie the saide rentes and kepe the saide houses {or te*n*ement*es*} in good and sufficient rep*a*racio*n*s, accordinge to the Covenaunt*es* grauntes payment*es* and agreement*es* mencioned in the saide leases, And not doe or suffer to be done, any acte or actes thinge or thinges whereby the saide leases or any of them maie be forfited, or thestate thereof whiche shall grow, be due, or remain*n*e to my saide brother Nicholas Hovell be in any Wise forfited impeached or debarred/ Item I give and bequeath vnto my sister Allice Alewood wife to Robert Alewood of Debden in essex ffyve Pounds of lawffull monie of England, Item I give and bequeath vnto my sister Margaret Rayner of Stow market in Suffolke ffive Pounds of like lawffull monie, Ite*m* I give and bequeath vnto my sister Ann ffyve pounds of like lawffull monie/ Ite*m* my will and mynde is that my executor shall for the good of my sister, Allice warner of Woodforde in the Countie of North hampton, bestow ffyfteene pounds of lawffull monie of England to buy a house for her selfe duringe her life, and to her three daughter after her decease equally amongest them, And my will is that the ffyve pounds a pece wh*i*ch I haue bequeathed vnto my three sisters first named shalbe paide vnto them w*i*thin one moneth next after my decease if the² come to demaunde the same or at any other tyme after when they shall demaunde (**p. 3**) the same/ Item I give and bequeath the somme of Thirteene Pounds of lawffull monie of England to be put forth for the benifitt of the poore of the libertie of the Clinke And my will is that my executor and overseers, w*i*th some other of the inhabitant*es* (if they shall think fitt) to ioyne w*i*th them to put out the said somme of xiij li, and the profitt whiche shall arise or grow by the same to be by them or there derection distributed weekly {or at there discretions} forever amongest the poore there inhabitinge And my Will is that this my gyfte shalbe sett downe for a rememberaunce in the Booke of the orders for this libertie Ite*m* I give and bequeath vnto my Brother Robe*r*te Alewood ffortie shillinges of lawffull monie of England, Item I give and bequeath vnto my saide brother Nicholas Hovell my best Gowne, and my signet or seale

Ringe Wherein is ingraven two le*tt*res for my name/ Item I give and bequeath vnto my lovinge frends, Mr Roger Cole fortie shillinges, to Mr Edwarde Griffin* a pece of gold of xxij s and to Mr Thomas Mansell a pece of gold of xxij s, to buy eych of them a Ringe requestinge them to weare them for my sake, Ite*m* I give and bequeath vnto Camilla Tod widdow Tenn shillinges of lawffull monie of England, Ite*m* my Will and mynde is, that all suche bills or bondes as I haue of Nathaniell Clayes* and of one Dobson*n*s shalbe delivered to them, and I doe freely forgive them all such somme or sommes of monie as they or eyther of them do owe vnto me, Ite*m* I give and bequeath vnto my app*r*entice Michael Bowyer* xl s/ And to my app*r*entice William Wilson* xx s/ Item I give and bequeath vnto Nathaniell Clay and Iohn podger* my fyfte parte of my stocke of app*a*rell and other thing*es* w*hi*ch I haue in the companie wherein they playe, and my horse which is w*i*th them, to be equallie shared or devided betwne them Two/ Item I give and bequeath vnto my maid servaunt Iane fortie shillinges of lawffull monie of England [to be paide her vppon the daie of her Marriage] Ite*m* my Will is that all such app*a*rell or other thing*es* whiche I haue of Nicholas longes* somtyme my servant, vppon whiche I haue lente him monie shalbe deliuered to him w*i*thout payinge any monie for the same, Ite*m* I give and bequeath vnto Mr Archer* the minister x s and to Mr Sutton the (p. 4) preacher x s/ <Item I give>[3] Item my funerall expences dischardged my debtes [and] legaseys and other charges beinge satisfyed and paide according to the discrec*i*on of my executor and over seyers [and] and this my will p*er*formed and done, All the rest of my goods ymplemente*s* plate ringes, Iewells and houshold stuffe {and [a] bon<.>es[4] in her possession} I give and bequeath vnto Ione hovell my saide Wife/ Item I doe ordaine and make the saide Mr Roger Cole my ffull and sole executor And the saide Edwarde Griffin, And Thomas Mansell my overseers/ In Witnes whereof I haue herevnto sett my hande the daie and yere firste above Written
                    Wylleam havill
Witnes herevnto Iohn X Taylors m*a*rke Thomas Bryan
md[5] that the Testator willed that there should be a friendlie mettinge amongst the greate Enquest of the Libertie of the Clyncke whereof he was a member {some time} after his decease as his Executor and Overseers thought fittinge for a repast amongst them
By me Thomas mansell[6]

1. Opening parenthesis omitted. 2. *the*: rightly *they*. 3. <*Item I give*>: ink smudged deliberately? 4. bon<.>es: *?bondes*. 5. *md*: mark of abbreviation omitted, rightly *memorandum*. 6. md . . . *mansell* subscribed in a second hand, signed by Mansell.

PRO PROB10/327. OW, note of registration marginated (p. 1), prob. clause and note of exhibition subscribed (p. 4). Single sheet folded to make four pages, unsealed with signatures. Text in rapid secretary, with subscription in small formal secretary.

Prob. PCC 22 Dec. 1615 to Roger Cole gent., executor. PAB (PRO PROB8/ 16 fo. 97v) notes exhibition of inventory.

fl. 1615. Licensee for second King's Revels Children 1615 (Murray II, 10, 340) but Bentley questions identification of company (II, 510). Actor apprentice, Bowyer, suggests Hovell was actor as well as financier, involved with boys' companies. (Chambers II, 324; Nungezer, p. 199.)

Henslow] 1616; see index.
wiffe] Joan Hovell (**1620**).
Cole] see index.
Griffin] scrivener, signatory with Cole to letter to Edward Alleyn from churchwardens and others of Liberty of Clink c.1616 (Warner, p. 102), acted as witness etc. for Henslowe 1599–1613; see index.
Clayes, Clay] actor; one of leaders of Children of Bristol 1618 (Murray II, 5), licensee for Children of King's Revels 1629 (Bentley II, 408).
Bowyer] actor with Queen Henrietta's from 1625 (**1645**).
Wilson] ?connected with Palsgrave's 1617 (Bentley II, 622–3).
podger] apparently actor but not noticed in standard sources.
longes] ?actor; N. Long (**A1622**) later associated with W. Perry, co-licensee with Hovell in 1615, in forming new Children of Queen's Revels (Murray I, 361).
Archer] James Archer, curate of St Saviour's; see index.

1616 Jan. 6 Philip HENSLOWE

In the name of God amen. I Phillipp Henslowe of the parrishe of St Saviours in the Burrough of Sowthwarke and Cowntie of Surrey Esq*uire* being sicke in bodie but of p*er*fecte mynd and memory, thanck*es* be vnto Almightie God, doe make and ordaine this my last Will and Testame*nt* in forme following V*idelice*t ffirst and principally I Com*m*end my Soule vnto Almightie god hopeing to be saued by thonly merit*es* of my Lord and Saviour Iesus Christ and my body to be buryed in the p*a*rish Church of St Saviours aforesaid at the discrec*i*on of my Executrix and Overseers herevnder named; And touching the dispos*i*cion of such Landes and goods as it hath pleased god to blesse me with all my Will and meaninge is as followeth. ffirst I giue and bequeath vnto Agnes Henslowe my loving wife, all and singuler my Landes, Teneme*ntes*, hereditame*ntes* and Leases whatsoever, To haue and to hould to her the said Agnes for and during the terme of her naturall life and [no] noe longer, And after her decease I giue and bequeath all that my messuage or Tenemente with thappurtenances and the Tenementes therevnto belonging Commonlie Called or knowen by the name of the Bores hed* scituate on the Banckeside in the parrishe aforesaid, which I purchased of one devonishe Raymod[1] gentleman vnto Ann Henslow alias Parson now wife of William Parson and vnto her Heires forever. Alsoe I giue and bequeath (after the decease of my said wife) vnto Phillipp Henslow my godsonn sonn of Iohn Henslow waterman, all those my landes and Tenementes with thappurtenances which I purchased of one Throckmorton being scituate in the parrishe aforesaid, To haue and to hould vnto the said Phillipp Henslowe and to his Heires for ever, Item I giue and bequeath (after the decease of my said wife) vnto my loving Sister Marie Walters alias Adlington, all those my Landes and Tenementes with thappurtenances which I purchased of one Mr Mvnson scituate on the Banckeside in the parrishe aforesaid, To haue and to hould the same and every part and parcell thereof for and during the Terme of her naturall life, And after the decease of the said Mary my sister my Will and meaninge tis, that all and singuler the premisses last recited and bequeathed, shall come and descend vnto my said godsonn Phillip Henslowe and to his Heires for ever, Item I giue and bequeath (after the decease of my said wife) vnto my loving brother William Henslow<e> and his Assignes. all that my messuage mansion house and lease called the Beare garden* with all the Tenementes and appurtenances therevnto belonginge, which I hould and enioye by vertue of a Lease from the Lord Bishopp of Winton'.[2] Item I giue and bequeath vnto my loving sister Margarett Cuxon one yearlie annuytie or somme of thirtie poundes duringe her naturall life, to be paied vnto her quarterlie by my Executrix or her Assignes by even porciones. the first paymente to beginn at the next quarter daye after my decease, Item I giue and bequeathe vnto fortie poore men of the Libertie of the Clyncke, to eache a moorninge gowne, to attend my bodie to buriall; I giue and bequeath vnto mr Iames Archer* fortie shillings to preach at my funerall; All the rest and residue of all and singuler my goods, chattells, debtes readie money plate and househouldstuffe not before given or bequeathed, I giue and bequeathe vnto my lovinge wife Agnes Henslowe whome I make and ordaine sole Executrix of this my last Will, And I appointe my lovinge Sonn Mr Edward Alleyn Esquire Mr Robert Bromfeild,* Mr William Austen* and Mr Roger Cole* to be my Overseers, And my Will and meaninge is and hereby I order and devise, that if any ambiguytie dowbt or question arise or growe Concerninge any Clause matter or Legacie herein mencioned or bequeathed that the same shalbe heard and determined by my said Overseers or the greater part of them, and that if any such person causinge suche dowbt or question shall refuse to be ordered as aforesaid, and to abide the Award and Censure of my said Overseers as aforesaid, then and in that case everie such person shall loose all benefitt whatsoever of and by this my Will, and his or theire Legacie or Legacies to be vtterlie voyde as if none such had bynn by me bequeathed, and given. And then and in that case I giue and bequeath all such guifte, Legacie or bequest of any such person soe refusinge vnto my said sonn Edward Alleyn and vnto his Heires for ever, And I doe vtterlie revoake, frustrate and make voyde by theise pre*sentes* all other former [Wills] Will or Will*es,** legacies, bequest*es* or guift*es.* Executor or Executors in wrightinge or otherwise, and I will that this onlie shall stand for my last Will and Testame*nt*. In wittnes whereof I haue herevnto sett my hand and seale the sixt daye of Ianuarie Anno do*m*ini stilo Anglie .1615. Signu*m* di*c*ti Phillippi Henslowe. Sealed and subscribed in the pre*se*nce of Iames Archer, Ro: Bromfyld, Roger Cole, Robert Meare, Edw: Alleyn, Nicho: Sheppard.*

1. *devonishe Raymod*: *Devenishe Raymond* in RegC (PROB11/127 fo. 45r).
2. *Winton'*: Winchester.

PRO PROB10/327. OffC, prob. clause and note of collation with original subscribed, note of registration marginated. Single sheet, unsealed; right margin crumbling and lower edge torn resulting in some loss of legibility. No significant endorsements. Text in set secretary with displayed matter in hybrid secretary.

Prob. PCC 'intra Burgu*m* De Southwarke' 7 Jan. 1616 to Agnes (Anne) Henslowe, relict and executor. Undated note subscribed on will records collation with original by Richard Hulet, notary public, and Thomas Taylor. PAB (PRO PROB8/16 fo. 106v) notes exhibition of inventory in eighth year of archbishopric of George Abbot (Apr. 1618–Apr. 1619).

Noted: Chalmers, *Apology*, pp. 390–1 fn. z.

fl. 1577–1616. Theatrical proprietor and manager; builder of Rose in 1587, Fortune with Edward Alleyn (**1626**) in 1600, and Hope in 1613 with Jacob Meade (**1624**) and Gilbert Katherens (**1619**), perhaps lessee of Whitefriars 1613; financier to Admiral's/Prince's to 1604, Worcester's 1602–4, Lady Elizabeth's 1611; father-in-law of Alleyn; mentioned in wills of Hugh Davis (**1608**), William Hovell (**1615**), Agnes Henslowe (**1616**). Died 6 Jan., buried St Saviour's Southwark 10 Jan. 1616. (Greg, *Henslowe's Diary*, II, 1–41 for biography; Chambers I, 358–68.) See William Rendle, 'Phillip Henslowe', *Genealogist* n.s., IV, 1887, pp. 149–59; C. J. Sisson, 'Henslowe's will again', *RES*, V, 1929, pp. 308–11; John Briley, 'Edward Alleyn and Henslowe's will', *SQ*, IX, 1958, pp. 321–30 for accounts of litigation arising from will, in which John Henslowe and others accused Alleyn, Agnes Henslowe and Roger Cole of collusion in making of will and valuation of estate by holding back leases, including that for Fortune theatre. Depositions in Chancery by witnesses to will, Archer, Bromfyld, Sheppard and others, including Jacob Meade, describe Henslowe's last hours and the drawing up of the will.

Bores hed] not the theatre pa. Whitechapel.

Beare garden] site of Hope theatre; Henslowe and Alleyn involved in bearbaiting on Bankside from 1594; associated with J. Meade, Keeper of Bears 1599; became joint Masters of Royal Game of Bears, Bulls and Mastiff Dogs 1604 (Chambers II, 448–71).

Archer] curate of St Saviour's, preached memorial sermon 16 Feb. 1618 (Rendle, p. 153); see index.

Bromfeild] tradesman who supplied Admiral's Men from 1601; for dealings with Henslowe and Alleyn see Greg, op. cit., II, 245–6.

Austen] possibly William Augusten, player, from whom Henslowe acquired boy 18 Dec. 1597 (*Diary*, p. 241); Rendle (p. 158) identifies him as William Austin, author of *Ecce Homo* (rightly *Haec Homo*, 1637) and *Godly Meditations* (rightly *Devotionis Augustinianae Flamma; or, Certaine Meditations*, 1635).

Cole] registrar of Bp. of Winchester (Rendle, p. 153); his will dated 2 Sept. 1625, proved 3 May 1628 (PRO PROB11/153 fos 362v–364r); see index.

Will or Willes] earlier draft said to have been made 4 Jan. ('Thursday before he died') in testator's own hand (Briley, p. 328) or dictated to Cole on 5 Jan. (Rendle, pp. 153–4).

Sheppard] Cole's clerk (Briley, p. 328).

1616 Feb. 15 Agnes HENSLOWE (abstract)

(Anne)* widow, late wife and executor* of Phillipp Henshlowe esq. Soul 'into the hand*es* of Allmighty God my Maker and vnto Iesus Christ my only savio*ur* and redeemer hopinge and confidently trustinge in by and throughe his only meritt*es* mercye death and passion*n* to have and enioye life everlastinge'. Burial without 'anye vayne pompe or shewe', at discretion of executor. £20 to be paid within twelve days after her death to eighty poor widows and women living in the Libertye of the Clynck pa. St Saviour co. Surrey, or elsewhere in same parish, 5s each, at election of her executor. 40s yearly from a lease, which she holds from Leonard Billson esq., to eighty poor widows and women living in the said Libertye of the Clynck or elsewhere in said parish, 6d each, at election of her executor, to be paid between feasts of St Thomas the Apostle and birth of our Lord God yearly during continuance of same lease. To John Russell,* of pa. St Gyles without Creplegate co. Middlesex, tailor, £10 to be paid within one year of her death. To Edward Laytonn and Henry Laytonn, sons of Edward Laytonn waterman, £80; to Edward £50, to Henry £30, to be paid at ends of their apprenticeships or at age of 24, as a stock to set up their trades. Rest to only and well beloved daughter Joane Allen, wife of Edwarde Allen* esq., whom she appoints sole executor. Wit. Edwarde Smythe, Thomas Foster, Mathias Alleyn,* John Kezar.

PRO PROB10/344. OW, prob. clause subscribed, note of registration marginated. Single sheet with testator's mark, signatures of witnesses, and remnants of seal; filing hole at top centre; bottom right corner of document damaged resulting in some loss of text. Text in facile secretary.

Prob. by sentence PCC 3 Jul. 1617 to Joan Allen, daughter and executor. Sentence (PRO PROB11/130 fos 67v-68r) (Joan Allen, promoter, v. William Henslowe) upholds validity of the will. Note endorsed on will dates exhibition of inventory on 13 Jun. 1617. PAB (PRO PROB8/17 fo. 54v) gives pa. of origin as Dulwich co. Surrey and valuation of inventory: 11d.

Printed: William Rendle, 'Phillip Henslowe', *Genealogist* n.s., IV, 1887, pp. 149–59 (p. 158) (abstract).

fl. 1572–1617. Widow of Philip Henslowe (**1616**). Buried Dulwich College chapel 9 Apr. 1617. (Greg, *Henslowe's Diary* II, 4–5.)

Anne] also known as Agnes (see husband's will).
executor] for litigation arising see husband's will (**1616**).
Russell] E. Alleyn paid legacy and appointed him gatherer at Fortune where his dishonesty provoked letter of complaint from William Bird (**1624**) (Bentley II, 558–9).
Edwarde Allen] (**1626**); see index.
Mathias Alleyn] first Warden of Dulwich College 1619–31; see index.

1616 Mar. 25 William SHAKESPEARE

T*estamentum* w*illel*mij Shackspeare[1]
Vicesimo Quinto die [I<anuar>ij][2] {m*a*rtij} Anno Regni D*o*mini n*o*stri Iacobi nunc R*egis* Anglie &c decimo quarto & Scotie xlixo Annoq*ue* d*o*mi*ni* 1616
In the name of god Amen I William[3] Shackspeare of Stratford vpon Avon in the countie of warr*wick* gentl*eman* in p*er*fect health & memorie god be praysed doe make & Ordayne this my last will & testame*nt* in manne*r* & forme followeing That ys to saye ffirst I Comend my Soule into the hand*es* of god my Creator hoping & assuredlie beleeving through thonelie meritt*es* of Iesus Christe my Saviour to be made p*a*rtaker of lyfe everlastinge And my bodye to the Earth whereof yt ys made Item I Gyve & bequeath vnto my [sonne in L] Daug<ht>er Iudyth One Hundred & ffyft<ie po>und*es* of lawf<ull> English money to be paied vnto her in manne*r* & forme followeing That ys to saye One Hundred Pound*es* {in discharge of her marriage porc*i*on} w*i*thin one yeare after my Deceas w*i*th consideraci*on* after the Rate of twoe shilling*es* in the pound for soe long tyme as the same shalbe vnpaied vnto her after my deceas & the ffyftie pound*es* Residewe thereof vpon her Surrendring {of} or gyving of such

sufficient securitie as the overseers of this my Will shall like of to Surrender or gra*un*nte All her estate & Right that shall discend or come vnto her after my deceas or {that shee} nowe hath of in or to one Copiehold ten*eme*nte with thapp*ur*ten*au*nces lyeing & being in Stratford vpon Avon aforesaied in the saied countie of warr*wick* being p*ar*cell or holden of the manno*ur* of Rowington vnto my Daughter Susanna Hall & her heires for ever Item I Gyve & bequeath vnto my saied Daughter Iudith One Hundred & ffyftie Pound*es* more if shee or Anie issue of her bodie be Lyvinge att thend of three Yeares next ensueing the daie of the Date of this my Will during w*hi*ch tyme my executo*urs* to paie her consideraci*on* from my deceas according to the Rate afore saied And if she dye w*i*thin the saied terme w*i*thout issue of her bodye then my will ys & I doe gyve & bequeath One Hundred Pound*es* thereof to my Neece Elizabeth Hall & the ffiftie Pound*es* to be sett fourth by my executo*urs* during the lief of my Sister Iohane Harte & the vse & p*r*offitt thereof Cominge shalbe payed to my saied Sister Ione & after her deceas the saied l li shall Remaine Amongst the children of my saied Sister Equallie to be Devided Amongst them But if my saied Daughter Iudith be lyving att thend of the saied three Yeares or anie yssue of her bodye the\<n\> my Will ys & soe I devise & bequeath the saied Hundred & ffyftie pound*es* to be sett out {by my executo*urs* & overseers} for the best benefitt of her & her issue & {the stock} not {to be} paied vnto her soe long as she shalbe marryed & Covert Baron [by my executo*urs* & overseers] but my will ys that she shall have the consideracon[4] yearelie paied vnto her during her lief & after her deceas the saied stock and consideraci*on* to bee paied to her children if she have Anie & if not to her executo*urs* or assignes she lyving the saied terme after my deceas Provided that if such husbond as she shall att thend of the saied three Yeares be marryed vnto or attaine after doe sufficientle Assure vnto her & thissue of her bodie land*es* Awnswereable to the porc*i*on by this my will gyven vnto her & to be adiudged soe by my executo*urs* & overseers then my will ys that the saied Cl li shalbe paied to such husbond as shall make such assurance to his owne vse Item I gyve & bequeath vnto my saied sister Ione xx li & all my wearing Apparrell to be paied & Deliu*er*ed w*i*thin one yeare after my deceas And I doe Will & devise vnto her {the house} w*i*th thapp*ur*ten*au*nces in Stratford wherein she dwelleth for her naturall lief vn\<der\> the yearelie Rent of xij d. Itm[5] I gyue & bequeat\<h\>[6] (**fo. 2**) vnto her three sonns William[3] Harte   [7] hart & Michaell Harte ffyve pound*es* A peece to be payed w*i*thin one Yeare after my deceas [to be sett out for her w*i*thin one Yeare after my Deceas by my executo*urs* with thadvise & direcc*i*ons of my overseers for her best p*r*offitt vntill her Marriage & then the same with the increase thereof to be paied vnto her][8] Item I gyve & bequeath

vnto [her] {the saied Elizabeth Hall} All my Plate {(except my brod silver
& gilt bole)} that I now<e> have att the Date of this my Will Itm⁵ I gyve
& bequeath vnt<o> the Poore of Stra<tf>ord aforesaied tenn pound*es* to
mr Thomas Combe my Sword to Thomas Russell Esquier ffyve pound*es*
& to ffrauncis Collins of the Borough of War*rwick* in the countie of
War<r*wick*> gent*leman* thirteene pound*es* Sixe shilling*es* & Eight pence
to be paied w*i*thin one Yeare after my Deceas Itm⁵ I gyve & bequeath to
[mr Richard Tyl< . . >⁹ theld*er*] {Hamlett Sadler} xxvj s viij d to buy him
A Ringe {to William³ Raynold*es* gent*leman* xxvj s viij d to buy him A
Ringe} to my godson Willi*a*m Walker xx s in gold to Anthonye Nashe
gent*leman* xxvj s viij d & to mr Iohn Nashe xx{vj s viij d} [in gold] {&
to my fellows Iohn Hemyn*n*ges* Richard Burbage* & Henry Cundell*
xxvj s viij d A peece to buy them Ring<*es*>} Item I Gyve Will bequeath
& Devise vnto my Daughter Susanna Hall {for better enabling of her to
p*e*rforme this my will & toward*es* the p*e*rformans thereof} All that
Capitall messuage or ten*eme*nte w*i*th thapp*ur*ten*au*nces {in Stratford
aforesaied} Called the newe place Wherein I nowe Dwell & twoe
messuag*es* or ten*eme*ntes w*i*th thapp*ur*ten*au*nces scituat lyeing & being
in Henley streete w*i*thin the borough of Stratford aforesaied And all my
barnes stables Orchard*es* gardens land*es* ten*eme*nt*es* & hereditam*en*tes
Whatsoeu*er* scituat lyeing & being or to be had Receyved p*er*ceyved or
taken within the townes Hamlett*es* villag*es* ffield*es* & ground*es* of
Stratford vpon Avon Oldstratford Bushopton & Welcombe or in anie of
them in the saied countie of warr*wick* And alsoe All that Messuage or
ten*eme*nte w*i*th thapp*ur*ten*au*nces wherein one Iohn Robinson dwelleth
scituat lyeing & being in the blackfriers in London nere the Wardrobe &
all oth*er* my land*es* ten*eme*nt*es* & hereditam*en*tes Whatsoeu*er* To Have
& to hold All & sing*u*ler the saied p*re*misses w*i*th their App*ur*ten*au*nces
vnto the saied Susanna Hall for & During the terme of her naturall lief
& after her Deceas to the first son<n>e of her bodie lawfullie Yssueing &
<to the> heires males of the bodie of the saied first Sonne lawfullie
Yssueinge & for defalt of such issue to the second Sonne of her bodie
lawfullie issueinge & [fr] to the heires males of the bodie of the saied
Second Sonne lawfullie yssueinge & for defalt of such heires to the third
Sonne of the bodie of the saied Susanna Lawfullie yssueing & of the heires
males of the bodie of the saied thir<d> sonne lawfullie yssueing And for
defalt of such issue the same s<oe> to be & Remaine to the ffourth [sonne]
ffyfth sixte & Seaventh sonnes of her bodie lawfullie issueing one after
Another & to the heir<*es*>¹⁰ (**fo. 3**) Males of the bodies of the saied
ffourth fifth Sixte & Seaventh sonne<s> lawfullie yssueing in such mann*er*
as yt ys before Lymitted to be & Remaine to the first second & third
Sonns of her bodie & to their heires males And for defalt of such issue

the saied pr*emiss*es to be & Remaine to my sayed Neece Hall & the heires Males of her bodie Lawful<lie> yssueing for Defa<lt of> such issue to my Daughter Iudith & the heires Males of her bodie lawfullie issueinge And for Defalt of such issue to the Right heires of me the saied Will*i*am Shackspere for ever {Itm[5] I gyve vnto my wief my second best bed w*i*th the furniture} Item I gyve & bequeath to my saied Daughter Iudith my broad silver gilt bole All the Rest of my good*e*s Chattel<les> Leases plate Iewels & household stuffe Whatsoeu*er* after my d*e*ttes and Legasies paied & my fun*er*all expences discharged I gyve Devise & bequeath to my Sonne in Lawe Iohn Hall gent*leman* & my Daughter Susanna his wief Whom I ordaine & make executo*ur*s of this my Last Will & testam*en*t And I doe intreat & Appoint {the saied} Thomas Russell Esquier & ffraunci<s> Collins gent*leman* to be overseers hereof An<d> doe Revoke All form*er* wills & publishe this to be my last Will & testam*en*t In Wit<nes> Whereof I have her<e>vnto put my [Seale] {hand} the Daie & Yeare first aboue Written./ By me William Shakspeare witnes to the publishing hereof Fra: Collyns Iulyus Shawe Iohn Robinson Hamnet Sadler Robert Whattcott

1. *T'* . . . *Shackspeare* marginated. 2. *[I<anuar>ij]* interpreted thus by Chambers, etc.; read by Malone and others as *Februarij* (Chambers, *William Shakespeare: A Study of Facts and Problems*, 2 vols, Oxford, 1930, II, 175). 3. *William*: otiose special sign for *a*. 4. *consideracon*: mark of abbreviation omitted, rightly *consideracion*. 5. *Itm*: mark of abbreviation omitted, rightly *Item*. 6. Signed bottom left *Willi<a>m <Shakespear>e*. 7. Blank in MS; rightly *Thomas*. 8. *[to be sett . . . her]*: originally began new page; what precedes on fo. 2 probably added when will revised. 9. *Tyl* . .: ?Tyler. 10. Signed bottom right *Willm Shakspeare*.

PRO PROB1/4. OW, note of registration marginated (fo. 1), prob. clause and note of exhibition of inventory subscribed (fo. 3). Three sheets, each bearing the signature of the testator, final page bearing signatures of witnesses. Text in facile Elizabethan secretary with revisions and interlineations in same hand, conjectured to be that of Francis Collins (Eccles, *Shakespeare*, p. 141), of Collins's clerk (E. K. Chambers, op. cit., II, 174), or Shakespeare's own (J. C. Jeaffreson, 'A new view of Shakspeare's will', *Athenaeum*, no. 2844, 29 Apr. 1882, pp. 539–40; most recently Charles Hamilton, *In Search of Shakespeare*, London, 1986, pp. 66–83). Transcript of OffC now in collection of Shakespeare Birthplace Trust, Stratford-upon-Avon (see Levi Fox, 'An early copy of Shakespeare's will', *ShS*, IV, 1951, pp. 69–77).

Prob. PCC 22 June 1616 to John Hall, one of executors, reserving power to Susanna Hall.

Discovered: George Vertue 1737; printed: Lewis Theobald, ed., *Works of*

Shakespeare, 3rd ed., 8 vols, London, 1752, I, 1–8 (facsimile in S. Schoenbaum, *William Shakespeare: A Documentary Life*, Oxford, 1975, pp. 243–5; for signatures see S. Schoenbaum, *William Shakespeare: Records and Images*, London, 1981, pp. 95–7).

1564–1616. Dramatist, actor; Strange's 1592, ?Pembroke's 1593, ?Sussex's 1594, Chamberlain's/King's Men from 1594; housekeeper in Globe and Blackfriars. Legatee of Augustine Phillips (1605). Buried 25 Apr. 1616 Holy Trinity, Stratford-upon-Avon. (For discussion of will see E. K. Chambers, op. cit., II, 169–80; B. Roland Lewis, *The Shakespeare Documents*, 2 vols, Stanford, CA, 1940, II, 471–507; S. Schoenbaum, *Documentary Life*, pp. 242–50; E. A. J. Honigmann, '"There is a world elsewhere": William Shakespeare, businessman', in *Images of Shakespeare: Proceedings of the Third Congress of the International Shakespeare Association 1986*, ed. Werner Habicht et al., Newark, NJ, 1988, pp. 40–6 and 'The second-best bed', *New York Review of Books*, XXXVIII, no. 18, 7 Nov. 1991, pp. 27–30. For beneficiaries see Leslie Hotson, *I, William Shakespeare, Do Appoint Thomas Russell, Esquire*, London, 1937, and Eccles, *Shakespeare*, pp. 111–30, 141–2.)

Hemynnges] 1630; see index.
Burbage] 1619; see index.
Cundell] 1627; see index.

1617 Mar. 3 Ralph REEVE

In the name of God, amen I Raphe Reeue beinge sicke in body but in good and perfect memory doe make this my last will and testament in manner & forme followinge fyrst I doe bequeath my soule vnto god my sauiour and redeamer and my body to be buried in the Church of St dunstons in the West next I make my deare friend Mr Robert Benfeild* my full & whole executor my deb*tes* beinge payd & theis ensuinge leagacies discharded Imp*rimis* I giue & bequeath to William Roe* somettymes my seruant ffyue pound*es* Item I giue to Richard Hunter ffyue pound*es* Item I giue to Richard ¹ Gryffithes ffoure pound*es* Item I giue to Daniell weller ffyue pound*es* all theis legacies to be payd att the feast of St mycaell tharke Angell next ensuinge & not before Alsoe I remitt vnto Tho*mas* Kendall* his wyddowe a bond wherein her husbandeth bound vnto me also I giue vnto ffrauncis Boulton Twenty Two shilling*es* presently to be payd Alsoe I giue to Iohn Bugge* fforty ffowre shilling*es* within one monthe After I ame buried to be payd also I giue to Margery Dale yf she be now liuinge eleuen shilling*es* to be payd vpon her demaund not by any deputy Also I giue to Elizabethe Kingman* Twenty Two shilling*es* presently to be payd In witnes that this ys my deede I haue

hereto put my hand the 3th day of Marche 1616 & in the xiijth yeare in the raigne of our soueraigne lord Iames by the grace of god of England Scotland ffraunce & Ireland Kinge defendor of the fayth &c
Rafe Reve auur²
Subscribed and deliuered in the presentes of Phillapp Kingman,* Willia' Chapman
& yat this ys the very same soe many of those as were presente haue noe leagacies giuen haue hearto put theyr handes
Robert Benfild Iohn Bugge³

1. Blank in MS.   2. auur: ?armiger.   3. & ... Bugge endorsed in same hand as text, with signatures.

GL MS 9172/29. OW, prob. clause marginated, note of registration endorsed. Single sheet folded to make four pages, with signatures of testator and witnesses, applied seal and executor's signature on dorse. Text in rapid secretary.

Prob. CCL 14 Mar. 1617 to Robert Benfield, executor. PAB (GL MS 9168/16 fo. 267v) gives pa. of origin as St Dunstan in the West, notes exhibition of inventory in 1618 and valuation at £746 13s 4d.

fl. 1603–15. Leader of company in Germany 1603–9; of Children of Queen's Revels company in provinces, 1611; one of patentees for Porter's Hall playhouse 1615. Probably son of Ralph Reeve of St Saviour Southwark, who made his will 1576 (GLRO DW PA 5/1576/137). Buried 5 Mar. 1617, St Dunstan in the West. (Nungezer, p. 294.)

Benfeild] actor, possibly Queen's Revels, then Lady Elizabeth's in 1613, then King's Men (Chambers II, 303; Nungezer, pp. 42–4; Bentley II, 374–6); see index.
Roe] ?actor in Germany, with Robert Reynolds's company in 1640, and in 1650 (Nungezer, p. 303; Bentley II, 553).
Kendall] patentee of Children of Queen's Revels 1604 (1608).
Bugge] actor, Queen of Bohemia's 1628; related by marriage to Robert Benfield above (J. G. Riewald, 'Some later Elizabethan and early Stuart actors and musicians', *English Studies*, XL, 1959, pp. 33–41 (p. 34)) (Bentley II, 393–4).
Kingman] ?related to Philip Kingman, witness.
Kingman] leader of company in Germany 1596; patentee of Porter's Hall (Nungezer, pp. 225–6 (Kingsman)).

1617 Sept. 1 Thomas GILES

Testamentum Thome Giles parochie sancti Martini in Campis¹
In the name of god Amen I Thomas Giles of London gentleman being weak in bodie but of perfect memorie doe make this my last will and

testament in wryting as followeth. ffirst I bequeath my sowle vnto god the father that created it, and vnto Ihesus Christ that rede[a]med it and vnto the holie ghost that sanctefied it three in one, and one in three, the indevided blessed and holie Trynitie in full assuraunce and confidence that my synnes are pardoned by the merrittes of christes sufferinges alone, and I commytt my bodie to the earth from whence it came there to be buried where it falleth in expectacion of a ioyfull resurrection at the last daye. Item my Will is that the CL li' in the hands of Mr Duppa made ouer by bond vnto my syster Elizabeth doughtie and Iane her daughter shall whollie be bestowed vpon my saied syster and her daughter and be ymploied for theire best benefitt during their lives as my executours in their discrecion shall best dyrect. Item my will is that all my plate be forthwith sould and the money thereof converted and emploied by my executoures to thvse of my syster & her daughter Item I giue vnto Iohn my man in money the somme of tenne poundes and all my wearing Lynnen. Item I doe forgeue vnto Mr Peter Edney oute of the debt which he oweth me the somme of xiiij l'. Item I doe giue vnto the poore of St Butholles without Aldersgate where I was borne the somme of five poundes to be distributed by the mynister and Churche Wardens there. Item I doe geve vnto the poore of St Ollyves in Silverstreet where my father and mother lieth buryed the somme of five poundes to be lykewise distributed by the mynister and churchewardens of the parrishe there Item I giue to the poore of the parrishe of ffulham the somme of xl s to be distrybuted at the discrecion of the mynister and churche Wardens there Item I doe freelie forgeue vnto mrs Anne kynderslye a debt of xxx l' which shee doth owe vnto me. Item I doe geue vnto my good frend Mr Rowland Rubbidge* the somme of Tenne poundes. Item I giue vnto my good[2] (p. 2) frend Mr Humphrey Nycolls and vnto his wief Tenne poundes a peece Item I doe giue vnto Roger Bolt, and his wief eache of them an Angell [of] {in} gould. Item I doe geue vnto Bennet White mayde servaunt vnto Mr Rowland Rubbishe xxij s in gold. And I doe hereby nomynate and appoynt my good frendes Rowland Rubbidge and Humfrey Nycolls Executours of this my last will and testament. Requesting them that theie wilbe contented with the Legacies which I have formerlie giuen them. And that the ouerplus of all my[3] goodes remaynyng vndeposed of maye whollye come and be ymployed to thuse and benefitt of my poore syster and her daughter accordynge to my true entent and meanyng. And I doe further hereby request Mr Iohn Read* and Mr William Perry* to be ouerseers of this my Will, gevynge eache of them for their paynes therein to be taken the somme of ffyve poundes tenne shillinges in gold In Witnes Whereof I have putto my hand and seale the first daye of September in the yeare of oure lord god 1617. Thomas Gyles/ Witnesses herevnto. Io' London. Phillippe King. ffrancis Mersh. Cor' Conquest/

1. T' . . . Campis: marginated. 2. Catchword frend. 3. originali sic (tr. thus in the original) marginated opposite line beginning my goodes; relates to vndeposed? PRO PROB10/345. OffC, note of registration marginated (p. 1) and prob. clause subscribed (p. 2). Single sheet folded in half to make four pages, unsealed.

Prob. PCC 5 Sep. 1617 to Rowland Rubbish (Rubbidge) and Humphrey Nicholls, executors. PAB (PRO PROB8/17 fo. 68v) notes exhibition of inventory.

fl. 1605–13. Musician, dancing master; appointed music master to Prince Henry 1605; participant in court masques (Paul Reyher, *Les masques anglaises: Étude sur les ballets et la vie de cour en Angleterre (1512–1640)*, Paris, 1909, p. 78. Identified with T. Giles, Master of Paul's Boys 1584–1600, by Hillebrand (*Child Actors*, p. 210) but Reavley Gair states that Giles was buried 4 July 1600 ('The conditions of appointment for Masters of Choristers at Paul's (1553–1613)', *N&Q*, CCXXV, 1980, pp. 116–24 (p. 122)).

Rubbidge] R. Rubbish (**1620**), violinist at court.
Read] ?actor, whose children were buried in St Botolph's Aldgate in 1600 and 1608 (Nungezer, p. 291).
Perry] unlikely to be actor, who was a boy with Lady Elizabeth's 1613 (Nungezer, pp. 278–9; Bentley II, 529–31).

1618 Jan. 13 Richard COWLEY

The xiijth of Ianuary 1617
Memorandum that Richard Cowley in the presence of vs herevnder written made and Constituted his Daughter Elizabeth Cowley sole Executrix of all his goods and Chattells
Witnes. Iohn heminges Cuthbert Burbadge Iohn Shancke Tho: Rauenscroft*

GL MS 9052/5. OW (nuncupative), prob. clause subscribed. Single sheet, sealed, with signatures of witnesses. Text in a facile secretary.

Prob. ACL 6 Apr. 1619 to Elizabeth Birch alias Cowley, daughter and executor. Note subscribed on will and PAB (GL MS 9050/5 fo. 101r) give pa. of origin as St Leonard Shoreditch.

Printed: H.R. Plomer, 'Richard Cowley the actor: witnesses to his will', *N&Q* 10th ser. VI, 1906, p. 369 (RegC); see also Bentley II, 642.

fl. 1590–1619. Actor; Strange's c.1590 and 1593, Chamberlain's/King's Men from 1601. Beneficiary of Augustine Phillips (**1605**) where termed Phillips's 'fellow'. Witnesses to will all involved in theatrical affairs: Heminges (**1630**), Burbage

(A1636), Shank (1635). Buried St Leonard Shoreditch 12 Mar. 1619. Unusual for nuncupative will to predate death so far, in this case by fifteen months. (Chambers II, 312–13; Nungezer, pp. 105–6; Bentley II, 414.)

Rauenscroft] may be Thomas Ravenscroft, madrigalist and former chorister of St Paul's (see W. J. Lawrence, 'Thomas Ravenscroft's theatrical associations', *MLR*, XIX, 1924, pp. 418–23).

[1618 c.Nov.] undated Edward JUBY

Memorandum that Edward Iuby late of the parishe of St Sauiours in Southwoke gent deceased did ye day whervppon he died declare his last will & Testament Nuncupatiue to this or the like effect followinge videlicet he saied that he would giue all his goodes vnto ffrances* his wiffe & yat she should be his executrix willinge her to burie him decently & pay his debtes and that his brother George Iuby & Alexander Kippynge his neighbor should be his ouerseers, & that he would giue them twentie shillinges a peice, beinge present at the premises ye said ouerseers mistris Kippinge & one Luce Wall as also ye said ffrances Iuby the Executrix ffraunces Iuby George Iuby Alexander Kippinge

GLRO DW/PA/7/10/fo. 47v. RegC with prob. clause.

Prob. ACS 19 Dec. 1618 to Frances, relict and executor.

fl. 1594–1618. Actor and sharer; Admiral's/Prince Henry's/Palsgrave's; among Palsgrave's men who leased Fortune from Alleyn Oct. 1618. Buried St Saviour Southwark 20 Nov. 1618. Registers also record baptisms of seven children 1599–1614, none of whom mentioned in will. (Chambers II, 325; Nungezer, pp. 213–15; Bentley II, 490.)

ffrances] Alleyn granted her lease of one half share in Fortune 20 May 1622 (Warner, p. 246) (Bentley II, 490).

1619 Mar. 12 Richard BURBAGE

Memorandum That on ffrydaie the Twelueth of March Anno Domini one thousand Six hundred and eighteene Richard Burbadge of the parish of St Leonardes in Shoreditch in the Countie of Middlesex Gentleman, being sick in body, but of good and perfect remembraunce, did make his Last Will and Testament nuncupative, in manner and forme following, videlicet He the said Richard, did nominate and appoint his welbeloued wife Winifride Burbadge, to be his sole Executrix of all his goodes and Chattelles whatsoeuer, In the presence and hearing of the persons herevnder named. Cuthbert* Burbadge brother to the Testater the marke of X Elizabeth his wife Nicholas Tooley* Ann Lancaster Richard Robinson* the mark X of Elizabeth Graues henry Iacksonn

PRO PROB1/32 (formerly PROB10/362). OW (nuncupative), prob. clause subscribed, note of registration marginated. Single sheet, unsealed. Text in rapid engrossing secretary with displayed matter in italic. Stopes (*Burbage*, p. 124) speculates that Cuthbert Burbage acted as scribe, probably due to fact that text and Burbage's 'signature' are in same hand. However comparison with MSS identified as written by Ralph Crane suggests that Crane wrote the text of the will and at least some of the signatures. (See F. P. Wilson, 'Ralph Crane, scrivener to the King's players', *Library*, 4th ser. VII, 1927, pp. 194–215, which includes facsimiles of Crane's work.)

Prob. PCC 22 Apr. 1619 to Winifred Burbage, relict and executor. Note of same date subscribed to will records oath of witnesses, Cuthbert Burbage, Anne Lancaster, and widow. PAB (PRO PROB8/18 fo. [30v]) records no valuation of inventory but Burbage said to have left 'better than 300^{li} land' (John Chamberlain to Sir Dudley Carleton [19 Mar. 1619], in *The Letters of John Chamberlain*, ed. N. E. McClure, 2 vols, Philadelphia, 1939, II, 222–3).

Printed: Malone (1790), I, pt 2, 186.

c.1573–1619. Actor; ?Admiral's and Lord Strange's c.1590, Chamberlain's/King's Men 1594–1619. Son of James Burbage (**A1597**) from whom, with brother Cuthbert (**A1636**), inherited interest in Theatre and Blackfriars; also shared moiety of housekeepers' interest in Globe. Executor of Augustine Phillips (**1605**), legatee of Shakespeare (**1616**). Died 13 Mar., buried 16 Mar. 1619 St Leonard Shoreditch. (Chambers II, 306–10; Nungezer, pp. 67–79; Bentley II, 395–7.)

Cuthbert] see index.
Tooley] actor with King's Men (**1623**); see index.
Robinson] actor with King's Men from c.1611, later married Burbage's widow, possibly his apprentice (Chambers II, 336–7; Nungezer, pp. 300–3; Bentley II, 550–3); see index.

1619 May 22 Gilbert KATHERENS (abstract)

Of pa. St Saviour in Southwarke co. Surrye, carpenter. Sick. Soul 'into the hand*es* of allmightie God my maker trusting through his mercie & for the meritt*es* of Iesus Christ my redeemer to have forgivenes of all my sinnes & after this life ended to be made p*a*rtaker of life eue*r*lasting in the kingdome of heaven'. Burial at discretion of executor. To sister Hellen Porter widow 12*d* and to each of her children 12*d*. To sister Agnes

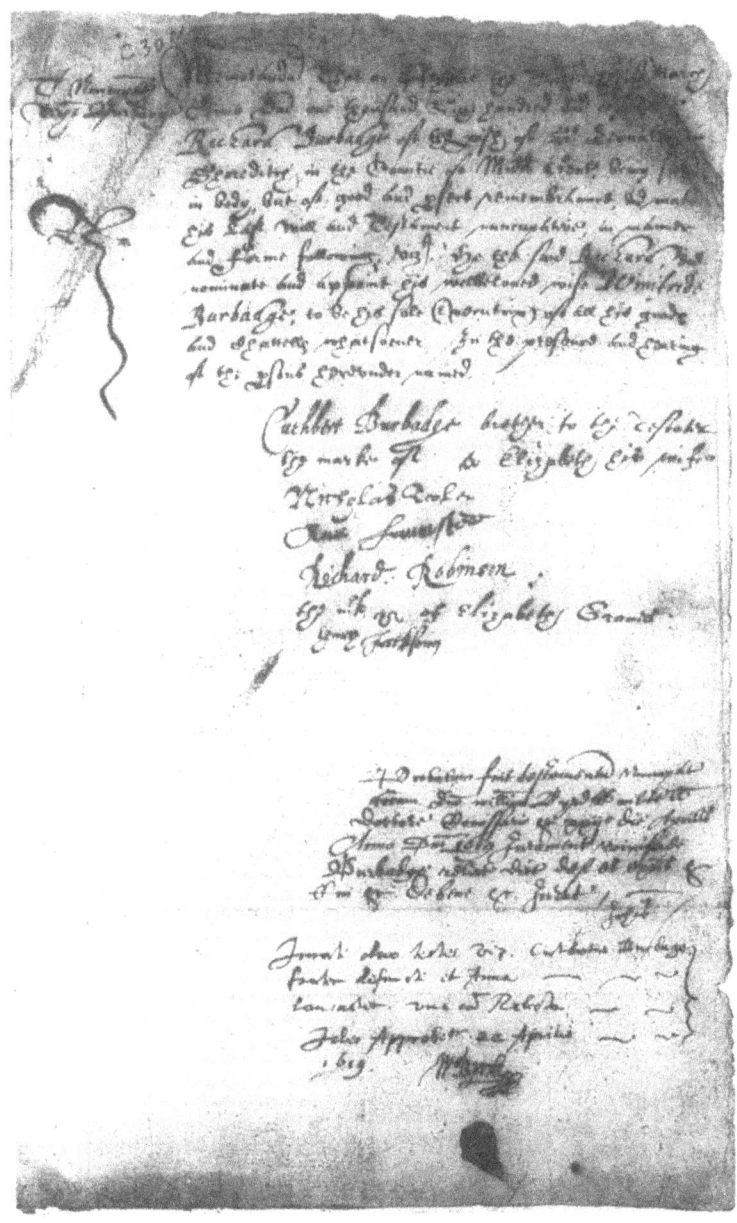

Figure 4 Richard Burbage 1619

Woolwright, wife of John Woolwright, 12*d* and to each of her three sons 12*d*. To John Woolwright 2*s* 6*d* and to said sister Agnes his Bible. To cousin Peter Katherens, son of brother Richard Katherens deceased, 12*d* and to his wife 12*d* and to each of their children 12*d*. To Joane Katherens, widow of brother Richard Katherens, 12*d* and to daughter 12*d*. To two daughters of brother John Katherens deceased, 12*d* each. Residue of goods and chattels to loving wife Jane Katherens whom appoints sole executor. Wit. James Reade scrivener, John Robinson,* Raphe Keyes.*

GLRO DW PA/5/1619/71. OW, prob. clause and note of registration endorsed (p. 4), note of exhibition of will marginated (p. 1). Single sheet folded to make four pages, with seal and mark of testator and signatures of witnesses. Small neat secretary probably hand of J. Reade.

Prob. ACS 26 June 1619, to Jane, relict and executor.

fl. 1613–19. Carpenter; 1613 entered contract with Philip Henslowe (**1616**) and Jacob Meade (**1624**) to pull down Bear Garden and erect Hope theatre. (Chambers II, 465–8.)

Robinson] possibly actor with King's Revels from c.1634 (**1641**) (Bentley II, 549–50).

Keyes] person of same name mentioned in list of thirty-nine defendants, chiefly actors, sued by Gervase Markham, 1623 (Bentley II, 682).

1619 Sept. 4 Samuel DANIEL

In the name of god amen. I Samuell Danyel sick in body but well in mynd make heere my last will and Testament
ffirst I comitt my Soule vnto god trusting to be saved by the pretious bloud and death of my redeemer Iesus Christe, and my body to the earth, to be interred in the parrish church where I dye.
Item I bequeath to my Sister Susan Bowre one ffeather bedd with the furniture thearto belonging and such linnen as I shall leave at my house at Ridge
Item I bequeath to Samuell Bowre x L.
Item to Ioane Bowre x L.
Item to Susan Bowre x L.
Item to Mary Bowre x L.
for the disposing of all other things I referr them to my faythfull Brother Iohn Danyel* whome I heere ordayne [to] my sole executor to whose care and conscience I comitt the performance thearof
And I lykewyse appoynt and ordayne my loving friend Mr Simon waterson* and my brother in-law Iohn Phillipps to be overseers of this

my last will and Testament. wherevnto I have sett my hand and Seale dated the 4th day of September 1619. Samuel Danyel witnesses of this my last will and testament[1] umphery Adlemes[2] mark. X william wheatlyes Marke. X

1. *Samuel . . . testament* in testator's hand. 2. *Adlemes*: all earlier transcripts erroneously print *Aldemes*.

PRO PROB10/371. OW, prob. clause subscribed, note of registration marginated. Single sheet folded in half to make four pages, with original signatures and remnants of seal. Text in facile secretary, with Daniel's signature and the phrase 'witnesses of this my last will and testament' in italic. *Index of English Literary Manuscripts*, vol. I, *1450–1625*, comp. P. Beal, 2 pts, London, 1980, I, 197 mistakenly implies that entire will is autograph.

Prob. PCC 1 Feb. 1620 to John Daniel, brother and executor. Note subscribed on will gives pa. of origin as Ridge co. Somerset.

Printed: Peter Cunningham, 'Will of Samuel Daniel, the poet, Shakespeare's rival and contemporary', *Shakespeare Society Papers*, IV, 1849, pp. 156–8 (pp. 156–7) (RegC).

1563–1619. Poet, playwright. Licenser of plays at second Blackfriars for Children of Queen's Revels 1604. In 1609 in dispute over payment for duties with Edward Kirkham and widow of Thomas Kendall (**1608**) (see Hillebrand, *Child Actors*, pp. 177–8, 334–8). Buried 14 Oct. 1619 Beckington co. Somerset. (Chambers III, 272–83; Joan Rees, *Samuel Daniel: A Critical and Biographical Study*, Liverpool, 1964.)

Iohn Danyel] patentee of Children of Queen's Chamber of Bristol, 1615–17 (Chambers II, 313; Nungezer, p. 110; Bentley II, 419–20).

waterson] bookseller; publications included many of Daniel's works; with J. Daniel published *The Whole Workes of Samuel Daniel Esq. in Poetrie*, 1623 (McKerrow, *Dictionary*, pp. 284–5).

1620 Jan. 9 Joan HOVELL (abstract)

(Iohane Havell) Of pa. St Saviour in Southwark co. Surrey widow. Sick. Soul 'into the hand*es* of Almighty God my maker & of his sonne Christ Iesus my Saui*our* & Redeemer, by whose pretious death and passion I hope to be saved and to enioy everlasting happynes'. Burial in churchyard of parish church of St Saviour, where first husband Edward Addison waterman was buried, as near to his body as convenient. To poor of Liberty of the Clinck in aforesaid parish twenty dozen of bread to be distributed on day of burial at discretion of executor and overseers. To Mr Sutton,* preacher of parish of St Saviour, 20*s* for a sermon on day of burial and to Mr Archer* minister of same parish 10*s*. To grandson

Thomas Tucker, son of John Tucker waterman deceased, £50 and one gold ring with death's-head engraven on it, one featherbed, four pairs of sheets, one tablecloth containing four ells in length, and one dozen napkins, to be paid at age twenty-one. To granddaughter Sara Tucker his sister, daughter of said John Tucker, £50 and one enamelled gold ring with burning heart engraven on it, one featherbed, four pairs of sheets, one tablecloth containing four ells in length and a dozen napkins, to be paid at age twenty-one or day of marriage, whichever first happens. If either of them dies before this, portion of him or her so dying to survivor. Said sums of £50 each and goods aforesaid to remain in hands of Richard Aylwood carpenter and wife Anna, daughter, mother of said grandchildren, for their education and for binding Thomas Tucker as apprentice to some fit trade as he likes and at discretion of executor and overseers. Said Richard Aylwood and Anna, upon receipt of said sums and goods, to become bound to overseers with sufficient surety for payment of same in good condition to Thomas Tucker and Sara Tucker at age twenty-one or her day of marriage; if they refuse, said sums and goods to remain in custody of overseers to be used for most profit for education and advancement of said grandchildren. Overseers on receipt to become bound to said Richard Aylwood and Anna, with sufficient surety for payment of same to grandchildren at age twenty-one or her day of marriage. To poor of Liberty of the Clinck £10 and odd money due to her from John Swynnerton* and John Edmondes,* two players, by obligations, which obligations she has assigned by letter of attorney in trust to Mr Roger Cole,* to use of poor of said liberty; and increase arising from it to be distributed to them for ever at discretion of her overseers and churchwardens and overseers of the poor. To Mary Tomlin her maid 20s to be paid within three months of death. To Edward Jacson writer of will and wife Blaunch 20s each, to be paid within three months of death. Residue of goods, chattels, etc. to Anna Aylwood, daughter, whom she apppoints sole executor. Appoints William Corden,* chandler, and William Wood, baker, overseers; to each 20s. William Corden, Thomas Bryan,* Edward Jacson public scrivener, Peter Newsam[1] his servant, Marie Tomlin (mark).

1. *Newsam*: RegC (GLRO DW PA/7/10/fos 135r–136r) has *Newsom*.

GLRO DW/PA/5/1620/67. OW, prob. clause subscribed, note of registration endorsed. Four pages sewn at top fastened with seal, with seal and mark of testator and signatures and marks of witnesses. Text in facile secretary with displayed matter in bastard secretary, hand of Edward Jackson.

Prob. ACS 1 Dec. 1620 to Ann Aylwood, executor and heir.

fl. 1615–20. Widow of William Hovell (**1615**), licensee for II King's Revels Children.

Sutton] see index.

Archer] see index.

Swynnerton] no actor of this name known; possible connection with Thomas Swinnerton, actor with Queen Anne's from 1604 and leader of provincial company from 1616 (Chambers II, 341; Nungezer, pp. 344–5; Bentley II, 588–9).

Edmondes] actor, associated with Nathaniel Clay (see index) as leaders of Children of Bristol 1618; with Queen Anne's from 1618 (Chambers II, 315; Nungezer, p. 128; Bentley II, 431); see index.

Cole] husband's executor; see index.

Corden] signatory with Cole to letter to Edward Alleyn from churchwardens and others of Liberty of the Clink, Southwark, c.1616 (Warner, p. 102); see index.

Bryan] see index.

1620 Mar. 1 Thomas CAMPION

Memorandum that Thomas Campion late of the parishe of St Dunstons* in the Weste {doctou*r* of phisicke} beinge in perfecte mynd and memory did w*i*th an intent to make and declare his laste will and Testament vpon the firste of March, 1619 and not [lay] longe before his death say that he did give all that he had vnto mr Phillip Rosseter,* and wished that his estate had bin [w*i*th one th] farre more, or he vsed word*es* to that effecte, being then and there present divers Credible Witnesses/

GL MS 9172/31. OW (nuncupative), grant of admon, note of exhibition and value of inventory (£22) subscribed, note of registration endorsed. Single sheet without seals or signatures. Subscribed are process notes relating to Rosseter's petition for letters of administration as Campion's principal beneficiary and one of his creditors.

Admon [with will annexed]. CCL 3. Mar. 1620 to Philip Rosseter, beneficiary, no executors named.

Noted: Gordon Goodwin, 'Thomas Campion and Philip Rosseter', *The Academy*, XLIII, 1893, p. 199; printed: P. Vivian, ed., *Campion's Works*, Oxford, 1909, p. xlvii.

1567–1620. Composer, writer of masques. Buried 1 Mar. 1620 St Dunstan in the West. (Chambers III, 239–47; *New Grove*.)

St Dunstons] lived in Fetter Lane in 1606, 1616 (Eccles, 'Brief lives', p. 21).

Rosseter] musician and theatrical manager (**1623**); first collection of Campion's songs to be printed published in Rosseter's *A Booke of Ayres*, 1601; Campion died in his house in Fleet St. (Goodwin, p. 199).

1620 Aug. 21 Rowland RUBBISH

25 Rubbish[1]

In the name of God amen, Memorandum that Rowland Rubbish of the parish of St Alphege nere Criplegate in London' Musicion on Mondaie [beinge] the xxjth daie of August Anno domini 1620. beinge of verie perfect minde & memorie, havinge an intent to declare & make his last will & testament, did then vtter & speake theis wordes, or the verie like in effect followinge videlicet: All the gooddes chattles & debtes whatsoeuer I haue, I do geve vnto Elizabeth my wife, savinge one peece of plate which I do geve vnto my daughter Ann Bradford, at my wife her discrecion. Beinge then present & hearinge the same, Humphry Nicholls,* & Vrsula Sturt, & Thomas Sherman, & others.

1. *25 Rubbish* superscribed.

GL MS 9052/5. OffC (nuncupative) with grant of admon subscribed. Single sheet, unsealed and unsigned. Text in rapid secretary.

Admon ACL 30 Aug. 1620 to Elizabeth, relict, no executors named. PAB (GL MS 9050/5 fo. 123r) gives valuation of inventory as £139 7s 11d.

fl. 1611–20. Violinist at court; took part in Jonson's masque *Oberon*, 1611; executor of court musician Thomas Giles (**1617**). (Chambers III, 385.)

Nicholls] executor with Rubbish of will of Giles.

1621 Jan. 8 William LEVESON (abstract)

Citizen and mercer of London. Sick. Soul 'into the handes of Almighty God stedfastly beleeueinge by the alone sufficient merrittes and death of his sonne and my sauiour Iesus Christ to obteyne remission and pardone of all my sinnes and to be made an heire with him in the kingdome of heauen'. To parson and churchwardens of pa. Aldermanbury, where he once lived, toward augmentation of parish stock 'some tymes in my hand[s] where in I might be mistaken', £4. To poor of pa. St Alphage, where he lives, 20s to be distributed by his executor. To Susan Hall 10s. To Robert Harrys 10s and forgives him all debts. To his servant Anne Curles 10s. He owes Robert Hall £4 for soliciting his business which his executor is to pay him and a cloak cloth of 4 nobles. These sums to be paid out of one third part of estate according to custom of the City of London. Residue of this to Mary, loving wife, with one third of his estate according to custom of the City of London. The other third of his estate to sons Thomas and James. Appoints Mary Leveson sole executor.

Wit. James Stonehouse, Richard Chapman servant to Charles Bostocke scrivener, Robert Hall, Thomas Stockwood.

PRO PROB 10/384. OffC, prob. clause endorsed, note of registration marginated. Single sheet, unsealed. Text in set secretary hand with displayed matter in italic.

Prob. PCC 21 June 1621 to Mary Leveson, relict and executor. PAB (PRO PROB8/19 fo. 41v) gives pa. of origin as St Alphage City of London.

Printed: Honigmann, 'Lost Years', p. 88 (abstract of RegC).

fl. 1586–1621. Merchant and financier; trustee with Thomas Savage (**1611**) for division of Globe shares in 1599 on behalf of Shakespeare and others. (Leslie Hotson, *I, William Shakespeare*, London, 1937, pp. 160–3; Honigmann, op. cit., pp. 87–9.)

1622 Sept. 23 Robert PAYNE (abstract)

Citizen and salter of London. Sick. Soul 'into the handes of allmightie god my maker and Creator trustinge throughe his mercies and the meritt*es* of my saviour Iesus Christe to receaue forgivenes of my sinnes and thereby to inheritt the kingdom of heaven'. Burial in church of St Mildred in Breadstreete near his first wife at night. To Corporation of Basingstoke £100 to be lent to three young men of town being clothiers for four years, 100 nobles to each, upon good security and paying 6s 8d p.a. to twenty of poorest people of said parish. To Company of Salters in London £100 to be lent to two young men of company, £50 to each for four years, upon good security and each paying 10s p.a. divided as follows: to Clerk of said Company 5s p.a., to Beadle of the Livery of said company 3s, and to Beadle of the Yeomanry of said Company 2s, 10s to almsmen of said Company. To Florentine Payne, brother, 40s. To John Wythers, sister's son, 40s. To William Paine, brother's son, 40s. To brother Thomas 40s. To son John 40s. To cousin Agnes Hopegood, brother Thomas's daughter, 40s. To George Paule 40s. To John Winge 20s. To John Greygoose gown faced with damask. To Robert Dyer gown lined with lamb and 40s. To Edward Tailor his workday gown and 40s. To Mr Currall preacher 40s. To clerk and sexton of St Mildred's church in Breadstreete 10s each. To poor pensioners of said parish 5s each, except woman who came last in as pensioner. To John Swanne, scrivener, 10s. Residue to wife Mary and daughter Elizabeth whom he makes executors. Stephen Woodford and Ellis Crispe to be overseers, to whom gives £3 each to buy rings. To brother Poole his ring which Mistress Skip gave him. To Mr Andrew his ring with toad stone. To neighbour Plott 4 marks for ring. To Ed Dalby and Susan Dalby £10, survivor to have benefit. To mother-in-law Avis

Payne £3, and executor to pay her 40s p.a. quarterly for her life. Wit. Thomas Mathew scrivener.

Memorandum: if any person standing surety for loans to three young clothiers of Basingstoke or two members of Salters' Company should die before repayment of the same, then other competent sureties should be procured. Wit. Thomas Mathew scrivener.

PRO PROB10/395. OffC, prob. clause subscribed, note of registration superscribed. Notes record 1. collation with original by Robert Erswells and Humfrey Dyson, signed; 2. receipt of original will by Mary Payne 2 Oct. 1622, signed; 3. both transactions witnessed by Robert Dawson, signed. Three sheets joined at the top, unsealed. Text in small engrossing secretary; subscriptions in three other hands with signatures.

Prob. PCC 1 Oct. 1622, to Mary Payne (Paine), relict and executor, reserving power to Elizabeth Payne, daughter and joint executor. PAB (PROB8/19 fo. 182v) gives pa. of origin as St Mildred Breadstreet.

fl. 1604–22. Possibly patentee for Children of Queen's Revels Feb. 1604, with Thomas Kendall (**1608**) and others. (Chambers II, 49, 332; Hillebrand, *Child Actors*, p. 177; Nungezer, p. 269.)

1623 Mar. 28 William JAGGARD (abstract)

Citizen and stationer of London. In health. Soul 'to Almighty god my Creator stedfastly beleeving to be saved by faith in Iesus Christ only, my blessed lord and Saviou*r*'. Burial at discretion of executor. To Isaack* Jaggard eldest son £150. To Thomas Jaggard youngest son £150 to be paid at age twenty-one. Whereas Jone eldest daughter, wife of Richard Coesar* yeoman, has been allowed £8 p.a. toward maintenance for two and a quarter years, the annuity to continue during his life, to said daughter Jone, sum which, together with all money already paid or which shall be paid at time of death, shall amount to £150. Son Isaac and daughter Jone to be paid within one year of death. To Alice youngest daughter £150, to be paid on day of marriage or age twenty-one whichever happens first. If one or more of said sons or daughters die before receiving portion, having no issue to inherit, portion of those so dying to survivor. To Hall of Worshipful Company of Stationers, very good friends and brothers, to use of said brotherhood, piece of silver plate called bullion weighing twenty ounces with following words engraved on it 'The Guift of William Iaggard Printer to the honourable Citty* of London', to be delivered to Master, Wardens and Assistants of said company at said hall within eighteen months of death. To Abraham

Woodford* his apprentice the last year's service of his indenture, provided he serve out the other years well. To ten poor people being householders to be chosen by executor, £10, that is 20s each, to be paid within three months of death or sooner. To Thomas Pavier,* stationer, and to John Evans, grocer, citizens of London, very good friends, towards* pains taken about will 40s, that is 20s each to be paid within one year of death. Residue of goods, chattels, etc. to wife Jane whom he makes sole executor. Appoints Thomas Pavier and John Evans overseers. Wit. W. Smith scriptor.

GL MS 9052/5. OW, prob. clause subscribed. Single sheet, with seal tag, and signatures of testator and witness. Document damaged along right margin with loss of text, readings supplied from RegC (GL MS 9051/6, fo. 114r). Text in engrossing secretary with displayed matter in bastard secretary and italic, hand of W. Smith.

Prob. ACL 17 Nov. 1623 to Jane, relict and executor. Note on will gives pa. of origin as St Botolph Aldersgate. PAB (GL MS 9050/5 fo. 170v) records valuation of inventory at £1238 18s 1d.

c.1568–1623. Printer and bookseller; published *Passionate Pilgrim* by Shakespeare 1599 and shared financial backing of publication of First Folio; printed playbills from 1602. Dead by 4 Nov. 1623. (McKerrow, *Dictionary*, pp. 153–4; E. E. Willoughby, *A Printer of Shakespeare: The Books and Times of William Jaggard*, London, 1934.)

Isaack] printer 1613–27; will dated 5 Feb. 1627, proved 13 Mar. 1627 (GL MS 9051/6 fo. 276v) (McKerrow, *Dictionary*, p. 152).
Coesar] Willoughby (pp. 175–6) gives name of Joan's husband as Yardsley.
Printer to . . . Citty] 1610–23.
Woodford] named in will of Jane Jaggard (GL MS 9051/6 fo. 217r) as Woodfall; not listed among testator's apprentices, but, as Woodhall, freed by Isaac Jaggard 15 Dec. 1626 (D. F. McKenzie, *Stationers' Company Apprentices 1605–1640*, Charlottesville, VA, 1961, p. 19).
Pavier] bookseller 1600–25; publisher of plays by Kyd, Peele, etc.; collaborated with Jaggard on production in 1619 of ten Shakespearean and pseudo-Shakespearean plays; will dated 29 Jun. 1625, proved 17 Feb. 1626 (PRO PROB11/148 fos 142r–142v) (McKerrow, *Dictionary*, pp. 211–12).

1623 May 5 Philip ROSSETER

Memorand*um* That Phillip Rossiter late whilest he lived of the parishe of St dunstans in the west London gent*leman* deceased beinge of perfect mind and memory (on the fifth day of May Anno d*omini* 1623 beinge the day of his death) vttered and declared theise word*es* followeinge or the like in effect for and as his last will and Testament nuncupative videlicet he gaue all his goodes and housholdstuffe and whatsoever elce he had vnto his loveinge wife Elizabeth Rossiter and made her his Executrix, Beinge present and heareinge the premisses the tyme aforesaid Hugh Rossiter, dudley Rossiter and Elizabeth Simpson wife of william Simpson

Hugh Rossetter Dudly Rosseter Elizabeth Simpson

PRO PROB10/401. OW (nuncupative) prob. clause subscribed, note of registration marginated. Note subscribed, signed by Richard Clarke, Surrogate, dated 21 May 1623, that H. Rossiter and D. Rossiter had sworn at the time of the declaration of the will and E. Simpson afterwards. Single sheet, folded to make four pages, unsealed, with signatures of witnesses. Text in rounded set secretary influenced by Chancery hand.

Prob. PCC 21 May 1623 to Elizabeth, relict.

Noted: Gordon Goodwin, 'Thomas Campion and Philip Rosseter', *The Academy*, XLIII, 1893, p. 199.

c.1568–1623. Musician and theatrical manager. Lessee of Whitefriars theatre 1609–15; patentee of Children of Queen's Revels 1610; associated with P. Henslowe (**1616**) in management of combined Revels and Lady Elizabeth's companies 1613–14; Porter's Hall patentee with others 1615; manager of Children of Queen's Revels with R. Lee (**1629**), N. Long (**A1622**) and others 1617; royal lutenist 1604–23, published *A Booke of Ayres* with Thomas Campion who named him principal legatee (**1620**). Died 5 May, buried 7 May 1623 St Dunstan in the West. (*DNB*; Chambers II, 337; Hillebrand, *Child Actors*, pp. 237–50; Nungezer, pp. 304–5; Bentley, II, 554; *New Grove*.)

1623 June 3 Nicholas TOOLEY alias WILKINSON

In the Name of God Amen I Nicholas Tooley of London gentleman being sicke in body but of perfect mynd and memorie praysed be God therefore doe make and declare this my last will and Testament in forme followeing That is to say ffirst I Commend my soule into the handes of Almightie God the ffather trusting and assuredlie beleeuing that by the merrittes of the pretious death and passion of his only sonne and my only Lord and Sauiour Iesus Christ I shall obtaine full and free pardon and forgiuenes of all my sinnes and shall enioy euerlasting life in the Kingdome of Heaven amongest the elect children of God My Bodie I Committ to the Earth from whence yt came to be buried in decent manner att the discrecion of my Executours herevnder named My worldlie substaunce I doe dispose of as followeth Inprimis I giue vnto my good freind Mr Thomas Adams preacher of Godes word whome I doe entreate to preach my ffunerall

Sermon the somme of Tenn poundes Item I doe release and forgiue vnto
my kinswoman Mary Cobb of London widdowe the somme of ffyve
poundes which she oweth me And I doe giue vnto her the somme of ffyve
poundes more Item I doe release and forgiue vnto her sonne Peter Cobb
the somme of Sixe poundes which he oweth me Item I doe giue vnto her
sonne Iohn Cobb the somme of Sixe poundes Item I doe giue vnto her
daughter Margarett Moseley the somme of ffyve poundes Item I doe giue
vnto Mrs Burbadge* the wife of my good freind Mr Cutbert Burbadge*
in whose house I doe nowe lodge)¹ as a remembraunce of my love in
respect of her motherlie care ouer me the somme of Tenn poundes ouer
and besides such sommes of money as I shall owe vnto her att my decease
Item I doe giue vnto her daughter Elizabeth Burbadge alias Maxey the
somme of Tenn poundes To be payd vnto her owne proper handes
therewithall to buy her such thinges as she shall thincke most meete (fo.
2) to weare in remembraunce of me And my will is that an acquittance
vnder her only hand and seale shalbe a suffitient discharge in lawe to my
Executours for payment thereof to all intentes purposes and construccions
and as fully as yf her pretended husband should make and seale the same
with her Item I giue to Alice Walker the sister of my late Mr Richard
Burbadge* deceased the somme of Tenn poundes To be payd vnto her
owne proper handes therewithall to buy her such thinges as she shall
thincke most meete to weare in remembraunce of me And my will is that
an acquittaunce vnder her only hand and seale shalbe a suffitient
discharge in lawe to my Executours for the payment thereof to all intentes
purposes & construccions and as fully as if her husband should make and
seale the same with her Item I giue vnto Sara Burbadge the daughter of
my said late Mr Richard Burbadge deceased that somme of Twenty and
Nyne poundes and thirteene shillinges which is oweing vnto me by
Richard Robinson* To be recouered detayned and disposed of by my
Executours herevnder named vntill her marriage or age of Twenty and
One yeares (which shall first and next happen) without any alloweaunce
to be made of vse otherwise then as they in their discrecions shall thinck
meete to allowe vnto her Item I giue vnto Mrs Condell* the wife of my
good freind Mr Henry Condell* as a remembraunce of my love the
somme of ffyve poundes I giue vnto Elizabeth Condell the daughter
of the said Henry Condell the somme of Tenn poundes Item whereas I
stand bound for Ioseph Tayler* as his suerty for payment of Tenn
poundes or thereaboutes My will is that my Executours shall out of my
estate pay that debt for him and discharge him of that bond Item I doe
release and forgiue vnto Iohn Vnderwood* and William Ecclestone* all
such sommes of money as they doe seuerally owe vnto me Item I doe giue
and (fo. 3) bequeath for and towardes the perpetuall releife of the poore

people of the parrishe of St Leonard in Shoreditche in the County of
Middlesex vnder the Condicion herevnder expressed the somme of
ffourescore poundes To remayne as a stocke in the same parrishe and to
be from tyme to tyme ymployed by the aduise of the Parson Churchwardens
ouerseers for the poore and vestrymen of the said parrishe for the tyme
being or the greater nomber of them In such sort as that on euerie Sunday
after morninge prayer for euer there may out of the encrease which shall
arrise by the ymployment thereof be distributed amongest the poorer sort
of people of the same parrishe Thirtie and Two penny Wheaten loaves
for their releife Prouided allwaies and my will and mynd is That yf my
said gift shalbe misimployed or neglected to be performed in anie wise
contrarie to the true meaning of this my will Then and in such case I giue
and bequeath the same Legacie of ffoure score poundes ffor and towardes
the releife of the poore people of the parrishe of St Gyles without
Criplegate London to be imployed in that parrishe in forme aforesaid Item
I doe giue and bequeath for and towardes the perpetuall releife of the
poore people of the said parrishe of St Giles without Criplegate London
vnder the Condicion herevnder expressed the somme of Twenty poundes
To remayne as a stocke in the same parrishe and to be from tyme to tyme
ymployed by the aduise of the Churchwardens Ouerseers for the poore
and Vestrymen of the same parrishe for the tyme being or the greater
nomber of them In such sort as that on euery Sunday after morninge
prayer for euer there may out of the encrease which shall arrise by the
ymployment thereof be distributed amongest the poorer sort of people of
the same parrishe Eight penny wheaten loaves for their releife Prouided
allwaies and my will and mynd is That yf my said gift shalbe misimployed
or neglected to be performed in anie wise contrarie to the (**fo. 4**) true
meaninge of this my will Then and in such case I giue and bequeath the
same legacie of Twenty poundes ffor and towardes the releife of the poore
people of the said parrishe of St Leonard in Shoreditche to be imployed
in that parrishe in forme aforesaid Item my will and mynd is and I doe
hereby devise and appoynt That all and singuler the legacies bequeathed
by this my will (for payment whereof noe certaine tyme is otherwise
limited) shalbe truly payd by my Executours herevnder named within the
space of One yeare att the furthest next after my decease All the rest and
residue of all and singuler my goodes chattelles Leases money debtes and
personall estate whatsoeuer and wheresoeuer (my debtes legacies and
funerall charges discharged I doe fully and wholly giue and bequeath vnto
my afore named loving freindes Cutbert Burbadge and Henry Condell to
be equally devyded betweene them parte and partelike And I doe make
name and constitute the said Cutbert Burbadge and Henry Condell the
Executours of this my last will and Testament And I doe hereby revoke

and make voyd all former willes testamentes Codicilles legacies executours and bequestes whatsoeuer by me att any tyme heretofore made named giuen or appoynted willing and mynding that theis presentes only shall stand and be taken for my last will and Testament and none other In witnes whereof to this my last will and Testament conteyninge foure sheetes of paper with my name subscribed to euerie sheete I haue sett my seale the Third day of Iune 1623 And in the One & Twentith yeare of the Raigne of our Soueraigne Lord King Iames &c. Nicholas Tooley Signed sealed pronounced and declared by the said Nicholas Tooley the Testatour as his last will and Testament on the day and yeares aboue written in the presence of vs The marke of Anne X Asplin The marke of Mary X Dover The marke of Joane X Booth The marke of Agnes X Dowson The marke of EB Elizabeth Bolton The marke of X ffaith Kempsall The marke of X Isabell Stanly Hum: Dyson* Notary Publique And of me Ro: Dickens servant vnto the said Notary

(fo. 5) Memorandum That Whereas I Nicholas Wilkinson alias Tooley of London gentleman haue on the day of the date of theis presentes by the name of Nicholas Tooley of London gentleman made my last will and Testament in writing conteyninge ffoure sheetes of paper with my name subscribed to euery sheete and sealed with my seale And thereby haue giuen and bequeathed diuers personall legacies to diuers persons and for diuers vses And thereof haue made named and constituted my loueing freindes Cutbert Burbadge and Henry Condell the Executours As thereby may more at large appeare Nowe for the explanacion cleering avoyding and determinacion of all such ambiguities doubtes scruples questions and variaunces about the validitie of my said last will as may arrise happen or be moued after my decease by reason of omission of my name of Wilkinson therein I doe therefore by this my presente Codicill by the name of Nicholas Wilkinson alias Tooley ratifie confirme and approve my said last will and euerie gifte legacie and bequest therein expressed and the Executours therein named as fully and amply to all intentes purposes and construccions as if I had byn soe named in my said last will Any omission of my said name of Wilkinson in my said last will or any scruple doubt question variaunce misinterpretacion cavill or [any] misconstruccion whatsoeuer to be had moved made or inferred therevpon or thereby or any other matter cause or thinge whatsoeuer to the contrarie thereof in any wise notwithstaing And I doe also hereby further declare That my will mynd and meaning is that this my presente Codicill Shalbe and shalbe by all Iudges Magistrates and other persons in all Courtes and other places & to all intentes and purposes expounded construed deemed reputed and taken to be as parte and parcell of my said last will and Testament In witnes whereof I haue herevnto sett my hand and seale the Third day of

Iune 1623 And in the one and Twentith yeare of the Raigne of our Soueraigne Lord king James &c.
Nicholas Wilkinson alias Tooley
Signed sealed pronounced and declared by the said Nicholas Wilkinson alias Tooley as A² Codicill to be annexed vnto his last will and Testament on the day and yeares aboue written in the presence of vs Symon: Drewe: The marke of Isabell X Stanley The marke of X ffaith Kempsall Hum: Dyson Notary Publique And of me Ro: Dickens servant vnto the said Notary

1. Opening parenthesis missing. 2. A: originally the, A overwritten.

PRO PROB10/412. OW, codicil of same date annexed, prob. clause endorsed (fo. 5), and note of registration marginated (fo. 1).

Will on four unnumbered sheets joined at the top, signed by testator on each page, unsealed with signatures of witnesses (fo. 4). Codicil on single sheet folded to make four pages, with applied seal, signatures of testator and witnesses. Text of both documents in same set secretary, hand of codicil more compressed; will has displayed matter in hyrid secretary, codicil in italic. Same hand writes will of H. Condell (1627), possibly of scribe, Robert Dickens.

Prob. PCC 17 Jun. 1624 to Cuthbert Burbage and Henry Condell, executors. PAB (PRO PROB8/21 fo. unnumbered (June 1624)) gives pa. of origin as St Giles Cripplegate.

Printed: Chalmers, *Apology*, pp. 450–6 fn. x; see also Bentley II, 649–51.

fl. 1605–23. Actor, King's Men c.1605–23; legatee of Augustine Phillips (1605), witness to will of Richard Burbage (1619). Buried St Giles Cripplegate 5 June 1623. (Chambers II, 346–7; Nungezer, pp. 374–6; Bentley II, 601–2.)

Mrs Burbadge] Elizabeth; see index.
Cutbert Burbadge] held shares in Globe and Blackfriars (A1636). Tooley was buried from his house; see index.
late Mr Richard] Tooley probably his apprentice.
Robinson] actor with King's Men from c.1611 (Chambers II, 336–7; Nungezer, pp. 300–3; Bentley II, 550–3); see index.
Mrs Condell] Elizabeth (1635); see index.
Henry Condell] (1627); see index.
Tayler] actor with King's Men from 1619 (Chambers II, 345–6; Nungezer, pp. 366–72; Bentley II, 590–8).
Vnderwood] actor with King's Men from 1608 (1624).
Ecclestone] actor with King's Men 1610–11, 1613–23 (Chambers II, 314–15; Nungezer, pp. 127–8; Bentley II, 429–31).
Dyson] see index.

1623 [c.Dec.] Robert BROWNE

In the name of god amen. I Robard Browne of the parish of St Lenard Shordish in the Countie of Middlesex yeoman being sick of bodie but of perfect Remembrance thankes be giuen to [god] Allmightie god, And Knowing that nothing is more Certaine then death, and nothing more vncertaine then the hower of death doe therefore make my last will and Testament in manner and forme ffollowing first bequeath by[1] sowle to Allmigtie god my maker hopeing for Remition of my [sims] sinns by the death and [pation] passion of Iesus Christ myne onely saviour and Redeemer for his Mercie onely and by[1] bodie ot the grownd from whence it cam to be buried in [Cri] Christian buryall in the Church of St Lenardes shordish if [Id . . .] I dye in Clarkenwell, and if I dye ells wheare then in the discretion of my executor[s] here after named And touching the disposition of Landes goodes and Chattells I giue devse[2] bequeath and dispose them in manner and forme ffollowing, that is to say I giue [power and Authoritie to my Trustey] {power and [ayth] authoritie to my Trustey} and wellloued [{brother} Iames Browne and] {mother} Cissalie* Robins [my mother] my Executour[s] {to giue these [legas] legaces hereafter mentioned} [and my will and intent is that my sd Executour[s] shall haue full power and Authoritie in Convenient time after my decease to bargaine and sell to the best [vallewe] these messuages and tenements scituate lying and being in {the} parish of St Lenardes shordish aforesd] Item I giue vnto my Mother Cissalie Robins, her heires Executours and assignes, all that one howse [f] messuage or tenement scituate lying and being in the parish of St Lenard shordish, in the Countie afore sd Item to my sister Iane Renaldes* Tenn powndes to be paide A yeare after my decease [by my Executours] Item giue and bequeath vnto [El] my sister Elizabeth* Browne Tenn pound to be paid at the day of her Maridge Item' to my brother Iames Browne Iudeth Browne and my sister Awedry Browne Ten pound to be devided equally amongst them at the day of their Maridges Item to my ffather {Willm} Robins* ffortie shillinges to by him a Ring to weare for my sake after my decease, all which legaces to be paid by my Executour[s] after my decease In witnes whereof I haue here vnto put to my hand and seale in the yeares[3] of our Lord god one thowsand six hundred and twentie three

The marke X of Robert Browne Miles Hill[4] The marke of X Katherine Swainestone <T>he marke of X Elizabeth Hill

1. *by*: rightly *my*. 2. *devse*: rightly *devise*. 3. *yeares*: rightly *year*. 4. *Hill*: possibly *Sill*; reading unclear in RegC (PRO PROB11/145 fos 30r–30v).

PRO PROB10/418. OW, note of registration marginated and oath of executor, dated 20 Jan. 1624/5, endorsed. Single sheet, torn at top and bottom resulting in loss of seal and prob. clause (information supplied from RegC), with marks of testator and witnesses. Text in secretary hand with corrections and insertions in same hand.

Prob. PCC 20 Jan. 1625 to Cicely Robins, mother and executor.

Printed: Schrickx, *Foreign Envoys*, pp. 221–2.

1595–1625. Son of Robert Browne, who acted on the Continent. (Berry (*Boar's Head Playhouse*, pp. 191–7) untangles the various Robert Brownes conflated in Chambers II, 304 and corrects identifications of Sisson, *Boar's Head*, and Willem Schrickx, 'English actors at the courts of Wolfenbüttel, Brussels and Graz during the lifetime of Shakespeare', *ShS*, XXXIII, 1980, pp. 153–68.)

Cissalie] wife, first of Robert Browne, then of William Robins, both actors; see index.
Renaldes] wife of Robert Reynolds, actor with Queen Anne's c.1616 then on Continent with R. Browne and others (Chambers II, 336; Nungezer, pp. 295–6; Bentley II, 543); see index.
Elizabeth] see index.
Robins] actor with Queen Anne's/Revels and its provincial company to 1625; married Cicely Browne July 1622 (Chambers II, 336; Nungezer, pp. 298–9; Bentley II, 547–9); see index.

[1624 c.Jan.] undated Francis GRACE

It is my will and desire that the benefitt of my share* which is to continew for two yeares after my decease shalbe disposd in this manner to the payment of my debtes as farr as the two yeares profitt of it do{th} come to, which is to Margoret Goborne* the somme of twentie two poundes. To Robert Gibbs* the some of fortie six shillinges, to ¹ Rhodes* the some of fortie shillinges. To Richard Witton the somme of six poundes. To Edward Coborne* the somme of three poundes, and to be disposd to em, by Andro Kene,* in an equall proportion, and my gatheringe place {the benefit of it} [in my] for the two yeares, I give vnto Tomazin Tomson, as allso all that is mine in her house, & if my share do amount to more then the satisfaction of these debtes aboue specified, I give it vnto my brother Richard Grace.* Franck Grace. Witnesses to this, [will] Iohn Peirson, Iohn ffishe,* Edward Knight.//.*

1. Blank in MS.

GL MS 25.626/4 fo. 230r. RegC. with admon grant.

Admon [with will annexed]. Court of Dean and Chapter of St Paul's 31 Jan. 1624 to John Goborne, creditor, no executor named.

Printed: S. P. Cerasano, 'New ... wills', pp. 301–2 (RegC); see also her 'The "business" of shareholding, the Fortune playhouses, and Francis Grace's will', *Medieval and Renaissance Drama in England*, II, 1985, pp. 231–51 (p. 249).

fl. 1610–24. Actor, sharer, gatherer. Prince Henry's/Palsgrave's from 1610; one of company who in 1618 signed lease of first Fortune from E. Alleyn. Buried St Giles Cripplegate 2 Feb. 1624. (Chambers II, 319; Nungezer, p. 158; Bentley II, 448–9.)

share] in second Fortune, although not listed in Alleyn's first division of shares 1622. Cerasano ('The "business" of shareholding', p. 246) suggests Grace's share originally that of Charles Massey, actor with Admiral's/Prince Henry's/Palsgrave's 1597–1625 (Bentley II, 507–8), who surrendered whole share to Alleyn Mar. 1623.
Margoret Goborne] presumably connected with his creditor and administrator.
Gibbs] hired man at Fortune (Bentley II, 442).
Rhodes] possibly John Rhodes who owned shares in second Fortune 1637 and 1648 and may have succeeded Gunnell as manager after 1634 (Bentley II, 544–6).
Edward Coborne] Colborne/Colbrand was actor with Prince Henry's/Palsgrave's from 1610 (Nungezer, p. 96; Bentley II, 408–9).
Kene] Andrew Cane, actor with Lady Elizabeth's and then Palsgrave's from 1622 (Nungezer, pp. 82–5; Bentley II, 398–401); see index.
Richard Grace] hired man with Palsgrave's from 1624 (Nungezer, pp. 158–9; Bentley II, 449–50).
ffishe] Alleyn granted John Fisher, barber-surgeon, lease of half share of Fortune 1622 (*Henslowe Papers*, ed. W. W. Greg, London, 1902, pp. 29–39).
Knight] witnessed agreement in 1616 between Prince's Men and Alleyn and Jacob Meade (**1624**) (Bentley II, 495).

1624 Jan. 17 William BIRD alias BORNE

In the name of God Amen I william Byrd al*ia*s Bourne of [1] although Sick in Bodie yett of p*er*fect memorie, thank*es* bee vnto allmightie God haue ordayned this my last will and Testament: ffirst I will and bequeath my Soule vnto allmightie God my Saviour and my Body to bee beryed in Christian Buriall: hoping through the death and passion of my Lord Ihesus Ch<rist> to haue euerlasting happines As Concerning my wordly estate and for th<e> disposing thereof this is my last will and Testament: ffirst I revoak<e> all former wills and Testament*es* whatsoeuer made heeretofore by mee: And now my mynd and will is [That] and I doe bequeath vnto my Eldest Sonne William Byrd my ash Culler Suite {& Cloake} of Cloth laced w*ith* Satin lace I giue and bequeath vnto my second Sonne Theophilus* [a]my wainscott Cupbo<rd> w*ith* particons therein and the Bookes nowe remayning [therin] in the same Item I giue

and bequeath vnto my Third Sonne Thomas Byrd* my ashe Coller Suite and Cloake trymmed with greene Silke and Silver lace all other of my goodes and Chattelles whatsoeuer {(my debtes and funeralles discharged)} I giue and bequeath vnto my dearly beloued wife Marie* Bird and I make and appoynt her my Sole executrix of this my last will and Testament. In wittnes wher<of> I haue heerevnto set my hand and Seale The Seventeenth day of Ianuarie 1623 In the presence of Edward Hobert
ffrancis B<.>ina² WM

1. Blank in MS. 2. *ffrancis B<.>ina* WM: omitted in RegC (PRO PROB11/143 fo. 21v).

PRO PROB10/407. OW, prob. clause subscribed, note of registration marginated. Single sheet, with signatures and remnants of applied seal. Text in facile mixed hand.

Prob. PCC 30 Jan. 1624 to Mary Bird (Byrd) alias Borne, relict and executor. PAB (PRO PROB8/21 fo. unnumbered (Jan. 1623/4)) gives pa. of origin as St Leonard Shoreditch.

Printed: S. P. Cerasano 'New . . . wills', pp. 299–301 (RegC).

fl. 1597–1624. Actor; Pembroke's 1597, Admiral's/Prince Henry's/Palsgrave's 1597–1622; one of company who in 1618 signed lease of first Fortune from E. Alleyn. Collaborated with Samuel Rowley (**1624**) as reviser of plays. Legatee of Thomas Towne (**1612**). Buried St Leonard Shoreditch 22 Jan. 1624. (Chambers II, 303; Nungezer, pp. 48–9; Bentley II, 379–80.)

Theophilus] actor (**1663**); see index.
Thomas Byrd] Cerasano (p. 301 fn. 14) suggests identification with player Thomas Bourne (Nungezer, p. 52; Bentley II, 384–5).
wife Marie] (**1625**).

1624 June 21 John CLARKE

22 Clarke¹
In the name of God Amen I Iohn Clarke Citizen and Musiconer of london beinge at this tyme weake and sick in bodie but of good and perfect remembraun<ce> prayse be given to allmightie god doe make and ordayne this my last Testament expressinge herein my last will in manner and forme followinge videlicet first and principally I Commend my soule into the handes of allmightie god my maker Redeeemer and Comforter hopinge by the only merittes of my said saviour Iesus Christ to inherit eternall life And I Committ my bodie to the earth from whence it Came to be buried in decent and Christian buriall in the parish church of

St Andrewe² in Holborne of the which parish I am a parishoner accordinge to the discresion of my executrixes hereafter named. As for those worldlie goodes which god hath lent [my] me I thus dispose of. Item I will that all such de<btes> that in Conscience I owe to any person or persons be truly paid within one moneth After my decease {Item} I give and bequeath vnto Henry Pike my sonne in lawe twoe shillinges of lawfull money of England and I forgive and remitt vnto him twentie shillinges he oweth me vpon the which I had a gowne of his in pawne but I let him haue it againe without my money Item I bequeath and give vnto Iohn Robbins my sisters sonne twentie shillinges sterlinge to be paid within six monthes after my decease. Item I give and bequeath [and] vnto Abel Call my lovinge freind tenne shillinges for a token of my love to be paid him within six monthes after my decease Item whereas I stand bound for the bringinge {vp} of Mary ffenn alias Batty. my will is that Ione the Mother of the said Mary shall have five poundes given vnto her by my said executrixes within six monthes after my decease for the bringinge vp of the said Mary provided that the said Ioane or her husband shall secure my executrixes for the discharge of the said bond wherein I and my executours & administratours stand bound for the somne All the rest of my goodes and Chattells whatsoever by this my will not disposed of my debtes beinge paid and funerall expences performed I give and bequeath vnto³ Alice Peters and lucye Ash widowes to be equally devided betwene them And I make and ordayne them to be executrixes of this my said will desiringe them to execute the same accordinge to my minde herein expressed. And I revoke & disanull all other former willes & executours by me formerly made and appointed In Witnes wherof I haue hereunto put my hand & seale dated the xxjth day of Iune 1624 in the twoe and twentie yeare of the Raigne of our Soveraigne lord Kinge Iames of England ffraunce & Ireland &c and of Scotland the seven & fiftieth.

By me Iohn Clark

Subscribed sealed & deliuered and published as the last will and testament of the said Iohn Clarke in presence of us Abel X Call and Iohn Carter Scrivener

1. 22 Clarke superscribed.   2. Andrewe: originally written Andrewes, es overwritten by e.   3. vnto: originally written vtto, t overwritten by n.

GL MS 9052/6. OW, prob. clause endorsed (date corrected from July to June). Single sheet, sealed, with signature and marks of testator and witnesses; damage to top right margin resulting in some loss of text. Text in facile secretary, probably hand of John Carter scrivener.

Prob. ACL 26 June 1624 to Alice Peters and Lucy Ash, executors. PAB (GL MS 9050/5 fo. 182r) gives valuation of inventory at £8 6s 3d.

fl. 1608–24. Perhaps boy actor; sworn in as member of Chapel Royal, Aug. 1608 (Hillebrand, 'Early history', p. 257).

1624 July 4 (codicil) (July 1) Jacob MEADE

In the name of god Amen. the fyrst day of Iuly in the year of our Lo{r}d god on Thowsand syx hundred and ffower and twenty I Iacob' mead of the parrysh of saynt saviours in the County of surry waterman' syck in body but of good and perfect memory (praysed bee god therfore) doe make and ordayne this my Last wyll and testament in manner and forme ffollowynge that is to say)¹ fyrst I Comend my soulle into the handes of Allmighty god my maker Assuredly hopinge through the only merryttes of Iesus Chryst my saviour to bee made partaker of Lyf everlastyng And I Comend my Body to the earth whearof it was made Item I wyll' that all' such deptes and duetyes as I owe of Ryght or of Conscyence to any person or persons bee well and truely Contented and payed by my executours heerafter named or els ordayne soe for to bee payd without Contradiction' And after my deptes payd and my ffunerall' expences performed I geeve and beequeath vnto my daughter Iudyth pyttes the sum of tenne powndes of Lawfull english money to bee by my executors soe disposed of as they shall think fytt soe as my sayd daughter may ffrom tyme to tyme have and receave som proffytt therby and the pryncipall to Remayne vnto and for the only vse and beehof of my sayd daughter so long as it shall' pleas allmyghty god that shee shall Lyve with her husband mychaell pyttes whom' I wyll' shall have nothing to doe or meddlle therwyth but yf it fortune that the sayd mychaell pyttes doe happen to depart out of this mortall Lyf bee fore my sayd daughter then the sayd sum of tenn powndes to bee payd vnto my sayd daughter Iudyth pyttes and yf it ffortune that my sayd daughter doe depart out of this mortall Lyf before my grandchyld Allis pyttes doe acomplish the full age of syxteen years then the sayd sum of tenn powndes to Remayne vnto my sayd grandchyld Allis pyttes and then after yf my sayd daughter do happen {to} depart this mortall Lyf beefor my sayd grandchyld then the sayd Legacy of ten poundes to Remayne vnto her my sayd grandchyld also I geeve and beequeath vnto my sayd grandchyld Allis pyttes the Lyck sum of tenn powndes of Lyck english money to bee by my executors soe disposed of that my sayd grand Chyld may have toward her education' som proffytt therby which I wyll' to bee payed vnto her mother for the same intent and purpos vntyll it shall please god that shee bee ablle to gett her own Lyvyng but yf it fortune that my sayd daught² Iudyth pyttes and Allis pyttes doe fortune to dye beefor the sayd allis pyttes shall' accomplish the full age of on and twenty years then the sayd Legacy of tenn powndes beequeathed vnto my sayd daughter and alsoe the Legacy beequeathed vnto my sayd grandchyld Allyce pyttes to Remayne vnto the next of kynn. Also I wyll and my mynd is that yf my sayd grandchyld do Lyve vntyll shee have acomplished the full age of on and twenty years then my mynd is that her Legacy of tenn powndes bee then payed vnto her or els in her marriag day or whether of them shall' (fo. 2) ffyrst happen' Item I geeve and beequeath vnto my syster Ioan Berrydge one peece of golld of two and twenty shillinges to bee payed vnto her vpon demaund after my decease. Item I geeve and beequeath vnto Katheryn Grevyll'* her daughter on other Lyck peece of golld of twoe and twenty shillinges to bee Lyckwyse payed vnto her vpon demaund after my decease Item I geeve and beequeath vnto Elizabeth strange the sum of ffyve powndes of Lawfull English money to bee payd vnto her at thend of three monethes next after my decease Item I geeve vnto the poor of the Lyberty of the Clynck in the parrysh of saynt saviours in sowthwork the summ of Thyrty shillinges of Lyck english money to bee by {my executour &} the overseers {for the poor} of that Lyberty geeven to the poor in Bread on my ffunerall day {or as they think good} Item I geeve vnto the poor of the parrysh of saynt Ollaves in sowthwork the Lyck sum of Thyrty shillinges of Lyck english money to bee Lyckwyse by the [by the] Overseers for the poor of that parrysh geeven to the poor in bread on my ffunerall day Item I geeve and beequeath vnto my breethren the overseers of the Company of Watermen the sum of fforty shilling of Lyck english money to bee spent Amongst them on' my ffunerall day Item I geeve vnto mr Roger Colle* Nycholas norman' and Andrew Lucas vnto every one of them on payer of gloves of the pryce of tenn shyllinges a payer And All other my goodes and Chattelles whatsoever now vnbeequeathed I geeve and bequeath vnto my three sonns Iacob' Edward and Rychard mead to bee equally devyded betwyxt my sayd three sonns part and part Alyck to bee payed vnto them severally when they shall have severally accomplished ther full age or ages of on and twenty years but yf it fortune that any of my sayd sonns Iacob' Edward or Richard mead doe happen to depart out of this mortall Lyf beefore hee or they shall accomplish the age or ages of one and twenty yars then the Legacy or[3] Legacyes of him or them heerby beequeathed to Remayne {to} hym, or them then' survyvyng equaly to bee dvyded And yf Any of my sayd sonns wyll' or shalbe Obstynat and disobedyent and wyll not bee governed and Ruled by my executours then hee or they soe Refusyng to bee governed to Loose the one half of his or ther Legacye or Legacyes heerby to him or them geeven', to bee and Remayne to hym (or them' equally) that wylbee governed by my executours Item ffurther my Wyll and my Intent is that my executours assone after my decease as Conveniently

{they} Cann or may shall put the portions of my sayd (fo. 3) Three sonns into the handes of the Churchwardens of the parrish of saynt saviours {or ellwher} takyng securyty for the same for the good of my sayd three sonns as my executors shall thinck fytt And further my wyll and my mynd is that my sayd sonns portions {shall} [shall Remayne in the vestery in the Chest ther and to] bee payd vnto my sayd three sonns when they shall have Accomplished ther {severall'} Ages of one and twenty years as affore sayd And ffurther my wyll and my mynd is that mr Roger Colle Nycholas norman' and Andrew Lucas shall' have the goverment and disposyng of my sayd sonns vntyll they may {bee} Conveniently placed with som honest masters whear they may Lyve in the ffear of god And for the good opinion I have of mr Roger Colle Nycholas norman and Andrew Lucas hoping they wylbee Carefull for performance of this my Last wyll & Testament I doe mak and ordayne mr Roger Colle Nycholas Norman & Andrew Lucas Ioynt and Coexecutors of this my wyll and Testament And I doe heerby Revoake and Adnull' all fformer wyll'es and Testamentes by mee at any tyme heertofor made In wyttnes wherof I have heer vnto sett my seall and subscribed my name the fyrst day of Iuly 1624   Ia mede[4]
Sealled and subscrybed in the presentes of vs./ William Checkley Iohn ffacye[5] Griffith hinton

(fo. 4) A Coddysell' made by mee Iacob' mead the fowerth day of Iuly 1624 to bee Anexed and Ioyned to my Last wyll and Testament & to bee by my Executours performed as ffolloweth

Imprimis[6] I ffreely fforgeeve Ralphe Iepson the dept hee oweth vnto mee by bond and the bond Wherin hee standeth bownd for payment of the same to bee Canceled or ells delyvered vnto hym

Item my wyll' and my mynd also is that the bond wherin the sayd Ralphe Iepson' and Iohn Bowen standeth bownd vnto mee for perfformance of Artycles of Agreement bee Canceled and delyvered vnto them'

Item that wheras Davyd sheeffell hath promysed vnto mee to take into his Chardg my youngest sonne Rychard mead to have hym brought vpp in the fear of god my mynd is yf my executors bee Contented therwth[7] that the sayd Davyd sheffell shall and doe Receave and take all' the proffyttes yshuing out of the Tementes which I hold by Lease in the parysh of saynt Ollaves duryng the wholle term therin vnexpryred for the further benyfytt of my sayd sonn Rychard mead

Item that the wyddow Brackes ffor the paynes that shee hath taken with mee in my sycknes bee well dealt wthall[8] by my executors

Item that my mayd servant Katheryn Reynoldes bee also by my executours well dealt wythall' for her paynes & servyce done

Item I fforgeeve my mother in law all' the Rent that she oweth vnto mee

Item I also forgyve vnto   [9] parssoll' fower pownd of the Rent wch[10] hee oweth vnto mee

Item I doe Allso forgeeve vnto Iohn ffacy all' dept*es* wch[10] hee oweth vnto mee and the bond wherin he standeth bownd for payment of the same to bee Canceled or Delyvered vnto hym
Item that Edward Collyns* for the paynes that hee hath taken in travelyng in my busynes bee also by my executo*u*rs well dealt wyth all'
Item I doe forgeeve the Wyddoe Tyrry of St olaves sempster all the Rent that shee oweth vnto mee
Item whearas the Legacy geeven by my wyll vnto my daught*er* Iudyth pytt*es* {Beyng x li} my mynd is that when my executo*u*rs shall bryng my estate togeather see whate the estate is I Reffer it to ther Discressions To geeve vnto my sayd daught*er* what mor they shall thynk ffytt for the Augmentati*on* of her portion'
Item I geeve vnto mr Roger Colle my new Redd saddlle and Brydlle w*i*th the saddll*e* Cloth and Coveryng belongyng to the same
Item I geeve vnto Nycholas Norman on peece of Chamlett of 13 yard*es* or therabout*es*
Item I geeve vnto Andrewe Lucas my horse and my old saddll & Brydll
Item I geeve vnto Gryffyth hynton my black grogoram suit Doblett hose and the Ierken therv*n*to beelongynge   Iacob Mede
Wyttnesses to this Coddysell Edw: Collins Griffith hinton Ioan X Brackes

1. Otiose parenthesis. 2. *daught*: mark of abbreviation missing, rightly *daughter*. 3. *or*: otiose superscript *r*. 4. *Ia mede*; written *Iacob Mede* (fo. 1) and *Iacob meade* (fo. 2). 5. *ffacye*: written *ffacy* (fo. 1). 6. *Imprimis*: otiose superscript *r*. 7. *therwth*: mark of abbreviation missing, rightly *therwith*. 8. *wthall*: mark of abbreviation missing, rightly *withall*. 9. Blank in MS. 10. *wch*: mark of abbreviation missing, rightly *which*.

PRO PROB10/412. OW, codicil annexed, prob. clause subscribed (fo. 4) and note of registration marginated (fo. 1). Will and codicil on four unnumbered sheets joined at the top, unsealed, each signed by testator and witnesses. Text of both documents in same facile secretary with many otiose marks of abbreviation.

Prob. PCC 19 July 1624 to Roger Cole, Nicholas Norman, and Andrew Lucas, executors. PAB (PRO PROB8/21 fo. unnumbered (July 1624)) gives pa. of origin as St Saviour's.

1557–1624. Theatre manager and owner, Keeper of Bears by 1599; closely associated with Philip Henslowe (**1616**) and Edward Alleyn (**1626**) in management of Bear Garden; part-owner of Bear Garden and Hope theatre. Buried St Saviour Southwark 9 Jul. 1624. (Chambers II, 452, 465–70; Nungezer, p. 250; Bentley II, 510.)

Grevyll'] perhaps wife of Curtis Greville, actor with Lady Elizabeth's and then Palsgrave's in 1622 and, from 1626, King's company (Nungezer, p. 165; Bentley II, 451–2).

Colle] churchwarden of St Saviour's Southwark, 1616 (Young, *Dulwich*, I, 32); see index.
Collyns] possibly Ned Collins, cousin of actor Charles Massey, who dined with Alleyn 1622 (Warner, p. 192); Edward Collins listed among attendants employed by players at Blackfriars 1637 (Nungezer, p. 97; Bentley II, 409).

1624 July 23. Samuel ROWLEY

In the name of God Amen the Three and Twentith daye of Iuly Anno domini 1624 <in the Two> and Twentith yeere of the raigne of owr Souereigne lord Iames by the grace of god king of England, ffrance, and Ireland, defendor of the ffaith &c And of Scot<land the seauen> and ffifteth./ I Samuell Rowley of the parishe of White chappell* in the County of Midelsex gentelman, being visited with sicknes, by the hand of Almigh<tie god yet> thorough his blessing, in perfect memorie, Laude and praise be therfore geuen to him for the same. Doe make, and ordayne this my last will and Testament <in manner and> forme ffollowing ffirst and before all thinges. I Commend my Soule into the handes of Almightie god, my only Sauiowr and Redemer. Humblie beseeching him to p<ardon and> forgiue me All my Synns And I will that my bodie shalbe buried in the parishe Church of White chappell abouesaid. And for the disposition of all my good<s and chattells> that god of his great goodnes hath bestowed on me in this world First I will that all my debtes be trwlie paid, and my funerall discharged Item I giue {will} and bequeath vnto Alice* my wife, for terme of her naturall life, my lease which I hold in Plowgh Alley of Iohn Hope gentelman, And alsoe all my Copiehold land l<ying> neere Ratcliff highe waye in the parishe of Stepney and County of Midelsex abouesaid which I purchased of George Howghton Citizen and Apothecarie of london, Item I giue and bequeath vnto Iane Adams my dawghter, the wife of Richard Adams my ffower Copiehold Messuages or Tenementes scituat in Artilerie lane in the parishe of White chappell and County of Midelsex abouesaid for terme of her naturall life. And also all my said Copiehold land lying neere Ratcliff highe waye in the parishe of Stepney and Countie of Midelsex abouesaid {and said lease in Plough Alley}¹ from and after the decease of the said Alice my wife, for the terme of her Naturall life, And after the decease of the said Iane my dawghter Then to her ffirst begotten sonne Samuell Adams, and to his heires males foreuer, And for default of such heires Males, Then to Richard Adams second sonne of the said Richard Adams and to his heires males for euer, And for default of such heires Males, Then to Iane Adams, dawghter of the said Richard Adams and to her heires Males Successiuelie as is before

expressed And for default of such heires Males then to the right heires of
me the said Samuell Rowley for euer, Item I giue and bequeath vnto my
Brother William Rowley* All my Bookes, Item I giue and bequeath vnto
my brother Thomas Rowley ffortie shilling*es* of lawfull mony of England
to be paid vnto him within one Moneth next after my decease Item I giue
and bequeath vnto my Nephewe Richard Rowley ffiue pownd*es* of lawfull
mony of England to be paid vnto him within six Monethes after my
decease. Item I giue vnto the most needie, A<ged> and impotent poore of
the parishe of White chappell abouesaid wheare I nowe dwell ffortie
shilling*es* of lawfull mony of England to be laide owt in bread and giuen
them in the daie of my buriall, or the next daie after, by the Churchwardens
for the tyme being of White chappell abouesaid All the rest of my good*es*
debt*es*, and Chattell*es* not geuen, nor bequeathed. I doe wholie giue and
bequeath vnto my louing wife Alice Rowley. she seing my debt*es* paid
and my funerall discharged And of this my pr*es*ent Testament and last
will I doe make the said Alice my wife, and the foresaid Richard Adams
my sonne in lawe my sole and only executo*ur*s. And I vtterlie revoke, and
Adnull all and euerie former Will*es* legasies, bequeast*es*, and Executo*ur*s.
by and before this tyme made named, and bequeathed And I will this to
stand for my last will and Testament and none other {or} otherwise In
witnes wherof I the said Samuell Rowley to this my pr*es*ent Testament
and last will, haue sett my hand, and Seale. Dated the daie and yeares
ffirst aboue written./ Samuell Rowlye.
<Memorandum that theis> woord*es* (and the said lease in <Plough> Alley)
enterlined betweene the <Eleaven>th & twelueth lines within written
<were en>terlined before thensealing and <deliuerie> heereof: <Io>hn
Collman <Wa>lter Baker Antho: Bodie scri*uener* Tho: Symonds seruant
to the said scri*uener*/²
Sealed and deliuered, and also published and declared, by the within
named Samuell Rowley for his last will and Testame*n*t in the pr*es*ence
Iohn Collman Walter Baker Antho: Bodie scr Tho: Symonds seruant to
the said Scri*uener*/³

1. *and* ... *Alley*: insertion in a second hand.   2. <*Memorandum* ... *scr:*
endorsed; refers to interlineation l. 26 above.   3. *Sealed* ... *Scr:* endorsed.

GL MS 9172/34. OW, prob. clause, note of registration endorsed. Parchment; single
sheet, seal tag (seal lost), with signatures of testator and witnesses. Top right corner
of document missing with loss of text; lacunae supplied from RegC (GL MS 9171/24
fo. 355v–356v). Text in set mixed hand with displayed matter in hybrid secretary.

Prob. CCL 4 Dec. 1624, to Alice, widow and executor, reserving power to Richard
Adams, executor. PAB (GL MS 9168/17 fo. 181v) notes pa. of origin as Stepney
and valuation of inventory at £32 8s.

Printed: J. A. B. Somerset, 'An edition of Samuel Rowley's *When You See Me You Know Me*', unpublished M.A. dissertation, University of Birmingham, 1964, pp. 326–30 (OffC); his 'New facts concerning Samuel Rowley', *RES* n.s., XVII, 1966, pp. 293–7 (RegC).

fl. 1597–1624. Actor, dramatist, sharer; Admiral's/Prince Henry's/Palsgrave's 1597–1613. Beneficiary of Thomas Towne (**1612**). Buried St Mary Matfellon 29 Oct. 1624. (Chambers II, 337, III, 472; Nungezer, pp. 305–6; Bentley II, 555.)

White chappell] resident pa. St Mary Matfellon, Whitechapel from 1601.
Alice] confirms marriage of 'Samewell Rowley' and Alice Coley, 7 Apr. 1594 St Michael Crooked Lane, was that of dramatist (Bentley II, 555).
William Rowley] perhaps the dramatist (**A1626**).

1624 Sept. 8 Sarah DAMBROOKE (abstract)

(Danbrooke) Of London widow. Sick. Soul 'into the hand*es* of God my Maker and Redeemer'. Burial at discretion of executor. Whereas stands indebted to children and to uncle Nathanael Torperley in various sums and also to others, said debts be paid in such order as money due to her is gathered in; surplus to said children and other friends to be distributed at discretion of executor. Appoints Nathanael Torperley executor. Revokes all other wills. Wit. John Shancke,* Winifrid Shanck, Anne Claye* (mark), Amye Sheparde (mark).

PRO PROB10/420. OW, prob. clause subscribed, note of registration marginated. Single sheet with signature of testator and signatures and marks of witnesses; remnants of seal. Text in facile secretary hand with displayed matter in italic.

Prob. PCC 23 Mar. 1625 to Nathaniel Torperley, uncle and executor. PAB (PRO PROB8/22 fo. unnumbered (Mar. 1624/5)) gives pa. of origin as St Giles Cripplegate.

Printed: Bentley II, 642 (summary).

fl. 1624. Possibly widow of John Shanbrooke, actor who may have been hired man with Palsgrave's. Buried from house of John Shank (**1635**) at St Giles Cripplegate 11 Sep. 1624. (Bentley II, 561–2; 564–5.)

John Shancke] actor with Prince Henry's/Palsgrave's 1610–14 (**1635**); see index.
Claye] possibly related to Henry Clay, functionary of King's company in 1624, resident in St Giles 1620–26 (Nungezer, p. 92; Bentley, II, 407–8).

1624 Sept. 10 John GARLAND

In the name of God Amen I Iohn Garland of Stratford Bowe in the County of Midd*lesex* gent being sicke in Bodie but of good p*er*fect health & memorie thanck*es* be to god for ye same doe make & ordeaine this my last will & Testament in manno*ur* & fourme followinge That is to saie first I Committ both bodie & soule into ye hand*es* of god my Creato*ur* Iesus Christ my Readermer & ye holie Ghost my sanctifier in w*hi*ch Three p*er*sons & it but one god I stidfastlie beleaue assuringe my selfe of Ever lastinge Salvation throught our lord & saviour[1] Iesus Christ w*hi*ch died for me My bodie I Committ vnto ye earth desiringe ye same may be decentlie Buried in the Chappell of Stratford Bowe so neare my wife as may best be done I Giue & Bequeath vnto Marie my wife Two Acker*es* & Three Roods of ground or there about*es* called by ye name of Tenter hill with house & Barne belonginge to ye same. beinge one ye North side of Stratford Bowe. & lyinge betweene ye land*es* of Iohn Eagelsfeild gent one ye North side & ye land*es* of mr William Gowge one ye south side & one ye {Easte} side leaden to Oldford. Also I Give vnto my Wife Marie Garland one lease w*hi*ch I haue ye residue of yeares it to come of a peace of Land contayninge Three Roodes[2] more or lesse lyinge att Milend w*hi*ch is more att large specified in ye lease Excepting & reservinge out of ye same Land ffortie foote in lenght & fortie foote in Breadth out of ye south ende Which I give & bequeath vnto my god sonne Iohn Reignall*es* sonne of [3] Reignalls of Milend in ye County of Midd*lesex* Smith duringe his naturall life & after his decease to come vnto my Daughter Elizabeth Garland & after hur decease {& hur heires} to my Heire Also I give vnto Marie my wife ye lease of ye ground w*hi*ch lieth in Barbinder Layne contayninge Sixe Acker*es* be it more or lesse. Also I Give vnto Marie my wife ye leasse of ye House w*hi*ch I {now} dwell in I Give vnto Marie my wife my ffive Acker*es* of ffreland lyinge in Oldford lyinge one ye North one ye land of Henery Iohnson and one ye South side one Barbinder Layne one ye East Side {of} Henery Iohnson & one ye west side of mr Pease [vnte] Vntell my Daughter Elizabeth Garland come two ye age of Eaighteene Yeares & then to goe vnto Elizabeth my Daughter duringe hur life {& hur heires} & if she doth dep*ar*te this life before hur Mother Marie my will is y*a*t it shall then come vnto my wife a gaine Duringe hur natureall life & after (fo. 2) hur Decease to Iohn Garland of Burnt Wood in the County of Essex Gardener & to his heires & for want of heires {of his bodie} two returne backe againe to my heires I Give & Bequeath vnto my Daughter Elizabeth Garland a ffeild Bedstid A ffether Bed & Boulster one Blancket a Couerlit of Tapstery to be Delivered to hur att Eaighteene yeares of age I Give vnto Marie my wife All my Cattell Bills bound*es* Or what so euer is left vnnamed in this my will eyther with in Doores or with out And doe also make hur my hole and sole Executrix of this my last will & Testament & y*a*t this is my will and last Testament I haue here vnto sett my hand and Seale this Tenth day of September 1624 And in the yeare of the Raigne of our Souerraigne lord Iames by the grace of god king of England ffrance and Ireland the Two and Twentie and of Skotland the Eaight and ffiftie defendo*u*r of the faith &c   Iohn garland Sealled & delivered as my last will & Testam*en*t contayninge a sheate & a halfe of paper in ye present*es* of vs./ Thomas Skoryer Walter Hutchinson

1. *saviour*: otiose superscript *r*.   2. *Roodes*: otiose special sign for *es*.   3. Blank in MS.

GL MS 9172/34. OW, prob. clause subscribed, note of registration endorsed (fo. 2). Two sheets fastened at top, each with signature and seal of testator, signatures of witnesses (fo. 2). Text in set secretary with displayed matter in italic; insertions in same hand.

Prob. CCL. 29 Sep. 1624 to Marie, relict and executor. PAB (GL MS 9168/16) records admon granted to widow Elizabeth Garland in 1608 cancelled because he was alive (fo. 73v) and gives valuation of inventory at £149 5s 6d (GL MS 9168/17 fo. 175v).

Noted: Eccles, 'Actors II', p. 455, but misdated 1614.

fl. 1583–1624. Actor; Queen Elizabeth's 1583–8, Lennox's 1605, Duke of York's/ Prince Charles's from 1610. Lived at 'ould forde' 1605; will does not mention the property, called Bromedown in Old Ford, leased to actor Robert Shaa, noted by Eccles (ibid.). Likely to have retired from theatre by 1616; no theatrical connections in will. (Chambers, II, 318; Nungezer, pp. 146–7.)

1624 Oct. 20 (codicil) (Oct. 4 and 10) John UNDERWOOD

In the name of God Amen, I Iohn Vnderwood of the parishe of Sainte Bartholomews the lesse in London gentleman being very Weake and sick in bodie but (thank*es* be giuen to Almightie god) in perfect minde and memorie doe make and declare my last Will and Testament in manner and forme followinge v*i*d*elicet* ffirst I Commend and committ my soule to Almightie God. and my bodie to the earth to be buried att the discretion of my Executors, And my Worldly good*es* and estate (which it hath pleased the Almightie god to blesse me w*i*th) I will bequeath and dispose as followeth That is to say to and amongst my fiue Children namely Iohn Vnderwood, Elizabeth Vnderwood Burbadge Vnderwood, Thomas Vnderwood and Isabell* Vnderwood (my debt*es* and other legacies heerin named paid and my funerall and other iust dues and duties discharged) all and singuler my good*es* houshould stuffe plate and other thing*es* whatsoeuer in or about my now dwelling house or elsewhere, and alsoe all the right title or interest part or share that I haue and enioy att this present by lease or otherwise or ought to haue, possesse, or enioy in any manner or kinde att this present, or heerafter w*i*thin the Blackfryers* London or in the Companie of his Maiesties Servan*tes* my louimg[1] and kinde fellows in theire house there or att the Globe* on the Bankside[2] (fo. 2) And alsoe that my part and share or due in or out of the playhouse Called the Curteine* scituate in or neere Holloway in the parish of Saint Leonard in Shoredich London or in any other place to my said fiue Children equally and proportionatably to be devided amongst them at theire severall ages of one and Twentye years. And during there and euery of theire minorities for and toward*es* theire education maintainance and placeing in the world ackording to the discretion direction and care which I repose In my Executors Provided allways and my true intent and meaning is That my said Executors shall not allienate change or alter by sale or otherwise directly or indirectly any my part or share wh*i*ch I now haue or ought to hould haue possesse or enioy in the sai[e]d playhouses Called the Blackfryers London The Globe on the Bankside and Curteyne aforemenc*i*oned or any of them but that the encrease or benefite out and from the same and euery of them shall come agrue and arise to my sai[e]d Executors as now it is to me to the vse of my said children equally to be devided amongst them Provided alsoe[3] (fo. 3) That if the vse and encrease of my said estate giuen (as aforesaid) to my said children shall proue insufficie{nt} or defectiue in respect of the young years of my Children for theire education and placeing of them as my said Executors shall thinke meete Then my will and true meaninge is, That when the eldest of my said children shall attaine to the age of one and Twentye years my said Executors shall pay or cause to be paid (vnto him or her soe surviueing or atteyninge) his or equall share of my estate soe remaining vndisbursed or vndisposed for the vses aforesaid in theire or either of theire hand*es* and soe for euery or any of my said Children attayning to the age aforesaid. Yet if it shall appeare or seeme fitt at the Compleac*i*on of my said children euery or any of them att theire said full age or ages which shall first happen my estate remaining not to be equallye shared or disposed amongst the rest surviueing in minoritie, Then my will is that it shall be left to my Executors to giue vnto my childe soe attaininge the age as they shall Iudge will be equall to the rest surviueing and accomplishing[4] (fo. 4) The aforesaid age, And if any of them shall dye or depart this life before they accomplish the said age or ages I will and bequeath theire said part share or portion to them him or her surviueing att the ages aforsaid equally to be devided by my Executors as aforesaid And I doe

heerby nominate and appoynte my louing freind*es* (in whome I repose my trust for *pe*rformance of the *p*remisses) Henry Cundey* Thomas Sanford and Thomas Smyth gentlemen my Executors of this my last Will and Testament, And doe intreate my louing freind*es* Mr Iohn Heming*es** and Iohn Lowyn* my fellows ouerseers of the same my last will and Testament, And I giue to my said Executors and Overseers for theire paines (which I intreat them to accept) the some of eleuen shilling*es* a peece to buy them rings to weare in remembrance of me, In wittnes wherof I haue heer vnto sett my hand and seale the fourth day of October in the yeare of our lord God <u>1624</u>   Iohn Vnderwood
(fo. 5) Codicill to be annexed to the last will and Testament of Iohn Vnderwood late of the parishe of little Ste Bartholomewes London deceased made the tenth day of the moneth of October Anno d*o*m*i*ni 1624 or therabout*es* v*i*d*e*lic*e*t his intent and meaning was And soe he did will dispose and bequeath (if his estate would thervnto extend, and it should seeme convenient to his executors) these *p*articulers following in manner and forme followinge scil*i*c*e*t to his daughter Elizabeth two seale Rings of gould one with a deaths head thother w*i*th a red stone in it, To his sonne Iohn Vnderwood a seale Ring of gould w*i*th an A and a B in it, To Burbadge Vnderwood a seale Ring with a blewe stone in it, To Isabell one hoope ring of gould, To his said sonne Iohn one hoope Ringe of gould, To his said daughter Elizabeth one weddinge Ringe, To his said sonne Burbadge one hoope Ringe black and gould To his said sonn Thomas one hoope ringe of gould and one gould ringe w*i*th a knott, To his said daughter Isabell one blewe saphire and one ioynt Ringe of gould, To Iohn Vnderwood one halfe dozen of siluer spoones and one gylt spoone, To Elizabeth one siluer spoone and three gylt spoones, To Burbadge Vnderwood his sonne aforenamed one great gylte spoone one plaine bowle and one roughe bowle. To Thomas Vnderwood his sonn one siluer porringer one siluer taster and one gylt spoone To Isabell his said daughter three siluer spoones two gylt spoones and one gylt Cuppe: Which was soe had and done before sufficient and Credible Witnesses the said Testato*u*r being of perfect minde and memorie./
The will of Iohn Underwood read published and acknowledged for his last will and testament the xxth day of October 1624 in the *p*resence of vs Antho: Marshall Henry Cundall Tho: Smyth Anthoni parrish Richard Lightma<a>ker[5]

1. *louimg*: rightly *louing*.   2. Catchword *And*; new fo. numbered 2.   3. Catchword *That*; new fo. numbered 3.   4. Catchword *the*; new fo. unnumbered.   5. *The will . . . Lightma<a>ker* endorsed fo. 4.

PRO PROB10/419. OW, codicil annexed, prob. clause subscribed (fo. 5) and note of registration endorsed (fo. 4). Will on four sheets joined at the top, the last with signatures of testator and witnesses (latter endorsed) and applied seal; codicil on single sheet, once sewn to rest, now detached. Text of both documents in same secretary, with displayed matter in italic.

Prob. PCC 1 Feb. 1625 to Henry Condell (Cundey), one of his executors, reserving power to other executors, Thomas Sanford and Thomas Smith.

Printed: Malone (1790), I pt 2, 212–15 (RegC); see also Bentley II, 651 (extracts).

fl. 1601–24. Actor; as boy with Children of Chapel in 1601, with King's Men from 1608; held shares in Curtain, Globe and Blackfriars theatres; mentioned in will of Nicholas Tooley (1623). (Chambers II, 348; Nungezer, pp. 384–5; Bentley II, 610–11.)

Isabell] see index.

Blackfryers] not known when testator acquired interest but one housekeepers' share held by an Underwood in 1635 (Bentley VI, 36).

Globe] Chambers speculates that testator succeeded to eighth share of Nathan Field (A1620) in 1619 (II, 424), while T. W. Baldwin suggests he may have secured shares 1612–24 in Globe and Curtain bequeathed to heirs by Thomas Pope (1603) (*Organization*, p. 102).

Curteine] no record of regular playing there after 1625; this reference is one of last indicating theatrical activity (Bentley VI, 137).

Cundey] Henry Condell passed on duties as Underwood's executor in own will (1627); see index.

Heminges] business manager of King's Men (1630); see index.

Lowyn] actor with King's Men from 1603 (Chambers II, 328–9; Nungezer, pp. 238–42; Bentley II, 499–506); see index.

1625 [c.Jan.] undated Robert YARINGTON

The last will' and Tessteementes of Robart yarrantonn. Item I bequee[1] vnto my sonn Thomas Yarrantonn ffoverscore pound: and my wiffe dorrotie yarrantonn full' and whole Exseckettour. Robert Yarranto Wittnes Richard Stretch.

1. *bequee*: rightly *bequeeth*.

PRO PROB10/418. OW, prob. clause subscribed, note of registration marginated. Note subscribed that relict sworn on 18 Jan. 1624, signed by William Sames. Single sheet with testator's signature. Text in facile secretary, probably the hand of Stretch.

Prob. PCC 18 Jan. 1625 to Dorothy Yarington (Yarranton), relict and executor. PAB (PRO PROB8/22 fo. unnumbered (Jan. 1624/5)) gives pa. of origin as St Dionis Backchurch.

fl. 1594–1625. Possibly author, more likely merely scribe, of *Two Lamentable*

Tragedies, conflation of two plays written for Admiral's company, printed 1601 with Yarington's name on title page. (Greg, *Henslowe's Diary*, II, 208–9; Chambers III, 518; B. M. Wagner, 'Robert Yarrington', *MLN*, XLV, 1930, pp. 147–8.)

1625 Aug. 5 Thomas DOWNTON

In the Name of God Amen I Thomas Downton of the Parish of St Gyles without Creplegate Vintner being sick in Body but of perfect mind & Memory, for which the God of heuen be glorifie[1] Do make this my last will & testament in maner & forme foloung,[2] ffirst I bqueth[3] my soule into the handes of Almighty god my Creator & into the Blessed Bosom of Ihesus Christ my Redemer tristing[4] in no other meanes to haue Remisson of my monstrous sims[5] & off<ences> but by his precious[6] shed for me vpon the Cross for me & being saintified & clensed by the grace of the holy Spiritt am assurd of a Ioy full resarecioon at the last to him be prayse & glorie for euer amen Item' I bequeath my body to be buried in the Churchyard of the Parrish Church of St Gylees where I yet liue as nere my first wyfe Ann* Downton as may be ffownd place which I leaue to the discression of my Executrix hereafter mamed[7] Item I giue to my sonn Thomas* Downton all my librarie of books both of Devinitie & humainitie except for[8] Books of Diuinitie & humanitie which my wyfe shall chose Item because my sonn hath bin a desperat sonn to me I giue a desperate legacy ffyfty powndes of one humdred[9] & 30 ll which I haue sude to a Iudgment in the Court of pleas in the Checker office a<l>so I giue him one Ring of gould with a lyon Rampant & the 2 great lettres of his name provided that he shall not Receaue thos legacyes but vpon such occasion as my Executrix shall think fitt no<r> shall he clame or seeke by aniy sinister meanes to wrest the said debt of ffifty powndes from my Executrix or assignes vntill he shall well approue the bond & monny to be in the posession of my Executrix or her Asignes but if he shall otherway do I do vtterly depriue him of any such legacy Item' I giue & bequeath to my sonn Ed my Muskett with the appurtenaiunces & the othe fffifty powndes of the said bond of one hundred & 30 ll vpon the lyke Condiciones to be performed [all as be] as be fore also I giue & bequeath to my Daughter Iaine Downton the som of thirty pondes which is full some of 130 ll du by that bond also I giue my said daughter Iane one bond of 60[10] [ll] pond bill of ffe 30 l' for the payment of 15 l'/[11] I [be] give & bequeathe to [my] all my dawghters some little Remembrance of Edward Shillings According to my poore Abeletie, And I do make & Constitvte Iayne my welbeloved [wife] & Constant wife my sole

Exectatrixe of <A>ll my personall Estate, or of whatsoever I did InIoye before I married her, or whattsoever I have inIoyed or possessed for hir & to her vse since my marriadge to her [being] {freing} my selfe <of> my promise [vder to them {Ether}] that I have not Altered Any Estate of hers since my marriadge to her so to this will I make my Lovinge Cossen Andrew wheatley & Richard waight my overseers Sealead with with my seale & subscribred with my hand this 5th of August 1625 And the the Raigne of our Soveraigne Lord [King] Charles the first of England Scotland ffrance & Ireland Kynge ettc.   Tho Downton
Signed, Sealed & delivered in the presence of vs The mark X of Abraham Sissers[12] Humfry marshall Robertt Baxter

1. *glorifie*: rightly *glorified*. 2. *foloung*: rightly *folowing*. 3. *bqueth*: rightly *bequeth*. 4. *tristing*: rightly *trusting*. 5. *sims*: rightly *sinnes*. 6. *blood* omitted. 7. *mamed*: rightly *named*. 8. *30 l* marginated in a second hand opposite line beginning *for Books* .... 9. *humdred*: rightly *hundred*. 10. *60*: originally *30*; 6 written over 3. 11. Hand changes. 12. *Sissers*: *Ressert* marginated in a third hand; Bentley reads *Rissers* (II, 643).

PRO PROB10/425. OW, grant of admon subscribed, note of registration marginated. Single sheet with signatures and mark of testator and witnesses, sealed. Text written by two hands: (a) to 'of 15 l' (n.11) in crabbed secretary; (b) thence to end in rapid secretary. Testator's signature in italic.

Admon PCC 19 Aug. 1625 to John Worsopp and John Sherrington, creditors, Jane Downton, relict and executor, renouncing. PAB (PRO PROB8/22 fo. unnumbered (Aug. 1625)) notes exhibition of inventory.

Printed: Bentley II, 642–3 (RegC).

fl. 1592–1625. Actor; Strange's 1593, Admiral's 1594, Pembroke's 1597, Admiral's/Prince Henry's/Palsgrave's from 1597 until retirement from stage c.1618. (Chambers II, 313; Nungezer, pp. 117–20; Bentley II, 426; Eccles, 'Actors I', p. 46.)

wyfe Ann] buried St Giles Cripplegate 14 Nov. 1617; Downton married Jane, widow of Oliver Easton, Feb. 1618.

sonn Thomas] possibly provincial actor with Queen Henrietta's 1628, King's Revels 1635 (Bentley II, 426–7).

[1625 c. Sep.] undated Mary BIRD alias BORNE

This is for Theophilus[1]*
The Cockpitt lease* after my yeres are owt* with my mother it is myne in the meane while it must paie debt*es* Also his fathers swoord the Presse of book*es* and print*es* the bed wherein she laye and a Canopie of Chyna

stuffe a payre of blanckettes a payre of sheetes the bolster and the pillowe, and the Orris Coverlidd & the Curtaines & Canapie and Vallance² And after my brother Toms* yeres is owt he must haue forty shillinges to sett vp his trade, To hir mayde Priscilla the petticoate & thirtie shillinges she owed hir for hir wages & also sheele make that vp of her benevolence three powndes for to buie hir a gowne & a yellowe Wastcoate & Mistres Linsle twenty shillinges & The Portall the closett and all the shelues must stand to the howse The next Quarter my sister Layton³* must paie the landlord/Twoe diamond Ringes I giue to Mall, & hir mother must haue the keeping of them till she comes of age and the suite of needleworke three boles & a salt of siluer & half a dosen of spoones of siluer./ Three suites of apparrell videlicet a purple clothe suite a chamlett doblett lay with gold lace & a payre of Tawny breeches and an Ashecolor doblett & a payre of black breeches to remayne & belonge To my Theophilus my sonne in lawe And all the rest of the thinges to my brother Laton & my sister his wife to thuse of the children to increase a stocke./ The marke of Mistris Mary Byrd Iames Holmes* The marke of Mistris Anne Greene.

1. *This is for Theophilus* marginated next to bracketed paragraph. 2. *The Cockpitt . . . Vallance* bracketed in margin. 3. *Layton*: spelled Lacan in admon clause, Laton in RegC (GL MS 9171/24 fo. 649v), Lacon in PAB (GL MS 9168/17 fo. 230r).

GL MS 9172/35. OffC, admon subscribed, note of registration marginated. Single sheet folded to make four pages, unsealed. Text, marginal additions and signatures in same facile secretary. No endorsements of note.

Admon CCL 28 Sep. 1625 to Richard and Catherine Lacan, principal beneficiaries (no executors named). PAB gives pa. of origin as St Giles in the Fields and valuation of inventory at £20 15s <.>.

fl. 1624–5. Widow and executor of actor William Bird alias Borne (**1624**).

Theophilus] (**1663**) actor, son of William Bird; see index. First part of will seems to be his words.
Cockpitt lease] Christopher Beeston leased Cockpit from John Best and his trustees for thirty-one years from 29 Sept. 1616; Hotson believed Beeston was sole lessee of building until death (**1638**) (p. 93). William Bird had no connection with companies known to have acted there and makes no mention in will.
after my yeres are owt] Theophilus, sixteen at time of mother's death, was with Queen Henrietta's Men (?as an apprentice) who played at Cockpit from formation in 1625, but unlikely that he would have a share, unless he had already married into Beeston's family.
my brother Toms] Thomas Bird, third son of William Bird, brother to Theophilus.

my sister Layton] probably sister of Mary Bird; remainder of will seems to be voice of testator.
Holmes] see index.

1625 Dec. 22 Mary BRYAN (abstract)

Of pa. St James at Clarken well co. Middlesex, widow. Sick. Soul 'vnto Almighty god my onely Saviour maker and redeemer by whome and thorough the merittes death and passion of whome I faithfully trust and assuredly beleive to be saved and made partaker with those which shall enter into his blessed Kingdome'. Burial at discretion of executors. To poor of pa. Martin and Mackworth co. Darby where she was born £10, £5 to be paid within one year of death, £5 the next year. To cousin Ann Walker, daughter of Robert Walker of Bredsoe co. Darby, £5 to be paid within three months of death. To cousin Francis Davis, wife of William Davis of London shoemaker, £5 to be paid within three months of death. To cousin John Ambrosse £10 with the bedstead, bedding and furniture thereto belonging on which she now lies. To poor of pa. St James at Clarken well aforesaid £5. To William Ploughman haberdasher, sometime her servant, 40s and one little featherbed. To cousin Hallingshead 20s and her old wearing apparel. To Margery Nash 20s. To Mistress Longford 10s. To Mr Richard Buckley, servant to the Earl of Sussex, £10. To very good friend George Longe* esq. two beer bowls of silver and her best silver salt. To cousin Francis Ashe, goldsmith, two silver bowls. To very good friend Mistres Longe, wife of the said George Longe, gold bracelets which said Mr Richard Buckley has. To Alice Cooke, wife of Richard Cooke fishmonger, one stammel petticoat with a gold lace. Remainder* to kinsman Joseph Coningham, citizen and haberdasher of London, whom she appoints sole executor. Revokes all former wills. Wit. Richard Cooke, Francis Bennit (mark), John Horne scrivener.

PRO PROB10/431. OW, prob. clause endorsed, note of registration marginated. Endorsement in eighteenth-century hand dates will 17 Jan. 1625. Single sheet, filing holes at top, with mark of testator, signatures and marks of witnesses; remnants of applied seals; right margin crumbling with some loss of legibility. Text in engrossing secretary, displayed matter in italic.

Prob. by definitive sentence. PCC 27 Jan. 1626 to Joseph Coningham, kinsman and executor. Sentence (PRO PROB11/148 fos 46r–46v) (Joseph Coningham, promoter, v. Francis Ashe, cousin) declares will valid and confirms Coningham as executor.

fl. 1624–5. Theatre investor; in 1624 granted one share in second Fortune by E. Alleyn (**1626**). Widow of actor, George Bryan (**A1612**). Buried 7 Jan. 1626 St James Clerkenwell. (Nungezer, p. 64; Bentley II, 392–3.)

Longe] Justice of the Peace in 1626 (Bentley I, 265–6).
Remainder] presumably included Fortune share granted for forty-nine and a quarter years 24 Mar. 1624 (Warner, p. 247), reassigned to Tobias Lisle 15 July 1639 (Warner, pp. 54–5).

1626 Nov. 13 Edward ALLEYN

In the name of God Amen the Thirtenthe day of November Anno Domini 1626 And in the second yeare of the raigne of our soveraigne Lord kinge Charles &c I Edward Alleyn of Dulwich in the countie of Surrey Esquire, beinge sicke in bodie but of perfect minde and memorie thanks be given to Almightie God, Doe make and ordaine this my present Testament, declaringe herein my last will in manner and forme followinge That is to saie, ffirst, and principally I commend my soule to Almightie God my [.] mercifull Creator, and to Iesus Christ my most lovinge Saviour and Redeemer, in whome and by whose meritts I onely trust to bee saved and made partaker of everlastinge life, and my body I will to the earth from whence it came without any vaine funerall pompe or shewe to bee enterred in the Quire of that Chappell, which God of his goodnes hath caused me to erect and dedicate to the honor of my Saviour by the name of Christes chappell in Gods–guifte Colledge, heretofore by me founded in Dulwich aforesaid Item my minde and will is, that all such debtes and dueties, which of right or in Conscience I doe owe and stand truely indebted in vnto any person or persons whatsoeuer shalbe truely payd and satisfied after my decease soe shortly and conveniently as may bee. And whereas I the said Edward Alleyn, and one Mathias* Alleyn (he (fo. 2) beinge a person by me putt in trust) for and in performance and assurance of one thousand and five hundred poundes, to and for my Deare and lovinge wyfe Constance* Alleyn, after my Decease haue by two seuerall deedes of Demise graunt and assignement bearinge Date the nyne and twenteth daye of Iune last past before the Date of theise presentes graunted assigned and sett over vnto Sir Nicholas Carew of Beddington and Sir Thomas Crimes* of Peckham in the Countie of Surrey knights theire executors and assignes; one Capitall messuage and tenemente or Inne called ye vnicorne* in St Saviours parishe in the burrough of Southwarke in the Countie of Surrey, and all other Messuages and Tenementes there &c And alsoe I the said Edward Alleyn and Mathias Alleyn by the other, of the said deedes, haue likewise graunted assigned and sett over vnto the said Sir Nicholas Carew and Sir Thomas Crimes theire executors and assignes Certaine Capitall Messuages and tenements called the barge the bell and the Cock, scituate and lyinge on[t] the banck–side in the parishe of St Saviours aforesaid And whereas likewise for further assurance of the said one thousand five (**fo.** 3) hundred poundes for my said wyfe as aforesaid I the said Edward Alleyn haue acknowledged a Statute of two thousand poundes bearinge the said Date of the nyne and twenteth Daye of Iune last, vnto the said Sir Nicholas Carew and Sir Thomas Crimes And whereas by a paire of Indentures of deseasance Dated the {said}[1] nyne and twenteth Daye of Iune last, betweene mee the said Edward Alleyn, and the said Sir Nicholas Carew and Sir Thomas Crimes knights wherein the said two knights haue covennaunted that if my said wyfe (in case she surviue mee) shall by me and out of my estate, be left the said summe of one thousand five hundred poundes in ready money, and that my Executor or Executors shall within three monethes after my decease paie to her the said Constance the said summe of one thousand five hundred poundes That then and not otherwise the said Statute of two thousand poundes to bee void and of none effect, together with the two deedes of assignement, or to reassigne them to such person or persons, as I the said Edward shall nominate and appointe. Nowe in full performance of the aforesaid assurance and to shewe my full desire, to haue [that] {it}[2] (**fo.** 4) really accomplished, I will and require my Executors Here vnder named That first and principally my lovinge wife Constance (in case she surviue mee) bee accordinge to my agreement fullie satisfied in the best manner that may bee, and then I desire the said two knights to reassigne and sett over the said two leases vnto my Executors Item I give and bequeath vnto my said lovinge wife Constance Alleyn in testimonie of my further loue vnto her, and for her present vse and benefitt, one hundred poundes more of lawefull money of England, which I haue already videlicet on the xxvith day of September laste in the presence of Mathewe Sweeteser[3] Edward Alleyn, Iohn Sanford and Iohn Casinghurst, deliuered to and for her vse into the handes and Custodie of the said Sir Thomas Crimes And moreouer I give vnto my said wife, all her Iewells and other ornamentes which she is nowe possessed with all Item I give and bequeath to the Corporation of Godes–guift Colledge* aforesaid these goodes and implementes followinge That is to saie ffirst my seale ringe with my Armes to bee worne by the master and his successors, next I appoint that a common seale shalbe made for the said Colledge at the the charge of my Executors, which said two seales (**fo.** 5) shalbee repayred by the Colledge[d] as often as neede shall require, alsoe all the wainscotts, hanginges, pictures, Carpetts, presses, tables, Chaires, formes, and stooles, in the said Colledge with all shelves, Desks, and seates, alsoe my bookes* and instruments, and likewise all the furniture in the twelue poore schollers Chambers, that is to saie sixe bedsteedes, sixe matts, sixe mattresses, sixe featherbedes, sixe feather boulsters twelue paire of sheetes Twelue blanketts, sixe ruggs, three dozen of bedstaues and sixe pewter Chamber potts Alsoe I giue vnto the said Colledge of my lynnen twelue table Clothes sixe dozen of napkins and sixe towells whereof one sorte or suite shalbe of damaske and other of Diaper likewise two dozen of pewter vessell with all other brasse and Iron vessell of furniture which shalbe in vse of the said Colledge at the hower of my Death in any roome of the said Colledge whatsoeuer Alsoe all implements & tooles of husbandrie together with two furnished teemes, the one with five horse, the other with sixe oxen: and my minde is that all theire goods by mee thus giuen to the said Colledge shalbee by my Executors presently by Inventory delivered vnto them to be continually by the said Colledge kept in good repaire Alsoe I will and require my Executors (**fo. 6**) hereafter named within two yeares after my decease to build ten Almes houses in the parishe of St Buttolph without Bishopsgate London for ten poore people of that parishe to be members of the aforesaid Colledge And likewise ten other houses in St Saviours parishe aforesaid for other ten poore people of the said parishe to be likewise members of the said Colledge, which said twentie poore people beinge placed in theire seuerall houses shall haue such releife and mainetenance, as in the Statutes* of the [a] foresaid Colledge is sett downe Item I giue to Thomas Alleyn* the sonne of Iohn Alleyn late of Willen in the Countie of Buckingham beinge my Cosen and next heire at the Common Lawe the summe of fiftie poundes Item I giue to Edward Alleyn Iunior of Newport the sume of twentie poundes and to his two sisters Elizabeth Newman and Anne Ashpoole twentie poundes a peece And I giue to my Aunt Iane Waldock of Water Eaton the sume of Tenne poundes Item I giue to Anne Alleyn the nowe wife of Iohn Harrison Clerke the sume of twentie pounds Item I will my Copyhold landes in Lambeth Marshe to Edward Alleyn my Godson and his heires males (which I hope the Custome there will allowe[4] and for want of such yssue (**fo. 7**) to Iohn Alleyn the sonne of Mathias Alleyn and his heires for euer Item I giue to Sir ffrancis Calton knight the sume of one hundred poundes and hereby forgive him Twentie poundes hee oweth me on his lettre due longe since Item I giue to Elizabeth Cutler my late wiues* Goddaughter the sume of Tenne poundes Item I giue to Hanna Pickerley the summe of Tenne poundes Item I giue to Elizabeth Russell a young girle that is nowe in my house, tenne poundes, Item I giue to all the rest of my houshold servantes that are in my service at the tyme of my death soe many poundes a peece as they seuerally haue bene and continued yeares in my seruice besides theire wages then due Item I will and bequeath to the Church=wardens of St Buttolphes without Bishopsgate* London and theire successors for euer a tenemente in Dulwich with th'appurtennaunces called the blew=house

nowe in the tenure of Edward Kippinge to and for the onely vse of the poore of theire said parishe to be by them imployed and (fo. 8) disposed of in such manner and forme as in the statutes of Gods Gift [C] Colledge aforesaid is sett downe and not otherwise And my will is And I doe hereby declare that after the said fifteene hundred poundes and all and every the [le] legacyes herein aboue bequeathed shabe[5] respectiuely paid that the said two leases soe assigned as aforesaid to the said Sir Nicholas Carew and Sir Thomas Crimes shalbe and remayne to the said Corporacion of Gods guift Colledge as an augmentacion vnto them duringe the termes thereof over and aboue what I haue already assigned and assured vnto them, To be imployed current accordinge to the intent of the statutes of the said Colledge; And I give and bequeath (after my legacyes [are] payed) to my two executoures herein to be named all my landes in Yorkeshire by what name or names or title soeuer called or knowne, which I lately purchased of George Cole Esquire in theire two names to hold to them and theire two heires and assignes ioyntly for euer And I doe by these presents give and bequeathe all the {rest and}[6] residue of my goods Chattells Cattells and ready money (fo. 9) whatsoeuer after my funeralls are discharged and my debtes payd with all the legacyes of this my will performed vnto Thomas Alleyn* and Mathias Alleyn my kinsmen whome of this my last will and Testament I make my sole executoures Charginge them as they will answeare yt before the face of Almighty God at the Dreadfull daie of Iudgment that they truely and punctually in euery particuler (soe farr forth as they possibly maie) performe this my last will and testament And I doe hereby revoke all former will and wills* by me at any tyme heretofore made, And in witnes of this my last will conteyninge two sheetes of paper I haue to the bottonn of each sheete [subch] subscribed my name and beinge both sheetes ioyned together at the foote thereof sett to my seale the daie and yeare first aboue written./
E Alleyn
Sealed [and] deliuered and published as his last will and Testament in the presence of vs/. Ioseph Redinge/ Mathew Sweeteser/ Henry Dell/ Iohn Casinghurst/ George Brome Scriuener

1. *said*: insertion in second hand. 2. *it*: insertion in same hand. 3. *Sweeteser*: originally *Sweetesi^r*, r struck through, *er* written over *i*. 4. Closing parenthesis missing. 5. *shabe*: rightly *shalbe*. 6. *rest and*: insertion in second hand.

PRO PROB10/443. OffC, note of registration marginated (fo. 1), prob. clause subscribed (fo. 9). Nine numbered sheets sewn at top, unsealed. Subscribed notes record collation with original by Henry Marten, and again by Peter Warde and Henry Daveis (*sic*), both undated, and receipt of original will for use of executors on 14 Dec. 1626, signed by Robert Daveis. Text in engrossing secretary, with displayed matter in hybrid secretary and italic.

Prob. PCC 13 Dec. 1626 to Thomas and Mathias Alleyn, executors. PAB (PRO PROB8/23 fo. unnumbered (Dec. 1626)) records exhibition of inventory.
Printed: *The Alleyn Papers*, ed. J. P. Collier, Shakespeare Society, London, 1843, pp. xxi–xxvi (modernised spelling).
1566–1626. Actor; Worcester's 1583, Admiral's/Prince Henry's from c.1589 until retired from stage c.1606; financial interest in Palsgrave's and Prince Charles's companies; builder/owner of both Fortune theatres; with father–in–law, P. Henslowe (**1616**), Master of the Royal Game of Bears, Bulls and Mastiff Dogs in 1604; founder of Dulwich College. Died 25 Nov., buried 27 Nov. 1626 Dulwich College chapel. Many of legatees and witnesses were officers or tenants of Dulwich College. (J. P. Collier, *Memoirs of Edward Alleyn*, Shakespeare Society, London, 1841; Warner; Young, *Dulwich*; Chambers, II, 296–8; Nungezer, pp. 4–11; Bentley, II, 346–9; G. L. Hosking, *The Life and Times of Edward Alleyn*, London, 1952.)

Mathias] son of Anthony, testator's first cousin, first Warden of College, 1619–31 and Master, 1631–42; left various bequests to College, including 'our ffounder's picture which I bought and now hangs in the dyneing Roome' 1642 (PRO PROB11/189 fos 66v–68r); see index.
Constance] daughter of John Donne, poet and Dean of St Paul's; possibly Alleyn's third wife; married 3 Dec. 1623.
Crimes] or Grymes, witness to deed of foundation of College 13 Sep. 1619, Constance Alleyn's uncle.
vnicorne] Dulwich Coll. Mun. 174 records dispute 25 June 1618 over this property 'late in the tenure of John Allen and others' between Attorney General and William Henslowe and Jacob Meade (**1624**) (Warner, p. 269).
Colledge] by letters patent, 21 June 1619, endowed in mortmain with most of Alleyn's property including Fortune which therefore not included in will.
bookes] Hosking (pp. 237–8) prints garbled list of Alleyn's books without source.
Statutes] reprinted in Young, op. cit., I, 65–92.
Thomas Alleyn] appointed Warden of College, Apr. 1631 (Young, *Dulwich*, I, 103), Master in 1642, not to be confused with first Master of same name.
late wiues] Joan Woodward, Henslowe's stepdaughter, married Alleyn 1592; died 28 Jun. 1623.
St Buttolphes without Bishopsgate] Alleyn baptised there 2 Sept. 1566.
Thomas Alleyn] first Master of Dulwich College, 1619–31; early draft of will refers to him as barber–surgeon; his will of 1631 survives (PRO PROB11/159 fo. 348v). Not to be confused with Thomas Alleyn, Warden in 1631 (see note above).
all former will and wills] two fragmentary drafts survive: 1. undated c.1616–19, Dulwich Coll. MS III fos 129v–130r (Warner, pp. 111–12; printed: Collier, *Memoirs of Edward Alleyn*, p. 183); 2. 1620 Nov. 3, Dulwich Coll. MS V fo. 104r (Warner, p. 143).

Wills

[1627 c.June] undated Henry EVESEED (abstract)

(Eviseede) Of London gent. To his child all his lands, and if child dies without heirs, to cousin John Bouger and his heirs for ever all lands in Delleshulden and Mungin. To cousin Joan Goulson £5 to be paid within two months of death by cousin John Bouger. To cousin Roger Coxe annuity which he had purchased from him. To cousin John Bouger his seal ring to wear for his sake 'prayinge to god for vs all this sicknes time'. Wit. William Johnson, Anne Larrat (mark), William Larratt

PRO PROB10/452. OffC, admon subscribed, note of registration marginated. Notes record 1. collation with original by Gabriel Lyon and Richard Browne, undated, signed; 2. receipt of original will by J. Bouger 25 Sept. 1627, signed. Single sheet folded in half to make four pages. Text in set secretary.

Admon [with will annexed]. PCC 24 Sept. 1627 to John Bouger, cousin and principal legatee, no executor named, Bouger having renounced admon 2 July 1627. PAB (PRO PROB8/24 fo. unnumbered (Sept. 1627)) gives pa. of origin as St Gregory near St Paul's Cathedral, notes renunciation by Bouger 3 July 1627 and sentence nullifying will 1633.

fl. 1615–27. Possibly boy actor; sworn as member of Chapel Royal Sept. 1615, dismissed Mar. 1621 (Hillebrand, 'Early history', pp. 258–9).

1627 Aug. 12 Thomas GILBOURNE (abstract)

(Gilborne) Citizen, and clothworker of London. Sick. Soul 'vnto {Iesus} Christ my sweete saviour, requestinge him to receaue it, as one of his redeemed, to bee satisfied for my sinnes, in his owne selfe, sacrificed, and to couer my vncleannes, with the robe of his righteousnes'. To daughter Anne Astley, wife of Richarde Astley of Chaldewell co. Essex, clerk, and her heirs, freehold land in pa. St Anne and Agnes near Aldersgate in London, which Peeter Betsworth and John Morley, citizens and goldsmiths of London, inhabit. To Tomasin and Margett, daughters of said Richarde and Anne Astley, five bonds, owing to him by the said Richarde Astley their father, in £90, to be equally divided between them. Further to said Tomasin and Marget £5 each to make up the abovesaid £45 to £50 each. To child which his daughter Anne Astley now carries, if born alive and baptised, £50, and if she bears more than one, the said £50 to be divided equally among them. To Allice, daughter of his daughter Marcye, wife of Andrew Barton, goldsmith, £20 to be paid to her two years after death. To cousin Marye Wood £10 to be paid to her at 25s a quarter, the first payment to begin two years after death. To cousin George Dennys, who was brought up in Christ's Hospital in

London, £10 to be paid to him three years after death. To Peter Betsworth, goldsmith, and to his wife 40s each to make each of them a ring, 'with this poesye: Aske not what my ringe did cost I had it by a frende I lost'. To Mr Bridges, brewer at The Labour in Vayne pa. St Marye Mounthawe London, 40s to make him a ring with same message. To poor of pa. Chaldewell in Essex 40s. Rest to daughter Anne Astley whom he appoints executor. Appoints Mr Bridges and Mr Betsworth as overseers. Wit. Peter Betsswth, William Skeath (mark).

PRO PROB10/632. OW, admon clause endorsed, note of registration marginated. Single sheet with applied seal, signatures and marks of testator and witnesses. Text in set Elizabethan secretary, with displayed matter and signature of testator in italic.

Admon PCC 5 Aug. 1642 to Thomasine Astley, niece by his daughter (rightly his granddaughter), Anne Astley alias Gilbourne, daughter and executor, having died. PAB (PRO PROB8/39 fo. unnumbered (Aug. 1642)) gives pa. of origin as St Anne and St Agnes Aldersgate and valuation of inventory at £10, as does note subscribed to admon on will.

Noted: Bentley II, 443 (confuses date of will with date of admon).

fl. 1624–7. Theatre investor; in 1624 granted one share of second Fortune by E. Alleyn. Possible family connection with Samuel Gilburne, actor with King's Men (see index). (Warner, p. 247 (Gibborne); Nungezer, p. 152 (Gibborne); Bentley II, 443 (Gilbourne).)

1627 Dec. 13 Henry CONDELL

<In the name of> God Amen I Henry Cundall of London gentleman being sicke in body but of perfect mynd and memorie laud and praise be therefore given to Almightie God Calling to my remembraunce that there is nothing in this world more sure and certaine to mankind then death and nothing more vncertaine then the houre thereof doe therefore make and declare this my last will and Testament In manner and forme followeing That is to say ffirst I Commend my soule into the handes of Almightie God trusting and assuredlie beleeueing that onlie by the merrittes of the pretious death and passion of my Lord and Saviour Iesus Christ I shall obtaine full and free pardon and remission of all my sinnes and shall enioy everlasting life in the Kingdome of Heaven amongest the elect Children of God My Bodie I Committ to the Earth to be decentlie buried in the night tyme in such parishe where yt shall please God to call me. My worldlie substaunce I dispose of as followeth And first concerninge all and singuler my ffreehold Messuages landes T<enementes> and hereditamentes whatsoeuer with their and euerie of their appurtenaunces whereof I am and stand seised of and manner of estate of inheritaunce I

give devise and (fo. 2) bequeath the same as followeth Inprimis I give devise and bequeath all & singuler my freehold Messuages landes Tenementes and hereditamentes whatsoeuer with their and euerie of their appurtenaunces scituate lying and being in Helmet Court in the Strond and elswhere in the County of Middlesex vnto Elizabeth* my welbeloued wife for and during the terme of her naturall life And from and ymediatlie after her decease [vnto my sonne] vnto my sonne Henry Cundall and to the heires of his bodie lawfully to be begotten And for default of such yssue vnto my sonne William Cundall and to the heires of his bodie lawfully to be begotten And for defalilt[1] of such yssue vnto my daughter Elizabeth ffinch* and to her heires and assignes for euer Item I give devise and bequeath all and singuler my freehold Messuages landes Tenementes and hereditamentes whatsoeuer with their and euerie of their appurtenaunces scituate lying and being in the parrishe of St Bride alias Bridgett neere fleetestreete London and elswhere in the Citie of London and the suburbes thereof vnto my welbeloued wife Elizabeth Cundall and to her assignes vntill m<y> sonne William Cundall his terme of Apprentishood* shalbe fully expired by effluxion of tyme And from and ymediatlie after the said terme of Apprentishood shalbe soe fully expired I give devise and bequeath the same Messuages and premisses (fo. 3) scituate in the Citie of London and the suburbes thereof vnto my said sonne William Cundall and to the heires of his bodie lawfully to be begotten And for default of such yssue vnto my said sonne Henry Cundall and to the heires of his bodie lawfully to be begotten And for default of such yssue vnto my said daughter Elizabeth ffinch and to her heires and assignes for euer And as concerninge all and singuler my goodes Chattelles Plate houshouldstuffe ready money debtes and personall estate whatsoeuer and wheresoeuer I give devise and bequeath the same as followeth videlicet Inprimis whereas I am Executour of the last will and Testament of Iohn Vnderwood* deceased and by force of the same Executorshipp became possessed of soe much of the personall estate of the said Iohn Vnderwood which is expressed in an Inventarie therof made and by me exhibited in due forme of lawe into the Ecclesiasticall Court and whereas also in discharge of my said Executorshipp I haue from tyme to tyme disbursed divers sommes of money in the educacion and bringing vpp of the [said] Children of th<e said> Iohn Vnderwood deceased As by my Accomptes kept in that behalf appeareth Nowe in discharge of my Conscience and in full performaunce of the trust reposed in me by the said Iohn Vnderwood I doe charge my Executrixe faithfully to (fo. 4) to pay to the survyving Children of the said Iohn Vnderwood All and whatsoeuer shalbe found and appeare by my Accomptes to belong vnto them And to deliuer vnto them all such Ringes as was their late fathers and which are by me kept by themselues a part in a little Caskett Item I doe make name ordaine and appoint my said welbeloued wife Elizabeth Cundall the full and sole Executrixe of this my last will and Testament Requireing and chargeing her as she will answere the contrarie before Almightie God att the dreadfull daie of Iudgement that she will truly and faithfully performe the same in and by all thinges according to my true intent and meaninge And I doe earnestlie desire my very loueing freindes Iohn Heminges* gent Cuthbert Burbadge* gent my sonne in lawe Harbert ffinch and Peter Saunderson Grocer to be my Ouerseers and to be ayding and assisting vnto my said Executrixe in the due execucion and performaunce of this my last will and Testament And I give and bequeath to euerie of my said ffoure seuerall Ouerseers the somme of ffyve poundes a peece to buy each of them a peece of Plate Item I gve² devise and bequeath vnto my said sonne William Cundall all the Cleere yearelie rentes and proffittes which shall arrise and come from the tyme of my decease of and by my Leases and termes of yeares of all my (fo. 5) Messuages houses and places scituate in the Blackfryers London and att the Banckside in the County of Surry vntill such tyme as that the full somme of Three hundred poundes by those rentes and proffittes may be raysed for a stocke for my said sonne William yf he shall soe long lyve Item forasmuch as I haue by this my will dealt very bountifully with my welbeloued wife Elizabeth Cundall considering my estate I doe give and bequeath vnto my sonne Henry Cundall for his maintemaunce³ either att the Vniversitie or elswhere One Annuitie or yearelie somme of Thirtie poundes of lawfull money of England To be payd vnto my said sonne Henry Cundall or his assignes during all the terme of the naturall life of the said Elizabeth my wife yf my said sonne Henry Cundall shall soe long lyve Att the ffoure most vsuall ffeastes daies or termes in the yeare That is to say Att the ffeastes of the Birth of our Lord Iesus Christ Thanunciacion of the blessed virgin Marie the Nativity of St Iohn Baptist and St Michaell Tharchaungell Or within th\<e\> space of Twenty and Eight daies next ensueing after euerie of the same ffeastes daies by euen and equall porcions The first payment thereof to begin and to be made att such of the said ffeastes daies as shall first and next happen after the (fo. 6) daie of my decease Or within the space of Twenty and Eight daies next ensueing after the same ffeast daie Item [Item] I give and bequeath vnto widdowe Martyn and widdowe Gymber to each of them respectyvelie for and during all the termes of their naturall lives seuerallie yf my Leases and termes of yeares of and in my houses in Aldermanbury in London shall soe long continue vnexpired One Annuitie or yearelie somme of Twenty shillinges \<a peece of\> lawfull money of England To be payd vnto them seuerallie by euen porcions quarterly att the ffeastes daies aboue mencioned Or within the space of Twenty and Eight daies next ensueing after euerie of the same ffeastes daies The payment of them seuerallie to begin and to be made att such of the said ffeastes as shall first and next

happen after my decease Or within the space of Twenty and Eight daies
next ensueing after the same ffeast Item I give devise and bequeath vnto
the poore people of the parrishe of ffulham in the County of Middlesex
where I nowe dwell the somme of ffyve poundes To be payd to Mr Doctor
Clewett and Mr Edmond Powell of ffulham gent and by them to be
distributed Item I give devise and bequeath vnto my said Welbeloued wife
Elizabeth Cundall and to my said welbeloued daughter Elizabeth ffinch
(fo. 7) All my houshouldstuffe Bedding Lynnen Brasse and Pewter
whatsoeuer remaineing & being aswell att my house in ffulham aforesaid
as also in my house in Aldermanbury in London to be equally devided
betweene them parte and partelike And for the more equall dealing in
that behalf I will appoint and request my said Ouerseers or the greater
nomber of them to make devision thereof and then my wife to haue the
preferment of the Choice Item I give and bequeath vnto my Cosen
ffraunces Gurney alias Hulse my Auntes daughter the somme of ffyve
poundes and I give vnto the daughter of the said ffraunces the like somme
of ffyve poundes Item I give devise and bequeath vnto such and soe manie
of the daughters of my Cosen Gilder late of newe Buckenham in the
County of Norffolk deceased as shalbe lyveing att the tyme of my decease
the somme of ffyve poundes a peece Item I give and bequeath vnto my
old servant Elizabeth Wheaton* a mourninge gowne and fforty shillinges
in money and that place or priviledge which she nowe exerciseth and
enioyeth in the houses of the Blackfriers London and the Globe on the
Banckside for and during all the terme of her naturall life yf my estate
shall soe long continue in the premisses And I give vnto the daughter of
the said Elizabeth Wheaton the somme of ffyve (fo. 8) poundes To be
payd vnto the said Elizabeth Wheaton for the vse of her said daughter
within the space of One yeare next after my decease And I doe hereby
will appoint and declare That an Acquittaunce vnder the hand and seale
of the said Elizabeth Wheaton vpon the receipt of the said legacie of ffyve
poundes for the vse of her said daughter shalbe and shalbe deemed
adiudged construed and taken to be both in lawe in equitie vnto my
Executrixe a suffitient release and discharge for and concerninge the
payment of the same Item I give devise and bequeath All the rest and
residue of my goodes Chattelles Leases money debtes and personall estate
whatsoeuer and wheresoeuer (after my debtes shalbe payd and my
ffunerall charges and all other charges about the execucion of this my will
first payd and discharged) vnto my said welbeloued wife Elizabeth
Cundall Item my will and mynd is and I doe hereby devise and appoint
That all such legacies giftes and bequestes as I haue by this my will given
devised or bequeathed vnto anie person or persons for payment whereof
noe certaine time is hereby before limited or appointed shalbe well and
truly payd by my Executrixe within the space of One yeare next (fo. 9)

after my decease ffinally I doe hereby revoke Countermaund and make voyd all former will*es* Testament*es* Codicill*es* Executo*u*rs legacies and bequest*es* whatsoeuer by me att anie tyme heretofore named {made} given or appointed willing and mynding that theis p*rese*nt*es* only shall stand and be taken for my last will and Testament and none other In Witnes whereof I the said Henry Cundall the Testato*u*r to this my present last will and Testament beinge written in Nyne sheet*es* of paper with my name subscribed to euerie sheete haue sett my seale the Thirteenth day of december In the Third yeare of the Raigne of our Soueraigne Lord Charles by the grace of God King of England Scotland ffraunce and Ireland defendo*u*r of the ffaith &c   Henry Cundall
Signed sealed pronounced and declared by the said Henry Cundall the Testato*u*r as his last will and Testament on the daie and yeare aboue written in the p*rese*nce of vs whose names are herevnder written Robart Younge Hum: Dyson* Notary Publiq*ue* And of me Ro: Dickens s*er*vant vnto the said Notary

1. *defalilt*: rightly *default*. 2. *gve*: rightly *give*. 3. *maintemaunce*: rightly *maintenaunce*.

PRO PROB10/457. OW, probate clause subscribed (fo. 9), note of registration marginated (fo. 1). Nine numbered sheets sewn together at top, each bearing Condell's signature; unsealed with signatures; right margin damaged with some loss of text. Text in engrossing secretary, with displayed matter in hybrid secretary, text enclosed within ruled frame; same hand writes will of N. Tooley (**1623**), possibly of scribe, Robert Dickens.

Prob. PCC 24 Feb. 1628 to Elizabeth relict and executor. PAB (PRO PROB8/25 fo. 19v) and note endorsed on will (fo. 9) gives pa. of origin as Fulham co. Middlesex.

Printed: Malone (1790), I pt. 2, 199–205; see also Bentley II, 640–2 (abstract).

fl. 1598–1625. Actor; Chamberlain's/King's Men from 1598; housekeeper in Globe and Blackfriars; compiler with John Heminges (**1630**) of First Folio. Mentioned in wills of King's Men: Augustine Phillips (**1605**), Alexander Cooke (**1614**), William Shakespeare (**1616**); named as executor by Nicholas Tooley (**1623**) and John Underwood (**1624**). Buried St Mary Aldermanbury 29 Dec. 1627. (Chambers II, 310–11; Nungezer, pp. 98–101; Bentley II, 410–12.)

Elizabeth] (**1635**); see index.
Elizabeth ffinch] see index.
Wil*li***am Cundall his terme of Apprentishood]** apprenticed to haberdasher Edward Pate 1625 (Bentley II, 413); see index.
Vnderwood] see index.
Heminges] fellow housekeeper in Globe and Blackfriars; see index.
Burbadge] fellow housekeeper in Globe and Blackfriars (**A1636**); see index.
Wheaton] gatherer (Bentley II, 616–17); see index.
Dyson] see index.

1628 June 7 Jaques JONES

In the name of God Amen The Seaventh day of Iune In the ffowerth yere of the reigne of our Souereigne Lord Charles (by grace of God King of England Scotland ffraunce and Ireland defender of the ffaith etc.[1] I Iaques Iones of london yeoman being att this pre*se*nte sick and weake in bodie [but of] but of good and p*er*fect minde and memory thank*es* be therefore given to Almightie God, And considering with my selfe the frailtie of this Transitorie life and the vncerteinty of the hower of my death, And being willing to settle and limitt a certeine course for the disposing of such worldly good*es* substance and other blessing*es* as it hath pleased God to bestow vpon mee, doe therefore make and ordeine this my pre*se*nte Testament Conteining therein my last will in manner and forme following That is to say: ffirst and principally I Comend my soule into the hand*es* of Almightie God in a constant faith and beleife and full assurance of the ffree remission pardon and forgiunes of all my sinns And that after this life ended I shall inheritt eternall life in the kingdome of Heaven with all the Elect Children of God And that by and through the mercie of Almightie God, and the most pretious death passion righteousnes and glorious resurrection of Iesus Christ my onely and alone savioure and none other nor otherwise, And my bodie I Comitt to the Earth from Whence it came to be buried in a decent Comly and *christi*anlike[2] mann*er* att and by the good discretion of my Executrix hereafter named Item my will and minde is that all such debt*es* as I shall truly owe and be indebted to anie p*er*son or persons att the time of my decease, shalbe forthwith soe soone after Conveniently may be paid and satisfied (or when and soe soone as the same shall grow due) by my said Executrix hereafter named And as concerning the disposition of all and singular such goods Chattells and other substance as it hath pleased God to bestow vpon mee I doe giue and bequeath the same as followeth (Vizt) Inprimis I giue and bequeath vnto my Daughter Mary Iones whoe (as I hope) now liveth in Virginia the somme of ffive Pounds of lawfull money of England to be paid vnto her att her lawfull age of Twentie and one* Yeres Item I giue and bequeath vnto my daughter Anne Iones the somme of Tenne pounds of like money Item giue and bequeath vnto my daughter Elizabeth Iones the somme of Tenn pounds of like money, to be paid vnto them and either of them att {their} seu*er*all and lawfull ages of Twentie and one yeres seu*er*all daies of Marriage which shall first happen come or bee And all the rest of my good*es* Chattells howshold stuff Plate money Iewells and all other thing*es* whatsoeu*er* I give will and bequeath vnto Alice, my loving wife whome I make full and sole executrix of this my pre*se*nte Testament and last Will hereby reuoking all former will and wills by mee

162 Playhouse wills, 1558–1642

made and doe pronounce and declare this and none other to be my verie true and last will and Testament In witnes whereof I haue herevnto sett my hand and seale the daie and yere aboue said.
 the marke of the X said Iaques Iones Sealed subscribed pronounced and declared by the said Iaques Iones as and for his last Will and Testament the day and Yere abouesaid in the presence of Rich: Alsope Scriuener Darby Yonge And of me Roberti Wallis seruant to the said Scriuener

1. Closing parenthesis omitted.   2. *christianlike*: xpanlike in MS.

GL MS 9052/7. OW, prob. clause subscribed. Single sheet, sealed, bearing the mark of the testator and the signatures of witnesses. Text in set secretary with displayed matter in hybrid secretary and italic.

Prob. ACL 20 Apr. 1629 to Alice, relict and executor. Note subscribed on will gives pa. of origin as St Katharine Coleman.

fl. 1602–28. Possibly actor; Admiral's Men 1602. Identification rests on 1. unusual form of Christian name, 2. Jack Jones appears in 1602 'plot' of *I Tamar Cam*. 3. John Jones 'a player' from Houndsditch resident 1615 in pa. St Botolph Aldgate which abuts St Katherine Coleman, 4. John Jones baptised daughter Mary St Botolph Aldgate 1610 (E.M. Denkinger, 'Actors' names in the registers of St Bodolph Aldgate', *PMLA*, XLI, 1926, pp. 91–109 (p. 101)). (Nungezer, p. 207; Bentley II, 485–6.)

Mary Iones . . . att her lawful age of Twentie and one] i.e. born after 1607.

1629 Jan. 30 Robert LEE

Leigh[1]
In the name of god amen I Robert Leigh of the <parish of St> Iames at Clarkenwell in the County of midd*lesex* gent beinge at this present tyme sicke & w<eak in> body but of sounde & perfect Remembrance thanckes be given to Almightie god for the same Doe here ordeyne and make this my last will & Testame*n*t in writinge in manner followinge v*id*elice*t* And first and principally I Comytt & Comende my Soule into the hand*es* of Allmightie God my Creator Trustinge & assuredly beleeveinge through the merritt*es* death and passion of Iesus Christ his only Sonne and my only and alone Saviour and redeemer, to haue full remission & forgivenes of all my synns and offences and to be saved vnto everlastinge <life> my body I Comytt to the grounde from whence yt came to be buryed in decent & Christia<n> manner at the discretion of myne Executrix herevnder named And as Concernin<g> the worldly good*es* which it hath pleased god of his goodnes to blesse me withall I doe bequeath and dispose of the

same in manner followinge (that is to say) Inprim<is> I give & bequeath
vnto the poore people of the parish of St Iames at Clarkenwell aforesai<d>
The some of ffortie shillinges of English money to be distributed amongst
them in bread vpon the next day after my buriall, by the appointment of
myne Executrix Item I give vnto my Sister Margarett Clarke dwellinge in
Greenewich ffortie shillinges of like English money to be payd vnto her
by myne Executrix within Three monethes nex<t> after my decease Item
I give vnto my [Sister] {Cossen} Anne Hill wife of Richard Hill the some
of Twenty shillinges of like money And to my Cossen Ione Baxter* wife
of Rich<ard> Baxter* of the said parish of Clarkenwell the like some of
Twenty Shillinges of l<ike> english money And vnto her Twoe Children
{William & Richard}* I give each of them Tenn shillinges a pee<ce> And
to my Cossen Audrey Potter wife of Henry Potter [Goldsmith] I give and
bequeath the some of Twenty shillinges of like money And vnto my
loveinge freind mr Robert Treat* {Goldsmith} I give & bequeath the
some of Twenty shillinges Item I give and bequeath vnto my addopted
daughter Darkas Woodgate alias Leig<h> The some of Three poundes of
lawfull money of England to buy her a gowne All which Legacyes (my
will & mynde is,) shall be payde by myne Executrix within Three
monethes next after my decease, The Rest and residue of all & singuler
my goodes Cattells, Chattells Landes Tenementes Leases plate Aparell
howseholdstuffe and all other my goodes whatsoever (my debtes and
Legacies beinge payde & my ffunerall expences discharged) I doe give and
bequeath vnto my loveinge wife Constance Leigh To have holde & enioy
the same duringe her naturall life And after her decease I {desire my wife
to} giue & bequeath the Remaynder[2] to my said Addopted daughter
Darkas to her & her assignes for ever And I doe hereby appoynt & make
my said loveinge wife Constance Leigh my full & sole Executrix of this
my last will And I doe renounce all former wills And this shall stand &
be my last will & Testament and none other nor other wise In witnes
whereof I haue herevnto sett my hand & Seale The Thirtieth daye of
Ianuary Anno Domini one Thousand Sixe hundred Twentie and Eight./
Sealed subscribed and deliuered by the Testator and declared to be his
last will & Testament in the presence of vs Rich: Gill Scr[3]

Rob't Leigh

1. *Leigh*: superscribed.   2. *Remaynder*: written over erasure.   3. *Scr*: mark of abbreviation omitted; rightly *Scrivener*.

GL MS 9052/7. OW, prob. clause endorsed with note of exhibition of inventory, valued at £212 8s 4d. Single sheet, with seal and signatures of testator and witness. Document damaged on right margin with some loss of text. Facile secretary with displayed matter in Chancery style, corrections in same hand and ink as text, probably hand of Richard Gill.

Prob. ACL 18 Jun. 1629 to Constance, relict and executor.

c.1569–1629. Actor; Admiral's or Strange's c.1590, Queen Anne's from 1604 in London and provinces; patentee for Children of Queen's Revels in 1617–18 with Nicholas Long (**A1622**), Philip Rosseter (**1623**) and William Perry; returned to Queen Anne's by 1619; with Players of Revels at the Red Bull 1622; licensed, with Thomas Basse (**1634**), Ellis Worth (**1659**) and others, to form company to be known as Children of Revels 1622; granted half of sixth share in new Fortune by E. Alleyn 1623. (Chambers II, 328; Nungezer, pp. 235–6; Bentley II, 496–7; Sisson, 'Notes', p. 28.)

Ione Baxter] Joan Ellit married Richard Baxter St James Clerkenwell 1614 (Bentley II, 361).
Rich<ard> Baxter] actor; fellow member of Queen Anne's 1605–6, Children of Queen's Revels 1624 (1623 according to Murray I, 362) (Nungezer, pp. 32–3; Bentley II, 360–2).
Richard] Richard, son of Richard Baxter, christened St James Clerkenwell 1618 (Bentley II, 361).
Treat] see index.

[1629 c.July] undated Thomas GOFFE (abstract)

Clerk, Batchelor of Divinity, late parson of Eastclandon co. Surrey. About four days before death. To son-in-law John Frances his horse. Remainder to wife Elizabeth Goffe. Wit. Mr William Quelch, clerk, parson of Easthorsley co. Surrey, Frances Wanham wife of Francis Wanham of Eastclandon (mark), John Frances.

GLRO DW/PA/5/1629/37. OW (nuncupative). admon clause subscribed, note of exhibition of inventory endorsed. Single sheet with signatures of witnesses.

Admon ACS 26 Oct. 1629 to Elizabeth Goffe, widow, by commission to William Quelch, vicar of Carshalton co. Surrey, no executors having been named.

c.1591–1629. Dramatist; no plays published before death although tragedies performed by students of Christ Church while at Oxford. *Careless Shepherdess* acted by Queen Henrietta's at Salisbury Court c.1638. Buried in chancel of East Clandon church 27 July 1629. (Bentley IV, 498–511.)

1630 Oct. 9 John HEMINGES

In the name of <god amen the> ixth day of October 163<0> and in the Sixth yeere of the raigne of our sou*e*raigne lord Charles by the grace of God kinge of England Scotland ffraunce and Ireland defender of the faith

&c. I Iohn Heminges Citizen and Grocer of London beinge of perfect minde and memory (Thankes be therefore given vnto Almighty God) yett well knowinge and Considering the frailty and incertenty of mans life doe therefore make ordeine and declare this my last Will and Testament in manner and forme following ffirste and principally I giue and bequeath my soule in to the handes of Almighty God my maker and Creator hopeinge and assuredly beleiving through the onely merittes death and passion of Iesus Christ my Saviour and redeemer to obteine remission and pardon of all my sinnes and to enioy eternall happines in the kingdome of heaven And my body I Comitt to the earth to be buried in Christian manner in the parrish Church of Mary Aldermanbury in London as neere vnto my loueinge wife Rebecca* Heminges who lieth there interred and vnder the same stone which lieth in parte over her there if the same Conveniently may be wherein I doe desire my Executor hereinafter named Carefully to see my Will performed and that my funerall (**fo. 2**) may be in decent and Comely manner performed in the Evening without any vaine pompe or Cost therein to be bestowed Item my Will is that all such debtes as I shall happen to owe at the time of my decease to any person or persons (being truly and properly mine owne debtes) shalbe well and truly satisfied and paid assoone after my decease as the same Conveniently may be And to that intent and purpose my will and minde is And I doe hereby lymitt and appointe that all my leases goodes Chattells plate and housholdstuff whatsoever which I haue or shalbe possessed {of} at the time of my decease ([Except the severall leases and termes for yeeres which I haue in the severall Playhowses of the Globe and Blackfriers* onely And also except such severall parcells of housholdstuff goodes and Chattells which I shall hereinafter by theis presentes particulerly giue and bequeath vnto and amongest my Children to be taken by them or any of them in kinde without alteracion]) shall imediatly after my decease be sold to the most and best benefitt and advantage that the same or any of them may or Can And that the moneys thereby raised shall goe and be imployed towardes the payment and dischardge of my said debtes assoone as the same may be Converted into moneys and be received without fraude or Coven And that if the same leases goodes and Chattells shall not raise so much money as shalbe sufficient to to pay my debtes Then my will and minde is And I doe (**fo. 3**) hereby will and appointe that the moity or one half of the yeerely benefitt and proffitt of the severall partes which I haue by lease in the severall Playhowses of the Globe and Blackfryers [aforesaid] for and during such time and terme as I haue therein be from time to time received and taken vp by my Executor[s] hereinafter named and by [them] {him} from time to time faithfully imployed towardes the payment of such of my said owne proper debtes which shall remaine vnsatisfied and that proporcionably to every person and persons to whome I shall then remaine indebted vntill by the said moity or one half of the said yeerely benefitt and proffitt of the said partes they shalbe satisfied and paid without fraude or Coven [And to that intent and purpose I the said Iohn Heminges by a Certen dede or writing in that behalf made sealed and delivered haue already assigned and Conveyed the s<ame> my partes in the said Playhowses which I doe hereby lymitt and appointe shalbe firste and principally towardes the payment of my said debtes being properly my owne debtes which {whereby} I hope if the same partes shalbe imployed in playing there wilbe sufficient moneye in reasonable time raised for payment thereof] And if the said moity or one half of the said yeerely benefitt of my said partes in the said Playhowses shall not in some Convenient time raise sufficient moneys to pay my said owne debtes Then my will and minde is and I doe hereby lymitt and appointe that the other moity or half parte of the benefitt and proffitt of my said partes in the said Playhowses be also received and taken vp by my said Executor[s] hereinafter named and faithfully from time to time imployed and paid towardes (fo. 4) the speedier satisfaction and payment of my said debtes And then after my said debtes shalbe so satisfied and paid then I lymitt and appointe the said benefitt and proffitt arrising by my said partes in the said Playhowses and the imployment of the same to be received and imployed towardes the payment of the legacyes by me hereinafter given and bequeathed and to the raising of porcions for such of my said Children as at the time of my decease shall haue received from me no advauncement And I doe hereby desire [aswell] my executor[s] herein after named [as also the Assignees to whome I haue {so} as aforesaid assigned my said partes] to see this my will and meaning herein to be well and truly performed according to the trust and Confidence by me in [them] {him} reposed Item I giue devise and bequeath vnto my daughter Rebecca Smith nowe wife of Captaine William Smith my best suite of linnen wrought with Cutworke which was her mothers And to my sonne Smith her husband his wives picture sett vp in a frame in my howse Item I giue and bequeath vnto my daughter Margarett Sheppard wife of Mr Thomas Sheppard* my red Cushions imbrothered with bugle which were her mothers And to my said sonne Sheppard his wives picture which is also sett vp in a frame in my howse Item I giue and bequeath vnto my daughter Elizabeth my greene Cushions which were her mothers Item I give and bequeath vnto my daughter Merefeild my Cloth of silver striped Cushions which were her mothers Item I giue and bequeath vnto so many of my daughter (fo. 5) Merefieldes and my daughter Sheppardes Children as shalbe living at the time of my decease ffifty shillinges a peece Item I giue and bequeath vnto my grandchilde Richard Atkins the somme of ffive poundes of lawfull money of England to buy him bookes Item I giue and bequeath vnto my sonne in lawe Iohn Atkins* and his nowe wife if they shalbe living at the time of my decease fforty shillinges to make them two ringes for remembrances of me Item I giue and bequeath vnto every of my fellowes and sharers* his Maiestes servauntes which shalbe living at the time of my decease the somme of Tenn shillinges a peece to make them ringes for remembrances of me Item I giue and bequeath vnto Iohn Rice* Clerke of St Saviours in Southwarke (if he shalbe living at the time of my decease) the somme of Twenty shillinges of lawfull English money for a remembrance of my loue vnto him Item I giue and bequeath vnto the poore of the parish of St Mary Aldermanbury where I longe lived and whither I haue bequeathed my body for buriall the somme of fforty shillinges of lawfull English money to be distributed by the Chuchwardens of the same parish where most need shalbe Item my will and minde is and I doe hereby lymitt and appointe that the severall legacyes and sommes of money by me herein before bequeathed to be paid in money be raised and taken out of the yeerely proffitt and benefitt which shall arrise or be made by my severall partes and shares in the severall playhowses Called the Globe and Blackfriers after my said debtes shalbe paid with as much speed (**fo. 6**) as the same Conveniently may be And I doe hereby will require and Chardge my Executor[s] hereinafter named especially to take care that my debtes firste and then those legacies be well and truly paid and dischardged assoone as the same may be so raised by the sale of my goodes and by the yeerely proffittes of my partes and shares and that my estate may be so ordered to the best proffitt and advantage for the better payment of my debtes and dischardge of my legacies before mencioned with as much speede as the same Conveniently may be according as I haue herein before in theis presentes [and in the said dede or writing before mencioned] directed and appointed the same to be without any lessening diminishing or undevaluing thereof Contrary to my true intent and meaning herein declared And for the better performance thereof my will minde and desire is that my said partes in the said Playhowses should be imployed in playing the better to raise proffitt thereby as formerly the same haue bine and haue yeilded good yeerely proffitt as by my bookes will in that behalf appeare And my will and minde is and I doe hereby ordeine lymitt and appointe that after my debtes funeralls and legacies shalbe paid and satisfied out of my estate That then the residue and remainder of my goodes Chattells and Credittes whatsoever shalbe equally parted and devided to and amongest such of my Children as at the time of my decease shalbe vnmarried or vnadvaunced* and shall not haue received from me any porcion in marriage or otherwise further then onely for (**fo. 7**) theire educacion and breeding parte and partelike And I doe hereby ordeine and make My sonne William Heming*es** to be the[1] Executor[s] of this my last Will and Testament requiring [them] {him} to see the same performed in and by all thing*es* according to my true meaning herein declared. And I doe desire and appoint my Loving freind*es* Mr Burbage* & Mr Rice—[2] to be the Overseers of this my last Will and Testament praying them to be ayding and assisting to my said Executor with theire best advice and Councell in the execuc*i*on thereof And I doe hereby vtterly revoke all former Wills by me heretofore made And doe pronounce publish and declare this to be my last Will and Testament In witnes whereof I haue herevnto put my hand and seale the day and yeere firste abouewritten.//

1. *to be the*: added at end of line after *Heminges*.   2. Space left in MS; *Rice* written in paler ink.

PRO PROB10/484. OW, prob. clause subscribed (fo. 7) and note of registration marginated (fo. 1). Eight sheets, each numbered, joined at the top, the last blank; unsigned and unsealed. Text in engrossing secretary with displayed matter in hybrid secretary; emendations (ll. 27–32, 41, 43–4, 49–56, 61, 70–2, 74, 108, 115–16, 131, 134), possibly in same hand as text but more carelessly written and in paler ink, change references to executors from plural to singular and remove references to earlier assignment of playhouse property. Some damage to the top of first sheet. No significant endorsements.

Prob. PCC 11 Oct. 1630 to William Heminges (Hemings), son and executor. Note subscribed to will (fo. 7) by William Sammes, dated 11 Oct. 1630, recording oath of John Rice and William Atkins 'de ver*i*tate huius test*a*ment*i*', has been deleted. The status of this document is unclear; it is neither sealed nor signed, no witnesses named, proof of authenticity has been deleted, but prob. clause marks its acceptance by the courts. PAB (PRO PROB8/27 fo. 100r) gives pa. of origin as St Saviour's Southwark.

Printed: Malone (1790), I pt 2, 191–5 (RegC which omits the deleted passages in OW); see also Bentley II, 643–5 (extracts).

fl. 1588–1630. Actor; Queen's, Strange's 1593, from 1594 Chamberlain's/ King's Men for whom acted as business manager; probably ceased acting by c.1612 although listed as company member until 1629. Named in wills of other King's Men: Augustine Phillips (**1605**), Alexander Cooke (**1614**), Richard Cowley (**1618**), John Underwood (**1624**) and Henry Condell (**1627**). Original housekeeper in Globe and Blackfriars. Trustee for Shakespeare's Blackfriars property in 1613 and legatee in his will (**1616**). With Condell compiled First Folio. Buried St Mary Aldermanbury 12 Oct. 1630. (Chambers II, 320–3; Nungezer, pp. 179–86; Bentley II, 465–9.)

wife Rebecca] formerly widow of actor William Knell (A1587), buried St Mary Aldermanbury 2 Sep. 1619.
Globe and Blackfriers] held one tenth of Globe in 1598, one seventh of Blackfriars in 1608; by 1630 increased share to four sixteenths of Globe and two eighths of Blackfriars (Baldwin, *Organization*, pp. 90–117).

Thomas Sheppard] see index.

Atkins] married Alice Heminges 1613, who presumably died before 1630; may be Atkins who held part of Globe property in trust for Heminges c.1615 and/ or scrivener of same name appointed overseer in will of John Shank (1635) (Bentley II, 351).

fellowes and sharers] members of King's company at that time included John Lowin, Robert Benfield, John Shank (1635), Richard Sharpe, Thomas Pollard (A1653), Joseph Taylor, John Thompson, Eyllaerdt Swanston (1651), Anthony Smith, John Honyman (1636), Alexander Gough, Richard Baxter (Bentley I, 84–5).

Rice] Heminges's apprentice; boy actor with King's 1607 and 1610, Lady Elizabeth's 1611, King's company 1619–c.1626 (Chambers II, 336; Nungezer, pp. 296–7; Bentley II, 546–7).

my Children . . . vnmarried or vnadvaunced] does not name daughter Thomasine, widow of actor William Ostler (A1614), with whom in dispute in 1615 over ownership of her husband's shares in Blackfriars and Globe.

William Heminges] dramatist; 1633–4 sold three shares in Globe and two in Blackfriars to John Shank (Bentley II, 470; IV, 539–47).

Burbage] Cuthbert Burbage (A1636); housekeeper in Globe and Blackfriars; see index.

1631 Nov. 12 Elizabeth HOLLAND

In the name of god Amen The Twelvth day of November in the yeare of our Lord god 1631 I Elizabeth Holland of St Iames Clerkenwell in the County of Middlesex widowe* beeinge sicke in body but of good and perfect remembrance thankes bee giuen to allmighty god therefore doe make and ordeyne this my last will and Testament in manner and forme followinge ffirst and principally I Committ my soule into the handes of Allmightie god my maker and reedeemer, my body to the Earth from whence itt came in hope of a certeine and Ioyfull resurreccion att the latter day: And for my mortuary as the Lawe willeth; As Concerninge that estate itt hath pleased god to beestowe vpon {me after my debtes payed and funeralls discharged} I giue and beequeath vnto Dorothy Waller my Sisters daughter my Gould Ringe: Item I giue vnto Elizabeth Waller her daughter and my Gooddaughter One feild beddstedd with Vallons and Curtaines beelonginge to itt, One ffetherbedd one Boulster two pillowes two Blanquettes, One paire of Holland Sheettes One greene Rugge and halfe my Pewter. Item I giue vnto Arthur Savill* Apprentize* vnto mr Cayne* Gooldsmyth London the summe of fforty shillinges lawfull English money to bee paid {vnto him} within Six monethes next after my deceasse [vnto Iohn Anthony of the parishe of the parishe of Clerkenwell Aforesaid yeoman for the vse of the Aforesaid Arthur Savill when hee shall Atteine his Age of One and Twenty yeares] Item I giue vnto William

Iohnson of Westminster Grocer, One ffetherbedd One Boulster, One Blanquett, And one Rugge Item I giue vnto Mathewe Bistowe my maide One ffetherbedd one Boulster, one Blanquett, One Rugge One paire of Tonges A ffire shovell, A Trucklebedd, And A Gowne Item I giue vnto Margery Anthony the wife of Iohn Anthony of St Iames Clerkenwell Aforesaid my best Ioyned Table One Court Cubbord And Cubbord Cloth beelonginge to itt standinge in the Roome next the streete one paire of Staires high: (p. 2) Item[1] I giue vnto Iustinian Rogers and Robert Rogers of Kingston each of them Twelve pence: All the rest of my goodes Cattells and Chattells not beefore giuen nor beequeathed I giue and beequeath them wholy to Robert Tompson my brothers Sonne dwellinge att Dowgate London whome I make and ordeyne the whole executor of this my last will and Testament. To pay my debtes discharge my Legaceis, and bringe my body honestly to the grownd In wittnes whereof I haue sett to my Hand the Day and yeare aforewritten./

Memorandum That theise wordes viz (me after my debtes payed and funeralls discharged) interlined vnder the tenth line[2] of this will [was] were soe interlyned before the subscribeing & sealeing & delivery hereof.

              marke Elizabeth X Holland

Sealed & her hand sett to: in the presence of Andrewe Kinge Iohn Anthonye

1. Catchword *It'm*. 2. Refers to interlineation ll.10–11.

GL MS 9052/8. OW, grant of admon subscribed (p. 4). Single sheet folded in half to make four pages, sealed, with mark of testator and signatures of the witnesses. Text in facile secretary with some characteristics of Chancery hand.

Admon [with will annexed]. ACL 23 Jan. 1632 to Robert Griffith, one of her creditors, executor renouncing. PAB (MS 9050/6 fo. 92r) names creditor as Thomas Griffith.

fl. 1581–1631. Widow of Aaron Holland (**A1631**), builder of Red Bull. Husband had sold all interest in theatre before 1623, retaining only annuity for his life (Sisson, *Lost Plays*, p. 100).

widowe] married Aaron Holland St Andrew's Holborn 1581 (Mark Eccles, 'George Wilkins', *N&Q*, CCXX, 1975, pp. 250–2 (p. 251); see index.
Savill] boy actor with II Prince Charles's Men; first role was in *Holland's Leaguer* Dec. 1631 (Nungezer, p. 312; Bentley II, 560); see Introduction p. 3.
Apprentize] bound on 1 Aug. 1631, made free by service 19 July 1639 (Goldsmiths' Hall Apprentice Register 1 fo. 305r; Court Book V fo. 3v).
Cayne] actor with Lady Elizabeth's, Palsgrave's, and from Dec. 1631 II Prince Charles's Men (Nungezer, pp. 82–5; Bentley II, 398–401); see index.

1633 Nov. 15 Nathaniel GILES

In the name of god Amen. I Nathaniel Gyles of the Castell of Windsore in the Countie of Berk*shire* Doctor of Musick being in health & memorie (thankes be to god) do make & ordaine this my last will & testament in man*ner* & forme followinge. ffyrst I bequeath & yeeld my soule to allmyghtie god trusting to be saved only by the mercy of god and merit*es* of Iesus Chryst. And my bodie I desire to be decentlie buried in the earth without any vaine pompe or ceremonie but for the place where & the man*ner* how I leave to the discretion of my Executrix. And as concerninge my wordly good*es* my will is that they be disposed as followeth. ffyrst whereas I have formerlie gyven by deed and Copie of Courte Roll to my Eldest sonne Nathaniel Gyles* Doctor in Dyvinitie dyverse Land*es* lying within the Parishes of Winckfeild & Warfeild in the Countie of Berk*shire* and some allso lyinge in the Parish of Wyrardsburie in the Countie of Buck*inghamshire* my will and meaninge now is that he shall enioy the same according to the tenor & true meaninge of those deed*es* & Copies & no otherwise Ite*m* I giue & bequeath to his sonne Nathaniel Gyles my Godsonn all those my Copiehold Land*es* in Winckfeild aforesayed w*hich* I lately bought of Stroude to be enioyed by him and his heyrs for ever according to the Custome of the Mannor: but my will & meaning is that he shall not enioy the same vntill after the decease of my lovinge wyfe Ann Gyles vnto who*m* I bequeath it for her lyfe only. Ite*m* I giue & bequeath vnto Charles Gyles the eldest sonne of my sayed sonne Nathaniel one Copiehold tenement & land*es* therevnto belonging lying in the Parish of Wyrardsbury & bought of Iohn Paltock to be inioyed by him and his heyrs for ever according to the custome of the Man*n*or but neverthelesse my will & meaninge is that he shall not enioy the same vntill after the decease of loving wyfe Ann Gyles to who*m* I bequeath the same during her lyfe only. Ite*m* I giue & bequeath to my sonne Robert Gyles and the heyrs of his bodie lawfullie begotten all my land*es* & tenement*es* lying in the Parish of Stanwell in the Countie of Midd*lesex* to be enioyed by him in such man*ner* as is expressed in a deed of ffeofment made to Thomas Horne Doctor in Dyvinitie Iohn Worsop Esquier & Willia*m* Brumskill Merchant being my three sonnes in lawe; Ite*m* I giue & bequeath to my lovinge Wyfe Ann Gyles all those my ffreehold & Copiehold land*es* and tenement*es* lying in the Parish of Langley Marish in the Countie of Buck*inghamshire* (Excepting those howses & landes w*hich* I have lately bought of Iohn & Edward Stiles in Reversion) the w*hich* land*es* & tenement*es* my will is that shee shall have & enioy during the terme of her naturall lyfe. And that after her decease I giue & bequeath all the sayed Land*es* & tenement*es* (Except before excepted) vnto my Sonne

Nathaniel Gyles and my three daughters videlicet Elyzabeth Worsop Ann Horne Susann Brumskill and theyr heyrs for ever equallie to be diuided amonge them. Item I giue & bequeath vnto my sayed loving wyfe Ann Gyles one Annuitie bought of[1] (**p. 2**) the old Lady Browne of the valewe of thirtie poundes per annum and all the arrerages which are or shallbe due therevppen. Item I giue and bequeath vnto my sayed loving wyfe Anne Gyles all that my lease of Landes lying in Sheer Green within the Parish of ffarnham Royall & Countie of Buckinghamshire with all the terme of yeers therein contayned which shall be vnexspired at my decease if the sayed Anne Gyles shall happen to liue vnto the end and Expiration of all the terme of yeers demised in the sayed lease. But if it shall happen that the sayed Ann Gyles shall depart this lyfe before the end and expiration of the sayed lease & terme of yeers therein demised then I do giue and bequeath the sayed Lease with all the remaynder of yeers therein contayned & not exspired at the death of the sayed Ann Gyles vnto my sonne Nathaniel Gyles and my three daughters videlicet Elyzabeth Worsoppe Ann Horne and Susann Brumskill equallie to be diuided between them. Item I giue and bequeath vnto my sayed lovinge wyfe Ann Gyles all that my Annuitie or rent charge which I purchased of Sir William Brooke Knight of the Honourable Order of the Bath (Excepting twentie poundes per annum which I have allready by my deed Indented made over vnto my sonne in lawe Thomas Horne Doctor in Dyvintie) if shee the sayed Anne Gyles my wyfe shall happen to liue vnto the full end and terme thereof. But if it shall happen that shee my sayed wyfe shall departe this lyfe before the full end and expiration of {the} terme thereof then I giue and bequeath the sayed Annuitie or rent charge vnto my sonne Nathaniel Gyles and my three daughters videlicet Elyzabeth Worsoppe Ann Horne and Susann Brumskill with all the remaynder of yeers therein contayned which shall be then to come and vnexspired at the death of my sayed wyfe Anne Gyles {equally to be diuided between them}. Item I giue & bequeath to my Eldest daughter Elyzabeth Worsoppe my house in Windsore wherein Mr Eveley now dwelleth & the lease thereof during so many yeers as shallbe to come after the decease of my sayed wyfe Ann Gyles. Item I giue & bequeath vnto my second daughter Ann Horne (my house in the hygh street of Windsore called Hunniwoodes house together with the lease thereof for so many yeers thereof as shall be to come after the decease of my sayed wyfe Ann Gyles. Item I giue and bequeath to my two daughters videlicet Ann Horne and Susan Brumskill and theyr heyrs for ever all my right title and Interest which I have or may have in and to all those houses & landes which I have lately bought of John & Edward Styles in Reversion Lying in the Parish of Langley Marrish and Countie of Buckinghamshire which howses and landes my will and meaninge is

that my sayed wyfe Ann Gyles shall have and enioy during her lyfe &
after her decease then my will & meaning is that my sayed two daughters
Anne and Susan shall have and enioy the same to them and theyr heyrs
for ever equallie to be diuided between them. Item I giue & bequeath to
my brother Iohn Gyles his daughters as followeth videlicet to Ann
Woodson* fortie shillinges. To Sarah Bell fortie shillinges To Elyzabeth
Charman six poundes: To Margaret[2] (p. 3) his fourth daughter fower
poundes. And to Mary his yongest daughter fower poundes. Item I giue
& bequeath to my Cosin Mary Starkey and her husband fortie shillinges
to make them two ringes to be worne by them in rememberance of me.
Item I giue & bequeath vnto my two sonnes Nathaniel Gyles & Robert
Gyles and to my three daughters Elyzabeth Worsoppe Ann Horne and
Susan Brumskill to every one of them twentie nobles a peece to buy them
mourninge apparrell. Item I giue & bequeath to the poore of the Parish
of Stanwell twentie shillinges. Item I giue & bequeath to the poore of the
Parish of new Windsore fortie shillinges. Item I giue & bequeath to the
poore of the Parish of Winckfeild twentie shillinges. Item I giue &
bequeath to the poore of the Parish of Langley Marrish twentie shillinges.
Item I giue & bequeath to the poore of the Parish of ffarnham Royall
twentie shillinges. All which my severall Legacis thus bequeathed to the
before mentioned severall Parishes my desyre is that they may be distributed
by {the} minister or Curate of each Parish with the Church wardens and
overseers or collectors for the poore to such poore of theyr severall
Parishes as they in theyr conscience shall thinke to have most need and
to deserve it best. And that it be gyven to them over and above that
weeklie or monethly almes which they do receave from theyr severall
Parishes. Item I giue & bequeath to the Gentlemen of the Kinges Chappell
royall fortie shillinges to drinke in wyne for my sake. Item I giue to the
Quire of St George his Chappell within the Castell of Windsore fortie
shillinges to be equallie diuided amongst them. All the rest of my Goodes
& Chattells Leases houshold stuffe plate mony or any thinge else which
is not allreadie bequeathed in this my last will & testament I giue &
bequeath to my lovinge wyfe Anne Gyles whom I do nominate & appoynt
to be my whole & sole Executrix of this my last will & testament. And
I do appoynt & ordaine my two sonnes in lawe Thomas Horne Doctor
in Dyvinitie and Iohn Worsoppe Esquier to be my Overseers thereof
intreatinge them to be helpfull to my Executrix in performance of this my
will And for a rememberance of me I giue to my sayed Overseers two
gold ringes of fifteen shillinges a peece Item my will & meaninge is that if
any bodie to whom I have bequeathed any legacie be not contented with
this my will, but shall seek to disturbe or disquiet my Executrix that then
any such person shall loose the benifit of this my last will and be as if he

or shee had not been named therein. In witnesse whereof as allso of all the rest of the particulars specified in this my last will & testament I have sett my hand & seale on the fyfteenth[3] of November in the nynth yeer of the raigne of our Soveraigne Lord Charles by the grace of god of England Scotland ffrance and Ireland Kinge Defender of the faith &c annoque Christi 1633. Nathaniell Giles
Sealed & signed in the presence of Tobias Burton Iohn Darknall

(p. 5) Whereas I have by my last will & testament bearing date the fyfteenth day of November in the nynth yeer of the raygne of our Soveraigne Lord Carles[4] by the grace of god of England Scotland ffrance & Ireland Kinge defender of the faith &c gyven & bequeathed to my lovinge wyfe Ann Gyles all those my ffreehold & Copie hold Landes & tenementes lying in the Parish of [G . . .] Langley Marish & Countie of Buckinghamshire (exccepting those howses & landes which I have lately bought of Iohn and Edward Stiles in Reversion) for and during the terme of her naturall life and after her decease I have gyven & bequeathed the sayed Landes & tenementes to my sonne Nathaniel Gyles and my three daughters videlicet Elyzabeth Worsoppe Ann Horne & Susan Brumskill and theyr heyrs for ever. Now in consideration that I do call to rememberance that my sonne Henry Gyles went out of England into forrayne Cuntries now about six yeers since of whose lyfe or death I am not fully assured to the end that if he be lyvinge and shall happen to returne into this realme at any tyme within fiue yeers after the decease of my sayed loving wyfe Anne Gyles {he may have some meanes of lyvinge} then I do giue and bequeath all the sayed Landes & tenementes vnto my sayed sonne Henry Gyles and his heyres for ever. But if that he the sayed Henry Gyles shall not happen to returne into this Realme within the tyme limited then my will is that all the sayed Landes and tenementes shall come vnto my sonne Nathaniel Gyles and my three daughters and theyr heyrs equallie to be diuided between them according as I haue ordayned in my last will before mentioned. And allso my will and meaning is that all the meane profittes rentes and issues of the sayed Landes & tenementes during those fiue yeers after the decease of my sayed wyfe Ann Gyles shall equallie be diuided between my sayed sonne Nathaniel and my three daughters before mentioned {if my sayed sonne Henry shall not returne}. And allso whereas I have in my sayed last will & testament gyven & bequeathed vnto my sayed lovinge wyfe Ann Gyles all that my lease of landes lying in Sheer Green within the Parish of ffarnham Royall & Countie of Buckinghamshire with all the terme of yeers therein contayned with condition if shee the sayed Ann Gyles shall liue vnto the end and expiration thereof or else that the sayed lease with all the remaynder of yeers which shall be to come & vnexspired at her death {shall} [to] come

vnto my sonne Nathaniel Gyles and my three daughters Elyzabeth
Worsoppe Ann Horne and Susan Brumskill equally to be diuided now in
the Consideration aforesayed my will is that all the remaynder of yeers
which shall be to come & vnexspired in the sayed lease at the death of
my sayed (**p. 6**) wyfe Ann Gyles shall come vnto my sayed sonne Henry
Gyles if he shall returne into this realme at any tyme within fiue yeers
after the decease of my sayed wyfe or otherwyse that the remaynder of
the yeers with the lease shall come vnto my sonne Nathaniel Gyles and
my sayed three daughters according as I have ordayned and appoynted in
my sayed last will & testament And allso my will and meaninge is that
all the meane profittes rentes & issues of the sayed lease & landes therein
demised during those fiue yeers after the decease of my sayed wyfe Ann
Gyles shall be equally diuided betweene my sayed sonne Nathaniel Gyles
and my sayed three daughters if my sayed sonne Henry do not come into
this realme. In witnesse whereof I have caused this Codicill to be made
and added vnto the before mentioned my last will and testament on the
fifteenth–day of November in the nynth yeer of the raigne of our
Soueraigne Lord Charles by the grace of god of England Scotland
ffrance & Ireland Kinge Defender of the fayth et[5] annoq*ue* Chri*sti* 1633.

Nathanell Giles

Sygned & delyvered in the presens of Tobias Burton Iohn Darknall

1. Catchword *the*. 2. Catchword *his*. 3. *fyfteenth*: added in darker ink by same
hand. 4. *Carles*: rightly *Charles*. 5. *et*: rightly *etc*.

PRO PROB10/523. OW, codicil annexed, prob. clause subscribed (p. 6), notes of
registration marginated (pp. 1, 5). Two sheets folded to make eight pages (pp. 4,
7, 8 blank); seal on will (p. 3). Text of will and codicil, with insertions and
corrections to both, in same facile secretary.

Prob. PCC 17 Feb. 1634 to Anne Giles, relict and executor. RegC (PRO PROB11/
169 fos 316r–316v) records confirmation of will by sentence, promulgated 2 Dec.
1635 (Elizabeth Gyles alias Worsopp, Anne Gyles alias Horne, Susan Gyles alias
Brunskill, daughters of deceased, promoters, v. Nathaniel Giles and Robert Giles,
sons of deceased, and others with claim on will). PAB (PRO PROB8/31 fo.
unnumbered (Feb. 1633/4)) notes exhibition of inventory.

c.1558–1634. Musician, composer, choirmaster. Master of Children of Windsor
1595–1634, of Chapel Children 1597–1634; with others managed Chapel
Children at Blackfriars 1600–4. Died 24 Jan. 1634, buried St George's Chapel,
Windsor. (Chambers II, 41–50, 64, 319; Hillebrand, *Child Actors*, pp. 158–9,
etc.; Nungezer, p. 153; Mary Elizabeth Smith, 'Nathaniel Giles "from Winsore":
Master of the Children in the Chapel Royal', *N&Q*, CCXXV, 1980, pp. 124–31;
New Grove.)

Nathaniel Gyles] later canon of Windsor and Worcester Cathedral.
Woodson] perhaps related to the Leonard Woodson who acted as deputy to Giles
in 1605, became organist of Eton College in 1615 (*New Grove*).

1634 Jan. 31 William FIDGE (abstract)

(Fitch) Citizen and goldsmith of London. Aged, ill and weak. Soul 'in to the hand*es* of Almighty God my heauenly father assuredly beleeuing to haue full remission & forgiuenesse of all my sinnes & to enjoy euerlastinge life in the kingdome of heauen by & through the onely meritt*es* death & passion of Iesus Christ myne onely Lord & Saviour In whose pretious bloud shedding I putt the onely hope of my Saluac*io*n'. Burial at discretion of executrix. Lease of dwelling house in Mugwell Streete in London and term of years to come, to loving wife Mary Fitch, for term of lease if she lives so long, wife to pay rent and perform covenants specified in lease; if she dies before expiry of lease, same to Agnes Wyborowe of London, widow, if she is alive and, if not, to Thomas Wyborowe, her son, for remainder of term. Said lease and possession of said house, together with wainscot and painted cloth in and about the same, to be delivered to Agnes or to Thomas within fourteen days at most after death of said wife. To said Mary Fitch all other goods, etc. to dispose of at her pleasure. Appoints her sole executor. Revokes all former wills. Wit. William Goulde, Samuel Walpole notary public.

GL MS 9052/8. OW, prob. clause endorsed together with note of exhibition of inventory, valued at £8 7s 2d. Single sheet, sealed, with mark of testator and signatures of witnesses. Text in a rapid secretary, with occasional italic *h*.

Prob. ACL 19 Aug. 1635 to Mary Fitch, relict and executor. Note endorsed on will gives pa. of origin as St Olave Silver Street.

fl. 1571–1634. Perhaps the William Fidge who bought playbooks in 1571, now 'aged'. (Chambers II, 316; Nungezer, pp. 134–5.)

1634 June 17 John MARSTON

In the name of god Amen I Iohn Marston of London Clarke being sicke in bodye, but of p*er*fecte and sound mynde & memorye do make my last will' and testament in manner & forme followeinge, Imprimis I give and bequeath my soule into the hand*es* of almightye god my maker & Redeemer, and my bodye to be buryed in Chirstian buriall' in some Convenient place where my executor hereafter named shall' appoynt It*em* I give and bequeath to Iames Coghill' & Iames Brynton boeth of Christchurche in the County of South*ampton* the some of fortie shilling*es* apeece to be paid w*i*thin six monethes after my decease, Item I give and bequeath to marye ffabian the wife of W*illia*m ffabian of Chirstchurch afforesaid toward*es* the educacon of her five sonnes the some of twentye eight pound*es* of Currant money of England to be paid vnto her w*i*thin

six monethes after my decease, Item I give to the parishe Churche of Christchurch* afforesaid the some of five poundes to be paid within six monethes next after my decease, Item I give and bequeath to my Cosen Hunt of ashford in the Countye of Salop* the somme of twentye poundes to be paid within six monethes after my decease, Item I give and bequeath to my Cosen Griffins daughter of* kingston in the Countye of Surrey the some of five poundes to be paid vnto her within six monethes after my decease, Item I gieve to Marye Collice the daughter of my Cosen anne Collice of Chauncery lane the somme of five poundes to be paid vnto her six monethes after my decease, Item I give and bequeath vnto my Cosen Richard Marston of new Inne in the County of Middlesex my silver Bason and Ewre, but my will' is that my wife shall have the vse of yt [during her life] vntil yt shalbe demanded of her by the said Richard, or his attorney in that behalfe Lawfully deputed Item I give and bequeath vnto George walley and Iames walley sonnes of mr Henrye walley* the some of five poundes apeece to be paid vnto the said Henry for their vse within six monethes after (p. 4) my decease, Item all' the Rest of my goodes and Cattells moveable and vnmoveable {my debtes & legacies [being discharde] & funerall expences dischardged} I give and bequeath to my welbeloved wife Marye whom I ordayne my sole executrix of this my last will' and testament, and I do hereby vtterly Renounce & make voyd all former wills by me heretofore made, In wittnes whereof I have herevnto putt my hand and seale the seaventeenth day of Iune in the tenth yeere of the Raigne of our soueraigne lord Charles by the grace of god of England Scotland ffrance and Ireland King defender of the ffaythe &c/ Annoque domini 1634/
signum predicti Iohannis Marston
Jho maston*
memorand that the wordes interlyned betweene the first & second lynes one this side the leafe[1] were interlyned before the subscribing publisheing and [delivery] {sealeing} hereof, and after Read published subscribed & sealed in the presence of Tho: Byrd Henry Walley

1. Refers to interlineation ll. 30–1 above.

PRO PROB10/528. OW, prob. clause endorsed, note of registration marginated. Single sheet, folded to make four pages (pp. 2 and 3 blank), sealed. Text in rapid secretary, signatures in italic.

Prob. PCC 9 July 1634, to Mary Marston, widow and executor. PAB (PRO PROB8/31 fo. unnumbered (July 1634)) gives pa. of origin as St Mary Aldermanbury, London and note of exhibition of inventory.

Printed: J. O. Halliwell, ed., *Works of John Marston*, 3 vols, London, 1856, I, viii–ix (RegC); corrected by A. B. Grosart in *Poems of John Marston*

(1598–1601), Manchester, 1879, pp. xxii–iii, who also prints abstract of wife's will (PRO PROB11/266 fos 96r–96v, dated 12 June, proved 31 July 1657) (p. xxiv), abstract of father's will (PRO PROB11/94 fos 276v–277r, dated 24 Oct., proved 29 Nov. 1599) (pp. x–xi).

1576–1634. Dramatist, shareholder in second Blackfriars c.1604–6. Died 25 June, buried 26 June 1634 Temple Church, London. (Chambers II, 50–4; III, 427–35; Nungezer, p. 245; R. E. Brettle, 'John Marston, dramatist: Some new facts about his life', *MLR*, XXII, 1927, pp. 7–14.)

Christchurch] Marston presented to living 10 Oct. 1616, resigned 13 Sept. 1631 (Brettle, p. 11).
Salop] Marston's father was from a Shropshire family (*Works of John Marston*, ed. A. H. Bullen, 3 vols, London, 1887, I, xii).
daughter of] Halliwell, misconstruing, leaves space after 'of' not present in RegC.
Henrye walley] eventually Master of Stationers' Company, named as executor by Marston's wife (see R. E. Brettle, 'Bibliographical notes on some Marston quartos and early collected editions', *Transactions of the Bibliographical Society*, VIII, 1927/8, pp. 336–48 (p. 340); Philip J. Finkelpearl, 'Henry Walley of the Stationers' Company and John Marston', *PBSA*, LVI, 1962, pp. 366–8); (Plomer, *Dictionary*, p. 188); see index.
Jho maston] R. E. Brettle ('Notes on John Marston', *RES* n.s., XIII, 1962, pp. 390–3 (p. 392)) corrects Halliwell's statement, repeated in all earlier accounts of will, that Marston made his mark instead of signing his name.

1634 Sept. 11 Thomas BASSE

Memorand*um* that on or <a>bout the eleuenth day of september Anno Domne[1] 1634: Thomas Basse of the p*a*rish of St Iames Clarkenwell in the Countye of Midlesex gent deceased whilest he liued beinge sicke in bodye but of perfect minde and memorye made and declared his last will and Testament {nuncupatiue in mann*er* and forme followinge}[2] v*i*delic*e*t He gaue and bequeathed to his Sister Iane the sume of fortye shillinges: To his Sister Vrsla a ringe of Tenn shillinge: To his Godsonn Thomas Axon the sonne of Robert Axon* the sume of fortye shillinge. He further gaue and bequeathed vnto his Louinge freind*es* Mr Christopher Beeston* and Elizabeth his wife: Mr William Robins* and Sislye* his wife. Robert Axon and {Mary} his wife. Richard Perkins:* Michaell Bower:* and William Beeston:* gent*leman* to each of them a ringe of the vallewe of tenn shillinges[3] a peece to weare in remembra*un*c of him: The rest and residue of all his estate whatsoeuer his deb*tes* and Legacies[3] beinge payed he gaue and bequeathed vnto his wife Dorcas* Basse whome he made his sole executrix which wordes[3] he the sayed Thomas Basse spake and vtered in the presence of us whose names are herevnder written/ Robert Axon Anne conisbey The marke X of Elizabeth Miller

1. *Domne*: rightly *Domine*. 2. *nuncupatiue in mann' and forme followinge*: marginated opposite line beginning *vizt*. 3. Otiose special sign for *es*.

GLRO Box DL/C/420. OW (nuncupative), note of registration marginated, note endorsed records swearing of Robert Axon and Elizabeth Miller on authenticity of will and of executor Dorcas Basse on 3 Oct. 1634, signed Thomas Wiborow scrivener. Single sheet folded, unsealed, with signatures of witnesses. Text in set secretary with displayed matter in italic; marginal insertion (l. 5) in smaller, less formal secretary.

Prob. ConCL 3 Oct. 1634 to Dorcas Basse, executor.

Printed: Bentley II, 631 (RegC).

c.1593–1634. Actor; Lady Elizabeth's 1611, 1613, Queen Anne's by 1617; licensed with Robert Lee (**1629**), Ellis Worth (**1659**) and others to form company to be known as Children of Revels 1622; Revels at Red Bull 1622. Bentley points out that apart from family all legatees members of Queen Henrietta's company. (Chambers II, 301; Nungezer, p. 31; Bentley II, 360; Sisson, 'Notes', p. 26.)

Robert Axon] (Axen) actor at Phoenix with Queen Henrietta's c.1630 and later with King and Queen's Young Company (Nungezer, p. 25; Bentley II, 353).
Beeston] owner of Cockpit/Phoenix and member of companies acting there including Queen Henrietta's which he probably organised (**1638**); see index.
Robins] actor with Queen Anne's 1616–19, Revels 1622, then Queen Henrietta's (Nungezer, pp. 298–9; Bentley II, 547–8); see index.
Sislye his wife] see index.
Perkins] actor with Worcester's/Queen Anne's from 1602, Revels 1622, King's 1623, Queen Henrietta's from 1625 (Chambers II, 332; Nungezer, pp. 274–8; Bentley II, 525–8); see index.
Bower] Bowyer, actor with Queen Henrietta's from 1625 (**1645**); see index.
Beeston] son of Christopher Beeston; actor and manager at Salisbury Court, Cockpit/Phoenix (**1682**); see index.
wife Dorcas] admon granted to William Atkinson, creditor, ConCL 18 Nov. 1635, inventory valued at £9 18s 2d (Bentley II, 631).

1634 Oct. 23 William BROWNE

In the Name of God Amen the Three and Twentyeth day of October 1634 And in the Tenth yeare of the Raigne of our Soveraigne Lord Charles by the grace of God Kinge of England Scotland ffrance and Ireland defendor of the faith &c I William Browne of the parish of St Iames Clarkenwell in the County of Midd*lesex* Gentl*eman*, beinge att this present sicke and weake of body but of perfect remembr<ance> (praised be God) doe make and declare this my present Testament and last Will in manner and forme followinge (that is to say) ffirst and before all thinges I commend my soule into the handes of almightie God my maker & Creat<or> from whome I had and receiued the same assuredly trustinge and beleeveinge by the death and merittes of Iesus Christ my Saviour and Redeemer I shall haue free remission and forgivenes of all my sinnes and Eternall life <in> the Kingedome of Heaven (amongest the elect Saintes of God,[1] and my body I comitt to the Earth from whence it came to be buried in decent and Christian manner in the Chancell of the parishe Church of St Iames Clarkenwell aforesaid soe neere as may be conveniently to my ffather Greene,* and for such worldly wealth where<euer> God of his goodnesse hath beene pleased to blesse me I dispose thereof as followeth (videlicet) Inprimis I giue and bequeath vnto my brother Robert Browne* Habberdasher the summe of ffive Powndes of lawfull money of England and alsoe my best suite of apparrell (videlicet) hose doublett and cloake the same to be paide and deliuered him within one Moneth nexte after my decease Item I give and bequeath vnto the Three Children of the said Robert Browne the summe of Tenn Powndes of lawfull money of England to be shared amongest them part and part like, and my will and minde is that if any of my said brothers Children shall depart this life before they shall accomplishe theire full ages of one and Twenty yeares, then his or theire part soe dyinge to remaine to the Survivor of them and if they shall all of them dye before the accomplishement of theire said ages of one and twenty yeares then I will the same shall remaine vnto my said brother Item I give to my brother in lawe Thomas Bond* my best blacke stuffe suite and cloake my wrought Gold Capp my best halfe shirt and my best band and my white Beaver hatt to be paid and delivered him imediately after my decease Item I give and bequeath vnto my Sister Susan* Bond wife of the said Thomas Bond the summe of ffower Powndes to be paide her within Three Moneths nexte after my decease, and I doe alsoe release acquite and discharge my said Sister of the debt of Twenty shillinges which she oweth me; Item I giue and bequeath vnto my dearely beloued mother Susan Greene alias Baskervile,* All such summe and summes of money debts dueties claymes chalenges and demaundes whatsoever, as either is ought or shalbe due owinge or belonginge vnto me forth out of and from the Redd Bull Playhouse* scituate in St Iohn streete in the County of Middlesex whereof I am a member and a fellow sharer, or of or by any {of the} sharers, or other person or persons players theire or owners thereof, and of in or to any hou<se> or houses to the said Playhouse adioyninge, And alsoe all bondes bills debts and other things as I haue formerly graunted or assigned vnto my said mother or wherein

by deed I haue declared any trust to be reposed in me for the vse and benefitt of my said mother, Item I further give and bequeath vnto my said mother my house Clocke my pockett watch my Gold seale ringe, my best beaver hatt, and all my wearinge apparrell aswell linnen as woollen, not otherwise herein and hereby given disposed willed or bequeathed Item I giue to the said company of Players* Twenty shillinges for to buy them blacke ribbons to weare in remembrance of me Item I giue and bequeath vnto Phillipp Massam my sonne in lawe the summe of Tenn Powndes of lawfull money of England to be paid him att his age of one and twenty yeares if he shalbe then liveing, and my will and minde is that if my said sonne shall depart this mortall life before he shall accomplishe his age of one and Twenty yeares aforesaid, That then the said Tenn Powndes which should haue beene paid to him shalbe paid within one Moneth nexte after the said Phillipps decease vnto my foresaid brother Robert Browne his executours or assignes Item I giue to the poore of the said parishe of St Iames Clarkenwell the summe of Twenty shillings to be distributed amongest them att the discretion of my Executrix hereafter named And all other my goodes chattells cattell plaite readye moneys debts and whatsoever else of mine, and not herein or by deed vnder my hand and Seale otherwise disposed of my due debts beinge first paid and my funerall expences and legacies discharged I give vnto my wife Anne Browne* And I doe make and ordaine my said mother Susan Baskervile alias Greene full and whole executrix of this my present Testament and last Will, And I doe hereby revoake and disanull all former wills and this onely to stand for and as my last Will and Testament, In Witnes whereof I the said William Browne haue herevnto sett my hand and Seale Yeouen the day and yeares first aboue written:/ per me Will'm Browne
Signed Sealed published and [declared] deliuered <by the sa>id Testator for and as his last Will and Testament <in the prese>nce of vs Robert Neale./* Josua: Hill Richard X Tuttells marke Rich: Merydale Scriuener

1. Final parenthesis omitted.

PRO PROB10/530. OW, prob. clause subscribed, note of registration marginated. Single sheet, with signatures and seal; right margin crumbling with some loss of legibility. Text in engrossing secretary hand with displayed matter in hybrid secretary.

Prob. PCC 10 Nov. 1634 to Susan Baskervile alias Greene, mother and executor. OffC at GL (MS 9052/8) with prob. ACL 21 Jan. 1635, recording collation with original in PCC.

Printed: Bentley II, 636–7 (RegC).

1602–34. Actor; Queen Anne's c.1616, II Prince Charles's 1631–2; son of Robert Browne, proprietor of Boar's Head (**A1604**); buried St James Clerkenwell

6 Nov. 1634. (Chambers II, 304; Nungezer, p. 63; Bentley II, 391–2; Berry, *Boar's Head Playhouse*, p. 209 fn. 18.) For involvement in lawsuit arising from stepfather's share in Queen Anne's see C. J. Sisson, 'The Red Bull company and the importunate widow', *ShS*, VII, 1954, pp. 57–68.

ffather Greene] stepfather, Thomas Greene (1612).
brother Robert] see index.
Bond] actor, Red Bull Revels company c.1622, Prince Charles's 1631 (Nungezer, pp. 51–2; Bentley II, 382–3).
Sister Susan] née Browne; see index.
Susan Greene alias Baskervile] widow of actors Robert Browne and Thomas Greene; married James Baskervile 1613; for disputes with Queen Anne's see Sisson, op. cit., with son's widow see Berry, op. cit.; see index.
Redd Bull Playhouse] William received pension from 1617 through stepfather's financial stake in company (Chambers II, 238).
Players] Prince Charles's company succeeded King's at Red Bull 1634; leading players were Ellis Worth (1659), Joseph Moore, Mathew Smith, Andrew Cane (Bentley I, 274–5, 310–11).
Anne Browne] second wife; identified by Bentley (II, 392) as Ann Baylie, married 1626, by Berry (op. cit.) as widow of Edward Neale, married 1634, subsequently wife of John Rhodes who, with Susan Baskervile, held leases of Fortune Theatre in 1648 (Bentley II, 544–6).
Neale] see index.

1635 Sept. 1 Elizabeth CONDELL

In the name of God Amen I Elizabeth Cundall of ffulham in the Countie of Midd*lesex* widdowe doe renounce all former will*es* made by me and {I} doe make this my last will (fo. 105r), and Testament, My soule I Committ into the Hand*es* of my Creato*ur* and my Bodie to the earth to be buried as shall seeme fitt to my Executors, My will and meaning is, That all the Moneyes which now I owe, and shall hereafter before my death be lyable to pay be it concerning Legacyes or otherwise shall first be satisfied and payd out of my estate, and after that this shalbee performed, and done; then I doe desire Mr Cutbert Burbidge,* and Thomas Seaman (whome I doe nominate make and appoynt the Executo*urs* of this my last will and Testament) to haue a Care vnto my grandchildren the now Children of my daughter ffynch,* and to performe this my last will and Testament in such manner as I shall lymitt and appoynt for certayne causes which I haue made knowne vnto my sayd Executo*urs* touching aswell my owne sonne William Cundall* as alsoe my sonne in lawe Mr Herbert ffynch* the which I hold fitt herein not to menc*i*on. And as I doe intend that my daughter Elizabeth ffinch during her life, and my said grandchildren after her death if the good*es* shall not then be worne out shall haue the vse of these good*es* (vi*delicet*) the vse of all my Lynnen and wearing apparrell except that which is hereafter menc*i*oned, and one strikeing Clocke two gold hattband*es* and One gold whistle, yet soe I doe intend the same as that my said sonne in lawe Mr Herbert ffynch shall neuer have possession of the same; and therefore my will is that my said executors shall keepe those good*es* in their hand*es* for the good of my said grandchildren vnles my said sonne in Lawe shall keepe house, and shall first giue good securitie to my said Executors that my said grandchildren shall haue those good*es* after their sayd mothers death, if in Case they be not worne out before then: And whereas I am possessed of seuerall messuages or Tenement*es* with their appurtena*u*nc*es* for certeyne yeares yetto come, the one of which is at ffulham, the which I now live in, and the other are in London, I doe hereby giue and bequeath vnto my sayd Executo*u*rs all my interest, and terme of yeares in all and singuler the said messuages, but with this trust that they nor either of them shall take any benefitt thereby to themselues or either of them but that all shall bee to, and for the ioynt benefitt and good of my said grandchildren vnlesse my said Executors, or the survivor of them shall in their or his the said survivors discretion and Iudgment see fitt to afforde some competency out of the same to my said daughter Elizabeth ffynch the which if they my said executo*u*rs or the survivo*u*r of them shall doe, then my said grandchildren shall noe wayes trouble my said Executo*u*rs touchinge the same, but my sayd grandchildren shall allowe of it, the same being done for their mother. And as touching my said sonne William Cundall, I doe giue vnto him twenty shillings to be paid vnto him within One weeke next after my death, but if my said Executors or the survivor of them shall in their, or his the said survivors discretion and Iudgment thinke fitt to giue vnto my said sonne William Cundall any more then the same which they shall agree vpon or the survivor thinke fitt for him to haue shalbee payd out of the interest lease or Terme of yeares which I haue in the Globe, and ffryers* at such tyme and tymes and in such manner as they my said Executo*u*rs or the survivo*u*r of them shall likewise thinke fitt, and my reason is for that I would haue noe parte of my estate neither prodigally spent, nor lewdly wasted by him, and the residue out of the same I doe giue vnto my said grandchildren, but if in Case my said Executo*u*rs or the survivor of them shall find and see that my said sonne William Cundall shall not amend his Courses, but spend that estate and meanes which hee now hath, then my will is that he shall onely haue the said Twenty shillings vnlesse his extreame poverty and need shall cause my said Executors, or the survivor of them to afford him what in charity they shall thinke fitt. Item I {doe} giue and bequeath vnto Elizabeth Cundall the wife of my said sonne William Cundall, One siluer Porringer, and my will is that they the said William and Elizabeth hauing noe interest att all in those Twelue messuages scittuat in the Strond in the Countie of Midd*lesex* which I haue sold to Iohn Hatt gent, shall leuy a ffyne of the same messuages, and (**fo.** [105v]) and assure the same {as} on their part*es* vnto the said Iohn Hatt or some other person, or persons which he shall nominate, and appoint, or els they nor either of them to take any benefitt by my will, for that otherwise my said Executo*u*rs and estate wilbee troubled and incumbred by that deed which I haue sealed to the said Hatt for more then One Thousand Pound*es* for the cleeringe of the Title, and freeing all Incumbrances vpon the said houses. Item I doe giue and bequeath vnto Elizabeth [Cundall] the child of my said sonne William Cundall ffiftie Pound*es* to be paid vnto her at her age of one, and twenty yeares or day of marriage which shall first happen with the Increase of the same. Item I doe give and bequeath vnto my said Executo*u*rs Tenn Pound*es* a peece for their paynes which they shall take herein, Item I doe giue vnto Mrs Burbidge,* a siluer forke, and a gold Purse, And vnto Mrs Seaman, my Case of strong waters with all that doe belong vnto it, togeither with a gold Purse, and because the said Thomas Seaman hath done the office of a true freind vnto me, therefore and in performance of my promise I doe give vnto him all my bookes. Item I doe give vnto Mr Iohn diodate* One Satten Capp, and a seale Ringe, and vnto Isabella Vnderwood* One guilt Cupp, Item I doe, give and bequeath vnto Mrs Norton two smocks, two Aprons, my Cotten Coate, a greene Apron, and a wheele. Item I doe give vnto Mary Norton Twentie shillings, Item I doe give and bequeath vnto Elizabeth Wheaton* widdowe the gatheringe Place at the Globe during my Lease {one} [my] featherbedd & blanketts two paire of Course sheet*es*, Two smocks, Two Aprons, a siluer Cupp and twenty Pound*es*, And vnto her daughter Tenn Pound*es*, and a paire of Course sheet*es*. Item I doe giue and bequeath to Iasper Smart Twenty Pound*es*, To Ioane Smart fforty Shillings, and to the mother of the said Iasper fforty shillings they all sealing on payment of the same such iust releases as my Executors shall crave, and require: Item I give vnto the poore of ffulham fforty shillings. Item I doe remitt vnto Mr Norton Twenty Pound*es* of the money which he oweth vnto me And I doe alsoe remitt vnto one Iones the fforty shillings which he oweth vnto me, And I doe nominate appoynte, and desire Mr Lowen,* and Mr Iohn diodate to be the Overseers of this my last will and Testament, and for the Care, and paines which they shall take herein I doe giue to each of them a Peece of plate worth ffiftie shillings, And what my Executo*u*rs shall expend touchinge this my will shalbe paid out of my estate, And I doe hereby declare, and make knowne {vn}to all men that I will haue none of the Legatees abouenamed hereafter to sue or trouble my said Executo*u*rs or either of them touchinge any thinge conteyned in this my will in regard I {doe} knowe that they will honestly, and faithfully performe the same to the vttermost of their power. And I doe Charge them as they will answere the same att the day of Iudgment that they, nor either of my said Executo*u*rs doe violate or breake anie the trust in them reposed, but that they and either of them p*er*forme the same to the best of their Power, And if in Case that any of the Legatees shall sue or trouble my said Executo*u*rs or either of them concerninge anie of the p*r*emisss, Then my will is, That such person, and persons shall have noe benefitt by this my will. And whereas the said Iohn Hatt hath bought of me the said Twelue Houses or Messuages in the Strond called the Helmett Courte for One Thousand ffower hundred, and ffiftie Pound*es*, And whereas hee the said Hatt hath already payd most parte of the same, and because the assurance in lawe is not as yet setled on him the said Hatt by reason of the vniust dealings of one Sir William Acton Knight and Barronett with mee, for releefe of which I haue now a Bill dependinge in the Chancery against him, therefore to the end that all people may knowe that it is my will and meaninge that hee the said Hatt should enioy his bargaine made (**fo. 106r**) with me, and alsoe haue the said houses I doe hereby give graunte, and deuise the said Twelue Messuages with their appurtena*u*nc*es* vnto the said Iohn Hatt, To haue, and to hold vnto him the said Iohn Hatt his heires and assignes for euer He or they paying vnto me or my Executo*u*rs the Remainder of the moneys in his hand*es* for the said purchase, and I doe hereby order and appoynt William danyell* and Walter Acton Trustees for the said Sir William Acton to seale, and deliver, and acknowledge in Chauncery that deed, and graunt of bargaine and sale of the said Twelue messuages which I have already sealed vnto the said Hatt, and acknowledged before Mr Page one of the Masters in Chauncery, In witnes whereof I haue herevnto put my hand and seale this ffirst daie of September. Anno domini. One Thousand six hundred thirty ffive, and I have published this to bee my last will, and Testament in the presence of vs, who are witnesses to the same v*idelice*t).[1] (Elizabeth Condell.) Robert Bl{u}mson, Thomas Blumson, The m*a*rke of Mary Cole.

1. Opening parenthesis omitted.

PRO PROB11/170 fos 104v–106r. RegC with prob. clause.

Prob. by definitive sentence, PCC 18 Feb. 1636 to Thomas Seaman, one of executors, reserving power to second, Cuthbert Burbage. PRO PROB11/170 fos 106r–106v records full sentence, promulgated 18 Feb. 1636 (Thomas Seaman, one of the executors, promoter, v. William Cundall and Elizabeth Finch, testator's children). Bentley gives date of probate incorrectly as 8 Feb. (II, 410, 640).

Printed: Bentley II, 638–40 (excerpts).

fl. 1599–1635. Widow of Henry Condell (**1627**), actor and manager of King's Men; by inheritance housekeeper in Globe and Blackfriars. Buried St Mary Aldermanbury 3 Oct. 1635. (Bentley II, 409–10.)

Burbidge] fellow housekeeper in Globe and Blackfriars (**A1636**); see index.
daughter ffynch] Elizabeth née Condell; see index.
William Cundall] legatee of father (Bentley II, 413).
Herbert ffynch] had fallen out of favour since being named as overseer of will by H. Condell.
Globe, and ffryers] at time of death testator held two sixteenth shares in Globe and one eighth share in Blackfriars (Baldwin, *Organization*, pp. 90–117).
Mrs Burbidge] Elizabeth, wife of Cuthbert; see index.
diodate] brother of Charles Diodati, friend of John Milton; married Isabel Underwood 28 July 1635 (D. C. Dorian, *The English Diodatis*, New Brunswick, NJ, 1950, pp. 155–6).
Vnderwood] daughter of actor John Underwood (**1624**), who appointed H. Condell executor.
Wheaton] legatee of H. Condell, who allowed her to continue privileges (of gatherer) at Blackfriars as well as Globe.
Lowen] actor with Worcester's 1602, King's Men from 1603; fellow housekeeper in Globe and Blackfriars (Chambers II, 328–9; Nungezer, pp. 238–42; Bentley II, 499–506); see index.
danyell] possibly the provincial player of same name who led King's Revels touring company from 1634 (Nungezer, p. 111; Bentley II, 420–1).

1635 Dec. 31 John SHANK

In the name of god Amen the Last day of december 1635 And in the Eleaventh yeere of the Raigne of our soueraigne Lord Charles by the grace of god king of England Scotland ffraunce and Ireland defender of the faith &c, I Iohn Shancke one of his M<*aies*ties> servants the players and Citizen and Weauer of london being sicke and weake in body but of good and perfect mind and memory (Thanck*es* be therefore giuen to Almighty god) doe make ordeine and declare this my last will and Testament in manner and forme following first and principally I give and Comend my soule into the hand*es* of Almighty god my maker and Creater hopeing and assuredly beleeueing through the onely merritts death and passion of Iesus Christ my sauiour to obteine remission and pardon of all my sinnes and to enioy eternall happines in the kingdome of heaven, And my body I Comitt to the Earth to be buried in *Christ*ian[1] {buriall} [like manner] in such place as it shall please god to appoint in decent and comely manner at the discrec*i*on of my Executrix hereinafter named, And as touching such worldly good*es* and estate as it hath pleased god to blesse me withall my will and mind is as (**fo. 2**) followeth, ffirst I will devise and appoint That all such debt*es* as I shall happen to owe at the time of my decease to any person or persons whatsoeuer be well and truly satisfied and paid assoone after my decease as the same Conveniently may be raised out of my estate Item I will devise and appoint that my debt*es* being paid and satisfied and my funeralle*s* discharged [that my] {my} loveing wife Winifride* Shancke haue and enioy to her owne vse One whole Third part of my cleere estate (the same being personall and Consisting in good*es* chattells and Leases) as being due and belonging vnto her my said wife according to the laudable Custome of the Citty of London whereof I am a ffreeman, And I also desire will devise and appoint that my said wife Winifride [Iohn] Shancke whom I doe hereby make the sole Executrix of this my Last Will and Testament [that she] doe take care that out of the other Two parts of my cleere estate theis Legacies by me hereinafter giuen and expressed be well and truly satisfied and paid according to my true meaning herein declared (V*id*e*licet*) ffirst I giue devise and bequeath vnto my Two sonnes Iohn* and Iames Shancke (**fo. 3**) vnto and for whom I haue already disbursed diuers som*m*es of money amounting together in the whole to a farr greater som*m*e then their part*es* in my estate would any way come vnto the seuerall som*m*es of Tenn pound*es* apeece of lawfull English money w*hi*ch I require them to rest satisfied with as my guift and bequeast vnto them leaueing them to their mother and my Executrix to deale better with them if they shalbe loveing and obedient vnto her Item I giue and bequeath vnto my daughter Elizabeth Bowen* the som*m*e of One hundred pound*es* in lawfull English money To be paid vnto her in manner and forme following (V*id*e*licet*) ffifty pound*es* thereof at her next day of marriage and the other ffifty pound*es* at the Birth of her next Child that she shall haue after such marriage Item I giue and bequeath vnto my Grandchild Winifrid Bowen* daughter of the said Elizabeth the som*m*e of Twenty pound*es* of lawfull English money To be deliuered into the hand*es* of mrs Morgan and shee to haue the benefitt of the yeerly interest thereof dureing the minority of the said Child & toward*es* her cost*es* and charges in the breeding and educac*i*on of her, And the same Twenty pound*es* to be paid vnto her my said Grandchild at her age of One and Twenty yeeres or day (**fo. 4**) of marriage w*hi*chsoeuer shall first happen And I further giue devise and bequeath vnto the said mrs Morgan the som*m*e of Tenn pound*es* in lawfull English money as a token of my gratitude and thanckfullnes vnto her for her loue and care in the educac*i*on and bringing vp of my said little Grandchild, And w*hi*ch said som*m*e of Tenn pound*es* I desire and appoint to be paid vnto her with asmuch Convenient speed as may be Together with the som*m*e of Threescore and Tenn pound*es* debt w*hi*ch I

doe owe vnto her the said mrs Morgan and for which she hath my bond
Item I giue and bequeath vnto my loueing Cozen Katherine Payne the
summe of fforty shillinges in lawfull English money to make her a Ring
for a remembrance; All the rest and residue of my goodes chattells and
Credditts vnbequeathed (my debtes funeralls and legacies being paid and
discharged) I doe hereby wholy giue devise and bequeath the same vnto
my said loveing wife Winifrid Shancke my Executrix desireing her that
she will take an especiall care that first and principally my debtes and
legacies be well and truly paid with asmuch convenient speed as may be
out of my estate which doth consist for the most parte in a Lease which
I haue for a few yeeres* of Two Eight partes in the Blackfriers playhowse
and of a lease which I am to haue of Three Eight partes in the moity of
the Globe* playhowse for the terme of [S ... n]² {Nyne} yeeres from
Christmas (fo. 5) last which I bought and paid deere for And by meanes
thereof haue bine putt into debt, And I doe devise desire and appoint that
the proffitts yeerly comeing and arriseing of and by the said partes may
goe and be ymployed for and towardes the payment of my debtes and
legacies aforesaid and that the same be not by my said Executrix
appraised at an vnder value and soe made part of my estate to the
diminution thereof thereby to hinder the payment of my debtes and
legacies And I doe desire my fellowes his Maiesties servantes the players*
that they doe not abridge my said wife and Executrix in the receiueing of
what is due vnto me and my estate amongst them as namely ffifty poundes
for my share in the stocke bookes apparrell and other thinges according
to the old Custome and agreament amongst vs, fforty poundes or more
by them receiued of my share taken vp and remayning in the handes of
Iohn Lowen* or some other of them which they haue for a good space
past receiued and taken vp of my share as I am a player and Sixteene
poundes and Twelue shillinges which they owe me for Two gownes and
Twoe and Twenty shillinges for Trigg* and my share in the Court monyes
behinde And that they will not goe about to hinder my wife in haueing
her assurance amongst them for my partes in the Globe playhowse (fo.
6) according to a decree in the Courte of Requestes* in that behalfe
obteined against Sir Mathew Brend* knight, And I doe hereby require
charge and Comand my said Two sonnes Iohn and Iames Shancke That
they nor either of them doe goe about to molest trouble or hinder my
wife their mother in the receiueing and takeing of this my estate or in
thexecucion of this my Will according to my true meaning herein declared
But that they and either of them be loveing and obedient vnto her which
if they soe be then I doubt not but she will as I doe and haue required
her be kind vnto and Carefull of them and doe them the best good she
can And I doe hereby desire and appoint my loveing freindes Phillip

Powell draper and Iohn Atkins* Citizen and Scriuener of London to be overseers of this my last Will and Testament desireing them to be aideing and assisting vnto my said wife and Executrix with their best advice and Councell in thexecuc*io*n of this my Will that the same may be pe*r*formed according to my true meaning (fo. 7) herein declared And I doe hereby Revoke all former Wills by me heretofore made and doe pronounce publish and declare this to be my last Will and Testament. In witnes whereof I haue hereunto putt my hand and seale the day and yeere first aboue written/.   Iohn Shancke
Signed sealed pronounced published and declared for and as the last Will and Testament of the said Iohn Shancke Conteyned in Seauen sheet*es* of paper in the presence of Will: Blagraue* Ionas Sage Iohn Atkins Scr*iuener*

1. *Christian*: MS has *xp'ian*. 2. *[S . . . n]*: original reading ?*Seauen* or *Sixteen*.

PRO PROB10/545. OW, prob. clause (fo. 7), note of registration marginated (fo. 1). Eight numbered sheets joined at the top, fos 1–7 bearing testator's signature; fo. 7 sealed, with signatures of witnesses. Text in set mixed hand with displayed matter in hybrid secretary, possibly hand of John Atkins.

Prob. PCC 28 Jan. 1636 to Winifred Shank (Shancke), relict and executor. Notes endorsed on will (fo. 8) and PAB (PRO PROB8/33 fo. 6v) give pa. of origin as St Giles Cripplegate; PAB notes exhibition of inventory.

Printed: Bentley II, 646–8 (RegC).

fl. 1597–1635. Actor, jig–maker and dancer; Pembroke's c.1597–1600, Queen Elizabeth's travelling company, Prince Henry's/Palsgrave's from 1610, King's Men 1619–36. Associated with large number of apprentice actors including Thomas Pollard (**A1653**) and John Honyman (**1636**). Shareholder in Globe and Blackfriars; 1635 sued by fellow members of King's company, for one share in each of Globe and Blackfriars (see 'Sharers' papers'). Witness to wills of Richard Cowley (**1618**) and Sarah Dambrooke (**1624**). Buried St Giles Cripplegate 27 Jan. 1636. (Chambers II, 338–9; Nungezer, pp. 316–20; Bentley II, 562–7.)

wife Winifride] subsequently married to a Fitch; see index.
Iohn] actor (**1655**).
Elizabeth Bowen] see index.
Winifrid Bowen] see index.
Lease . . . for a few yeeres] for four years in Blackfriars, one year in Globe ('Sharers' papers', p. 367).
Blackfriers . . . Globe] testator still held all his shares, purchased 1633–4 from William Heminges, son of John Heminges, despite Lord Chamberlain's order 1 Aug. 1635 that two shares be transferred to petitioners ('Sharers' papers', pp. 367, 373).
his Ma*iesties* servant*es* the players] King's company.

Lowen] actor with King's from 1603, one of managers of King's company after death of Heminges (Chambers II, 328–9; Nungezer, pp. 238–42; Bentley II, 499–506); see index.

Trigg] William Trigg, actor with King's from 1626, probably Shank's apprentice (Nungezer, p. 380; Bentley II, 604–6); see index.

decree in the Court of Requestes] for extension of lease of Globe for nine years from March 1635 ('Sharers' papers', pp. 364, 368).

Brend] owner of Globe site, by inheritance from Nicholas Brend (**1601**) (see Berry, *Playhouses*, pp. 75–119).

Atkins] possibly son–in–law of John Heminges (**1630**) and/or Atkins who held part of Globe property in trust for him (Bentley II, 351); responsible for writing out will.

Blagraue] deputy to Master of Revels Sir Henry Herbert (**1673**) 1624–35; partner of Richard Gunnell (**A1634**) in building and management of Salisbury Court 1629–36 (Nungezer, p. 50; Bentley II, 380–1, VI, 94); see index.

1636 Apr. 7 John HONYMAN

In the Name of God Amen I Iohn Honyman one of his Ma*ies*ties Servant*es* the Players being weake & infirme in body but, of sound & p*er*fect memory (thankes for the same to be giuen to Allmightie God) doe ordaine constitute & make this my last will & Testam*ent* in manner & forme following, ffirst I bequeath & recom*m*end my soule into the handes of my All=mercifull God & Maker & of his onely Sonne & my sole Saviour[1] Iesus Christ who spilt his most precious bloud & dyed for my sinnes, by whose onely meritt*es* I trust & rest assured to be acquited from all my offences and misdeedes & to be receiued into eu*er*lasting blisse & glory w*i*th him my deare Redeemer & all the holy Saint*es* departed in his peace, & to haue a ioyfull resurrection at the last day: And next I bequeath my body to be decently & Christianly buried in the Church yard of St Giles w*i*thout Criplegate, as neere as may be to the place where my owne ffather lyeth buried. And for that estate wherew*i*thall itt hath pleased God to blesse mee in this world I dispose of itt in manner & forme following v*i*d*elicet* (after my ffunerall expences discharged & my debt*es* paid wh*i*ch I desire may faithfullie be done to all my Creditou*r*s) [e] I giue & bequeath the one halfe or moitie of all my good*es*, whether ready money debt*es* Apparrell bookes or what some or som*m*es shall grow due vnto mee from & amongst my ffellowes the Players,* or any other thing whatsoeuer equally to be devided to my deare & loving Mother Ellen Sweetman, & the other halfe I bequeath & com*m*itt into the handes & custody of my said Mother to be disposed of by her as shee in her discretion shall thinke fittest to the onely vse behoofe & best benefitt of

Wills 191

my onely Brother Richard Honyman* & to noe other vse whatsoeu*er*
Item I giue & bequeath to my loving ffather in law Iohn Sweetman twentie
shillinges to buy him a ring w*i*thall, Item I giue to eu*ery* one of my
ffellowes* the Players a ring of ten shillinges price. Item I giue & bequeath
twentie shillinges to the poore of the Parrish of St Giles w*i*thout Criplegate
aforesaid to be distributed amongst them according to the discretion of
the Church wardens of the said Parrish. And I doe hereby will declare &
make my said Mother the sole Executrix of this my last will & Testame*nt*
not doubting but that out of her motherly care & pietie shee will faithfully
execute this my last will according to my true intent & meaning. In
wittnesse whereof I haue here vnto set my hand the seauenth day of Aprill
in the Twelft yeare of the Raigne of our[1] Soue*r*aigne Lord Charles by the
grace of God of England Scotland ffraunce & Ireland King defendor of
the faith &c & in the yeare of our[1] Redemption 1636/   Iohn Honyman
Signed subscribed & published in the p*r*esence of Will: Browne Robert
Benefeild* Will: Burbage*

1. Otiose superscript *r*.

PRO PROB10/547. OW, prob. clause endorsed, note of registration marginated.
Single sheet folded to make four pages, with signatures of testator and witnesses,
unsealed. Text in mixed hand, possibly that of William Browne.

Prob. PCC 26 Apr. 1636 to Ellen Sweetman, mother and executor. PAB (PROB8/
33 fo. 33r) gives pa. of origin as St Leonard Shoreditch.

Printed: Bentley II, 645 (RegC).

1613–36. Boy actor; King's Men from 1626. Possibly dramatist, though no work
survives. Buried St Giles Cripplegate 13 Apr. 1636. (Nungezer, pp. 196–8; Bentley
II, 476–8.)

my ffellowes the Players] King's Men.
Richard Honyman] hired man with Prince's company 1640 (Bentley II, 478–9).
eu*ery* one of my ffellowes] in May 1636 included William Trigg, Alexander
Gough, William Penn, Richard Baxter, Thomas Hobbes (**A1640**), William Hart,
Richard Hawley, William Patrick (Bentley I, 86–7).
Benefeild] actor; King's Men from 1616 (Chambers II, 303; Nungezer, pp. 42–4;
Bentley II, 374–6); see index.
Burbage] son of former King's man, Richard Burbage (**1619**) and part owner of
Blackfriars (Stopes, *Burbage*, pp. 127, 135, 141).

1638 Oct. 7 (codicil) (Oct. 4) Christopher BEESTON alias HUTCHINSON

In the name of god Amen The ffourth day of October 1638 And in the
ffourteenth yeare of the Raigne of o*u*r Soueraigne Lord Charles by the

grace of god King of England Scotland ffraunce and Ireland defendor of the faith &c I Christopher Hutchinson of the parish of St Gyles in the feildes in the County of Middlesex Gentleman being sick and weake in body, but of sound and perfect memorie praise bee therefore give vnto Almightie god, doe make and declare this my last will and Testament in manner and forme following (that is to say) First and principally and aboue all earthlie thinges I Commend my soule into the handes of Almightie god my Creator, and to his sonne Iesus Christ my only sauior and redeemer, by the merrittes of whose most bitter death and bloody passion I doe assuredlie trust to bee saued and haue remission for all my sinnes, And my body to the earth from whence it came to bee buried in Christian buriall in the parish {Church} of St Gyles in the feildes aforesaid: And as touching such temporall goodes where with the Lord hath endowed mee I dispose thereof followeth:[1] Imprimis I {forth with} give will and bequeath vnto my loving sonne William Hutchinson* his heires and assignes foreuer All and singuler my freehould Land and the Messuages or Tenementes therevpon erected and built or vpon anie parte or parcell thereof {scytuate lying and being in the parish of St Leonard in Shorditch* in the Countie of Middlesex} And all and singuler the deedes writinges and euidences concerning the same, and all leases there of made to anie person or persons whatsoeuer: More I give and bequeath vnto him all my parte or parcell of ground now inclosed with a Brick wall lying and being in Lincolnes Inne feildes in the parish of St Gyles in the feildes aforesaid: The deedes whereof were by mee deliuered vnto mr Thomas Vaughan to keepe in trust for mee, Item I give and bequeath vnto my eldest daughter Anne Bird wife of Theophilus Bird* Gentleman, and to her sonne (my godsonne) Christopher Bird the somme of Three hundred poundes of lawfull money of England if my Twoe howses lately erected and built, in Couent garden in the parish of St Martine in the feildes in the said County of Middlesex shalbee assured to amount vnto the somme of Six hundred poundes sterling: And by reason I doe owe many greate debtes, and am engaged for greate sommes of money, which noe[t] one but my wife vnderstandes, where or how to receaue pay or take in, I therefore make her, my [loving] beloued wife Elizabeth* Hutchinson my full and sole executrix of this my presente Last and {will}[2] Testament And doe hereby give vnto my said executrix after my debtes paid, leagacies performed, and funerall Chardges defrayed the residue of all and singuler my goodes and Chattells whatsoeuer; And Ouerseers hereof I doe make, nominate and appoynt, my noble freind Captaine Lewes Kirk,* and my worthie respected freind Thomas Shepheard* Esquire entreating them, in the loue of a true & dying freind that to their utmost (as occasion shall serve) they wilbee aiding and

assisting to my Executrix for the performance of this my last will
and Testament, according to my true intent and honest meaning
heere specified: And I doe give vnto either of them a Gould ring to
weare in remembrance of mee: And whereas I stand possessed of
ffower, of the Six shares in the Company for the King and Queenes
service,* at the Cockpitt in drury lane I declare, that twoe of my
said ffower shares bee deliuered vp, for the advancement of the
said Companie, and the other twoe [be] to remaine vnto my said
Executrix, as fully and amplie as if I lived amongest them; And I
will that my said executrix shall for the said twoe shares prouide
and finde for the said Companie, a sufficyent and good stock of
apparell fitting for theire vse; shee allowing and paying to my said
sonne William Hutchinson for his Care and industrie in the said Companie
Twenty poundes of lawfull money of England per Annum: And I doe
hereby Chardge him, by the loue of a Childe to his father that hee, for
my sake doe all good (concerning this, or anie other busines) to my said
wife and her twoe daughters; And I doe hereby will and order that the
leagacies by mee hereby given willed and bequeathed bee paid by my said
Executrix within Eighteen monethes next after my decease: In witnes
whereof I the said Christopher Hutchinson, to this my presente Last will
and Testament haue sett my hand and seale Dated the day and yeares first
aboue written   C Hutchimson
Read, signed, sealed and as the last will and Testament of the said
Christopher Hutchinson published, and deliuered in the presence of
Bartho: Bramfeld Scriuener The marke of MH Mary Haines The marke
of M Mary Wilkes Bor:[3] Church
7o die Octobris 1638
Memorandum that whereas I {the within named Christopher Hutchinson}
haue willed ordred and devised [that] by my last will and Testament
within written That my executrix within named should pay vnto my
within named sonne William Hutchinson[i] the yearely {somme} of
Twenty poundes of lawfull money of England for his Care and industrie
to bee taken in and about the Companie within mencioned now my will
and mynde is, [th] and I doe hereby order and devise that my sayd
executrix in liew of the said Twenty poundes per Annum shall[. .] allow
vnto him my said sonne William Hutchinson one half share of the Twoe
shares (in the said Company within mencioned[4] {for his Care in the
busines} shee finding & providing a stock of apparell for the said
Companie as is within declared; Witnes my hand the day and yeare
abouesaid   C Hutchinson
Subscribed in the presence of Bor: Church: The marke of MH Mary
Haines The marke of M Mary Wilkes Bartho: Bramfeld Scriuener[5]

1. *followeth*: rightly *as followeth*. 2. Caret mark incorrectly positioned after *and*. 3. *Bor:* RegC has *Bar:* (PRO PROB11/178 fos 450v–451v). 4. Closing parenthesis omitted. 5. *7o . . . Bramfeld Scr'* endorsed.

PRO PROB10/582. OW, codicil and prob. clause endorsed, note of registration marginated. Single sheet with signatures of testator and witnesses and remnants of seal. Text of will, including corrections, and codicil in rapid secretary with displayed matter in italic, hand of Bartholomew Bramfeld.

Prob. by definitive sentence PCC 3 Dec. 1638 to Elizabeth Hutchinson, relict and executor. Prob. clause first subscribed to text of will, then cancelled and rewritten in another hand after codicil adding 'vnacum codicillo ann*exo*'. Endorsement, signed by the surrogate, Charles Tooker, records first presentation of will for probate four days after Hutchinson's burial: 'Iurat Elizabetha Hutchinson al*ias* Biston 19o die mens*is* O*ct*obris 1638 sup*er* Test*ame*nto & Codicillo'. PROB11/178 fos 451v–452r records full sentence promulgated 3 Dec. 1638 (Elizabeth Hutchinson alias Beeston, promoter, v. William Hutchinson alias Beeston, Anne Hutchinson alias Beeston alias Bird, Margaret Hutchinson alias Beeston and Elizabeth Hutchinson alias Beeston, children of the deceased). PAB (PRO PROB8/35 fo. unnumbered (Dec. 1638)) notes exhibition of inventory.

Printed: Hotson, pp. 398–400; see also Bentley II, 631–3 (mistakenly dates probate 30 Dec. 1638) (both RegC).

c.1580–1638. Actor and theatre manager; Lord Chamberlain's c.1598, apprentice of Augustine Phillips who mentions him in his will (**1605**), Worcester's/Queen Anne's 1602–19; succeeded as leader Thomas Greene, in whose will is named overseer (**1612**). Built Cockpit/Phoenix 1617 and was member of each company that occupied theatre: Prince Charles's 1619–22, Lady Elizabeth's c.1622–5, Queen Henrietta's 1625–37, King and Queen's Young Company (of which was governor) from 1637. Executor of George Pulham (**1611**) and legatee of Thomas Basse (**1634**). Suspected recusant. Buried St Giles in the Fields 15 Oct. 1638. (Chambers II, 302; Nungezer, pp. 36–8; Bentley II, 363–70; Eccles, 'Actors I', pp. 39–40.)

Hutchinson] William Beeston, actor and manager (**1682**); see index.
freehould Land . . . in Shorditch] Beeston leased piece of Curtain estate which included Curtain theatre (Hotson, p. 92).
Theophilus Bird] actor with Queen Henrietta's 1625–37, stayed on at Cockpit after company broke (**1663**); see index.
wife Elizabeth] subsequently married Capt. (later Sir Lewis) Kirk and with him continued to run Cockpit as late as 1647 (Bentley II, 370; Hotson, pp. 94–5); see index.
Kirk] gentleman pensioner and Royalist officer in Civil War (Hotson, p. 94); left £100 to his 'dear wife' Dame Elizabeth, and properties in the Savoy and Covent Garden (will dated 21 Aug., proved 7 Oct. 1663 (PRO PROB11/312 fos 131v–132v)).
Shepheard] possibly legatee of John Heminges (**1630**); see index.
Company for the King and Queenes service] the King and Queen's Young Company or Beeston's Boys (Bentley I, 324–42).

1639 Aug. 26 Richard BENFIELD (abstract)

(Benefeild) Of Grayes Inn co. Middlesex, gent. Sick. Soul 'into the handes of Almightie God my Maker and to his sonne Iesus Christe my Saviour and Redeemer by whose painfull passion, cruell death and glorious Resurrection I stedfastly beleeve and assuredly trust to be saved and to enioye everlastinge life in the Kingdome of Heaven'. Burial in pa. St Saviours in Southwarke co. Surrey. Executors to spend £100 on funeral and erect monument with his figure represented for £40. To Thomas French, son, and to Anne and Sarah French, daughters of sister Rebecca French deceased, £30 equally divided between them. To Anne, daughter of kinsman Robert Benefeild* gent., £25. To Mrs Elizabeth Bowen,* widow, £30 to buy gown and ring. To her daughter Winifred Bowen* £20 for same purpose. To loving friend John Bugges,* doctor of physic, £15. To friend Robert Woodford £5. To gossip Eliardt Swanston* and Thomas Pollard* 40s each. To Mrs Winifred Fitche* and her son Mr John Shancke* 40s each. To Edward Goodale and wife 40s to be equally divided between them. Intent that money bequeathed to said friends Robert Woodford, Eliardt Swanston, Thomas Pollard, Winifred Fitch, John Shancke, Edward Goodale and wife shall buy them rings to wear for his sake. To Katharine Sadler, servant to said kinsman Robert Benefeild, 40s. To liberty of the Clincke pa. St Saviours in Southwarke co. Surrey, liberty of White Crosstreete pa. St Giles Cripplegate co. Middlesex, liberty of Grayes Inne Lane pa. St Andrews Holborne co. Middlesex, £10 each to be paid by executors to churchwardens of said parishes as a perpetual stock; money arising to be disbursed for bread to be distributed by the churchwardens or overseers to such poor people within same liberties as they think suitable on Sunday following 23 Nov. each year for ever. To executors for funeral expenses and payments of debts and legacies, rents and profits from several tenements as later described. Whereas now seised of estate of inheritance in fee simple in Grayes Inn Lane alias Perpoole Lane pa. St Andrewe in Holborne co. Middlesex, to Richard Leake, son of sister Sarah Leake, and heirs for ever, all messuages in tenures of George Read, innholder, and Thomas Cady, clerk, and all outhouses belonging to them; also one fourth part of tenements now in tenure of Raph Browne, white baker. To Edward Sturt, son of sister Anne Luke, widow, and heirs for ever, tenement in tenure of Humphrey Wiggan, chandler; also three other parts, residue of aforesaid tenements in tenure of Raph Browne. To Mary and Bridgett, daughters of sister Sarah Leake, to Anne, daughter of sister Anne Luke, and to kinsman Robert Benefeild, and their heirs for ever, inn called the Spread Eagle, with all houses, etc. belonging to it, to be equally divided between them. Aforesaid Edward and Richard to enjoy tenements etc. bequeathed to them at age twenty-one; said Mary, Bridgett, and Anne to enjoy lands etc. at same age or day of marriage, whichever happens first. All rents and profits arising from same premises to be received by executors on behalf of same children and yearly to expend £10 toward maintenance and education of each of same children until reach age of twenty-one; surplus to be kept by executors until that time and then be paid to them without delay; if either of children of sister Anne die before this, portion of deceased to survivor of same children; if any of children of sister Sarah die before this, portion of deceased to survivor of same children without further limitation; if only one of children survives, then solely to such person and heirs and assigns for ever; if more than one, equally between them and heirs and assigns for ever. If all children of either of said sisters die but that sister survives them, then portions of such children to go to surviving sister during her life, and after her decease equally to children of other sister and survivor of them and their heirs for ever. In default of such issue, to sister whose children die last, during her life, and after her death to testator's next of kin. If all said children die before reaching twenty-one, all their portions to said sisters in the proportions bequeathed to their children; if only one of sisters survive, portions of all same children to survivor during her life; and, in either case, after her or their deaths, the same to go to testator's next of kin at death of last of sisters. To loving friend John Heydon gent., one horse with a war saddle with all armour and appurtenances belonging to it. Appoints said Robert Benefeild and John Heydon executors. Revokes all former wills. Wit. Roger Miller scrivener, James Holmes* servant to said scrivener, Elizabeth Bayeley.

PRO PROB11/181 fos 339r–340v. RegC with prob. clause.

Prob. PCC 18 Nov. 1639 to kinsman, Robert Benfield (Benefield), and friend, John Heydon, executors. PAB (PRO PROB8/36 fo. unnumbered (Nov. 1639)) notes exhibition of inventory and gives pa. of origin as once of Gray's Inn co. Middlesex but at time of death of pa. St Giles Cripplegate.

Printed: Bentley II, 633–5 (in part).

fl. 1619–39. Friend of members of King's Men, making bequests to both sides in sharers' dispute of 1635, i.e. family of John Shank (**1635**) and to Robert Benfield, Eyllaerdt Swanston (**1651**) and Thomas Pollard (**A1653**). Father, William Benfield, held extensive property on Bankside (will dated 17 Oct., admon granted 27 Oct. 1619 (PRO PROB11/134 fos 91v–93r)). (Bentley II, 374.)

Robert Benefeild] actor, possibly Queen's Revels, Lady Elizabeth's in 1613, King's Men from 1616 (Chambers II, 303; Nungezer, pp. 42–4; Bentley II, 374–6); see index.

Elizabeth Bowen] daughter and legatee of John Shank; see index.
Winifred Bowen] granddaughter and legatee of Shank; see index.
Bugges] actor, Queen of Bohemia's 1628 (Bentley II, 393–4); related by marriage to Robert Benfield (J. G. Riewald, 'Some later Elizabethan and early Stuart actors and musicians', *English Studies*, XL, 1959, pp. 33–41 (p. 34)); see index.
Swanston] actor, Lady Elizabeth's in 1622, King's Men from 1624.
Pollard] actor, King's Men from 1617, apprentice of John Shank.
Winifred Fitche] widow and executrix of John Shank; see index.
Shancke] actor at Fortune (**1655**).
Holmes] witness to will of Mary Bird alias Borne (**1625**) who had purchased lease of property in Gray's Inn Lane from testator's father (see his will).

1639 Sept. 4 Adam ISLIP (abstract)

Citizen and stationer of London. Revokes all former wills. To kinsman Kenelme Islip all copies after death of wife, she to have use of them during her life. To Company of Stationers £10 to be bestowed on day of funeral as they please. If Richard Herne* his late servant gives executor such release as her counsel shall advise, then to him £100 to be paid within six months of death. To Elizabeth Monger* £20, and £30 more on her marriage day or his wife's death whichever happens first. To Mr Arthur Collins, wife's nephew, 40 marks. To Mr Lightfoot and his wife, to his brother Purfoot and his wife, and to Mr Henry Wally* 50s each, to buy rings to wear in remembrance. To Margrett, Susan, and Dorithie, his late servants, and to all his other servants and apprentices 40s each. To godchildren Adam (or John) Taylor, Swanston and Sara Namecott 20s each. Appoints Mr Lightfoot, his cousin Collins, and Mr Wally overseers; to each of them £10 more. Appoints Susan, loving wife, executor; rest of estate to her.
Codicil: To said Richard Hearne, after his wife's death, his printing presses, letters and implements used for printing. Wit. Arthour Throkmorton, Robert Bell.

PRO PROB10/593. OW, prob. endorsed, note of registration marginated (p. 1). Single sheet folded to make four pages, with signatures and remnants of seal tag (p. 1). Text in rapid secretary.

Prob. PCC 25 Sept. 1639 to Susan Islip, relict and executor. PAB (PROB8/36 fo. unnumbered (Sep. 1639)) notes exhibition of inventory and gives pa. of origin as St Sepulchre without Newgate.

Noted: McKerrow, *Dictionary*, p. 149.

fl. 1591–1639. Printer and theatre investor; in 1622 E. Alleyn granted him lease of one share of second Fortune. Legatees are printers and booksellers. (Bentley II, 481, VI, 157; McKerrow, *Dictionary*, pp. 148–9).

Herne] one of Islip's apprentices, printer in London 1632–46 (Plomer, *Dictionary*, p. 95).
Monger] Islip sold printing house in 1606 to John Monger and Robert Raworth, who were deprived for unlicensed printing of *Venus and Adonis*, and immediately set up another (McKerrow, *Dictionary*, p. 149).
Wally] bookseller in London 1608–55 (Plomer, *Dictionary*, p. 188); see index.

1640 Jan. 3 Sir John ASTLEY (abstract)

Of Maidstone co. Kent, kt. Master of the Revels and one of gentlemen of his Majesty's Privy Chamber. Soul 'to the pleasure of my good God my father and maker to Iesus Christ my Saviour and Redeemer and to the holy ghost my Sanctifier and comforter hoping with assurance by that glorious worke of the holy Trinitye in mans redemption which was wrought by my Saviour Iesus Christ his bitter death and passion to obtayne a full and free remission of all my Sinns and that at my Gods blessed and appointed tyme I shall bee receyved to raigne with the blessed in the Kingdome of Heaven'. To a hundred poor persons, inhabitants of Maidstone and in parishes of Boxley, Maidstone, Ailesford, and Allington, co. Kent, £33 6s 8d, to each 6s 8d within six weeks of funeral. To Francis Bourne, servant, £20. To Anne Dearing £10. To each of his men servants £5; each of his maid servants £3. To cousin Alice Cage, daughter of sister Elianor Knachbull, in widowhood and on demand £100. To cousin Edward Henton of Gray's Inne esq. £50 within seven months of death. To cousin John Knachbull, godson, eldest son of cousin Norton Knachbull esq., £100 at age twenty-one. To cousin Ruth Rogers, daughter of Anthony Nevile of Mattersey co. Nottingham esq., £100 within seven months of decease if unmarried or, if married, in widowhood on demand within twenty-one days. To each child of cousin Curteys by late niece Bridget, daughter of sister Elianor, 20 marks. To each child of cousin Tucke by late niece Margaret, daughter of sister Eleanor, £10. To each child, if any, of cousin Allen by late niece Susan, daughter of sister Elianor, £10. To niece Disney, daughter of late sister Margaret Nevile, 40 marks in widowhood. To cousin Nevile Hall, son of late Dame Margaret Hall, daughter of late sister Margaret, £200 on condition that he immediately pay same to cousin Debora Hall, his sister, towards portion given her by her late father Sir William Hall kt. unless already paid, in which case he is to have sum himself. To cousin Debora 40 marks. To other unnamed children of said Dame Margaret Hall then living 40 marks to be shared equally between them. To cousin Sir Jacob Astley kt. 500 marks if then living; if not, same to cousin Elizabeth Astley, daughter of Sir Jacob, at age twenty-one, if then living; if not, same to eldest child of Sir Jacob, at age twenty-one, if then living. To cousin Anne or Agnes Bridges 'by what name soever shee bee called', niece to wife, £1000; if dead, £500 to said Sir Jacob Astley if living; if not, same to eldest child of Sir Jacob, at age twenty-one, if then living; the other £500, residue of said £1000, to be equally divided between cousins, Thomas Astley, one of sons of uncle Thomas Astley esq. deceased, and Drew Astley, or survivor of them; if both die, to eldest child of said Drew Astley then living, at age twenty-one. To said cousin Thomas Astley, son of uncle Thomas Astley esq., £100; if dead, same to Thomas Astley, eldest son of cousin Andrew Astley esq., if living, at age twenty-one; if not, same to eldest child of said Thomas, son of Andrew, at age twenty-one. To cousin Drew Astley, one of sons of late uncle Richard Astley esq., 40 marks. To cousin Norton Knachbull esq., son of late sister Elianor, 200 marks. To cousin Thomas Knachbull, brother of Norton, £100. To cousin Edward Astley, son of Drew Astley, 40 marks. To godson John Clifford, son of George Clifford of London gent., £20. Dame Katherine his wife to pay to Bridgett Cherson alias Wainwright during her life £4 per quarter after his decease so that she 'may have the whole benefitt thereof to her selfe with out her husband or any other inter medling with the same'. To John Devorax, son of Jone Devorax, sometime his servant, £10 for binding him to a trade unless already done in his lifetime. To cousin John Nevile, on certain conditions, 1000 marks if living; if not, same to eldest son of said John then living, at age twenty-one; if none living, to eldest child of said John then living, at age twenty-one; if no children of said John live to twenty-one, same 1000 marks to said Sir Jacob Astley if surviving them; if not, to eldest child of said Sir Jacob then living after death of all children of said John Nevile, at age twenty-one. Unless otherwise specified, all legacies to be paid by executor within twenty-one days of receipt of due debts as follows: £2000 from Norton Knachbull, £1500 from Sir James Oxinden* kt., £1000 from Sir Jacob Astley, priority of payment to be at discretion of executor. Penalties for servants named as legatees who remove goods without informing the executor. Within eighteen months of decease executor to set up in chancel of church in Maidstone near monument of his late father John Astley esq., or in another convenient place in chancel, monument of his father, mother and self at cost of £100 or within £10 of that sum. Terrier book and 'greate Mappe of all my lands and {all my} originall writings and pattents which doe or shall touch or concerne all or any of my said lands tenements or hereditaments whatsoever', conveyed to said Sir Jacob Astley during life of his wife or after her death to Sir Jacob or his heirs. Executor to take care of those writings concerning wife's jointure. To wife, Dame Katherine, his silver plate and household stuff belonging to his house called the Pallace, 'of the sortes aforesaid propperlye belonging to and ordinarilye vsed in the roome now commonly vsed to dyne and sup in, in the little red chamber thereto adioying, in the roome where my said wife now vsually lyeth, in the little roome or closett thereto adioyning in the greate dyning roome, [in the greate chamber dyning roome], in the greate {lodging} chamber thereto next adioyning toward the North, in the little chamber with in the same in the chamber where my selfe doth now vsually lodge, in the chamber next adioyning where my maid servants doe now vsually lye and in the chamber with in the same where my said cosen Agnes Bridges did heeretofore vsually lye'. All household stuff to be divided into four equal parts, three parts to wife and one to executor. If he dies when farm rents are unpaid, to wife £150 to be paid after executor has received said rents from his tenants. To friend William Harison of upper Eache pa. Woodnes boroughe co. Kent gent. following rooms in his house called the Pallace in Maidstone, 'The roome which I vse for my closett where all or the most part of my books and writings now are the inner roome with in the same and the roomes and places with in the said closett and inner roome the little closett going vp the gallerye and the whole gallerye and little chamber at the end thereof with all the roomes to the said gallerye belonging the chamber over the closett aforesaid sometymes called the schoolehouse [and the inner roome] and the inner roome thereto, the chamber next the buttrey where my sister Elianor Knachbull vsually did lye with all the inner roomes to bee gone into out of the same and the Hovell which is at the end of the greate stable for horse and beasts to stand' for one year after his death without repairs or rent and with stabling for his horses 'for the benefitt of my executor that hee may have the more ease in the execution of my will'. Appoints said William Harison sole executor and residuary legatee. Appoints Sir Humfrey Tufton kt. and aforenamed cousin Edward Henton overseers. To Sir Humfrey Tuffton 'my booke of Ortelius his mapps and my booke of postures for the warres sent mee out of the low cuntreys by my cosen Sir Iacob Astley as {a} token of my love towards him'. To William Harison 'what advantage soever can or may redound to my said executor by this my last will ... for a further recompence'. Wit. Jo. Urrick, Jo. Fletcher, John Harrison, John Ducke.

PRO PROB10/599. OW, note of registration marginated (fo. 1), prob. clause subscribed (fo. 20). Twenty numbered sheets each bearing testator's signature, last sealed and signed by witnesses. Text in facile italic, with distinctive broken–backed *l* also found in testator's signatures, with corrections and interlineations in the same, some, in darker ink, probably made at a later date. Possibly holographic.

Prob. PCC 10 Feb. 1640 to William Harrison, executor.

Noted: Malone (1790), I pt 2, 46.

fl. 1603–40. Master of the Revels 1622–40, active from Mar. 1622 to July 1623. Sir Henry Herbert (1673) purchased life interest in post which he took over Aug. 1623, although Astley held title until he died. Became prominent figure in Kent politics as Puritan; legatees are members of family and Kent neighbours. Died 26 Jan. 1640, buried All Saints Maidstone co. Kent. (Dutton, *Mastering the Revels*, pp. 218–34.)

Oxinden] of Barham co. Kent; friend and correspondent of Samuel Hartlib (Peter Clark, *English Provincial Society from the Reformation to the Revolution: Religion, Politics and Society in Kent 1500–1640*, Hassocks, 1977, p. 217).

1641 Apr. 18 John ROBINSON

Memorandum That on or about the Eighteenth day of Aprill Anno domini 1641. Iohn Robinson late while he lived of the parish of St Giles without Cripplegate London deceased Being of perfect minde and memory and haveing an intention to settle his estate did make and declare his will nuncupative in the manner and the Words following or to the like effect Videlicet he said that all the estate that he had he gave and bequeathed to Elizabeth* Robinson his wife and made her sole Executrix of his will Which words or the like in effect he spoke in the presence of Richard ffowler* & Roger Nore.* Richard ffowler. Roger Nore.//

GL MS 25,626/5 fo. 204v. RegC (nuncupative) with prob. clause.

Prob. Peculiar of Dean and Chapter of St Paul's 29 Apr. 1641 to Elizabeth, relict and executor.

Printed: Cerasano, 'New . . . wills', pp. 302–3.

fl. 1634–41. Actor; King's Revels from 1634 at Salisbury Court and in provinces. Buried St Giles Cripplegate 27 Apr. 1641. (Nungezer, p. 300; Bentley II, 549–50.)

Elizabeth] (1641) widow of Richard Gunnell (A1634), actor with Palsgrave's 1613–22, manager of King's Revels at Salisbury Court.
ffowler] actor, associated with Gunnell in Palsgrave's from 1618 and later at Salisbury Court in II Prince Charles's (Nungezer, pp. 145–6; Bentley II, 439–40).
Nore] actor, II Prince Charles's 1640 (A1649).

1641 Nov. 27 Elizabeth ROBINSON

In the name of God Amen, I [Elizat] {Elizabeth} Robinson of london widdowe beinge sick in body but of sound and good memory, doe make

this my last will and testament in manner and forme followinge, that is to saye first I bequeath my soule to Christ my Redeemer and my bodye to the earth to be buryed in decent buryall: and all my worldley goods and estate I giue and bequeath vnto and amongst my three Chilldren: that is to saye vnto my daughter margeret Sherry* widdowe I giue and bequeath one halfe share that I haue in the playhouse in Salsbury Court:* Item I giue to my daughter Anne Gonnell one other halfe share that I haue in the foresayd playhouse: Item I doe giue one other halfe share that I haue in the sayd house vnto my sonne Iohn Robinson,: and all my goods to be [equally] equally diuided amongst them: and my Will is that my two dawghters shall keepe and maynteyne my sonne, and giue him such breedinge as shallbe fittinge vntill he Come to [age] the age of one and twenty yeeres with the proffitts arriseinge from the halfe share that as aforesayd I haue giuen vnto him, and with his parte of my goods: And my will is that all my debts (which they shallbe necessaryly bownd to paye) shallbe payd by the proffitts issueing from the three halfe shares aforesayd equally: And I doe make and ordayne my sayd two daughters margaret sherry widdow and Anne Gonnell full and sole Executresses of this my last will and testament, and my loueinge kinsman William Waluyn ouer seer of the same: in wittnesse where of I haue hereunto set my hand and seale this seauen[o] and twentith day of nouember 1641
                    the marcke of Elizabeth [off c..] Robinson X
Sealed and published in the presence off William Walwyn Humphery Brooke Edward Lambert

GL MS 9172/48. OW, prob. clause subscribed, note of registration marginated. Single sheet folded in half to make four pages, with mark of testator and signatures of witnesses; applied seal now lost. Text in facile mixed hand of W. Walwyn, corrections in same hand as text.

Prob. CCL 8 Dec. 1641 to Margaret Sherry (Sherrey) and Anne Gunnell (Gonnell), executors. PAB (GL MS 9168/19 fo. 69v) gives pa. of origin as St Bride and valuation of inventory at £34 18s 8d.

fl. 1634–41. Widow of actors Richard Gunnell (**A1634**) and John Robinson (**1641**); shareholder in Salisbury Court by inheritance. Will used as evidence in dispute in 1654 between Andrew Cane and Margaret and William Wintershall, of the Wintershalls' right to debt due to Richard Gunnell from agreement with Palsgrave's in 1624 (Hotson, pp. 52–3).

margeret Sherry] married William Wintershall, actor at Salisbury Court before 1642 and, after Restoration, in King's company under Killigrew (Bentley II, 623–4).
share ... in Salsbury Court] theatre built by Richard Gunnell and William Blagrave 1629. Gunnell and possibly Robinson among seven sharers in King's Revels company at Salisbury Court in 1634 (Bentley VI, 99–100) but division of shares in fabric of theatre unknown.

1645 Sept. 26 Michael BOWYER

In the name of God Amen, ye six and twentith day of September Anno Domini .1645. et Regis Caroli 21 I Michael Bowyer of Hounslow in the Countie of Middlesex gent being sicke & weake in bodye but of good and perfect memorie (thankes be giuen to god therfore) Doe make and ordayne this my last will and Testament in manner and forme following ffirst I bequeath my soule into the handes of allmightie god my Creator hopeing to be eternally saved thorough his infinite mercie and {by} the pretious death and suffering of Iesus Christ my alone Saviour, and my body to be decently buried at the discrecion of my executer hereafter named, Item I giue to my loveing frend mr Richard Perkins* of St Giles in the feildes London ffyftie poundes of currant English money to be payed vnto him by fyve shillinges a weeke, yf he shall soe long lyve as to receave the same as aforesaid But if he shall decease byfore the said summe soe to be receaved Then the sayd payment alsoe to cease likewise. But yf ye said Richard Perkins shall overlive the full receipt of the said summe as aforesaid. Then he shall haue foure shillinges a weeke dureing his naturall life to be paied out of my landes in Worcester sheire Item I give to Henry Mildmay of Heston Esq.* my Nagg which he gave vnto me with new Bridle Sadle & Cloth. Item to Iames Totnell in Shoe lane london in the parrish of St Brides my blacke lace suite and Cloake Item I giue to Nicholas Awnsham* of Hownslowe generosus twentie shillinges Item I give vnto my loveing wife Elizabeth* Bowyer all my landes tenementes and hereditamentes whatsoever in Worcester=sheire in Kiddermaster. with their appurtenaunces to her and her heires forever And alsoe I giue and bequeath all other my goodes and Chattles whatsoeuer (not before bequeathed) vnto my said loveing wife Elizabeth Bowyer whome I make and ordaine full and whole executrix of this my last will and Testament In witnes whereof I the sayd Michaell Bowyer haue hereunto set my hand and seale the day and yeare aboue written Michael Bowyer Signed sealed published and declared as the last will and testament of the said Michael Bowyer in the presence of vs Nicholas Awnsham ffrancis Harpar./

PRO PROB11/194 fo. 204v. RegC with prob. clause and marginal note recording grant of administration to Thomas Morrison, second husband of Elizabeth Bowyer, 7 May 1658.

Prob. PCC 6 Nov. 1645 to Elizabeth Bowyer, relict and executor.

Printed: Bentley II, 635–6.

fl. 1621–45. Actor; Queen Henrietta's from 1625, King's by 1641; legatee of Thomas Basse (**1634**) and William Hovell (**1615**) to whom he was apprenticed. (Nungezer, pp. 53–4; Bentley II, 385–7.)

Perkins] fellow member of Queen Henrietta's from 1626; acted as trustee for Bowyer for loan to King's company c.1635 (Chambers II, 332; Nungezer, pp. 274–8; Bentley II, 525–8); see index.
Mildmay of Heston Esq.] mistakenly identified in index to Bentley (II, 728, VII, 292) as Sir Henry Mildmay, Master of the Jewel House under Charles I, knighted in 1617.
Awnsham] Bentley (II, 461) tentatively identifies legatee as Nicholas Hanson, provincial player with King's Revels in 1620s.
wife Elizabeth] married Thomas Morrison 1 Apr. 1646, died 28 Aug. 1656; from 1655 involved with second husband in suit with Theophilus Bird (**1663**) over bond due to Bowyer for loan to King's company (Hotson, pp. 31–4).

1650 July 22 Inigo JONES (abstract)

Of pa. St Martin in the Feilds co. Middlesex, Surveyor of Works to late King and Queen, aged seventy-seven. Perfect health but weak. Soul 'to Almighty God, hoping by ye death and passion of my Saviour Christ Iesus to haue remission of my sinnes, and attayne vnto eternall life'. Burial in church of St Bennett Paul's Wharfe London. £100 for funeral expenses and £100 for erecting monument of white marble in said church. To Richard Gammon of pa. St Mary Savoy co. Middlesex, who married Elizabeth Jones his kinswoman, £500 and half his wearing apparel. To Mary Wagstaffe, kinswoman, £100 to be reserved by executor or Richard Gammon for her preferment either by marriage or otherwise. £100 to be equally divided among five children of said Mary Wagstaffe by Henry Wagstaffe, her late husband, to be used for their preferment as thought best by executor and Richard Gammon; if any of children die before portion paid, portion of that child to be equally divided toward advancement of survivors. To John Damford of pa. St Martin in the Feilds, carpenter, £100. To Stephen Page for faithful service, £100. To Anne Webb, kinswoman, £2000 as jointure, to be paid by executor within one year of proving of will. To five children of executor by said Anne Webb, £1000. Of debt owing to him for entertainment and service to late King and Queen, to Henry Wicks esq., Paymaster of the Works, £50 to be paid within one month of receipt of debt; remainder to be equally divided between executor and Richard Gammon. To poor of pa. St Martin's £10 to be paid within one month of proving of will. To poor of pa. St Bennett's £10 to be paid within one month of proving of will. Appoints John Webb* of pa. St Martin in the Feildes co. Middlesex, who married Anne Jones his kinswoman, sole executor; Henry Cogan of said parish esq. and Henry Browne of pa. St Mary Savoy esq. overseers, to whom £10 each.

Makes void all former wills. Wit. William Bell, Henry Browne, H. Cogan, William Gape, Godfrey Austinson scrivener.

PRO PROB1/39. OW, prob. clause subscribed, note of registration and of exhibition, in 3rd session of Trinity term 1652, endorsed. Single sheet, sealed. Text in small fluent mixed hand with signatures of testator and witnesses. Some loss of legibility along folds.

Prob. PCC 24 Aug. 1652 to John Webb, executor.

Printed: Peter Cunningham, *Inigo Jones: A Life of the Architect*, Shakespeare Society 39, London, 1848, pp. 49–51 (RegC).

1573–1652. Architect, designer of masques, King's Surveyor in Office of Works 1615–43, designed Cockpit theatre 1616. Died 21 June at Somerset House, buried St Benet 26 Jun. 1652. Legatees, Gammon, Damford and Wicks, colleagues at Works. (*DNB*; H. M. Colvin, D. R. Ransome, and John Summerson, *The History of the King's Works*, vol. III, *1485–1660 (pt 1)*, London, 1975, pp. 129–59; John Orrell, *The Theatres of Inigo Jones and John Webb*, Cambridge, 1985.)

Webb] Jones's pupil, assisting in Works from 1630 (H. M. Colvin, *A Biographical Dictionary of English Architects 1660–1840*, London, 1954, pp. 653–8).

1651 June 24 Eyllaerdt SWANSTON

Memorandum that Eyllœardt Swanstone late of the parish of St Mary Aldermanbury London gent, deceased, in the tyme of the sicknesse whereof he dyed, and vpon or about the fower and twentith day of Iune in the yeare of our Lord 1651, beinge of perfect mynde and memorie, with an intent to make his will, and to settle, and dispose of his estate did by worde of mouth declare his will and mynde to be as followeth, and in the wordes followeinge, or in words to the like effect v*idelice*t I will, or my will and desire is that my estate be divided, and shared equally amonge my children and further (speakinge to his daughter Sara the wfe[1] of Ioseph wilson, w*h*ich Sara was then, and there pr*es*ent) he the said Eyllœardt Swanstone vsed theise or the like wordes v*idelice*t. I leave this to your care to see it be performed and to take care of my children. W*h*ich wordes, or the like in effect the said Eyllœart Swanstone beinge then of perfect mynde and memorie did vtter and speake with an intent that the same should stand and be as, and for his last will and testament in the pr*es*ence and hearinge of Ioseph Wilson Elizabeth Vasely. Elizabeth Swanstone and of the said Sara Swanstone/
Ioseph Wilson Iunior the marke of Elizabeth X Vaseley Sarah willson

1. w/e: rightly *wife*.

PRO PROB10/734. OW (nuncupative), grant of admon endorsed (p. 1). Single sheet folded in half to make four pages, unsealed, with signatures of witnesses. Text in facile secretary with displayed matter in italic.

Admon [with will annexed]. PCC 3 July 1651 to son, John Swanston, and daughter, Sarah Wilson. RegC (PRO PROB11/217 fos 370v–371r) has marginal note recording grant of administration of goods unadministered 18 Apr. 1666 to Joseph Wilson, husband of Sarah, both administrators having died.

Printed: Hotson, p. 73 fn. 48 (abstract of RegC), reprinted Bentley II, 648.

fl. 1622–51. Actor; Lady Elizabeth's 1622, King's Men by 1624. Held one-third of one share in Blackfriars before 1635; in 1635, with Robert Benfield and Thomas Pollard (**A1653**), petitioned for and won share of Globe and Blackfriars from John Shank (**1635**) and others ('Sharers' papers'). Legatee of Richard Benfield (**1639**). During Civil War sided with Puritans, took trade of jeweller. Buried St Mary Aldermanbury 28 June 1651. (Hotson, p. 15; Nungezer, pp. 342–4; Bentley II, 584–8.)

1652 Sept. 28 (codicil) (1651 Aug. 1) Arthur WILSON (abstract)

Of Felsted co. Essex gent. In health 'knowing by Diuine Truth that man is as the flower of the ffeild, as a Vapor, as dust, as a shadow that passeth away; and by humane Experience as a brittle glasse, soone broken'. Soul 'to God, that gaue it, and to my lord and Sauiour Iesus Christ that redeemd it, by whose most blessed Merrits, I hope to attaine to that hapines in Heauen, which no Tongue nor pen can expresse, nor can it euer enter into the Heart of Man to conceiue it. And to the Holie Ghost the Comforter doe I resigne my Spirit. To which three Persons, and one God, bee all Honor, Glorie, and Praise, for Euer'. Burial at wife's pleasure 'Knowing wheresoeuer it lyes, it must resolue to its first Principles till the last great Restitution that the Earth shall make in giving vp her Dead, when I hope to see with theise Eyes, and heare with theise Eares, to the Comfort of my Soule, the glorious Sauiour and Iudge of the World, setting vpon a Throne of Mercie pronouncing his Venite. And because this Bodie of Mine hath so many yeares clogd' my Soule, and Chaind it to Vanitie, that it Could not so Clearely mount vp with the Wings of Loue to that Diuine Loue that made it. My Will is that it bee interred priuately, without any Outward Ostentation. ffor St Paul telleth the Corinthians that the Body is sowne in Corruption, but it is raisd in incorruption, it is sowne in Dishonor; it is rais'd in Glorie, it is sowne in weakenes, it is raisd in Power, It is sowne a Naturall Bodie, it is raisd a Spirituall Bodie, and hee assures him that is in Christ Quod transformabit corpus suum humile &c That his vile Body shalbe changed that it may be fashioned like vnto Christs glorious Body, which is farr aboue all the State and Glorie that the World Can afford'. Sixteenth part of ship costing £30 (and £10 in money) to use and disposal of sister Judeth or her children. To sister Marie £40 and lease of house in Perpole lane. To youngest daughter of deceased sister Katherine £30. To cousin Robert Nixon £10. To cousin Mr Richard Nixon £10, 'Camdens Britania and all my English Chronicles in English'. To son–in–law Mr William Web 'my Statute Bookes and all my other Bookes which Doe Concerne the Lawe'. Remainder of books except those hereafter mentioned to his lord's library at Leeze* 'to be Continewed there to that Noble ffamelie, for the Benefitt of the Chaplaines to that house'. To son Web £10 for a ring. To daughter Webb £10 for a ring. To good friend Mrs Sidney Humfries £10 for a ring, 'my Concaue glasse with the foot, Gerrardes Herball and my Phisick Manuscript with the blew strings'. To poor of pa. Little Leeze 40s. To poor of pa. Felsted £3. All legacies to be paid within twelve months of decease by 'my deare and loving wife to whome the bondes of Nature and affection ties mee, with whome I haue liued a quiet and Contented life, for whome I blesse God, And to whome I giue and [bef] bequeath the rest of my estate', that is profits from house and land in Felsted called Drinkalls for her life and, after her decease, same to poor of pa. Felsted for ever; yearly revenue to ministers and churchwardens of said parish to be divided weekly every Sunday morning among poor in bread. To wife house and land in Felsted on Cleuelandes greene commonly called Cleuelandes for her life and, after her decease, said house and land to cousin Mr Richard Nixon and heirs for ever provided that, within six months of receiving property, Nixon pays to testator's sister Marie £20, to daughter of his late sister Katherine £20, to eldest son of his sister Judeth £20, and to cousin Capt. Robert Nixon £10, and to cousin Mr John Nixon £10, or their children if they die before he inherits, reverting to Richard Nixon if they die without issue. Remainder to wife whom makes sole executor. Appoints son Mr William Webb and cousin Mr Richard Nixon supervisors. To grandchild Elizabeth Spittie his best diamond ring. No more to son and daughter Webb because wife's part will go to them and their children. Wit. John Sorell, John Snowe (mark). Codicil: Entire library to Earl of Warwick desiring him to apppoint a 'fitt place for disposeing {ther} of [them] with safety and Chayning the[m] {bookes} so as they {[s . . .]} may be Continued to the vse and Seruice of that nob<le> ffamily'. To Countess of Warwick £50 in gold for piece of gold plate. Instead of bookes mentioned in will, to Mrs Sydney Humphryes (Humfrye) 'the great Cabinett in my Closett with all thinges whatsoeu*er* therin being'. To good friend Mrs Gregory £10 for a ring. To maid Mary besides her wages £10. To William Bland besides his wages £10. To servant Richard Archer besides his wages 40*s*. To Arthur Nixon, son of cousin Robert Nixon, £20 to be paid to his father for buying plate. All money bequeathed to be paid within one year of death. To good friend Mr William Jessop his best diamond ring which he had bequeathed to his grandchild Elizabeth Spittie since deceased. As his wife had died since making of will appoints kinsman Mr Richard Nixon sole executor. Wit. William Bland, W. Jessop, Richard Archer (mark).

PRO PROB10/775. OW, codicil annexed, prob. clause subscribed (fo. 3). Three sheets, each signed by the testator and numbered, with applied seals on fos 2 and 3 and signatures of witnesses. Text of will in testator's fluent mixed hand, with displayed matter (headings, quotations, and significant nouns) in italic. Codicil in second hand.

Prob. PCC 16 Oct. 1652 to Richard Nixon, kinsman and executor.

Printed: Arthur Wilson, *The Swisser*, publié après un manuscrit inédit, avec une introduction et des notes par A. Feuillerat, Paris, 1904, pp. cvi–cx (RegC).

1595–1652. Dramatist; three plays performed by King's company at court and Blackfriars 1630–2 but unpublished until after death. Secretary to Robert Devereux, third Earl of Essex, 1614–30; steward to Robert Rich, second Earl of Warwick, 1632–52. Trained in court and chancery hands by John Davies of Hereford; several holograph MSS extant. Buried Felstead church co. Essex, date unknown. (Bentley V, 1267–74.)

lord's library at Leeze] Little Leighs, Warwick's estate near Felstead.

1655 Dec. 1 John SHANK Jr

Memorandum That Iohn Shanncke late of the parish of St Botolph without Aldersgate London deceased did on or about the first day of December In the yeare of our Lord One thousand six hundred fifty five, he then being (though sicke in body) of perfect mind, memory and vnderstanding and having an intent and purpose to settle or dispose of his estate, make and declare his last Will and testament Nuncupative in manner and forme following, videlicet; He gave and bequeathed all that he had and whatsoever was due vnto him vnto Henry Hasard of the parish of St Iames Clarkenwell in the County of Midd*lesex* gent*leman*, whom he the sayd deceased desired to haue a care to bury him; Which words or the like in effect he did nuncupate and declare with a mind of making his Will in the p*r*esence of divers credible wittnesses.

Hen Geery Ri: Wright

On the first of August 1656 The sayd Henry Geery and Richard Wright were sworne upon the truth of the abovewritten Nuncupative will Henry Geery & Richard wright sworne before me G Cock[1]

1. On . . . Cock subscribed, including 'signatures' of witnesses, in hand of Cock.

PRO PROB10/837. OW (nuncupative), grant of admon and note of registration endorsed (p. 4). Single sheet folded to make four pages, with signatures of witnesses. Text in fluent mixed hand with displayed matter in italic.

Admon [with will annexed]. PCC 10 Sept. 1656 to Henry Hasard, universal legatee, no executor named. PAB (PRO PROB8/50 fo. 267v) notes exhibition of inventory.

1616–55. Possibly the actor, son of King's Man John Shank (**1635**). With Red Bull provincial company 1635, at Fortune 1640; legatee of father and of Richard Benfield (**1639**). The John Shank buried St Giles in the Fields Oct. 1641 unlikely to be the actor as 'one Shanks a player' deserted Parliamentary forces Oct. 1642. (Nungezer, pp. 320–1; Bentley II, 567–9.)

1659 Apr. 9 Ellis WORTH

In the name of God Amen. I Ellis Worth of the parish of St Giles without Cripplegate in the County of Middlesex gent being at this present weak of body but of competent memory blessed be God)[1] doe make & ordein this my last will & testament first comending my Soule to almighty God my Creator hoping through the merrites of Iesus Christ my Redeemer to haue pardon of all my sinnes & be saved, My Body I commit to the Earth to be buried in the parish Church of St Giles aforesaid in the middle Isle by my Relacions there lying. And although I haue already advanced the Children of my Body and given them sufficient porcions of my Estate, yet out of my naturall loue and affeccion to them & theirs I giue & bequeath amongst them the seuerall Legacyes herein after mencioned (that is to say), Tenn poundes to my daughter Iane Alsopp wife of Peter Alsop in the Barbados, Item to hir eldest sonne Ellis Ricroft [by] which she had by hir former husband Henry Ricroft deceased also Tenn poundes, And to hir other Children Tenn poundes equally amongst them. Item [I] to my sonne in law Peter Alsopp afore–named Tenn shillinges to buy him a Ring. And to my sonne Elizeus Worth Tenn poundes, And to his 2 Children Katheren & Blandina ffiue poundes apeece. Item to my wifes sister Mary woodall widow fforty shillinges to buy hir a Ring, And to my daughter in law Katheren worth wife of my said sonne Elizeus Tenn shillinges {also for a Ring} Item I giue to the Churchwardens of the said parish of St Giles in the County of Middlesex & to their successors ffifteen poundes to be imployed by them for the vse & benefit of the Poore of the

said parish within ye (fo. 2) Lordshipp of ffinsbury, and to distribute the Interest & benefit thereof [to] yearly to such of the said Poore on the ffeast day of Allsaintes comonly called Alhallowday as the Church wardens & Overseers of the Poore in the said Lordship shall finde to haue most need thereof. Item I giue to Susan Heale* widow fforty shillinges and to dorothie ffowler* widow [also] Twenty shillinges, and to my Goddaughter Elizabeth Morgan Tenn shillinges, and to hir husband Charles Morgan also Tenn shillinges to buy each of them a Ring. And all the rest and residue of my goodes chattells Leases tenementes houses howsholdstuff and estate whatsoeuer I giue will & bequeath {vn}to my loving wife Frances Worth,* and I make & appoint hir my full & sole Executrix willing hir to pay the said Legacyes aboue by me given at or before th'end of one yeare next after my decease, And the Legacyes of such of the Legatees as shalbe then vnder the age of xxjtie yeares I appoint to be paid to their Parents or Guardians and whose Acquittances shalbe a sufficient discharge to my said Executrix for the same. And in witnes and confirmacion of this my last will conteined in two sheetes of paper I haue to each sheet set my hand & seale the Nyneth day of Aprill in the yeare of our Lord Christ One thousand six hundred fiftie nyne./   Ellis woorth
Signed sealed & published on the day of the date in the presence of Richard White Hen: Travers Scriuener in Smithfield./

1. Opening parenthesis missing.

PRO PROB10/912. OW, grant of admon subscribed (fo. 2), note of registration endorsed (fo. 3). Three sheets, joined at top, numbered, fos 1 and 2 bearing signature of testator, with signatures of witnesses and applied seals. Text in facile secretary.

Prob. PCC (at London before Judges for Probate) 7 May 1659 to Frances Worth, relict and executor. Undated note written and signed by Tho: Trice, endorsed on will (fo. 3): 'deceased 14 dayes since fully past'.

Printed: Cerasano, 'New ... wills', pp. 303–4 (Reg C).

c.1587–1659. Actor; member and sharer in Queen Anne's c.1612–19, with Players of Revels at Red Bull 1622, II Prince Charles's 1631–42. Buried St Giles Cripplegate 19 Apr. 1659. (Nungezer, pp. 401–2; Bentley II, 625–7; Sisson, 'Notes', p. 29.)

Heale] Cerasano reads Neale; possible connection with Robert Neale, witness to will of William Browne (1634) who was sharer in Red Bull company.
ffowler] not widow of fellow actor at Fortune, Richard Fowler, who married Elizabeth Freeman 1627 (Bentley II, 439).
Frances Worth] formerly widow of Thomas Holcomb, actor with King's company 1616–25 (Nungezer, p. 194; Bentley II, 475).

1663 Mar. 20 Theophilus BIRD

In the name of God Amen the twentieth of March in the fiueteenthe[1] yeere of the Raighne of our Soveraigne Lord Charles the Second by the Grace of God King of England Scotland ffrance and Ireland Defender of the faith etc, the yeare of our Lord 1662[2] I Theophilus Bird of the Parish of St Giles in the feilds of the County of Midelsex, Gentleman, being in perfect health of Minde though not of Bodey Thanked bee our Lord therefore: ffor the Setling and dispossing of those Portions of Goodes which it hath pleaced God of his Goodness to bestowe on mee for the helpe of me, my Wiffe & poore Children, Doe ordaine and make my last Will and Testament in maner and fforme ffollowing: ffirst I Humbley[3] besech our Lord God and Saviour that out of his Infinite Mercy it Will pleace him to fforgiue me all my wicked sinnes and offences, and that for his owne mercy Sake it will pleace him to receiue me into the number of his Elect and Chosen companie and according to the ffull trust and Beleife which I haue reposed only in his Ineffable mercy through the Sheding of his most pretious blood, and through the same faith I haue ffull hope and trust I shall liue againe and see my Lord and Redeemer:/

And I will that my Body shall be buried in the parish Church of St Giles in the ffeildes, if it pleace God I die with in tenn miles off the a fforesaid parish, otherwise in some Church or ChurchYard neer the place off my Decease as it shall seem convenient to my Executrex, the which my Buriall when soever it shall bee I will shall bee done without any Charges more then of Necessity must bee Imployed/

ffirst and formust I doe giue to my Daughter Ann Mohun* Wiff to Micheall Mohune* Gentleman twenty shillings.

and I doe giue to my Daughter Mary Bird twenty Shillings.

and I doe giue to my Sonne Theophilus Bird* twenty Shillings.

and I doe giue to my Sonne George Bird twenty Shillings.

and I doe giu\<e\> to my Daughter Elizabe\<th\> Bird twenty Shillings

and I doe giue to the poore, those that my Excutrex shall thinke fitt twenty Shillings.

Moreover I doe giue to my Sone Theophilus Bird and to my Sonne George Bird all my right and tytle[4] in all the playes and playbookes that are mine by payment and Survivourshipp:

My Will is that the residue of my goodes, Plate, Houshould stuff, leases, mouables and Redy Mony or mony's Worth not otherwayes being disposed of shall bee and remaine to my Well beloued wiffe Ann Bird* which I doe giue vnto her owne proper vse and behoof, and doe make her ffull and whole Executrex for the Exeuting and performance of this my Last Will and Testament:/ And in Witnesse that this is my true and last will and Testament

I haue Subscribd my name and Sett my Seall
Theo: Bird
Sealed and published to be the last will and Testament of the aboue named Theophilus Bird in the presence off, Will: Cowper ffran:[5] Cotton Hugh Greene Alce broadhead George Bird

1. *fiueteenthe*: added in paler ink. 2. *1662*: 2 added in paler ink. 3. *ffirst I Humbley*: written over erasure. 4. *tytle*: originally *title*, y written over *i*. 5. *ffran*: RegC (GL MS 9171/31b fos 242v–243v) has *Anne*.

GL MS 9172/55. OW, prob. clause and note of registration endorsed. Single sheet, sealed, with signatures of testator and witnesses. Text in round hand with insertions in same.

Prob. CCL 30 June 1663 to Ann Bird, relict and sole executor.

1608–63. Actor, son of actor William Bird alias Borne (**1624**) and Mary Bird (**1625**); Queen Henrietta's c.1625–37, Beeston's Boys from 1637; King's 1641–2; King's 1662, with acting share in Theatre Royal Drury Lane. In dispute with widow of Michael Bowyer (**1645**) over dissolution of King's company in 1642 (Hotson, pp. 31–3). Agent for brother–in–law William Beeston (**1682**) in lease of Salisbury Court theatre 1652 (Hotson, p. 103). (Nungezer, pp. 46–8; Bentley II, 377–9; Highfill et al. II, 133–5.)

Ann Mohun] buried 2 Jan. 1702; will dated 13 Oct. 1701, proved 23 Jan. 1702 (PRO PROB11/463 fos 61r–63r).
Micheall Mohune] fellow actor in Queen Henrietta's, Beeston's Boys; King's company after Civil War (Nungezer, pp. 252–4; Bentley II, 511–2; Highfill et al. X, 271–6).
Theophilus Bird] actor, King's company 1664–74 (Highfill et al. II, 135).
Ann Bird] daughter of Christopher Beeston (**1638**).

1666 July James SHIRLEY

In the Name of God Amen. I Iames Shirley of Whitefryers londo*n* gent being of perfect mind & memory do make and declare this my last will & Testament in manner & forme following, First I resigne my soule into the hands of Almighty God my Creator, with full beliefe to haue remission of all my sinnes, by ye merits death & passion of my Redeemer Iesus Christ. My body I remit to the E[e]arth, to be decently buryed according to the discretion of my Executor hereafter named. As to the disposition of my worldly estate, I giue and bequeath the same {(my debts if any shall appeare, & funerall charges {first} defraid)} as followeth [First]
I giue and bequeath to my oldest son Mathias Shirley 200 l' [< ... >] sterl*ing* to be paid him within 6 moneths after my decease, I likwise giue him my Cornelian seale ring, my silver watch, and my best wearing

clothes. I giue and bequeath to my son Christopher Shirley [one] {180 l'} to be paid him likewise within 6 moneths after my decease. [I giue him also one peece of plate marked. & ye remainder of my wearing clothes.] I giue and bequeath to my son Iames Shirley the somme of 150 l' [three score pounds] sterl*ing* to be paid him w*i*thin 6 moneths as aforesaid (**fo. 2**) I giue and bequeath to my daughter Mary now wife of Standerdine Shirley als[1] Sachell, the somme of [< . . . >] {200 l'} sterl*ing* to be paid as aforesaid I also giue her a silver Tankard marked,   [2] [and 6 silver] spoones, I giue unto Standardine abouenamed one gold ring with fiue Turkie stones, and Idoe release & forgiue to him [all former debts, & in particular I doe release to him] a debt of fifty pounds, w*hi*ch I lent him upon his bond, dated.[3]
I giue and bequeath to my daughter Laurinda [now wife] {ye relickt}[4] of Edward Fountaine the somme of 200 l'
Item I giue to her [one peece of plate marked]   [2] my litle diamond [ring, and 3 silver spoones].
I giue and bequeath to George Shirley ali*as* Sachell son of the said Standardine and Mary the summe of thirty pounds to be paid as abouesaid.
I giue and bequeath to my worthy freind mr Iohn Warter (**fo. 3**) of the Inner Temple the summe of   [2].
I giue to mistres Warter wife of the said Mr Iohn Warter to buy her a ring
I giue to mr George Warter sonne of the said Mr Iohn the summe of   [2]
I giue to mr Vincent Cane* my loving freind the summe of twenty pounds to be disposed by him, according to a former agreement betwixt us.
[I giue to m*ist*ris Mary Polton now wife of Mr Richard Polton of Vpney[5] in Essex gent 40 s to buy her a ring.
I giue to mr Robert Sturges of Whitefryers ye summe of   [2]
I giue to the {poore of ye} parishe of St Dunstane in the west five pounds to be disposed, & distributed according the prudence of my Executrix (**fo. 4**) And further my will is {& I doe give & bequeath}[4] that all the residue of my estate, and whatsoeuer shall remaine in any kind whatsoeuer, {herein not}[4] undisposed of, ouer and {aft} aboue the legacyes by me formerly in this my present will bequeathed, {firste being paid}[4] shall remaine] unto my [loving wife Frances] Shirley, And I do by this my will giue & bequeath unto {my loueing wife ffrance*es* Shirley}[4] [her] all the remainder of my estate {in specialtyes plate money Iewells, linnen woollen bedding brasse pewter, or goods of any kind whatsoeuer} {my debt*es* & legacye*es* being first paid}[6] [(after the discharge of my debts funerall charges, & payment of [my] the legacyes aboue said)] in confidence that she will be kind to my children, and at her death, if it shall please God that any of them survive her, I doubt not, but that she will leaue upon them some Testimony of her Loue for my sake. And I doe hereby

nominate constitute & appoint my said loving wife Frances Shirley, Executrix of this my last will and Testament. In witness whereof I haue subscribed my name and affixed my seale, the ² day of Iulie. A*nno* domi*ni* 1666 And in the eighteenth[7] yeere of the Reigne of o*u*r Soue*r*aigne Lord King Charles the second.
Signed sealed & published in the presence of   ²

Iames Shirley

1. *als*: mark of abbreviation omitted, rightly *alias*. 2. Blank in MS. 3. End of line; space for insertion of date?. 4. Insertion by second hand in darker ink. 5. *Vpney*: originally written *Epney*. 6. *my debt'* . . . *paid*: insertion by second hand. 7. *eighteenth* in second hand.

PRO PROB10/993. OW, grant of admon, note of registration and exhibition of inventory endorsed (fo. 4). Four loose sheets, each numbered, with signature of testator on last. Appears to be an incomplete draft in Shirley's hand, lacking witnesses and seal. Text in rapid mixed hand, with some alterations made in the course of writing and others made later in a different style (predominantly secretary) and on fo. 4 in a darker ink. There seem to be three levels of emendation: 1. in same hand and ink as main text; 2. second secretary hand using blacker ink correcting phraseology especially evident on fo. 4, probably later than original draft, e.g. change of status of daughter Laurinda from wife to relict (see ll. 25, 42, 44, 45, 47, 49–50, 58); 3. final substantive revision involving deletion of whole sections, especially on fo. 3 (see Figure 3, p. 16). We suggest that Shirley wrote the first draft, another person corrected common form, and then Shirley revised, cutting out Poultons, changing wording of responsibilities of his wife, etc. Second hand bears some similarities to the first, for example in forms of *t* and *y* but elsewhere diverges, for example ampersand, *e*, and *th* in 'give & bequeath' (fo. 1 passim and fo. 4). W. W. Greg describes will as 'to all appearance autograph' (*English Literary Autographs, 1550–1650*, Part 3: *Prose Writers and Appendix*, London, 1932, no. XCV).

Admon PCC 3 Nov. 1666 to Mary Poulton, wife of Richard Poulton, niece by her sister and next–of–kin to the late Frances Shirley, relict and executor, who died before taking up duties (Mary identified as daughter of Frances Shirley's brother, John Blackburne, by Sandra A. Burner, *James Shirley: A Study of Literary Coteries and Patronage in Seventeenth–century England*, Lanham, MD, 1988, pp. 212–3 fn. 104); gives pa. of origin as 'whitefryars sed in p*aro*chia S*an*cto Egidi in Campis Mid*d*lesex de*functus*'.

Printed: A. H. Nason, *James Shirley Dramatist: A Biographical and Critical Study*, New York, 1915, pp. 158–60 (RegC); W. W. Greg, op. cit. (OW in part with facsimile).

1596–1666. Dramatist; wrote some twenty plays for companies of Christopher Beeston (**1638**) at Cockpit 1625–36, including Lady Elizabeth's, Queen Henrietta's; may have been under contract to theatre. Wrote for Irish theatre 1636–40. Dramatist to King's Men at Blackfriars 1640–2. Became clergyman before 1618 but converted to Catholicism by 1625. Shirley and wife buried St Giles in the Fields

29 Oct. 1666, driven from home near Fleet Street by Great Fire (2–6 Sept. 1666). (Bentley II, 573; V, 1064–1170; Burner, op. cit., pp. 198–202 discusses will and identifies legatees.)

Cane] John Vincent Canes, Catholic apologist, possibly testator's confessor (see Aline M. Taylor, 'James Shirley and "Mr. Vincent Cane", the Franciscan', N&Q, CCV, 1960, pp. 31–3).

1673 Apr. 9 (codicil) (Jan. 1) Sir Henry HERBERT (abstract)

Of Ribbesford co. Worcs., kt. Good health. Soul to 'rich mercyes of the blessed Trinity'. Burial in day time 'in full assurance of the Resurrection of my Body and of the reunion of itt with the soule, for Solvation through the sole and precious merritts of my Iesus. And I give my most humble thankes to the holy spiritt for enabling me to liue and dye in the Christian Religion established and profesed in the Church of England'. To son Henry Herbert esq. and his heirs all messuages, malthouses, etc. in Bewdley co. Worcs.; in default of such issue, to his own male heirs; in default of such issue, to his daughters Magdalene Herbert and Elizabeth Herbert and their heirs; in default of such issue, to his own right heirs for ever; upon trust that any person to whom property descends employs profits etc. of said property for provision of twenty threepenny loaves of bread to be given weekly for relief of ten poor men and ten poor women of Bewdley for ever and for repair of said messuages etc. for ever. Loaves to be made weekly at Ribbisford house or in said borough and brought to church of Ribbesford, and not to chapel of Bewdely nor to any other church or chapel, every Sunday throughout the year at time of divine service in the morning, and set on table in said church provided for that use, and not on Communion Table, and distributed to said poor persons by churchwardens and overseers of poor of said parish. If loaves made at Bewdley, to be paid for half yearly by son Henry Herbert or such other person or persons to whom said messuages etc. descend. Poor men and women to be chosen out of eldest, poorest and most sober persons of said parish only and loaves to be given only to such poor persons as shall come to church of Ribbesford every Sunday successively before morning divine service and sermon as aforesaid and attend there devoutly and diligently during morning service and sermon in said church, unless hindred by sickness or other necessary impediment duly notified to his said son etc. and allowed as just cause of absence. Whereas, by indenture dated 16 Dec. 24 Chas. I between testator on one part and Sir Francis Lawley of Spynnell co. Salop bart. and William Lloyd of Westminster co. Middlesex esq. of the other, testator granted to said Sir Francis Lawley and William

Lloyd his manor of Hanslape otherwise Stoakes in Hanslape and site of said manor in co. Bucks and Northants, manor of Greate Sutton and Little Sutton co. Salop, the site, capital messuage, and mansion house of said manor of Greate Sutton and Little Sutton, manor of Whitchcott co. Salop, and site, capital messuage and mansion house of said manor, farm and farmhouse in Coldweston co. Salop, mill called Sparsfold Mill in pa. Didlebury co. Salop, and all other lands etc. of testator in Salop for twenty-one years from date of indenture at peppercorn rent, allowing testator to receive during his lifetime all rents etc. of premises mentioned in indenture, with condition that, if testator dies during term of indenture, his executors and administrators to receive all rents etc. to be disposed of to such uses as directed in will, instructs Sir Francis Lawley and William Lloyd as his trustees to allow executor to pay out of rents etc. £2000 to his daughter Magdalene Herbert at age of twenty-one or at marriage and £2000 to his daughter Elizabeth Herbert at age of twenty-one or marriage, each to have other's share if she predeceases before fulfilling conditions of inheritance. If both die before attaining age of twenty-one or marriage all rents etc. from this property to son Henry Herbert or, if his son pays to his daughters, Magdalene and Elizabeth, £2000 each at twenty-one or at marriage, or £4000 to survivor if one dies before reaching twenty-one or marriage, then son to receive all the rents etc. from property for residue of term of twenty–one years. If rents etc. from manor of Ribbesford fall short of £500 a year after his decease, same be made up by his son and paid to testator's wife for her life from rents etc. from property in manor of Alton alias Alnington co. Worcs. or from testator's personal estate. To daughter Magdalene Herbert £1000 more to be paid to her by son Henry Herbert at age of twenty-one or marriage. To daughter Elizabeth Herbert £1000 more to be paid her by said son at age of twenty-one or marriage, each to have other's share if she predeceases before fulfilling conditions of inheritance. To wife use of his plate and goods at Ribbesford and Hanslop for her life and, after her death, to his son Henry Herbert. To wife all his jewels, plate and goods in his house at Westminster. If his son dies before his mother, plate and goods at Ribbesford and Hanslop to his daughters Magdalene and Elizabeth to be equally divided between them if they are both living, but if either of them be dead, then to survivor of them after the death of his wife. To daughters, Magdalene Herbert and Elizabeth Herbert, £60 each to be paid them respectively by son Henry Herbert out of testator's personal estate for their respective maintenance until they reach age of twenty-one or are married. Manors of Greate Sutton and Little Sutton and of Whitchcott, farm called Englishes Farme, mill called Sparsfords Mill, farm and farmhouse called Coldweston co. Salop and all his other lands, etc. in said county and all rents etc. from them, and messuages etc. in manor of Alton alias Alnington co. Worcs. and all rents etc., and his third part of Kederminster heath and his pools there, lately purchased of Mr Humfrey Wildey of city of Worcester, to said son Henry Herbert and his male heirs; in default of such issue, to said daughters Magdalene and Elizabeth and their heirs; in default of such issue, to daughter or daughters of said son and their heirs; in default of such issue, to daughter or daughters of his daughter Dame Vere Every and their heirs; in default of such issue, to his right heirs for ever. Whereas, by marriage agreement dated 8 Mar. 23 Chas. I between Sir Henry Every bart. and testator, before marriage of his daughter Vere Herbert with said Sir Henry, it was agreed that upon marriage and settlement mentioned, £4000 should be paid by testator to Sir Henry Every as a marriage portion, of which £2000 were to be paid upon said settlement and £2000 more six months after testator's death, and, whereas settlement had been made by said Sir Henry Every of only some of lands mentioned, Sir Henry having sold, as soon as he came of age, lands in Buckenham sheire worth £100 p.a. which ought to have been settled according to said agreement, nevertheless testator had paid £2000 to Sir Henry Every and now wills that said £2000 payable six months after his death be duly paid to Sir Henry Every, Sir Henry giving an acquittance for the said £4000 marriage portion, and not otherwise. To wife Dame Elizabeth £1000 and mourning, £500 to be paid out of his personal estate six months after burial, the other £500 to be paid out of money due to him from King Charles I and King Charles II. To the Lady Garrard, wife's aunt, 10 guineas and mourning. To nieces, Magdalene and Katherine Vaughan, 5 guineas each and mourning. To nephew and godson, the Honourable Capt. Henry Herbert esq., 20 guineas and mourning. To Sir Henry Every bart. 1 guinea and mourning. To daughter Every 50 guineas and mourning. To godson and grandchild, Henry Every, 5 guineas and mourning, and to his brothers and sisters 1 guinea each and mourning. To servants their wages and mourning. To poor of parish where he dies £20 to be preserved as a stock for them by churchwardens and overseers of poor of same parish for ever. To twenty poor persons under his exhibition at Ribbesford 1s each. To son, Henry Herbert, 20 Queen Elizabeth pieces of gold and mourning. To daughters, Magdalene and Elizabeth, 10 guineas each and mourning. To cousin, William Lloyd esq., 1 guinea and mourning. To Mrs Mary Bouchee £5 and mourning. To servant Walter Vaughan £10 and mourning. To kinsmen Sir Francis Lawley bart. and William Harboard esq. 5 guineas each and mourning. Remainder of personal estate to son Henry Herbert. Appoints son Henry Herbert and kinsmen Sir Francis Lawley and William Harboard joint executors, son to receive residue of his personal estate as well as money due on mortgages, arrears of rents etc. on Privy Seal, and accounts of the Office of the Revels. Wit. Bennett Gyles, Walter Gyles, William How, Walter Vaughan.

Codicil: Confirms will. To wife Dame Elizabeth Herbert bracelets, gold watch, silver basin, and other things bequeathed to her by last will and testament of Dame Jane Garrard widow deceased. To son Henry Herbert esq. silver skillet and its silver cover and pair of silver candlesticks with silver snuffers and silver snuff dish given him by said Lady Garrard's will. Appoints said son to sell for cordwood all such runnel oaks fit for cordwood growing in his manor of Ribbesford and farms belonging to it; money raised by sale to be used for payment of portions given by his will to daughters Magdalene and Elizabeth Herbert respectively and not to any other use. To Mrs Ellinor Strong debt she owes of £25 and interest on it, assignment of lease of her house and bill of sale of her goods, on which debt was secured, to be returned to her. Wit. Mary Bouchee, Walter Vaughan.

PRO PROB11/342 fos 51v–55r. RegC with codicil and prob. clause.

Prob. PCC 15 May 1673 to executors, Henry Herbert esq., son, and Lord Francis Lawley bart. and William Harberd esq., kinsmen. PAB (PRO PROB8/66 fo. 66v) gives place of death as City of Westminster.

1595–1673. Master of Revels; 1623 purchased life interest in office from Sir John Astley (**1640**) (Dutton, *Mastering the Revels*, pp. 222–48, discusses Herbert's involvement with Revels to 1626); held office in own right 1639–42, 1660–73. Shareholder in Salisbury Court 1631. Died 27 Apr. 1673, buried St Paul's Covent Garden. (*DNB*; J. Q. Adams, *The Dramatic Records of Sir Henry Herbert, Master of the Revels, 1623–1673*, New Haven, 1917; Bentley II, 471.)

1675 July 26 Lodowick CARLELL (abstract)

(Carliel) Of St Martin's in the Fields co. Middlesex, esq. Weak. Soul to God 'who gaue it trusting in and through the Righteousnes and Merits of my Lord and Saviour Iesus Christ to obtaine eternall life and glory when this fraile life shall haue an end'. Burial at discretion of wife* whom appoints sole executor. All debts owed at death to be paid from moiety of money due to him from his Majesty as fast as executor shall receive same; other moiety for her subsistance. Wit. Frances Burwell, Penelope Palmer, John Fisher, Dorothy Tracy.

PRO PROB10/1068. OW, prob. clause subscribed, note of registration endorsed. Single sheet with seal and signatures of testator and witnesses. Text in fluent mixed hand. 'My Dear husbands Will' endorsed in hand of Joan Carlell.

Prob. PCC 25 Sept. 1675 to Joan Carlell, relict and executor.

Printed: Charles H. Gray, *Lodowick Carliell His Life, A Discussion of His Plays and 'The Deserving Favourite'*, Chicago, 1905, p. 176 (abstract).

c.1601–75. Dramatist and courtier; plays produced for court performance 1622–38, some acted by King's Men at Blackfriars. Buried Petersham co. Surrey 21 Aug. 1675. (Bentley III, 111–24; Gray, op. cit., pp. 1–45 (identifies witnesses as members of family, p. 176).)

wife] Joan née Palmer; will dated 13 Dec. 1677, proved 17 Aug. 1681 (PRO PROB11/367 fos. 177v–178v; printed: Gray, op. cit., p. 177 (abstract)).

1682 Aug. 23 William BEESTON

In the name of God Amen I William Beeston of the parish of St Leonards Shoreditch in the County of Midd*lese*x Gent being sick and weake in body but of sound and perfect memory doe make this my last will and testament in manner and forme followeing That is to say ffirst I doe commend my soule into the hands of Allmighty God my Creatour and to his Sonne Iesus Christ my only Saviour and Reedeemer by the meritts of whose death and passion I doe assuredly trust to bee saved and have remission for all my sinnes And my body I committ to the earth from whence it came to be decently buryed in the parish Church of St Leonard Shoreditch aforesaid And as touching such worldly estate both reall and personall as God hath blessed mee withall I dispose thereof as followeth Imprimis I doe give and bequeath vnto my Sonne Sackfeild* Beeston the sum of seaven pounds p*er* Annu*m* dureing his life to bee issueing and payeable out of my messuages and tenements in Kings head Yard in the said parish of Shoreditch and all other my estate hereafter bequeathed by mee to my loveing wife Alice* Beeston to be paid by my said wife by foure quarterly payments Item I doe give and bequeath vnto my Godsonne Thomas Mahonne* the sum of tenne pounds to bee paid him within eighteene moneths next after my decease Item I doe give and bequeath vnto Benaniah Beeston the reputed sonne of George Beeston* my Sonne all the rents issues and proffitts of the house wherein I now dwell and inhabite and allso the rents issues and proffitts of the house called the black Swanne in the said parish of Shoreditch after the decease of my said wife Alice Beeston togeather with all housholdstuffe and other things which now are or shall bee in the said house wherein I now inhabite att the time of my decease but my said wife is to enjoy both the said houses and housholdstuffe and other things in the said house dureing her life she said Alice Beeston takeing care and provision for the mayntenance of the said Benaniah dureing the life of the said Alice Beeston Item I doe give vnto Mr Thomas Shippey* for the care he hath and shall take about clearing Mrs Crouches business concerning money due to mee from her husband the summe of five pounds to be payable out of the first money shall be received of the said Mrs Crouch And I hereby presse him to bee carefull and sollicitous of itt till he hath seene itt effected Item I doe giue and bequeath vnto Anne Chubb for her greate care and trouble in my sickness the sum*m*e of five pounds of lawfull money of England All the rest of my estate whatsoever both reall and personall herein and hereby not bequeathed I doe hereby give and bequeath vnto my said wife Alice Beeston her Heires and Assignes for ever whom I doe hereby make my sole Executrix of this my last will and testament And I doe hereby revoke all former wills by mee made In Witnesse whereof I the said William Beeston have hereunto sett my hand and seale this Three and twentith[1] day of August In the yeare of our Lord One thousand six hundred Eighty and twoe Annoq*ue* Regis Caroli secundi tricesimo quarto

Will Beeston

Signed sealed and published in the presence of Tho: Shepey Cha: Blount Ann Chubb

1. *Three and twentith* inserted in second hand into space in text.

GL MS 9052/23. OW, prob. clause endorsed, inventory attached (see **In1683**). Single sheet, with signatures of testator and witnesses and applied seal. Text in set round hand.

Prob. ACL 7 Sept. 1682 to Alice Beeston, widow and executor. Note endorsed: 'This will was shewed to Mr Charles Blount {Mr} Thomas Shepey & Anne Chubb at the tyme of theire exa*m*inac*i*ons taken in Chancery on the behalfe of Alice Beeston wido*w* Compla*i*nant ag*ain*st Sackvill Beeston de*fendan*t Edw. Reade'. Inventory exhibited 28 Apr. 1683.

c.1606–82. Actor, theatre manager; son of Christopher Beeston (**1638**); associated in management of Salisbury Court 1632; with King and Queen's Young Company at Cockpit 1637 and inherited from father twelfth share in company of which appointed governor 1639 (replaced briefly by Sir William Davenant (**A1668**)); tried unsuccessfully to buy Cockpit 1650; purchased lease of Salisbury Court 1652, formed own company there in 1660 and owned theatre until destroyed by fire 1666; acted with King's company 1664–82. Legatee of George Pulham (**1611**), Thomas Basse (**1634**). Cited in list of recusants 1680. Died c.24 Aug. 1682 at home in Bishopsgate Street. (Hotson, pp. 95–114; Nungezer, pp. 39–42; Bentley II, 370–4; Highfill et al. I, 414–19.)

Sackfeild] b. 1654, named after Earl of Dorset with whom testator negotiating over Salisbury Court lease (Hotson, p. 104).

wife Alice] will dated 24 May, proved 20 Oct. 1686 (PRO PROB11/384 fos 275v–276v).

Mahonne] possible connection with actor Michael Mohun, who was with Beeston at Cockpit 1637–40 and married to Anne, daughter of Theophilus Bird (**1663**), brother–in–law of testator; see index.
George Beeston] actor, possibly with father's company at Salisbury Court 1660; King's company 1667–75 (Highfill et al. I, 413–14).
Shippey] actor in Duke's company from 1660 (Hotson, pp. 206–7); named as sole executor by Beeston's wife.

1683 July 10 Charles HART

In the name of God Amen the Tenth day of Iuly in the yeare of our Lord God One Thousand Six hundred Eighty three And in the ffive and thirtieth yeare of the Reigne of our Sovereigne Lord Charles the Second by the grace of God of England Scotland ffrance and Ireland King Defender of the ffaith &c I Charles Hart of the parish of Stanmore Magna in the County of Midd*lesex* Gent being sick and weake in body but of sound and perfect mind and memory (Thanks be therefore given to Almighty God) but knoweing the uncertainty of this mortall life and being now minded to settle things in order whilest I have opportunity and convenient time to doe the same I doe make this my last will & testament in manner and forme following (that is to say) First and principally I give and commend my soul to Almighty God my Creatour assuredly beleiving that I shall receive full pardon and free Remission of all my sins And be saved by the pretious death and meritts of my blessed Saviour and Redeemer Iesus Christ And my body to the earth from whence it came to be buried in such decent and Christian manner as to my Executor hereafter named shall be thought meet and convenient And as touching such worldly estate as Almighty God in his mercy hath lent me my will and meaning is the same shall be employed and bestowed as hereafter by this my will is expressed Item I will that all such debts and duties that I owe or am indebted in right or in conscience unto any person or persons whatsoever be first well and truly satisfied and paid Item I give and bequeath unto the Minister that shall preach my ffunerall sermon the sum*m*e of fforty shillings Item I give and bequeath unto my servant Alice Girdler Twenty peeces of Gold com*m*only called Guinneys And also All my plate (vi*delice*t) One Great Silver Tankard One silver plate One silver Pottinger, six silver salts six silver fforks and six silver spoons Item I give and bequeath unto the said Alice Girdler The Bed with the appurten*a*nces and all other the furniture now standing and being in the Roome hung with purple and white druggett (The Looking glasse there onely excepted which I give and bequeath unto my good friend Mrs. Carpendar) Item

I give and bequeath unto the said Alice Girdler The Bed with the appurten*an*ces and all other the furniture now standing and being in the roome she lies in and also the bed with the appurten*an*ces and all other the furniture now standing and being in the roome there next adjoyning where my servant Iames Allen usually lies Item I give and bequeath unto the said Alice Girdler All my Brasse, Pewter, Spitts, Andirons, and all such other things as properly belong unto and usually stand in the Kitchen Item I give and bequeath unto the said Alice Girdler All my vessells, Tubbs, Bottles, Wood, and Coales whatsoever now remaining and being in and about my now dwelling house Item I give and bequeath unto the said Alice Girdler my Linnen of all sorts (vi*delicet*) Points, Laces, Sheets, Tableclothes, Napkins &c And like wise All my wearing Apparell Item I give and bequeath unto my very loveing ffriend Thomas Napper of Edgworth in the County of Midd*lesex* aforesaid Esq*uire* my embroidered bed with the appurten*an*ces, and the Tapestry hangings Eight pictures, One Marcetree table and stands and all other the furniture now standing and being in the Roome or Chamber com*m*only called the Bestchamber Item I give and bequeath unto the said Thomas Napper my two large pictures that hang in the entry One being a peece of ffishes and the other of a ffarmehouse Item I give and bequeath unto Barbara ffenn daughter of mr. Iohn ffenn of Stanmore Magna aforesaid The Bed with the appurten*an*ces together with the Tapestry hangings and other hangings, pictures, and all other the furniture now standing and being in the Roome or Chamber com*m*only called my Bedchamber Item I give and bequeath all my Books now being in the Clossett to the said Chamber belonging unto my very good ffriends mr. ffenn mr Carpendar and mr. Norwood equally to be devided betweene them Item I will and desire that all and every my goods, pictures, furniture, and other things standing and being in the Little Parlour; The Hall, and the withdrawing Roome (the Looking glasse in the withdrawing Roome excepted which I doe hereby give unto Mrs. Norwood) be valued and apprized by two honest and able men within one moneth next after my decease And be sold at the full value by my Executor hereafter named within three moneths next after such apprisement soe directed to be made as aforesaid And my will is that the moneyes ariseing by sale of the same shall be devided into three equall parts or shares Two parts whereof I give unto the Poor of the parish of Stanmore Magna aforesaid and the other third part I give and bequeath towards the repairing of the highwayes of the said parish All and every which said goods, pictures, furniture and other things herein before by me given & bequeathed are standing remaining and being in my now dwelling house at Stanmore Magna aforesaid Item I give and bequeath unto [1] Hart daugher of Matthew Hart late Clerke of the parish of St.

Botolph Bishopsgate London the summe of Twenty Pounds And I doe hereby farther give and bequeath unto the said [1] Hart the summe of ffive pounds to be distributed by her according to her discrecion to any person or persons that she knoweth to be of my relacion or kindred But in case she knoweth not any such person or persons then I wholly give the said summe of ffive pounds to her the said [1] Hart over and besides the said summe of Twenty pounds herein before bequeathed unto her Item I give and bequeath unto Edward Kynaston* of the parish of St. Giles in the ffields in the County of Middlesex Gent All my estate right title and interest of in and unto One full part or share* (the whole being devided into six and thirty parts) of the ground or soyle and of the messuage or tenement thereupon erected and built commonly called or knowne by the name of the Theatre Royall or the Kings Playhouse scituate lying and being betweene Bridges street and Drury lane in the parishes of St. Martin in the ffields and St: Paul Covent Garden in the County of Middlesex aforesaid and in both or one of them To have and to hold unto the said Edward Kynaston his Executors Administrators and Assignes from and imediately after my decease for and dureing all the rest and residue of the terme of One and fforty yeares which I have therein yett to come and unexpired provided alwayes And my will and meaning is that the said Edward Kynaston his Executors Administrators and Assignes shall yearely and every yeare dureing the remainder of the said terme of One and fforty yeares which shall be to come and unexpired at the time of my decease pay or cause to be paid unto the Right Honourable William Earle of Bedford his heires and Assignes One full part (the whole being into six and thirty parts devided) of the yearely rent of ffifty pounds reserved and payable to the said Earle for and in respect of the ground or soyle whereon the said Theatre or Playhouse is built at such dayes and times as the same shall from time to time become due and payable Or other wise on default of payment thereof I give and bequeath the said premisses soe given and bequeathed to the said Edward Kynaston as aforesaid And all my right interest and terme therein unto my Executor hereinafter named Item I give and bequeath unto the said Edward Kynaston the summe of ffive pounds to buy him mourning Item I give and bequeath unto my loveing ffriends mr. Gilbert Sopor* and mr Henry Hales* the summe of Tenn pounds a peece Item I give and bequeath unto my loveing ffriends mr Thomas Betterton* mr William Smith* and Thomas Coffyn the summe of ffive pounds a peece to buy them mourning Item I give and bequeath unto my very loveing ffriends The Lady Drax the Lady Digby, mrs. Rogers Lake, the aforesaid Thomas Napper Esquire mr. Prideaux and his wife, mr. ffenn and his wife, mr. Norwood and his wife, mr. Carpendar and his wife, mr ffowke and his wife, mr Hooke and his wife, Capt. Lloyd* and

his wife, mr ffrench and his wife, mr. Nicholls and his wife, mr. Awborne and his wife mr. Iordan, mrs. Hooke Widd*ow* mrs. Mary Norwood, mrs Anne Carpendar, mrs. Ellen Lloyd {mrs. Bircher mr. Powell* mrs. Powell} mrs. Betterton* and mrs Cory* To every of them One Gold Ring of the value of Twenty shillings Item I give and bequeath unto my servant Iames Allen the sum*m*e of ffive pounds which I desire to be forthwith paid by my Executor hereafter named into the hands of Iames Allen ffather of the said Iames for the use of the said Iames the Son when he shall attaine to the age of One and twenty yeares Item I give and bequeath unto the aforesaid Thomas Napper Esq*uire* the sum*m*e of ffive pounds to buy him mourning The Rest and residue of my estate both Reall and Personall not herein or hereby before bequeathed (after my debts legacies and funerall charges shall be fully satisfied and paid) I give and bequeath unto the said Thomas Napper Item I doe hereby make the said Thomas Napper full and sole Executor of this my last will and testament And I doe hereby absolutely revoke renounce and make void all and all manner of former and other Wills testaments and devises at any time by me heretofore made And doe declare this tobe my last will and testament in the presence of those persons whose names are hereupon endorsed as witnesses hereunto In witnes whereof I the said Charles Hart have to this my last will and testament putt my hand and seale the day and yeare first above written./
                                                                                           Charles Hart
Signed Sealed Published and Declared to be the last will and testament of the Within named Charles Hart in the p*r*esence of Benjamin Long Thomas Rich Nic: Strawbridge[2]*

1. Blank in MS.   2. *Signed . . . Strawbridge*: endorsed.

PCC PROB10/1142. OW, prob. clause with notes of registration of will and exhibition of inventory endorsed. Single sheet with seal of testator and signatures of testator and witnesses. Text and insertion (ll. 118–19) in same mixed hand, with displayed matter in italic.

Prob. PCC, 6 Sept. 1683, to Thomas Napier, executor.

c.1630–83. Actor; King's Men to 1642 (Richard Robinson's apprentice); after Civil War acted at Cockpit, Red Bull; from 1660 actor/sharer in King's company with building shares in Bridges St theatre and then Theatre Royal, 1662–83; retired from stage 1682. Died 18 Aug., buried 20 Aug. 1683 at Stanmore. (Hotson, passim; Nungezer, pp. 175–7; Bentley II, 462–3; Highfill et al. VII, 147–53.)

Kynaston] fellow member of King's company (Highfill et al. IX, 79–85).
part or share] testator held two building shares in June 1683 (Hotson, p. 282).
Sopor] member of King's company 1674–5 (Highfill et al. XIV, 196).
Hales] member of King's company 1674–5 (*London Stage*, p. 220).
Betterton] member of Duke's company (Highfill et al. II, 73–96).
Smith] member of Duke's company from 1662 (Highfill et al. XIV, 168–73).
Lloyd] a John Lloyd acted with Duke's company 1669–70 (*London Stage*, p. 166).

mr. Powell] Martin Powell, member of King's company 1669–82 (Highfill et al. XII, 119–20).
Betterton] Mary Betterton née Saunderson, member of Duke's company 1662–82 (Highfill et al. II, 96–9).
Cory] Katherine Corey née Mitchell, member of King's company to 1679 (Highfill et al. III, 493–5).
Strawbridge] held building shares in Theatre Royal 1682–3 (Hotson, pp. 273, 282).

1686 Dec. 12 William CARTWRIGHT

4ta schedula in 26 articulo mencionata[1]*
The resolucion of William Cartwright gentleman/
That he will pay into ye hands of ye Most Reuerend ffather in God the Lord Arch Bishopp of Canterbury or such other person or persons as his Grace shall appoint the summe of foure hundred pounds to purchase Landes of Inheritance of 20 li perannum for him selfe for life the remainder for ye benefitt of Dullwich Colledge founded by mr Allen
That he will giue two guilt Siluer Tankards, one Indian Silk Quilt, one large Damask table Cloth with other Convenient Linnen for ye Communion table & the beautifying of ye Chappell & alsoe a large turkey–worke Carpett for ye Dyneing Roome, & seuerall pictures of storyes & Landskips for ye beautifying the Dyning Roome & Gallary, and alsoe such of his Bookes convenient for a liberary as ye Master Warden, & Schoolmaster shall approve of for ye Service of them & ye Schollers
Hee is contented to be buried in the place entring into ye Chappell which the Master & Warden haue told him of & desires that if it shall please God to enable him to goe Sometimes to ye said Colledge, he may [at] at such times haue a roome in the Colledge for himselfe & a place for his Man paying ye Colledge for their diett
If he findes occasion he may doe more
That ye Master & Warden shall for their care & kindenes haue the profitt of the Landes purchased with ye said 400 li or ye Interest thereof for the first yeare after his decease to be equally devided (p. 2)
That the foure fellowes of the said Colledg {for their respect & kindnes} shall haue the profitt of the [the] Lands purchased with the said 400 li or the Interest there of for the second yeare after his decease to be equally devided
[December 12th 1686]
this is a true Copy of mr Cartwrights paper which he sent to his Grace* the Lord Arch Bishopp of Canterbury Examind by William Sancroft* Raphe Snowe/. Iohn Alleyn

[Exam*in*ed 14:86]²
december 12:86* a Copie of ye Clause of mr Cartwrights will relateing
to Dullwich Colledge³

1. 4ta ... *menconat*': marginated in a second hand.   2. *Exam*ᵈ *14:86* marginated in same hand as text.   3. *december* ... *Colledge* endorsed in same hand as text.

PRO PROB10/1177. Copy of excerpt from will, grant of admon subscribed (p. 2). Single sheet folded to make four pages, with signatures of witnesses. Rapid mixed hand.

Admon PCC 28 Apr. 1687, to John Alleyn, Warden of God's Gift College, Dulwich, no executors named. Admon Act Book (PRO PROB6/63 fos. 3r–4r) records grant 'pendente lite' 29 Jan. 1687 to John Taylor of pa. St Martin in the Fields, tailor, and its expiry Apr. 1687 with end of dispute and probate, and gives pa. of origin as St Giles in the Fields co. Middlesex. Sentence (PRO PROB11/389, fos 268v–269v), promulgated 28 Apr. 1687, (Master, etc. of God's Gift College, beneficiaries under the will, promoters, v. Margaret Harris, niece by his sister and next of kin) upholds validity of will and confirms College as beneficiary. Inventory exhibited 29 Nov. 1687 (see **In1687**).

Printed: Eleanore Boswell, 'Young Mr Cartwright', *MLR*, XXIV, 1929, pp. 125–42 (p. 136) (RegC).

c.1606–86. Actor; son of actor William Cartwright, one of Palsgrave's who leased Fortune from Edward Alleyn 1618; possibly with King's Revels 1635; at Salisbury Court before Civil War. Bookseller during Interregnum. Actor and sharer with King's 1663–82; with United Company from 1682; shareholder in Theatre Royal Drury Lane. Died 17 Dec., buried St Paul's Covent Garden 18 Dec. 1686. For explanation of absence of properly executed will and of legal proceedings, brought by Dulwich College in PCC and Chancery, see Boswell, op. cit., pp. 133–42; Young, *Dulwich*, I, 182–7. (Nungezer, pp. 87–9; Bentley II, 404–5; Highfill et al. III, pp. 89–93.)

4ta ... **menc*i*onata**] quoted in allegation of Warden and College, see sentence (PRO PROB11/389 fo. 269r).
sent to his Grace] to approve revised burial arrangements at Dulwich which were a condition of his legacy to college (Boswell, op. cit., p. 135).
Sancroft] Abp. of Canterbury 1678–90.
december 12:86] not the date of composition as testator unconscious from 9 Dec. until death. Boswell surmises date 'must have been endorsed by Butler [testator's solicitor] when he took possession of the paper' (op. cit., p. 135 fn. 3).

Some administrations of interest

1585 Feb. 9 Richard HICKES (Hyxe) of St Olave, Southwark

PCC, to Margaret Hunningborne alias Hixe, daughter, in the person of Christopher Robinson, notary public, her proctor.
PRO PROB6/3 fo. 132r (old numbering fo. 129r).
Noted: William Ingram, 'The playhouse at Newington Butts: A new proposal', *SQ*, XXI, 1970, pp. 385–98 (p. 397).
fl. 1576–85. Owner of site of Newington Butts playhouse according to Ingram (op. cit., p. 394) who disagrees with the conjecture of Ida Darlington (*St George's Fields*, Survey of London 25, London, 1955, p. 86) that Hickes built theatre between 1566 and 1580.

1587 Dec. 12 William KNELL of St Mary Aldermanbury

CCL, to Rebecca Knell, widow, with undated note of exhibition of inventory.
GL MS 9168/14 fo. 144r.
fl. pre-1587. Probably actor with Queen's, murdered 13 June 1587 (Eccles, *Shakespeare*, pp. 82–3); widow married John Heminges (1630) 10 Mar. 1588. (Chambers II, 327–8; Nungezer, pp. 228–9.)

1594 Dec. 30 Thomas KYD of St Mary Colechurch

ACL, renounced by Anna and Francis Kyd, mother and father.
GL MS 9050/3 fo. 11v.
Printed: F. S. Boas, ed., *The Works of Thomas Kyd*, Oxford, 1901, pp. lxxvi–lxxvii.
1558–94. Dramatist. (Chambers III, 394–7.)

1596 May 5 John ALLEYN of St Andrew Holborn

ACL (intestate) to Margaret Allen, relict, in the person of Richard Stubbs, notary public, with note of valuation of inventory at £13 19s 5d dated 8 June 1596.
GL MS 9050/3 fo. 36r.
Letters of administration survive in Dulwich College Mun. 110 (Warner, p. 255).
c.1556–96. 'If not actually a performer, at least closely engaged in theatrical affairs' (Nungezer, p. 11); brother of Edward Alleyn (**1626**). (Chambers II, 298–9; Nungezer, pp. 11–12.)

1597 Feb. 3 James BURBAGE

ACL, to Helen Burbage, relict, with note of exhibition of inventory, valued at £37 14d, on 27 July, and of accounts 21 Nov. 1597.
GL MS 9050/3 fo. 52v.
Noted: Eccles, 'Actors I', p. 43.
c.1530–97. Actor; Leicester's from 1572; owner of the Theatre 1576, second Blackfriars 1596; father of Richard (**1619**) and Cuthbert (**A1636**); buried 2 Feb. 1597 St Leonard's Shoreditch. (Chambers II, 305–6; Nungezer, pp. 66–7.)

1598 July 21 George ATTWELL (Attywell) of St Leonard Shoreditch co. Middlesex

ACL, to Catherine, relict, with note of valuation of inventory at £3 27d.
GL MS 9050/3 fo. 94v.
Noted: Eccles, 'Actors I', p. 39.
fl. 1590–8. Actor; Strange's 1591, ?Queen's 1595; author or singer of *Mr Attowel's Jigge*, printed as *Francis's New Jig* (1595). Chambers (II, 300–1) and Nungezer (pp. 22–3) identify as actor a 'Mr. Otwell' who lived in St Saviour's Close in 1599.

1602 July 24 Francis LANGLEY (Langlie) of St Saviour, Southwark

PCC, to Jane Langley, relict, in the person of Alexander Serle, notary public, her proctor.
PRO PROB6/6 fo. 128v.
Noted: Ingram, *London Life*, p. 281.
1548–1602. Theatre owner; builder and owner of Swan in Paris Garden 1594–5; purchased interest in Boar's Head playhouse 1599 (see Sisson, *Boar's Head*, pp. 50–74 and Berry, *Boar's Head Playhouse*, chapters 4–6, for accounts of Langley's lawsuits over its ownership). Buried St Saviour's 9 July 1602. (Nungezer, p. 234.)

1604 Jan. 9 Robert BROWNE of St Mary Matfellon alias Whitechapel

PCC, to Susan Browne, relict, in the person of John Ivat, notary public, her proctor, with note of exhibition of inventory.
PRO PROB6/6 fo. 183v.
Noted: Berry, *Boar's Head Playhouse*, p. 70.
fl. 1599–1603. Actor and theatre proprietor; buried St Mary's Whitechapel 16 Oct. 1603. Widow married actor Thomas Greene (**1612**). (Chambers II, 304; Nungezer, pp. 60–3 conflate career of this R. Browne with that of actor on Continent; see Berry, op. cit., pp. 191–7.)

1606 Mar. 3 Henry LANMAN of Westhrope co. Suffolk

PCC, to Christopher Lanman, son, with note of exhibition of inventory and submission of accounts 1606.
PRO PROB6/7 fo. 30r (old numbering 31r).
Noted: William Ingram, 'Henry Lanman's Curtain playhouse as an easer to the Theatre 1585–1592', in *The First Public Playhouse: The Theatre in Shoreditch 1576–1598*, ed. Herbert Berry, Montreal, 1979, pp. 17–28 (p. 23).
c.1538–1606. Theatre owner; proprietor of Curtain; buried St Mary Woolchurch Haw 17 Feb. 1606. (Wallace, passim; W. Ingram, op. cit.)

1608 Apr. 21 Giles ALLEN of Hazeleigh co. Essex

PCC, to Sara Allen, relict, with note of exhibition of inventory 1609.
PRO PROB6/7 fo. 111v (old numbering 113v).
Noted: Berry, 'Handlist', p. 108.
fl. 1576–1608. Owner of site of Theatre 1576. Died 27 Mar. 1608. (Berry, 'Handlist', passim.)

1609 Mar. 31 William PAVYE (Pavy) of St Botolph Aldgate, gent.

ACL, to Elizabeth Pavy, relict, with note of valuation of inventory at £10 14s 7d.
GL MS 9050/4 fo. 358r.
fl. 1597–1608. Actor; Admiral's 1597–8, Prince's 1608; buried St Botolph Aldgate 8 Sept. 1608. (Nungezer, pp. 268–9.)

1612 Apr. 16 George BRYAN of St James Clerkenwell

PCC, to Mary Bryan (Brian), relict (**1625**), with note of exhibition of inventory in 1613.

PRO PROB6/8 fo. 56v.
Noted: Eccles, 'Actors I', p. 42.
fl. 1586–1612. Actor; Denmark and Germany 1586–7, Strange's 1590–1, 1593, Chamberlain's 1596. Chambers (II, 304) identifies actor with Groom of the Chamber named in Chamber Accounts 1603, 1611–13, but latter date inconsistent with date of death. (Nungezer, pp. 63–4.)

1612 John MASON

1. of St Andrew by the Wardrobe
ACL, 6 May to Elizabeth, relict, with note of exhibition of inventory, undated.
GL MS 9050/5 fo. 16r.
2. of St Leonard Shoreditch
ACL, renounced 5 Oct. by Prudence Mason, relict.
GL MS 9050/5 fo. 33v.
c.1581–1612. Dramatist, theatre investor. Eccles ('Brief lives', p. 93) speculates that one of these is probable author of *The Turk* acted by King's Revels Children. Held half share in King's Revels syndicate at Whitefriars 1608. (Chambers III, 435.)

1613 June 1 John DUKE of St James Clerkenwell

ACL, renounced by Suzanna Duke, relict.
GL MS 9050/5 fo. 27v; described as 'histrio'.
Noted: Eccles, 'Actors I', p. 47.
fl. 1590–1613. Actor; Strange's 1590–1, Chamberlain's 1598, Worcester's/Queen Anne's 1602–9. Buried St James Clerkenwell 31 May 1613. (Chambers II, 314; Nungezer, pp. 121–2; Bentley II, 428–9.)

1614 May 7 John DUTTON of St Botolph Bishopsgate

PCC, to John Dutton, son.
PRO PROB6/8 fo. 146v.
Noted: Eccles, 'Actors I', p. 48.
fl. 1575–91. Actor; Warwick's 1575–6, Oxford's c.1580, Queen's 1583, 1588–91. Elizabeth, daughter of John Dutton 'player', baptised in St Botolph's in 1586. (Chambers II, 314; Nungezer, pp. 123–4.)

1614 Dec. 22 William OSTLER of St Mary Aldermanbury

PCC, to Thomasine, relict, with note of exhibition of inventory.
PRO PROB6/8, fo. 176v.

Noted: Chambers II, 322.
fl. 1601–14. Actor and sharer; Children of Chapel Royal 1601, King's 1610. Acquired shares in Blackfriars 1611 and Globe 1612. Married in 1611 to Thomasine, daughter of John Heminges (1630). Died 16 Dec. 1614. (Chambers II, 331; Nungezer, pp. 261–2.)

1618 Oct. 14 George WILKINS of St Sepulchre

CCL (intestate) to Catherine Wilkins, relict, with undated note of exhibition of inventory.
GL MS 9168/16 fo. 311v.
Noted: Mark Eccles, 'George Wilkins', N&Q, CCXX, 1975, pp. 250–2 (p. 252).
c.1576–1618. Dramatist. Married in 1601/2 to Katherine Fowler or Fowles. Died between 3 Sept. and 2 Oct. 1618. (Roger Prior, 'The life of George Wilkins', ShS, XXV, 1972, pp. 137–52; Roger Prior, 'George Wilkins and the young heir', ShS, XXIX, 1976, pp. 33–9; Chambers, III, 513.)

1619 June 26 Francis BEAUMONT (Beamont) of City of Westminster

PCC, to Ursula Beaumont, relict.
PRO PROB6/10 fo. 26v.
Noted: A. B. Grosart, *DNB* (gives date wrongly as 20 June).
c.1584–1616. Dramatist. Died 6 Mar., buried Westminster Abbey 9 Mar. 1616. (C. M. Gayley, *Francis Beaumont, Dramatist: A Portrait*, London, 1914; Chambers III, 215–35.)

1620 Aug. 2 Nathan FIELD of St Giles in the Fields, Middlesex, bachelor

PCC, to Dorcas Rice alias Field, sister, with note of exhibition of inventory 1621.
PRO PROB6/10 fo. 80r.
Printed: R. F. Brinkley, 'Nathan and Nathaniel Field', *MLN*, XLII, 1927, pp. 10–15 (p. 13) (in translation).
1587–1620. Actor, sharer, dramatist; Children of Chapel Royal/Queen's Revels/Lady Elizabeth's 1600–15, King's 1615–19. (Chambers II, 316–18 (confuses him with brother Nathaniel), III, 313–14; Nungezer, pp. 135–41; R. F. Brinkley, *Nathan Field, the Actor–Playwright*, Yale Studies in English 77, New Haven, 1928; Bentley, II, 434–6.)

1622 Feb. 8 Nicholas LONG of St Giles Cripplegate

PCC, to Prudence Long, relict, with note of exhibition of inventory valued at £33 14s.
PRO PROB6/10 fo. 163r
fl. 1612–22. Actor/manager; led touring companies of Queen's Revels (in association with Philip Rosseter (1623)) 1612, 1617, Lady Elizabeth's 1614, unnamed provincial company with Robert Lee (1629) 1620. Legatee of William Hovell (1615). Buried 21 Jan. 1622 St Giles Cripplegate, where named as 'player'. (Chambers II, 328; Nungezer, p. 237; Bentley, II, 498.)

1625 Sept. 10 William CARPENTER of St James Clerkenwell

ACL, during minority and for use of Elizabeth Carpenter, daughter, to her maternal uncle, William Adkins.
GL MS 9050/5 fo. 205r.
1625 Oct. 4 ACL admon during minority and for use of Elizabeth Carpenter, daughter, to her mother Prudence Carpenter, former administrator Robert Ladkins [sic] now deceased.
GL MS 9050/5 fo. 210v.
1625 Nov. 10 ACL renunciation of admon by Prudence, relict.
GL MS 9050/5 fo. 217v.
fl. 1612–25. Actor; Lady Elizabeth's 1611, Prince Charles's 1619–25; Bentley identifies actor with gent. recorded mainly in St Giles Cripplegate, but notes burial of this W. Carpenter in St James, 9 Sept. 1625 (II, 401–2). (Nungezer, p. 85.)

1625 Oct. 12 Thomas LODGE of St Mary Magdalen, Old Fish St

PCC, to Joan Lodge, relict, with note of exhibition of inventory in 1626.
PRO PROB6/12 fo. 20v (old numbering 23v).
Printed: E. A. Tenney, *Thomas Lodge*, Cornell Studies in English 26, Ithaca, NY, 1935, p. 191, fn. 1.
1558–1625. Dramatist. Died Sept. 1625. (Chambers III, 409–11.)

1626 Feb. 15 William ROWLEY of St James Clerkenwell

ACL, renounced by Grace Rowley, relict, in the person of Henry Durham, notary public.
GL MS 9050/5 fo. 231r.
Noted: M. J. Dickson, 'William Rowley', *Times Literary Supplement*, 28 Mar. 1929, p. 260 (dates mistakenly as 16 Feb.).
fl. 1607–25. Actor, dramatist; Duke of York's/Prince Charles's from 1609, King's 1623–5. Possibly brother of Samuel Rowley (1624). Buried St James Clerkenwell

Administrations 233

11 Feb. 1626. (Chambers II, 337, III, 473–5; Nungezer, pp. 306–7; Bentley II, 555–8; Eccles, 'Brief Lives', pp. 116–17.)

1631 Apr. 2 Aaron HOLLAND of St James Clerkenwell

ACL, to Elizabeth, relict (1631), with undated note of exhibition of inventory.
GL MS 9050/6 fo. 83r.
1556–1631. Owner of ground rents and builder of Red Bull. (Nungezer p. 194; Sisson, Lost Plays, p. 100; Bentley II, 475.)

1632 Sept. 4 Thomas DEKKER (Deckers) of St James Clerkenwell

ACL, renounced by Elizabeth, relict.
GL MS 9050/6 fo. 103v.
Printed: Mark Eccles, 'Thomas Dekker: Burial place', N&Q, CLXXVII, 1939, p. 157.
c.1572–1632. Dramatist and pamphleteer; buried St James Clerkenwell 25 Aug. 1632. (Chambers III, 289–305.)

1634 Oct. 18 Richard GUNNELL of St Bride Fleet St

PCC, to Elizabeth Gunnell, relict [later Robinson] (1641).
PRO PROB6/15, fo. 61r with note of exhibition of inventory valued at £9.
1654 29 Sept. Admon of goods unadministered to Margaret Wintershall alias Gunnell, daughter, after death of Elizabeth Gunnell, relict.
PRO PROB6/28 fo. 122r.
fl. 1613–34. Actor, dramatist, theatre manager and owner; Palsgrave's 1613–22; wrote several plays, now lost, for company at second Fortune in which held full share and of which acted as manager; with William Blagrave built Salisbury Court theatre 1629. Accused of recusancy. Buried St Bride 7 Oct. 1634. Incorrectly identified with R. Gunnell buried in St Giles Cripplegate 22 Jan. 1630 (Nungezer, p. 169). (Chambers II, 320; Hotson, pp. 52–3; Nungezer, pp. 168–70; Bentley II, 454–8, VI, 94.)

1636 Oct. 25 Cuthbert BURBAGE of St Giles Cripplegate

PCC, to George Bingley, esq., and Elizabeth Bingley, his wife, daughter of deceased, with note of exhibition of inventory 1637.
PRO PROB6/16, fo. 26v.
Noted: Mary Edmond (private communication).
c.1566–1636. Theatre owner; held leases of Theatre, shares in Globe and

Blackfriars. Elder son of James (**A1597**), brother of Richard (**1619**) whose will he witnessed. Mentioned in wills of William Sly (**1608**), Richard Cowley (**1618**), Nicholas Tooley (who died in his house) (**1623**), John Heminges (**1630**), Elizabeth Condell (**1635**) and Henry Condell (**1627**). Buried St Leonard Shoreditch 17 Sept. 1636. Widow, Elizabeth, buried there on 1 Oct. of same year, hence administration to daughter as next–of–kin. Admon describes Burbage as 'decendent*es* apud Hayes in Com*itatu* Kantij habentis'. (Chambers II, 306; Nungezer, p. 65; Bentley II, 394–5.)

1637 Aug. 22 Ben JONSON of City of Westminster

Court of Dean and Chapter of Westminster, to William Scandret, creditor, with undated note of exhibition of inventory valued at £8 8*s* 10*d*.
City of Westminster Archive Dept., Victoria Library, London, Act Book 4, 1632–44, fo. 53r.
Printed: *Ben Jonson*, edited by C. H. Herford, P. and E. Simpson, 11 vols, Oxford, 1925–52, I (1925), 249.
1572–1637. Dramatist. Died 6 Aug., buried Westminster Abbey 9 Aug. 1637. (Chambers III, 352–94; Bentley IV, 603–77.)

1640 May 12 Thomas HOBBES of St Leonard Shoreditch co. Middlesex

ACL, to Anne, relict, with undated note of exhibition of inventory valued at £103 1*s*.
GL MS 9050/7 fo. 56r.
fl. 1610–40. Possibly the actor; Duke of York's/Prince Charles's 1610–25, King's from 1625; named in Markham's suit in 1623 as 'att the vpper end of Shoreditch' (Bentley II, 683) although Bentley prints register entries from St James Clerkenwell including marriage to Mary (II, 473–4). (Nungezer, p. 193.)

1649 July 20 Roger NORE of St Giles Cripplegate

Peculiar of Dean and Chapter of St Paul's, to Angelica, relict, with note of valuation of inventory at £3 15*s* 4*d*.
GL MS 25,625/1 fo. 19v.
Noted: Cerasano, 'New . . . wills', p. 303 fn. 27.
fl. 1640–9. Hired man with II Prince Charles's 1640. Witness to will of John Robinson (**1641**). Buried St Giles Cripplegate 19 Mar. 1649. (Bentley II, 517.)

1652 Jan. 17 Samuel THOMPSON of St Giles Cripplegate

PCC, to Grace Thompson, relict, with undated note of exhibition of inventory, 'pau*per*' marginated.
PRO PROB6/27 fo. 1v.
fl. 1634–52. Actor; King's Revels at Salisbury Court 1634, possibly sharer. May be 'Thomson the player [who] died of the govvt, 1652' (Ralph Desmus's *Merlinus Anonymous* (18 Nov. 1653) quoted by H. E. Rollins, 'A contribution to the history of the English commonwealth drama', *SP*, XVIII, 1921, pp. 267–333 (p. 304)). (Bentley II, 600–1.)

1653 Sept. 28 Thomas POLLARD of St Bride Fleet St

PCC, to Anne Perrin, wife of Richard Perrin, sister, 'by order of Court' marginated.
PRO PROB6/30 fo. 132r (old numbering 109A and 37).
fl. 1617–53. Actor; King's Men 1617–42, apprentice of John Shank (**1635**); in 1635 with Robert Benfield and Eyllaerdt Swanston (**1651**) petitioned for and won share of Globe and Blackfriars from Shank and others ('Sharers' papers'). Legatee of Richard Benfield (**1639**). In 1655 Chancery suit (Theophilus Bird v. Thomas Morrison) alleged 'that Pollard died worth £500' (Hotson, p. 33). (Nungezer, pp. 284–5; Bentley II, 532–5.)

1668 May 6 Sir William DAVENANT of St Clement Danes, Middlesex

PCC (intestate) to John Alway, principal creditor, with consent of Lady Mary Davenant, relict.
PRO PROB6/43 fo. 52r (old numbering 68r).
Printed: J. G. Nichols and J. Bruce, ed., *Wills from Doctors' Commons*, Camden Society vol. 83, London, 1863, p. 160 (abstract).
1606–68. Dramatist, theatrical manager; succeeded William Beeston (**1682**) as manager of King and Queen's Young Company 1640; led Duke's company from 1660. Died 8 Apr., buried Westminster Abbey 9 Apr. 1668. For dispute arising from admon see Hotson pp. 226–8, Appendix pp. 356–76. (Nungezer, pp. 112–14; Bentley II, 421–2; Highfill et al. IV, 170–87; Mary Edmond, *Rare Sir William Davenant*, Manchester, 1987.)

1684 Nov. 3 Robert SHATTERELL

CCL, to Anne, relict.
GL MS 9168/24 fo. 160r.
Noted: Mary Edmond, *Rare Sir William Davenant*, Manchester, 1987, p. 207.
c.1615?–84. Actor; as boy under William Beeston (**1682**) at Cockpit 1639; actor/sharer in King's company at Theatre Royal 1661–80. (Nungezer, p. 322; Bentley II, 571–2; Highfill et al. XIII, 287–9.)

Inventories

1638 Jan. 17 Thomas SACKVILLE

Anno 1638 den 17 Ianuarij sein folgende Bücher Iohan Wilhelm Sehll. nacher Hamburgk geschicket worden

The Worcks of that famous and Wortie minister oft Christ, etc:	in folio,
The institution of Christian religion	in fol*i*o
Hepapla in Genesin	in fol*i*o
The Workes both morall and naturall	in fol*i*o
A display of Heraltrie	in fol*i*o

[**new page**] Mehr Englische Bücher,

The misterie of iniguitie	in folio
The faerie queen the	in fol*i*o
The Workes of Beniamin Ionson	in fol*i*o
A Concortance Apiomaticall	in foll*i*o
The Essages off morall Politille	in fol*i*o
Englische Bibell zum theill	in foll*i*o
A Commentharie te Epistole	in fol*i*o
Troia Britania or Creat	in foll*i*o
The tives Banket	in 4*to*
Saint Peters Prophetie	in 4
Iuristiction Regall	in 4
A Commentaire or Exposition	in 4
The Encoanter against	in 4
the true honor	in 4
Ephues and his Engellandt	in 4
A part off a Register	in 4
Wits Private	in 4
A Briefe Discourse	in 4
the Kings Maiesties	in 4
the mount of Caluarie	in 4

Inventories

Microcomos	in 4
A learned	in 4
A True and perfect	in 4
Philomela	in 4
An Apologie	in 4
A treatsche of tre Conuulsions halb	4
Abuses Stript halb	4
Homely	in 4
Anansuuer	in 4
A ful satisfaction	in 4,

[new page] Noch mehr Englische Bücher

The Wonter full	in 4,
the Conflut of Iob	in 4,
A true Report of the tisputation	in 4,
the kastel of Knolesge	in 4
Metitationes of Vovves	in 8, klein,
the Image	in 8
the Doctrine	in 8
the Sermons	in 8
A Reform: Catholike	in 8
Ignatius his Conclace	in 8 klein,
Summa dießer Bücher in allem sein	45,
Alß in folio	13,
in 4to	26,
in 8to	6,

Niedersächsisches Staatsarchiv, Wolfenbüttel MS 7 Alt S 2189, Fasc. 5. Copy list of books (not a formal inventory) together with other of Sackville's belongings, dated ten years after his death. Will untraced.

Printed: Paul Zimmermann, 'Englische Komödianten am Hofe zu Wolfenbüttel', *Braunschweigisches Magazin*, 4, Apr. 1902, pp. 37–45; 5, Mai 1902, pp. 53–7 (p. 57) (argues that transcript shows signs of having been copied from an earlier version by someone who could not read it properly).

fl. 1592–1628. Actor, also in Germany (Schrickx, *Foreign Envoys*, pp. 184–200 gives detailed account of Sackville's activities in Germany until 1602). In service of Duke of Brunswick 1602–17 and traded as merchant in Frankfurt. Died 1628. (Chambers II, 277, 337; Nungezer, pp. 308–9; Bentley II, 559.)

1683 Apr. 28 William BEESTON

An Inventory of all and singuler the goodes Chattelles and credittes of William Beeston late of the parish of St Leonard Shoreditch in the

County of Middlesex taken vallued & appraised by vs Richard Garnon and William Kidgell as followeth vizt

Inprimis in the Cellar a parcell of old fire wood	vj s viij d
It 2 dozen of glass bottles[1] at 2s per dozen	iiij s
In ye Kitchen	
It 4 pewter dishes tenn plates[1] ditto 4 pottes ditto	j li
It 3 old brass Kettles and 2 iron pottes	xij s
It j pare of grates & other fyer irones	xij s
It 3 spittes j Iacke and frying pann	viij s
It 3 brass candlesticks and other small brass	vj s
It j old cupboard j settlebedd & other Lumber	v s
In the first Chamber	
It j featherbedd Blanckettes & a rugg	j li xv s
It j old bedstead curtains & vallens	v s
It j old couch 4 chaires[1] & 2 old tables[1]	viij s
It 2 glass cases[1] 4 old pictures[1] and 1 looking glass	j li
It j pare of old fashioned fire irones	iiij s
In the jst chamber 2 pare of staires./	
It j feather bedd 2 blankettes & j rugg	j li
It j old bedstead curtains & vallenes	v s
In ye 2d Chamber 2 pare of staires	
It j old chest of draweres & other Lumber	iiij s
It 2 old featherbeddes	j li xv s
It j rugg & bedstead	vij s
It j trunke & 2 stooles[1] & closestoole	vj s
It old Lumber in ye Garrett	v s
It 2 pare of sheetes & table Lynnen	j li
Summa totalis hujus Inventarij	xij li vij s viij d

1. Otiose special sign for es.

GL MS 9052/23. Inventory (office copy) annexed to OW (see above **1682**), note of exhibition subscribed. Single strip of parchment, no endorsements. Text in rapid mixed hand; mark of abbreviation in Item omitted throughout (not individually noted).

Exhibited ACL 28 Apr. 1683 by Pet' Barrett (prob. granted 7 Sept. 1682).

1687 [Apr.–Nov.] (undated) William CARTWRIGHT

A true and perfect Inventorij of all and singular ye goodes chattlles & credits of William Cartwright late of ye parishe of St Gyles in ye feilds in

Inventories 239

ye County of midx deceased, taken, & appraized before Iohn Allen*
obtained letters of administration of ye said deceased estate much whereof
was afterwards purloined* embeazelled & never came to ye said
administrators hands ye perticulers & values of which purloined part is
here sett downe & inserted at ye foot of this Inventorij

In the dining room:
Inprimis 8 books of printed cutts	iij l iij s
Item 6 copies after bassan[1]	ij li viij s
Item 5 peices of old painting	j li j s
Item 22 peices of painting in landscript & figures	j li vj s
Item 2 pictures	iiij s
Item 3 peices of old tapistry hangeings j dozen of old turkey worke chairs 1 large turkey Carpet j folding table [x] {1} cupboard 2 old green elbow chaires, 2 old red chaires 1 red stool 1 old chest of drawers j court cupboard j looking–glasse 6 brasse candelsticks 1 pair of bellows, j firegrate, j pair of andirons, 2 Iron fireshovels, 2 pair of tongs, 1 Iron fender, j brasse fireshovel, j bras pair of tongs – little grated shovell, j Iron forke, & jo little bird cages —	v li xix s
Item one little feather bed, & 2 bolsters, j pillow a little flockbed j halfe headed [.] bedsted j old rug & some small lumber	j li j s vi d

In ye Closset in ye Dining room
Item 55 pictures of painting, & j print	v li x s
Item 2 cups of mother of pearl	l li j s vj d
Item little box with severall toies, & pictures in small boxes	j li v s

In ye first room 2 pair of staires
Item 19 pictures of painting	l li x s
Item 2 old peices of tapistry hangings	xv s
Item j old bedstead, mat & cord feather bed bolster, rug, j blancket & 3 old curtains & vallens	j li– j s
Item 4 old green chairs, 4 old stools Irons for the chimney, with other small lumber	x s

In the second room two pair of staires
Item 38 pictures, whereof 2 are printes, & 2 are drawings	v li x s
Item 10 small plaister–figures	iiij s
Item 2 small peices of tapistry hangings, & baies	xviij s
Item j old looking glasse	j s

Item one Indian bedsteed inlaid with shells, cord, &
matt two curtain–rods 2 old feather beds 2 old feather
bolsters, j flock bolster, j old turkey carpet, j feather
pillow, 2 old blankets, 2 flannen curtains, &
j brasse–pan   ij li x s
Item j tin {chaffing} dish, & some small lumber   iiij s
Item 3 callico curtains lined with silk & j silk quilt for
ye bed   ij li
Item j blew indian silk quilt   v s
 In the garret
Item 16 pictures   j li
Item a parcell of plaister–figures   –j li– v s
Item   ² heads in wax, & j blackmores head   xv s
Item 18 prints in frames   j s
Item j old cupboard, & lumber & striped hangings   ij s vj d
 In the stair case & parlor
Item 28 pictures of painting   ij li x s
 In another garret
Item lumber & old rotten stuffe   –v s
Item j damaske table cloath & j dozen & halfe of
damask napkins   j li
Item a parcell of old linnen   ij s– vj d
 In the parlor
Item 5 old green chaires 3 wooden chairs, j old drawing
table, j grate fireshovel, forke, spitt, Iack, 6 pewter
dishes 2 porringers, j dozen of plates, 3 pewter
chamber pots 3 pewter basons, 2 drinking pots &
one leaden cistern in the cellar   iij li x s
Item 2 silver tanckards guilt   vij li xv s
{All which were so valued the 14th of Ianuary 1686 by
Iohn Grosvenor, & Richard Tonson}³*
 The sum totalle of ye premisses is 57 li*   Lvij li
  In the closset one pair of stairs
  bookes* as follow
Item Downhams Warefare, babingtons works Halls works
an old edition of the first volum–2 Bea{u}mont &
ffletchers plaies an old edition Davenants workes prins
life of King Iohn, 3 Ben Iohnson, 1st volume, 1 second
vol–Lestranges life of King Charles ye first, woodalls
Surgery 1655–sterlings poems, Shakespears—plaies
imperfect, 3 martins Cronicle old edition, Mountaignes
Essayes, Mayer on the prophets, mercators Atlas pot',

Inventories

5 Lisander & Callista—Loves Sacrifice, Kellet on the Sacrament, Iuleta pastorall, Iustin Historia latina, Hookers Ecclesiastical polity, the five books, Haywood of Angells Eusebius Ecclesiastical history, an old edition fourth Tome of ye holy court [of] Bacons Henry ye 7th; an old edition, Huletts Dictionary history of China Herberts travels old edition, Hackluits voiages, j volume Gusman ye rogue History of Hungary, Hackvills apology old edition 3 Godfrey bulleign, Grand Cyrus ye 4th part, Growers confession ² fabians chronicle, ffullers holy war, holy state, ffelthams resolutions 1661 fonsecas contemplations, Elton on ye colossians, Greyes horseman 2 Eromena, a Romance extravagant shepheard, ffairfax history Orlando furioso, Sydnies Arcadia old edit 2 dr{a}ytons poems Daniells poems, Diall of princes, Guillams Heraldry old ed{i}tion defensive against prophesies, Dooms day or ye day of judgment, 3 Cornelius Tacitus English 2 old common praiers, Chapmans hymnes, a peece of Cesars commentaries {Lushington on hebrewes Cranmer against Harding pareius on revelations Cesars commentaries}⁴ English Carpenters merchants accounts Cassandra, a romance, compleat Embassador. Clarks Martyrology, part Britaines Troy Bifeild on ye colossians exemplary Novells Bacons natural history old edition barcklayes argenies Brooks heraldry Boccaline parnassus, old book of Honor Blundell of Sybill, Bentivoleo & Urania, part of it, Grimstons history of ffrance 2 Ariana, a romance, Andrews lectures, weavers monument old edition, Austins meditations, eng, Amadis de Gaule, Astrea, 3d volume Bentroliglio & urania plutarchs lives old edition, perkins works, 3d volume ffulk on ye rem' Test', Howells 3 monarchs of christendom, Heylins cosmography, August pharmacopea, Phillips world of worlds, pembrooks arcadia 2 ovids metamorphosis pot' folio Mason of consideration, pembles works, Rogers on Naaman 2 Rogers 7 treatises Ramsies Astrology, slaters Hist of Brittain purchas pilgrimage, history of venice, Salust in english, Thomas Taylors 1st volume smiths conquest of virginia 2 sandys travels exemplary novells, spencers fairy queen, whites reply to fisher Zanchius, in epistle,

old scapulas Lexicon old peece of origen, Maxian
Hispania, old peice of St Ierom Sandersons sermons, old
[old] dionisius in latin, Calvins institutions, Hemings
commentaries, buntinges Chronology Areties in epist',
musculus on mathew, Bullingers commentary [Iohnsons
3 plaies] Hipperius on ye Hebrewes Calvins
Commentary Iohnsons 3 plaies, 2 old latin bookes,
Brookes plaies, History of Goths and vandalls, 2 spanish
baud, Howards five plaies, 4 plaies, old martins
Chronicle, arcana, old edition of Shakespear old french
bible, old latin bookes, cuts, 43 old folio bookes in ye
presse, 2j old folios in or by ye windows about 350 old
4o books, 3 bundles of sticht 8o, 55 more 4os j bundle
of sticht 4o about 800 old books in 8o. 12o. 24o/
 In the room j pair of stairs
ogilby Homer oddisses folio Iliads folio, Stows chronicle,
 38 old folios. 35 bundles of old books in 4: 8. 12 &c
 abt^s 20 loose bookes
  over ye bed
21 volumes of plaies in 4o 32 bundles of books in 4o. 8o.
 et 12o &c 7 books loose
  In the garret
abt^s 50 bundles of 8o 12o &c abt^s 30 other loose bookes
 In the garret–staircase
abt^s 17 or 18 bundles stitcht
 In ye other garret staircase
Item 2 bundles of stitcht books folio 22 bundles of 4o sticht
 books
  In ye staircase of ye dineing room
30 bundles of 4o 8o 12o &c.
 In ye box in ye dining room
old plutarchs lives folio Eng purchas pilgrims folio 3d vol
 a bible in 4o English a welsh bible in 8o 2 english bible
 in 8o a greek testament in 8o English bible in 12o
 testament psal. in 24o
  In another box
speeds chronicle 3 english bibles 4o 4 testament & psal in
 24 an old latin bible jst part of Doways bible
  In ye dining room under the table
about 100 Manu Scripts of plaies 18 old folios 4 more, 16
 bundles of — 4o, & large 8o all which bookes together
 were appraised by Wm brook* & Rowland Reynolds*
 ye 14th of Ianuary 1686 37 li 15 s   xxxvij li xv s

Inventories 243

The summ totall of this Inventory is   92 li   15 s*
92 li– 15 s–

A note of such of ye perticulers before mencioned as on ye
31th of Ianuary 1686 could not be found,* but are
supposed to have been purloined, & embeazelled away by
some of those, who had ye power & custody thereof, &
which never came to ye hands & possession of ye said Iohn
Allen
One Bishop–Halls works in folio ye jst volume of an old
    edition, one Ben: Iohnsons workes ye second volume
    two Shakespears plaies, 1647 3 Ben Iohnsons works ye
    jst volume all valued by ye said William Brooke at   ij li v s
Item 46 peices of painting & other books of printed
    cuttes   jx li x s
Item 46 peices of painting & other bookes of printed
    cutts 9 li–10 s–0 d
Item 2 silver gilt tanckards 7 li –15 s– 0
Item j long carpet 3–10–0
Item severall medalls of painting & other curious &
    ancient things in a blew box, as figures in marble.
    & ingraven on coper 6 li–10 s–0 d
All which goods were so valued by ye said Iohn
    Grosvenor on ye 31 of Ianuary 1686 & amount in
    ye whole to 27 li –5 s   xxvij li v s
And theres great reason to suspect that other parts of ye said estate
set down in ye foregoeing Inventory were, in like manner purloined,
& embeazelled away & never came to ye said Iohn Allen ye said
Administrators hands or possession.
    Io: Hungerford*

1. *bassan*: could be *baswin*. 2. Blank in MS. 3. *All ... Tonson* inserted in different hand. 4. *Lushington ... com'entaries* inserted in different hand. 5. *abt*: mark of abbreviation missing, rightly ab*ou*t.

PRO PROB4/3022. Inventory (office copy), certificate of exhibition subscribed. (For will see above **1686**.) Parchment roll, four sheets joined serially. Text in late seventeenth–century engrossing hand with some corrections and insertions in more cursive style but same ink, with signature of John Hungerford.

Exhibited PCC 29 Nov. 1687. (Admon 'pendente lite' granted 29 Jan. and 28 Apr. 1687.)

Allen] John Alleyn, Warden of Dulwich College.

purloined] by Cartwright's servants Francis and Jane Johnson (see Young, *Dulwich*, I, 182–7 for account of the College's attempt to retrieve the legacy).

Tonson] bookseller 1675–89? (Plomer, *Dictionary* . . . *1668 to 1725*, pp. 292–3).

57 li] correct total is £56 13s.

bookes] quantity confirms John Aubrey's statement that Cartwright was a bookseller (*Natural History and Antiquities of the County of Surrey*, 5 vols, London, 1718–19, V, 356).

brook] bookseller 1661 (Plomer, *Dictionary*, p. 34).

Reynolds] bookseller 1667–91 (Plomer, *Dictionary*, p. 153; Plomer, *Dictionary* . . . *1668 to 1725*, pp. 251–2).

92 li 15 s] correct total is £94 15s or, using corrected figure for first part of inventory, £94 8s.

could not be found] Dulwich Coll. Alleyn MS VI fo. 136r lists items still missing c.1690 (Warner, p. 154; printed: Young, *Dulwich*, I, 187).

Hungerford] notary public, syndic of Warden and College in dispute over will in PCC.

APPENDIX 1
ACTING COMPANIES TO 1642

Actors whose wills or administrations are printed in this volume are marked with an asterisk. Some actors stayed with one company, others moved around. Most of the companies changed patrons several times. Information is drawn from Chambers, Bentley and *The Reader's Encyclopedia of Shakespeare*, ed. O. J. Campbell and E. G. Quinn (New York, 1966). (* Indicates willl or admon.)

The Queen's Men (1583–1603)
The most important London company until about 1588: it included *John Bentley, *John Dutton, *John Garland, William Johnson, *William Knell, *Richard Tarlton, John Towne, Robert Wilson, possibly *George Attwell, etc. Played in inn–yards and probably at the Theatre and the Curtain.

The Lord Chamberlain's Men (1594–1603); Lord Hunsdon's Men (1596–7); thereafter King's Men (1603–42)
Formed from the earlier Lord Strange's Men, the company's leading actors in 1594 were *George Bryan, *Richard Burbage, *John Heminges, William Kempe, *Augustine Phillips, *Thomas Pope, *William Shakespeare, *William Sly. Other leading actors who joined the company at various times included *Robert Armin, *Christopher Beeston, *Theophilus Bird, *Michael Bowyer, *Henry Condell, *Alexander Cooke, *Richard Cowley, *John Duke, *Nathan Field, *Charles Hart, *Thomas Hobbes, *John Honeyman, John Lowin, *William Ostler, *Thomas Pollard, *William Rowley, *John Shank, *Eyllaerdt Swanston, *Nicholas Tooley, *John Underwood. Played at the Theatre and the Curtain, at the Globe (from 1599), at the Blackfriars (from 1609).

Worcester's Men (1555–1603); Queen Anne's Men (1603–19); Players of the Revels (1619–22)
Included *Edward Alleyn, Robert and Edward Browne, and *James Tunstall (who all, except Robert Browne, later joined the Admiral's Men). Also, at various times, Richard Andrewes, *Thomas Basse, *Christopher Beeston, Robert Beeston, *William Browne, John Cumber, *John Duke, *Thomas Greene, Thomas Heywood, William Kempe, *Robert Lee, John Lowin, Richard Perkins, *George Pulham, William Robbins, *Ellis Worth. Played at the Boar's Head, the Rose, the Red Bull, and the Phoenix.

The Lord Admiral's Men (1585–96); Earl of Nottingham's Men (1596–1603); Prince Henry's Men (1603–12); Palsgrave's or Elector Palatine's Men (1612–25)
Led by *Edward Alleyn, included at various times *William Bird or Borne, *Thomas Downton, *Francis Grace, *Richard Gunnell, *Jaques Jones, *Edward Juby, *William Pavye, *Samuel Rowley, *John Shank, *Thomas Towne, *James Tunstall. Played at the Theatre, the Rose, the Fortune, etc.

Appendix 1

The Duke of York's Men (1608–12); Prince Charles's Men (1612–16)
Led by *William Rowley, included at various times *John Garland, *William Carpenter, *Thomas Hobbes. In 1616 borrowed from *Jacob Meade and *Edward Alleyn to buy a stock of apparel worth £400. Probably played at the Boar's Head.

Lady Elizabeth's Men (1611–25); Queen of Bohemia's Men (1628–41)
Financed by *Philip Henslowe. Actors included *Thomas Basse, *William Carpenter, *Nathan Field, Joseph Moore, John Rice, Joseph Taylor, John Townsend. They 'broke' several times; in 1613 they amalgamated with *Philip Rosseter's Children of the Queen's Revels, in 1615–16 with Prince Charles's Men; in 1614 *Jacob Meade joined Henslowe as company's financier. 1614–24 a Lady Elizabeth's company toured provinces under *Nicholas Long and then John Townsend. 1622 a new company was formed by *Christopher Beeston which included Joseph Moore, *Eyllaerdt Swanston, Andrew Cane. In 1628 reformed as Queen of Bohemia's Men, which included Richard Brome, John Bugge, Alexander Foster, Joseph Moore. Probably played at the Swan, the Rose, the Whitefriars, and (from 1622) the Phoenix. *James Shirley wrote his early plays for this company.

King and Queen of Bohemia's Men (1626–30)
Company included, Andrew Cane, William Cartwright sen., Richard Fowler, *Richard Gunnell. Probably played at Fortune of which Gunnell was manager.

Queen Henrietta's Men (1625–42)
Formed by *Christopher Beeston. Among actors in the company were William Allen, Robert Axen, *Theophilus Bird, *Michael Bowyer, Hugh Clark, William Robbins, John Sumner, William Sherlock, Anthony Turner. Played at Cockpit where *James Shirley wrote for them. In 1637 reformed at Salisbury Court.

King's Revels (also known as Children of the Revels, Company of the Revels, Company of his Majesty's Revels) (1629–35)
Company contained both adults and children with more of the latter than usual in men's companies, included *William Cartwright, *John Robinson, *Samuel Thompson. Played at Salisbury Court and Fortune.

Prince Charles's Men II (1631–42)
Licencee was Andrew Cane, included Thomas Bond, *William Browne, Richard Honyman, Joseph Moore, Arthur Savill, Mathew Smith, *Ellis Worth. Played at Salisbury Court, Red Bull, Fortune.

King and Queen's Young Company or Beeston's Boys (1637–41)
Founded by *Christopher Beeston, succeeded by son *William who was briefly replaced by *William Davenant. Company contained both adults and children, included Robert Axen, *Theophilus Bird, Michael Mohun, *Robert Shatterell. Played at Cockpit.

CHILDREN'S COMPANIES

The Children of St Paul's

*Sebastian Westcott, master of the song school at St Paul's, was 'schoolmaster of Paul's' by 1557. After Westcott's death (1582) *Richard Farrant transferred productions to the Blackfriars theatre. Thomas Giles became master of the song school in 1584; succeeded by Edward Pearce. John Lyly and *John Marston wrote plays for them.

The Children of the Chapel (1501–1603); Children of the Queen's Revels (1603–5); Children of the Revels (1605–6); Children of the Blackfriars (1606–9); Children of the Whitefriars (1609–10); Children of the Queen's Revels (1610–16)

Masters included *Richard Bower (1545–61), William Hunnis, *Richard Farrant (acting master, 1576–80), *Nathaniel Giles (1597–1634). Other masters included Robert Keysar, *Philip Rosseter (1610–16). James Robinson was a partner with Giles in managing the Children from 1600, and *Thomas Kendall and *Robert Payne joined as partners a little later. *Ralph Reeve and *Nicholas Long led provincial companies. *John Marston invested in the company and wrote plays for it, as did *Edward Sharpham. *Samuel Daniel was appointed official censor for the company's plays in 1604, and seems to have had a financial interest in it. *Henry Eveseed, *John Clarke were choristers. *Nathan Field, *William Ostler and *John Underwood acted with the companies as boys.

The Children of Windsor

Gave performances under *Richard Farrant (master 1564–80) and *Nathaniel Giles (1595–1634).

The Children of the King's Revels

Existed briefly before 1609. *John Mason invested in company. A second company travelled outside London with a licence dated 27 Feb. 1615, made out to *William Hovell, William Perry and Nathan May.

APPENDIX 2
PRINTED INDEXES TO WILLS

We have identifed hitherto unknown wills chiefly from the following indexes:

Prerogative Court of Canterbury
Index of Wills Proved in the Prerogative Court of Canterbury
   Vol. III: *1558–1583*, ed. S. A. Smith and Leland L. Duncan, Index Library 18, London, 1898
   Vol. IV: *1584–1604*, ed. S. A. Smith and E. A. Fry, Index Library 25, London, 1901
   Vol. V: *1605–19*, ed. E. Stokes, Index Library 43, London, 1912
   Vol. VI: *1620–9*, ed. R. H. Ernest Hill, Index Library 44, London, 1912
   Vol. VII: *1653–1656*, ed. Thomas M. Blagg and Josephine S. Moir, Index Library 54, London, 1925
   Vol. VIII: *1657–1660*, ed. Thomas M. Blagg, Index Library 61, London, 1936
   Vol. IX: *1671–1675*, ed. John Ainsworth, Index Library 67, London, 1942
   Vol. X: *1676–1685*, ed. C. Harold Ridge, Index Library 71, London, 1948
Prerogative Court of Canterbury Wills, Sentences and Probate Acts 1661–1670 (inclusive), ed. J. H. Morrison, London, 1935
Abstracts of Probates and Sentences in the Prerogative Court of Canterbury, 1620–1624, ed. John Matthews and George F. Matthews, London, 1911
Abstracts of Probate Acts in the Prerogative Court of Canterbury 1630–1655, ed. John Matthews and George F. Matthews, 8 vols, London, 1902–1927
Sentences and Complete Index Nominum (Probate and Sentences) for the Years, 1630–1639, ed. John Matthews and George F. Matthews, London, 1907
Administrations in the Prerogative Court of Canterbury 1559–1580, ed. R. M. Glencross, 2 vols, Exeter, 1912–17
Index to Administrations in the Prerogative Court of Canterbury
   Vol. I: *1649–1654*, ed. John Ainsworth, Index Library 68, London, 1944
   Vol. II: *1655–1660*, ed. C. Harold Ridge, 3 vols, Index Library 72, 74–5, London, 1949–53
   Vol. III: *1581–1595*, ed. C. Harold Ridge, Index Library 76, London, 1954
   Vol. IV: *1596–1608*, ed. Marc Fitch, Index Library 81, London, 1964
   Vol. V: *1609–1619*, ed. Marc Fitch, Index Library 83, London, 1968
   Vol. VI: *1631–1648*, ed. Marc Fitch, Index Library 100, London, 1986
Prerogative Court of Canterbury: Letters of Administration, 1620–1630 (inclusive), ed. J. H. Morrison, London, 1935

Archdeaconry Court of London
Index to Testamentary Records in the Archdeaconry Court of London now Preserved in Guildhall Library, London,
  Vol. I: *(1363)–1649*, ed. Marc Fitch, Index Library 89, London, 1979
  Vol. II: *1661–1700*, ed. Marc Fitch, Index Library 98, London, 1985

Commissary Court of London
Index to Testamentary Records in the Commissary Court of London (London Division) now Preserved in Guildhall Library, London, Vol. III: *1571–1625*, ed. Marc Fitch, Index Library 97, London, 1985

Court of Husting
Calendar of Wills Proved and Enrolled in the Court of Husting, London, A.D.1258–A.D.1688, ed. Reginald R. Sharpe, 2 pts, Part II *A.D. 1358–A.D.1688*, London, 1890

Archdeaconry of Surrey
Union Index of Surrey Probate Records which Survive from before the Year 1650, ed. Cliff Webb, Index Library 99, London, 1990

INDEX

This is an index of sixteenth- and seventeenth-century persons mentioned in the introduction, documents and notes, excluding the lists of testators and appendices. We have not indexed persons when they are referred to as subjects, for example as authors of books in inventories. In the absence of other distinctions, we identify by number persons bearing the same name. Unknown forenames are indicated by ellipses. References to testators are in bold type.

(b. brother; d. daughter; f. father; m. mother; s. son; w. wife)

Acton, Walter, 185
Sir William, 185
Adams, Jane (d. of Richard), 138
Jane (w. of Richard), 138
Richard, 138–9
Richard (s. of Richard), 138
Robert, 7, 57–8
Samuel, 138
Thomas, 124
Adderley, William, 86
Addison, Edward, 117
Adkins, William, 232
Adleme (Aldeme), Humphrey, 117
Adlington, Marie Walters alias, *see* Walters
Agmansam, John, 39
Aldeme, *see* Adleme
Alewood (Aylwood), Allice, 99
Anna, née Hovell, 118; *see also* Hovell, Ann
Richard, 118
Robert, 99
Allen, Giles, 9, 27, 62, 84, **229**
James, 222, 224
James (s. of James), 224
John, 6
Lowin, 6
Sara, 229
Susan, and husband, 198
Alleyn (Allen), Anne Harrison née, 152
Anthony, 154
Constance, née Donne, 150–1, 154
Edward, 2, 6, 17, 27, 89–90, 101–5, 113, 119, 131–2, 137–8, **150–4,** 155, 164, 197, 225–6, 228

Edward (f. of Edward), 6
Edward (godson of Edward), 152
Edward, of Newport, 152
Joan, née Woodward, 104–5, 154
John (b. of Edward), 6, 154, **228**
John (cousin of Edward), 152, 225–6, 239, 243
John (s. of Mathias), 152
Margaret, 228
Mathias, 104–5, 150, 152–4
Thomas, Master of Dulwich College (1619), 153–4
Thomas, Master of Dulwich College (1642), 152, 154
Alsop (Alsopp, Alsope), Jane, formerly Ricroft, 209
Peter, 209
Richard, 162
Alway, John, 235
Ambrosse, John, 149
Andrew, . . ., 121
Andrewes, John, (i) 44; (ii) 90
Anne, queen-consort of James I, 3–4
Anthony (Anthonye), John, 169–70
Margery, 170
Archer, James, 100–4, 117, 119
Richard, 208
Armin (Armyn, Armyne), Alice, 97–8
John, 97
Robert, 3, 11, 18–19, 73–4, **96–8**
Robert (s. of John), 97
Tabitha, 97
Ash (Ashe), Francis, 149
Lucy, 133
Ashpoole, Anne, 152
Askew, Robert, 78
Asplin, Anne, 127

Astley, Andrew, 199
  Anne, née Gilbourne, 155–6
  Drew, 199
  Edward, 199
  Elizabeth, 198–9
  Sir Jacob, 198–9
  John, 199
  Sir John, 15, 17, 20, **198–201,** 218
  Dame Katherine, 199–200
  Margett, 155
  Richard, 199
  Richard, clerk, 155
  Thomas, 199
  Thomas (s. of Andrew), 199
  Thomas (s. of Thomas), 199
  Thomasine, 155–6
Atkins, Alice, née Heminges, *see* Heminges
  John, 167, 169, 189–90
  Richard, 166
  William, 168
Atkinson, William, 179
Attwell (Attowell, Attywell, Otwell), Catherine, 228
  George, 228
Augusten, *see* Austen
Aundersone, John, 50
  Robert, 50
Austen (Augusten, Austin), William, 102, 104
Austinson, Godfrey, 205
Awborne, . . ., and wife, 224
Awnsham, Nicholas, 203–4
Awty, Thomas, 86
Axon, Mary, 178
  Robert, 178–9
  Thomas, 178
Aylwood, *see* Alewood

B<.>ina, Francis, 132
Babham, Abigail, 28
  Christopher, 28
Baker, Walter, 139
Baldwine (Bowldwin), Raphe, 63, 67
  Raphe (s. of Raphe), 67
Banckworth, Robert, 68

Barker, Edward, 47
Barnard, Charles, 58
  Helen, née Tarlton, 58
Barrett, Elizabeth, 91
  Peter, 238
Barsey, Thomas, 50
Barton, Allice, 155
  Andrew, 155
  Marcye, 155
Baskervile, James, 92, 182
  Susan, formerly Greene, formerly Browne, *see* Browne; Greene
Basse, Dorcas, 178–9
  Jane, 178
  Thomas, 92, 164, **178–9,** 194, 203, 220
  Ursla, 178
Batty, *see* Fenn alias Batty
Baxter, Jone, née Ellit, x, 163–4
  Richard, x, 163–4, 169, 191
  Richard (s. of Richard), 163–4
  Robertt, 147
  William, 163
Baylie (Bayeley), . . ., 50
  Anne Browne, née, *see* Browne
  Elizabeth, 196
Beale, . . ., fishmonger, 39
Beaumont (Beamont), Francis, 231
  Ursula, 231
Beawsoe, . . ., 93
Bedcher, William, 84
Beden, Richard, 39
Bedford, William Russell, Earl of, 223
Beeston (Beeson, Bescon, Bestone, Biston), Alice, 219–21
  Anne Bird, née, alias Hutchinson, *see* Bird
  Benaniah, 219–20
  Christopher, alias Hutchinson, 6, 18–19, 21, 26–7, 29–30, 73–4, 84–5, 91–2, 148, 178–9, **191–4,** 212, 214, 220
  Christopher (s. of Christopher), 84–5
  Elizabeth, alias Hutchinson (d. of Christopher), 194

Index 253

Elizabeth, alias Hutchinson (w. of Christopher), 21, 178, 192–4
George, 219, 221
Margaret, alias Hutchinson, 194
Robert, 6, 84–5
Sackville, 219–20
William, alias Hutchinson, 6–7, 17, 27, 29, 84–5, 178–9, 192–4, 212, **219–21**, 235, 237–8
Beighton, *see* Brighton
Belchen (Belcher), William, 59–60
Bell, Robert, 197
  Sarah, 173
  William, 205
Benfield (Benefeild, Benfeild, Benfild), Anne, 195
  Richard, 20, **195–7**, 206, 209, 235
  Robert, 109–10, 169, 191, 195–7, 206, 235
  William, 196
Benger, Dame Dorothy, 43–4
  Margaret, 44
  Susan, 44
  Sir Thomas, 17, 21, **43–5**
  William, 44
Bennett (Bennit), Agnys, 73, 75
  Francis, 149
Bentley (Bently), Edward, 55–6
  Elizabeth (d. of John), 55
  Elizabeth (m. of John), 56
  Johan, 56–7
  John, 3, **55–7**
  Richard, 55–6
  Steven, 55–6
  Thomas, 55
  Thomas, of Newmarket, 56
Berrydge, Joan, 135
Best, John, 148
Bestone, *see* Beeston
Betsworth (Betsswth), Peter, 155–6
Betterton, Mary, née Saunderson, 224–5
  Thomas, 223–4
Bilson (Billson), Leonard, 104

Thomas, bp. of Winchester, *see* Winchester
Bingley, Elizabeth, alias Maxey, née Burbage, 233–4; *see also* Burbage
  George, 233
Birch, Elizabeth, née Cowley, *see* Cowley
Bircher, Mrs . . ., 224
Bird (Byrd), Anne, née Beeston alias Hutchinson, 6, 192, 194, 211–12, 221
  Christopher, 192
  Elizabeth, 211
  George, 5, 211–12
  Mary, alias Borne (w. of William), 4, 11, 17, 27–8, 132, **147–9**, 197, 212
  Mary (d. of Theophilus), 211
  Theophilus, alias Borne, 5–6, 27, 75, 131–2, 147–8, 192, 194, 204, **211–12**, 221, 235
  Theophilus (s. of Theophilus), 5, 211–12
  Thomas, 75, 132, 148, 177
  William, alias Borne, 6, 26–7, 71, 75, 88–9, 105, **131–2**, 147–8, 212
  William (s. of William), 75, 131
Biston, *see* Beeston
Bistowe, Mathewe, 170
Blackburne, John, 214
Blagrave, Thomas, 40–1
  William, 189–90, 202, 233
Blake, William, 67
Bland, William, 208
Blinco (Blinko), . . ., fellmonger, 98–9
Blount, . . ., of Arlaston, and wife, 93
  Charles, 220
Bluet, Thomas, 50
Blumson, Robert, 185
  Thomas, 185
Blundevell, George, 97
Bodie, Anthony, 139
Bodley, John, 63–4, 67–8

Bolt, Roger, and wife, 111
Bolton, Elizabeth, 127
Bond, Albyn, 66
  Susan, née Browne, 180, 182; see also Browne, Susanna
  Thomas, 180, 182
Booth (Boothe), Joan, 127
  Thomas, 39
Borne, Margery, 73
  Myles, 73
  Phillipps, 73
  see also Bourne; Bird alias Borne
Bostocke, Charles, 121
Bouche (Bouth), Roger, 46
Bouchee, Mary, 217–8
Bouger, John, 155
Boult (Boulte), John, 48, 52
Boulton, Francis, 109
Bourne, Francis, 198
  Thomas, 132
  see also Borne; Bird alias Borne
Bouth, see Bouche
Bowen, Elizabeth, 187, 189, 195, 197
  John, 136
  Winifred, 187, 189, 195, 197
Bower (Bowere, Bowre), Agnes (Anne) Farrant, née, see Farrant
  Elizabeth, 41–2
  Joan, (i) 41–3; (ii) 116
  Katherine, 41–2
  Mary, 116
  Raffe, 41–2
  Richard, 6, 19, 41–3
  Samuell, 116
  Steven, 41–2
  Susan, 116
  see also Bowyer
Bowldwin, see Baldwine
Bowre, see Bower
Bowryng, Gregory, 50, 53
Bowyer (Bower), Elizabeth, later Morrison, 203–4
  Michael, 100–1, 178–9, **203–4**, 212
Brackes, Joan, 136–7

Bradelei, John, 66
Bradford, Ann, 120
Braine, see Brayne
Bramfeld, Bartholomew, 193–4
Branfor, Sir Thomas, 93
Brayne (Braine), Ellen Burbage, née, see Burbage
  John, 7, 9–10, 17, 45–7, 62, 84
  Katherine, 61–2
  Margaret, 4, 7, 28, 45–7, **60–2**, 62
Brend, Anne, 63–4
  Frances, 64–7
  Frauncis, 63
  Jane, 64, 67–8
  John, 64, 67–8
  Judith, 63–4
  Katheren Seares, née, see Seares
  Margaret, née Strelly, later Zinzan, 64, 68
  Matthew, 64, 68, 188, 190
  Mary Maylard, née, see Maylard
  Mercy (Mary) (d. of Nicholas), 64, 67
  Mercye (d. of Thomas), 63
  Mercy (w. of Thomas), 64
  Nicholas, 2, 10, 63–4, **67–8**, 190
  Thomas, 63–4, 68
  Thomas (b. of Thomas), 63
Brian, see Bryan
Brice, William, 97
Bridges, ..., brewer, 156
  Anne or Agnes, 199–200
Brighton (Beighton), Nicholas, 47–8
Britton, Mother ..., 66
Broadhead, Alce, 212
Brome, George, 153
Bromeham, ..., 50
Bromfeild (Bromfyld), Robert, 102–4
Bromley, Thomas, 69–70
Brooke (Brook), Humphery, 202
  William, 242–4
  Sir William, 172
Brookes, ..., 59
Browne (Broune, Brown, Brownes), Lady ..., 172

Alis, 39
Anne (d. of Robert), 90–2
Anne, ? née Baylie, 181–2
Anthony, 40
Awedry, 129
Cicely (Sisley), née Sands, later Robins, 80–1, 84; *see also* Robins
Elizabeth, 84–5, 90–1, 129–30
Henry, 204–5
James, 129
Jane *or* Jeane Reynolds, née, 80–1, 84–5; *see also* Reynolds
John, 39, 60
Judeth, 129
Sir Mathewe, 67–8
Raph, 195
Richard, 155
Robert, actor in Germany, 80–1, 85, 130, 229
Robert (s. of Robert, actor), 24, 90–2, **129–30**
Robert, haberdasher, 180–2
Robert, notary public, 78
Robert, proprietor of Boar's Head, 66, 92, 181–2, **229**
Susan, later Greene, later Baskervile, 229; *see also* Greene
Susanna Bond, née, 90–1; *see also* Bond, Susan
Thomas, 39
William, 191
William, actor, 19, 21, 23–4, 90–2, **179–82**, 210
Brumskill, Susan, née Giles, 172–5
William, 171
Brunswick, Henry Julius, Duke of, 237
Bryan (Brian), George, 149, **229**
Mary, 4, 28, 30, **149–50**, 229
Thomas, 100, 118–19
Brynton, James, 176
Buck, Sir George, 4, 26
Buckley, Richard, 149
Bugge (Bugges), John, 109–110, 195, 197

Bund, Margerett, 83
Burbage (Burbadge, Burbaige, Burbidge), **Cuthbert**, 6, 9, 80–1, 84, 112, 114, 125–8, 158, 160, 168–9, 182–6, 228, **233–4**
Elizabeth, 114, 125, 128, 184, 186, 234
Elizabeth Bingley alias Maxey, née, 125; *see also* Bingley
Ellen (Helen), née Brayne, 9, 228
James, 5, 9, 46–7, 62, 84, 114, **228**, 234
Richard, 5–6, 7, 9, 10, 17, 74–5, 107, 109, **113–15**, 125, 128, 191, 228, 234
Sarah, 125
William, 191
Winifred, née Turner, 5–6, 113–14
Burton, Tobias, 174–5
Burwell, Frances, 218
Butler, Robert, 226
Byrd, *see* Bird
Byshopp, Barbary, 61
Nicholas, 61–2

Cady, Thomas, 195
Cage, Alice, 198
Calfehill, James, 40
Call, Abel, 133
Calton, Sir Francis, 152
Campion, Thomas, 13, **119**, 124
Cane (Kene, Cayne), Andrew, 3, 130–1, 169–70, 182, 202
Canes (Cane), John Vincent, 213, 215
Canis, John, 44
Canterbury, William Sancroft, abp. of, 225–6
Caper, Francis (Frances), 95
Carew, Sir Nicholas, 150–1, 153
Carey, Henry, Lord Hunsdon, *see* Hunsdon
Carlell (Carliel), Joan, née Palmer, 218–19
Lodowick, 218–19
Carleton, Sir Dudley, 114

256   Index

Nicholas, 50, 53
Carpenter (Carpendar), . . ., 68
 . . ., and wife, 221–3
 Anne, 224
 Elizabeth, 232
 Joane, 68
 Prudence, 232
 William, 232
Carter, John, 133
Cartwright, Margarett, 82
 William, 5, 30, 225–6, 238–44
 William (f. of William), 226
Casellman, John, 63
 Sence, 63
Casinghurst, John, 151, 153
Castelton, Baldwin, 54
Cawerden (Cawarden), **Sir Thomas**,
 39–41
 Dame Elizabeth, 40–1
 John, 39–40
Cayne, see Cane
Chamberlain, John, 114
Chambers, Roger, 82
Champion, . . ., 89
Chapman, Richard, 121
 William, 110
Chappell, Thomas, 86
Charles I, king of England, 204, 217
Charles II, king of England, 217
Charlett, Gregory or George, 54–5
Charman, Elyzabeth, 173
Checkley, William, 136
Cherson alias Wainwright, Bridgett,
 199
Chester, . . ., and wife, 54
Chubb, Anne, 220
Church, Bor., 193–4
Clarke (Clarcke), Dority, 70
 George, 66
 John, 132–4
 Katheren, 89
 Margarett, 163
 Mary, alias Wood, 69–71
 Richard, 124
 William, 67
Clay (Claye, Clayes), Anne, 140

Henry, 140
John, 45
Nathaniel, 21, 100–1, 119
Clewett, Dr . . ., 159
Clifford, George, 199
 John, 199
Clinton, Edward, Earl of Lincoln see
 Lincoln
Clunye, Frydiswide, 50
Cobb (Cob), John, 125
 Mary, 125
 Peter, 125
 William, 54
Cobhead (Cobhed), Thomas, 46
Coborne, see Colbourne
Cock, G., 209
Coesar, Jone, née Jaggard, 122–3
 Richard, 122–3
Coffyn, Thomas, 223
Cogan, Henry, 204–5
Coghill, James, 176
Colbourne (Coborne, Colbrand),
 Edward, 130–1
Cole (Colle), George, 153
 Mary, 185
 Roger, 98, 100–4, 118–19, 135–8
Coley, Alice Rowley, née, see Rowley
Collett, John, 63
Collice, Anne, 177
 Marye, 177
Collins (Collyns), Arthur, 197
 Edward, 137–8
 Francis, 7, 19, 107–8
Collman, John, 139
Combe, Thomas, 10, 107
Condell (Cundall, Cundell, Cundey),
 Elizabeth (w. of Henry), 4, 10,
 19, 28, 30, 125, 128, 157–60,
 182–6, 234
 Elizabeth (w. of William), 183–4
 Elizabeth (d. of William), 184
 Elizabeth Finch, née, 125; see also
 Finch
 Henry, 7, 12, 17, 20, 22, 24,
 73–4, 95–6, 107, 109, 125–8,
 144–5, **156–60**, 168, 186, 234

Henry (s. of Henry), 157–8
William, 157–8, 160, 182–6
Coningham, Joseph, 149
Conisbey, Anne, 179
Conquest, Cor., 112
Cooke (Cook), . . ., 59
  Alexander, 3, 16–17, 73–4, **94–6**, 160, 168
  Alice, 149
  Ellis, 95
  Francis, 94
  John, 95
  Rebecca, 94–5
  Richard, 149
Cooper, Edward, 51
Corden, William, 89–90, 118–19
Corey (Cory), Katherine, née Mitchell, 224–5
Cotton, Anne, 212
  Francis, 212
Cowley (Coweley), Elizabeth Birch, née, 112
  Richard, 17, 73–4, **112–13**, 168, 189, 234
Cowper, William, 212
Coxe, Roger, 155
Crane, Martyn, 63
  Ralph, 17, 114–5
Creake, Thomas, 51
Crimes, see Grymes
Crispe, Ellis, 121
Crouche, Mrs . . ., 220
Cumbere, John, 91–2
Cundall, Cundell, Cundey, see Condell
Curles, Anne, 120
Currall, . . ., preacher, 121
Curteys, Bridget, and husband, 198
Cutler, Elizabeth, 152
Cuxon, Margaret, 102

Daighton, John, 93–4
Dalby, Ed, 121
  Susan, 121
Dale, Margery, 109
Dambrooke (Danbrooke), **Sarah**, 28, 140, 189

Damford, John, 204–5
Daniel (Danyel, Danyell), John, 116–17
  Samuel, 6, 79–80, **116–17**
  William, 185–6
Dansey, see Dauncey
Darknall, John, 174–5
Dauncey (Dansey), [John], 44–5
Davenant, Lady Mary, 25, 235
  Sir William, 25, 220, **235**
Davies (Daveis), Henry, 153
  John, of Hereford, 208
  Robert, 153
Davis, . . ., d. of Mrs Skynner, 66
  Anne, 76–7
  Frances (Francis), 149
  Hugh, 28, **76–7**, 103
  William, 149
Dawson, Robert, 122
Dearing, Anne, 198
Dekker (Deckers), Elizabeth, 233
  Thomas, 233
Dell, Henry, 153
Denham, Sir John, ix
Dennys, George, 155
Devereux, Robert, Earl of Essex, see Essex
Devorax, John, 199
  Jone, 199
Dickens, Robert, 17, 127–8, 160
Digby, Lady . . ., 223
Dighton (Dyghtonn), Hugh, 54–5
Diodati (Diodate), Charles, 186
  John, 184, 186
Disney, . . ., niece of J. Astley, 198
Dobsonns, . . ., 100
Dodmer, Bryan, 39–40
  Thomas, 39
Dolytell, . . ., sister of T. Giles, 54
Donne, John, 154
  Constance Alleyn, née, see Alleyn
Dorset, Charles Sackville, Earl of, 220
Doughtie, Elizabeth, 111
  Jane, 111
Dover, Mary, 127

Downton (Dowton), Ann, 146–7
  Ed, 146
  Jaine (d. of Thomas), 146
  Jane (w. of Thomas), formerly Easton, 15, 28, 146–7
  Thomas, 5, 8, 15, 19, 21, 28, 88–9, **146–7**
  Thomas (s. of Thomas), 146–7
Dowson, Agnes, 127
Drax, Lady . . ., 223
Drewe, Symon, 128
Ducke, John, 200
Duffelde, . . ., 39
Duke, John, 92, **230**
  Suzanna, 230
Duppa, . . ., 111
Durham, Henry, 232
Dutton, Elizabeth, 230
  John, **230**
  John (s. of John), 230
Dyer, Robert, 121
Dyghtonn, *see* Dighton
Dyson, Christopher, 62
  Humphrey, 17, 87–8, 122, 127–8, 160

E.,T., 28, 30
Eagelsfeild, John, 141
Easton, Jane Downton, formerly, *see* Downton
  Oliver, 28, 147
Eaton, Thomas, 5
Ecclestone, William, 125, 128
Edmonds (Edmondes, Edmans), John, 70–1, 118–19
Edney, Peter, 111
Edward VI, king of England, 44
Elizabeth I, queen of England, 3–4, 12, 43–4
Elizabeth, princess, 4
Ellam, Brian, 20, **62**
  John, 62
Ellit, Jone Baxter, née, *see* Baxter
England, John, 54
  Robert, 54
Engleton, Davie, 64
  Margaret, 64–5
Erswells, Robert, 122
Essex, Robert Devereux, Earl of, 208
Evans, Henry, 50–1, 53, 80
  John, 123
Eveley, . . ., 172
Even, *see* Ewen
Every, Sir Henry, 217
  Henry (s. of Sir Henry), 217
  Dame Vere, née Herbert, 217
Eveseed (Eviseede), Henry, 155
Evor, Ellen, 64–5
  Oliver, 64
Ewen (Even), Thomas, 70–1

Fabian, Marye, 176
  William, 176
Facy (Facye), John, 136–7
Fantrat, Elizabeth, 87
  Peter, 87
Farrant (Farrante), Agnes (Anne), née Bower, 25, 41–3, 47–8
  Richard, 6, 25–6, 41, 43, **47–8**
  Richard (s. of Richard), 47
Farthing, Elizabeth, 50
Feeldhowse, Dorathie, 88
Felles, William, wife of, 79
Fenn, Barbara, 222
  John, and wife, 222–3
  Jone, alias Batty, 133
  Mary, alias Batty, 133
Fidge (Fitch), Mary, 176
  William, 176
Field, Dorcas Rice, née, *see* Rice
  Nathan, 26, 145, **231**
  Nathaniel, 231
Finch (Fynch), Elizabeth, née Condell, 157, 159–60, 182–3, 185–6; *see also* Condell
  Herbert, 10, 158, 182–3, 186
Fishe, John, 130–1
Fisher, John, 218
  John, barber–surgeon, 131
Fitch (Fitche), Winifred Shank, later, 195, 197
  see also Fidge

Fletcher, John, 200
  Lawrence, 73–5
  Richard, 59
Flint, Sara, 87
Fortescue, Bridgett, 78
Foster, Thomas, 104
Fountaine, Edward, 213
  Laurinda, 213–14
Fowke, . . ., and wife, 223
Fowler, Catherine Wilkins, née, (or Fowles), see Wilkins
  Dorothie, 210
  Richard, 201, 210
Foxe, John, 63
Frances, John, 164
Freeman, Elizabeth, 210
French, . . ., and wife, 224
  Anne, 195
  Rebecca, 195
  Sarah, 195
  Thomas, 195
Fugall, Thomas, 21, 44–5
Fynch, see Finch

Gafford, William, 51
Gall, Richard, 56
Gammon, Elizabeth, née Jones, see Jones
  Richard, 204–5
Gape, William, 205
Garland, Elizabeth (d. of John), 141
  Elizabeth (w. of John), 142
  John, 141–2
  John, of Burntwood, 141
  Marie, 141–2
Garnon, Richard, 238
Garrard, Lady Jane, 217–18
Garton, William, 83
Gasking (Gasquine, Gasqune), Susan, 69, 70–1
Gautres, . . ., baker, 91
Gayton, William, 78–9
Geery, Henry, 208–9
Gerrarde (Gerrade), Gilbarte, 40
Gibborne, see Gilburne
Gibbs (Gibbes), Anne, 66
  Henrie, 65–6
  Marie, 65
  Robert, 130–1
Gilbourne (Gilborne), Anne Astley, née, see Astley
  Thomas, 17, 155–6
Gilburne (Gilborne, Gibborne), Samuel, 73–5, 156
Gilder, . . ., 159
Giles (Gyles), Ann, 171–5
  Anne Horne, née, see Horne
  Bennett, 218
  Charles, 171
  Elizabeth Worsop, née, see Worsop
  Henry, 174–5
  John (b. of Thomas), 54–5
  John (b. of Nathaniel), 173
  Margaret, 173
  Mary, 173
  Nathaniel, 18, 30, 80, 171–5
  Nathaniel (s. of Nathaniel), 171–5
  Nathaniel (grands. of Nathaniel), 171
  Robert, 54
  Robert (s. of Nathaniel), 171, 173, 175
  Susan Brumskill, née, see Brumskill
  Thomas, haberdasher, 14, 19–20, 48, 52, **53–5**
  Thomas, musician, **110–12**, 120
  Thomas (s. of Thomas, haberdasher), 54–5
  Walter, 218
Gill, Richard, 163
Girdler, Alice, 221–2
Glascocke, William, 65
Goborne, John, 130
  Margoret, 130–1
Godfrey, Edmond, 67
  Edward, 68
Godman (Goddman), Thomas, 82
Goffe, Elizabeth, 164
  Thomas, 164
  see also Gough
Golding, Persivall, 79–80

Gonnell, *see* Gunnell
Gooddall (Goodale), Edward, and wife, 195
   Richard, 60
Good, Mistress . . ., 51
Goodhand, Fraunces, 80
   Harte, 80
Goodinow, Jaqnet, 50
Goodridge (Goodridges), Richard, 40
Goteham, Richard, 78
Gough (Goughe), Alexander, 169, 191
   Elizabeth, 73, 75
   Robert, 70–1, 74–5
   see also Goffe
Goulde, William, 176
Goulson, Joan, 155
Gowge, William, 141
Grace, Francis, 17, 24, **130–1**
   Richard, 130–1
Granwall, Richard, 47–8
Graves, Elizabeth, 114
Greene (Green, Greenes), Anne, 148
   Honnor, 90
   Hugh, 212
   Jeafferey, 91
   John, 91–2
   Susan, formerly Browne, later Baskervile, 4, 91–2, 180–2; *see also* Browne
   Thomas, 20–1, 85, **90–2**, 180, 182, 194, 229
Gregory, Mrs . . ., 208
Gressopp, Nicholas, 54
Greville (Grevyll), Curtis, 137
   Katheryn, 135, 137
Greygoose, John, 121
Griffin, . . ., of Kingston, daughter of, 177
   Edward, 89–90, 100–1
Griffith, Robert or Thomas, 170
Grome, John, 17, 87–8
Grosvenor, John, 240, 243
Grove, John (b. of Jane Poley), 66
   John (nephew of Jane Poley), 66
Gryffithes, Richard, 109

Grymes (Crimes), Sir Thomas, 150–1, 153
Grynkyn, John, 65
Guest, Ellis, 7
   Ellis (s. of Ellis), 7
Gunnell (Gonnell), Anne, 202
   Elizabeth, later Robinson, 233; *see also* Robinson
   Richard, 8, 131, 190, 201–2, **233**
Gurney alias Hulse, Fraunces, and daughter, 159
Gyles, *see* Giles
Gymber, . . ., widow, 158

Haines, Mary, 193
Hales, Henry, 223–4
Hall, Debora, 198
   Elizabeth, 106–8
   John, 108
   Dame Margaret, 198
   Nevile, 198
   Robert, 120–1
   Susan, 120
   Susanna, née Shakespeare, 9, 106–8
   Sir William, 198
Hallingshead, . . ., 149
Halse, Thomas, 67
Hammon, Maudley, 68
Hancocke, William, 79
Hanson, Nicholas, 204
Harboard (Harberd), William, 217–8
Hardye, Richard, 80
Harison, *see* Harrison
Harlam, . . ., 68
Harpar, Francis, 203
Harris (Harrys), Mrs . . ., 66
   Margaret, 226
   Robert, 120
Harrison (Harison, Harryson), Anne, née Alleyn, *see* Alleyn
   George, 61
   John, (i) 152; (ii) 200
   William, (i) 2, 26; (ii) 200–1
Harrys, *see* Harris
Hart (Harte), Charles, 221–5

Joan, 106
Matthew, daughter of, 222–3
Michaell, 106
[Thomas], 106, 108
William (nephew of W. Shakespeare), 106
William, actor, 191
Hartlib, Samuel, 201
Hassard (Hasard), Anne (w. of Robert), 82
Anne (d. of Robert), 82
Edmond, 82
Henry, 208–9
Robert jun., 82–3
Hatt, John, 184–6
Haughton (Hawghton, Houghton), Alice, 75–6
George, 138
Henry, 56
Raphe, 62
William, 75–6
Havell, *see* Hovell
Hawes (Hawe), Thomas, 39–40
Hawley, Richard, 191
Hayman, Robert, 79
Heale, Susan, 210
Hearne, *see* Herne
Heckste, George, 78
Helyard, . . ., aunt and uncle to E. Pudsey, 94
Heminges (Hemings, Hemynges, Hemynnges, Hennings), Alice Atkins, née, 169
Elizabeth, 165–7
John, 3, 5, 20–2, 24, 27, 74–5, 86–8, 95–6, 107, 109, 112, 144–5, 158, 160, **164–9**, 189–90, 194, 227, 231, 234
Rebecca, formerly Knell, 5, 165, 168; *see also* Knell
William, 5, 165–9, 189
Henrietta Maria, queen consort of Charles I, 4, 204
Henry, prince of Wales, 112
Henrye, John, 63
Henslowe (Henslow, Henshlowe, Henshelowe, Hinchlowe), **Agnes** (**Ann**), 20, 28, 30, 101–3, **104–5**
Ann, alias Parson, 102
John, 102–3
Philip, 2, 6, 8, 10, 17, 20–1, 24, 27–8, 76–7, 83, 89–90, 98–9, **101–5**, 116, 124, 137, 154
Philip (s. of John), 102
William, 102, 105, 154
Henton, Edward, 198, 200
Herbert, Elizabeth (d. of Sir Henry), 215–18
Dame Elizabeth (w. of Sir Henry), 216–18
Sir Henry, 10, 15, 18, 20, 190, 201, **215–18**
Henry (s. of Sir Henry), 215–18
Capt. Henry (nephew of Sir Henry), 217
Magdalene, 215–18
Mary, Countess of Pembroke, *see* Pembroke
Dame Vere Every, née, *see* Every
Herne (Hearne), Richard, 197–8
William, 39
Hesketh, Thomas, 86–8
. . ., widow of Thomas, 87
Heydon, John, 196
Heywood (Heyward), Thomas, 91–2
Hickes (Hixe, Hyxe), Margaret Hunningborne, née, *see* Hunningborne
Richard, 227
Higgens, Lawrence, 54
Hill, Anne, 163
Elizabeth, 129
Josua, 181
Miles, 129
Richard, 163
Robert, 87
Hillton, Charles, 63
Hinchlowe, *see* Henslowe
Hindes, Matilde, 55–6
Hinton (Hynton), Griffith, 136–7
Hobbes, Anne, 234
Mary, 234

Thomas, 191, 234
Hobert, Edward, 132
Hodges, Leonard, 58
Hoghton, Alexander, 3, 27, 88
Holcomb, Frances Worth, formerly, see Worth
  Thomas, 210
Holland (Holand), Aaron, x, 170, 233
  Elizabeth, x, 3, 4, 18, 28, 169–70, 233
  John, 69–71
Holmes, James, 148–9, 196–7
Honyman, Ellen, later Sweetman see Sweetman
  John, 3, 19, 24, 26, 169, 189, 190–1
  Richard, 191
Hooke, . . ., and wife, 223
  Mrs . . ., widow, 224
Hope, John, 138
Hopegood, Agnes, 121
Horne, Ann, née Giles, 172–5
  John, 149
  Thomas, 171–3
Houghton, see Haughton; Hoghton
Hovell (Havell), Ann Alewood, née, 99; see also Alewood, Anna
  Joan, 4, 19–20, 28, 98–101, 117–19
  Nicholas, 98–9
  William, 3, 7, 19–21, **98–101**, 103, 119, 203, 232
How, William, 218
Howghton, George, 138
Howghton, see also Hoghton
Howson, . . ., and wife, 54
Hublethorne, Dorothie, 80
Hudson, Richard, 62
Hulet, Richard, 103
Hulse, see Gurney alias Hulse
Humphryes (Humfrye, Humfries), Mrs Sidney, 207
Hungerford, John, 243–4
Hunningborne, Margaret, née Hickes, 227

Hunsdon, Henry Carey, Lord, ix, xi
Hunt (Hunte), . . ., of Ashford, co. Salop, 177
  Elizabeth, 61
Hunter, Richard, 109
Huse, Richard, 50, 52
Hutchinson, Walter, 142
Hutchinson, see also Beeston alias Hutchinson
Hynton, see Hinton
Hyxe, see Hickes

Ireland, Jacob, 61
Islip, Adam, 6, 19, **197–8**
  Kenelme, 197
  Susan, 197
Ivat, John, 229

Jackson (Jacksonn, Jacson, Jacsun), Blaunch, 118
  Edward, 118
  Henry, 114
  John, 70–2, 87–8
Jaggard, Alice, 122
  Isaac, 122–3
  Jane, 123
  Jone Coesar, née, see Coesar
  Thomas, 122
  William, 122–3
James I, king of England, 3
Jeffes, Humfrye, 88, 90
Jepson, Ralphe, 136
Jessop, William, 208
Jewell, Simon, 58–60
Johnson, . . ., 59–60
  Francis, 244
  Henry, 83–4
  Henry, holding land in Oldford, 141
  Jane, 244
  Peter, 57
  Thomas, 83–4
  William, 155
  William, actor, 57–8
  William, grocer, 169–70
Jones, . . ., 184

Index

Alice, 161–2
Anne (d. of Jaques), 161
Anne Webb, née, *see* Webb
Elizabeth (d. of Jaques), 161
Elizabeth Gammon, née, 204
Inigo, 7, **204–5**
Inigo (f. of Inigo), 7
Jack, 162
Jaques, 28, **161–2**
John, 162
Mary, 161–2
Thomas, 39
Jonson, Ben, 5, 7, 60, 120, **234**
Jordan, . . ., 224
Juby (Jubye), Edward, 88–9, 113
Frances, 113
George, 113

Katherens, Gilbert, 103, 114, 116
Jane, 116
Joane, 116
John, 116
Peter, 116
Richard, 116
Kempe, William, 71
Kempsall, Faith, 127–8
Kendall, Anne, 79–80, 109, 117
   Christopher (b. of Thomas), 79
   Christopher (cousin of Thomas), 79
   Edmond, 79
   Edward, 79
   John, 79
   Marmaduke, 79
   Thomas, 19, **79–80**, 109–10, 117, 122
Kene, *see* Cane
Kennett, John, 80
Keyes, Raphe, 116
Kezar, John, 104
Kidd, *see* Kyd
Kidgell, William, 238
Killigrew, Thomas, 202
Kinge, Andrew, 170
   Philip, 93, 112
Kingman (Kingsman), Elizabethe, 109–10
   Philip, 110
Kippinge, (Kippynge), Mrs . . ., 113
   Alexander, 113
   Edward, 153
Kirk (Kirke), Lewes, 192, 194
Kirkham, Edward, 79–80, 117
Knachbull, Elianor, 198–200
   John, 198
   Norton, 198–9
   Thomas, 199
Knell, Henry, 7
   Rebecca, later Heminges, 227; *see also* Heminges
   William, 5, 7, 168, 227
Knight, Edward, 130–1
   Robert, 50, 53
Knocke, George, 56
   Katherne, 55–6
Kyd (Kydd, Kidd), Anna, 227
   Francis, 227
   Thomas, 123, **227**
   Justinian, 50–3
Kynaston, Edward, 223–4
Kynborowghe, . . ., d. of Mrs Good, 51
Kynderslye, Anne, 111

Lacan, Lacon, *see* Layton
Ladkins, Robert, 232
Lake, Mrs Rogers, 223
Lambert, Edward, 202
Lambertonn, Richard, 54
Lancaster, Ann, 114
Laneham, John, 56–7
Langeworthye, William, 78
Langhorne, Richard, 5
Langley (Langlie), Francis, 66, 69, 71, **228**
   Jane, 228
Lanman, Christopher, 229
   Henry, 229
Larratt (Larrat), Anne, 155
   William, 155
Laton, Latton, *see* Layton
Lawes, Anthony, 52
Lawley, Sir Francis, 215–18

Layton (Laytonn, Laton, Latton, Lacan, Lacon), . . ., sister of Mary Bird, and husband, 148–9
  Blase, 41
  Edward, 104
  Edward (s. of Edward), 104
  Henry, 104
Leake, Bridgett, 195–6
  Mary, 195–6
  Richard, 195–6
  Sarah, 195–6
Leather, Elizabeth, 80
  Peter, 80
Lee (Leigh), Constance, 162–4
  Robert, x, 92, 124, **162–4**, 179, 232
  see also Woodgate, alias Lee
Leedham (Leedhame), Thomas, 79–80
Legatt, John, 5
Leie, *see* Leys
Leigh, *see* Lee
Leland, Ann, 87
Leveson, James, 120
  Mary, 120–1
  Thomas, 120
  William, 14, 87, **120–1**
Lewes, Elizabeth, 75
Leys (Leye, Leie), Richard, 39–40
Lightfoot, . . ., and wife, 197
Lightmaaker, Richard, 144
Lincoln, Edward Clinton, Earl of, 40–1
Linsle, Mrs . . ., 148
Lisle, Tobias, 150
Lister, . . ., doctor, 68, 87
Litler, Laurence, 71
Lloyd, Capt. . . ., and wife, 223–4
  Ellen, 224
  John, 224
  William, 215–17
Lodge, Joan, 232
  Thomas, 232
London, John, 112
Long (Longe, Longes), Anthony, 53–4
  Benjamin, 224
  George, and wife, 149–50
  Nicholas, 100–1, 124, 164, **232**
  Prudence, 232
Longford, Mrs . . ., 149
Lowin (Lowyn, Lowen), John, 3, 6, 144–5, 169, 184, 186, 188, 190
Lucas, Andrew, 135–7
Luke, Anne, 195–6
  Anne (d. of Anne), 195–6
Lyon, Gabriel, 155

Mahonne, Thomas, 219, 221
Mansell, Thomas, 100
Manser, John, 83
Markham, Gervase, 116, 234
Marmion, Shakerley, 3
Marsh (Mersh), Francis, 112
  William, 44
Marshall, Anthony, 144
  Humfry, 147
Marston, John, 19, 79, **176–8**
  Mary, 177–8
  Richard, 177
Martyn (Marten), . . ., widow, 158
  Henry, 153
  Joan, 67
  Nicholas, 67
Mary I, queen of England, 44
Mason, Bartholomew, 47
  Elizabeth, 230
  John, 230
  Prudence, 230
Massam, Phillipp, 181
Massey (Mercie), Charles, 88, 90, 131, 138
Mathew, Thomas, 122
Matthewes, . . ., 59
Maxey, Elizabeth Bingley, alias, née Burbage, *see* Burbage; *see also* Bingley
Maye, Elizabeth, 56
Maylard (Maylarde), Mary, née Brend, 63, 67
Mayne, Sir Jasper, ix
Meade (Mead, Mede), Edward, 135–6

Jacob, 10, 18–20, 103–4, 116, 131, **134–8**, 154
Jacob (s. of Jacob), 135–6
  Richard, 135–6
Meare, Robert, 103
Mercie, *see* Massey
Merefield (Merefeild), . . ., d. of J. Heminges, 166
Mersh, *see* Marsh
Merydale, Richard, 181
Mihell, William, 42
Mildmay, Henry, 203–4
  Sir Henry, 204
Miles (Myles), Robert, 7, 46–7, 61–2
Miller, Elizabeth, 179
  Elizabeth (d. of Jane Poley), 66
  Roger, 196
Milton, John, 186
Mitchell, Katherine Corey, née, *see* Corey
Moden, John, 69
Mohun (Mohune), Anne, 6, 27, 211–12, 221
  Michael, 6, 211–12, 221
Monger, Elizabeth, 197–8
  John, 198
Moore, Joseph, 182
More (Moore), Sir William, 39–40, 48
Morgan, Mrs . . ., 187–8
  Charles, 210
  Elizabeth, 210
Morley, John, 155
Morrison, Elizabeth Bowyer, later, *see* Bowyer
  Thomas, 203–4, 235
Moseley, Margarett, 125
Mottershedd, Rose, 68
Munson, . . ., 102
Myles, *see* Miles

Namecott, Sara, 197
  Swanston, 6, 197
Napier (Napper), Thomas, 222–4
Nashe (Nash), Anthonye, 107
  John, 107
Margery, 149
Nasyon, [?Henry], 50, 53
Neale, Edward, 182
  Robert, 181–2, 210
  Susan, 210
Nevile, Anthony, 198
  John, 199
  Margaret, 198
Newman, Elizabeth, 152
Newsam (Newsom), Peter, 118
Nicholls (Nicolles, Nycholles, Nycolls), . . ., and wife, 224
  Humphrey, 111–12, 120
  Humphrey, wife of, 111
  Robert, (i) 51–2; (ii) 59–60
Nicoll, Basell, 70–1
Nixon, Arthur, 208
  John, 207
  Richard, 207–8
  Robert, 207–8
Nore, Angelica, 234
  Roger, 201, 234
Norgate (Norgatte), Daniell, 88
  Phillis, 88
Norman, Nycholas, 135–7
Norton, . . ., and wife, 184
  Mary, 184
  Thomas, ix
Norwood, . . ., and wife, 222
  Mary, 222, 224
Nycholles, Nycolls, *see* Nicholls

Ordyner, Robert, 46
Ore, John, 51
Ostler, Beaumont, 6
  Thomasine, 5, 169, 230–1
  William, 5, 169, **230–1**
  William (s. of William), 5
Otwell, *see* Attwell
Owen, John, 78–9
Oxenden (Oxinden), Sir James, 199, 201

Page, . . ., master in Chancery, 185
  Stephen, 204
Paine, *see* Payne

Palmer, Mrs . . ., 66
  Joan Carlell, née, *see* Carlell
  John, 86
  Katherine, 86
  Penelope, 218
Paltock, John, 171
Paris (Parys), George, 52
  Raphe, 51
Parkines, *see* Perkins
Parrish, Anthoni, 144
Parson, Ann Henslowe alias, *see* Henslowe
  William, 102
Parssoll, . . ., 136
Partridge, Marie, 87
Parys, *see* Paris
Pate, Edward, 160
Paternoster, Robert, 42
Patrick, William, 191
Pattesonn, John, 61
Paule, George, 121
Pavier, Thomas, 123
Pavye (Pavy), Elizabeth, 229
  William, 229
Payne (Paine), Avis, 121–2
  Elizabeth, 121–2
  Florentine, 121
  John, 121
  Katherine, 188
  Mary, 121–2
  Robert, 121–2
  Thomas, 121
  William, 121
Peacock (Peacocke), Ambrose, 86
  Cicelie, 86
  Thomas, 86
Pease, . . ., 141
Peele, George, 123
Peirson, John, 130
  Jone, 63
  William, 86
Pembroke, Mary Herbert, Countess of, 60
Peningtone, James, 76
Penn, William, 191
Perkins (Parkines), John, 28

Richard, 91–2, 178–9, 203–4
Perrin, Anne, 235
  Richard, 235
Perry, William, 101, 111–12, 164
Peters, Alice, 133
Phillips (Phillipps), Anne (d. of Augustine), 72
  Anne (w. of Augustine), 72–5
  Augustine, 3–4, 21, 72–5, 81, 96, 98, 109, 112, 114, 128, 160, 168, 194
  Elizabeth, 73
  John, 116
  Maudlyne, 72
  Peter, 50, 52
  Rebecca, 72
Pickerley, Hanna, 152
Pigot (Pigete), William, 66
Pike, Henry, 133
Plott, . . ., 121
Ploughman, William, 149
Podger, John, 21, 100–1
Pole, . . ., 51
Poley (Pooley, Poolie), Edmund, 66
  Jane, 28, 65–7
  Sir John, 65–7
Pollard, Thomas, 169, 189, 195–7, 206, **235**
Polton, *see* Poulton
Poole, . . ., 121
Pooley, Poolie, *see* Poley
Poollam, Poollame, *see* Pulham
Pope, John, 69–70, 75
  Thomas, 20–1, 29, **68–72**, 75, 145
  William, 70, 75
Porter, Hellen, 114
Potter, Audrey, 163
  Henry, 163
Poulton (Polton), Mrs . . ., 94
  Mary, 213–14
  Richard, 213–14
Powell, Mrs . . ., 224
  [Martin], 224–5
  Edmond, 159
  Philip, 188–9
Pratt, Alexander, 91

Prideaux, . . ., and wife, 223
Pudsey, Amy, 93
  Edith, 92–4
  Edward, ix, 18, 92–4
  Edward (s. of Edward), ix, 92–4
  Elener, 93
  Margery, 93
  Martha, 93
  Nicholas, 93
  Richard, 93
  Samuell, 93
  Thomas, 93
Pulham (Poollam, Poollame),
  Francis, 84
  George, 84–5, 194, 220
  John, 84
  Timothie (b. of George), 84
  Timothie (f. of George), 84
Purfoot, . . ., and wife, 197
Pyford, Gregory, 62
Pyttes, Allis, 134–5
  Judith, 134–5, 137
  Mychaell, 134

Quelch, William, 164
[Quiney], Judith, née Shakespeare,
  105–6, 108
  Thomas, 11, 105

Rabbett (Ralbett), [Michael], 82–3
Radcliffe, Robert, Earl of Sussex, *see* Sussex
Rapers, Alice, 45
Ravenscroft, Thomas, 112–13
Raworth, Robert, 198
Raymond (Raymod), Devonishe, 102–3
Rayner, Margaret, 99
Raynoldes, *see* Reynolds
Read (Reade), Edward, 220
  George, 195
  James, 116
  John, 111–12
Redford, Bartholomew, 50, 52
  Henry, 50, 52
  John, 52
Redinge, Joseph, 153

Reeve (Reve), Ralph (f. of Ralphe), 110
  Ralphe, 109–10
Reignalles, Reignalls, Reignoldes, *see* Reynolds
Resert, *see* Sissers
Reynolds (Raynoldes, Reignalles,
  Reignalls, Reignoldes, Renaldes,
  Rennoldes, Renolds, Reynoldes)
  . . ., smith, 141
  Goodwife . . ., 66
  Jane *or* Jeane, née Browne,
    129–30; *see also* Browne
  Joan, 83
  John, 141
  Katheryn, 136
  Robert, 81, 110, 130
  Rowland, 242, 244
  William, 107
Rhodes, [John], 130–1, 182
Rice, Dorcas, née Field, 231
  John, 167–9
Rich (Riche), Eleanor, Countess of
  Warwick, *see* Warwick
  Margaret, 50
  Robert, Earl of Warwick, *see*
    Warwick
  Thomas, 224
Ricroft, Ellis, 209
  Henry, 209
  Jane Alsop, formerly, *see* Alsop
Ringsted, Robert, 54
Rissers, *see* Sissers
Robins (Robbins), Cicely, née Sands,
  formerly Browne, 129–30,
  178–9; *see also* Browne
  John, 133
  William, 81, 129–30, 178–9
Robinson, Christopher, 227
  Elizabeth, formerly Gunnell,
    8, 28, 201, 201–2; *see also*
    Gunnell
  John, 8, 116, 201, 202, 234
  John (s. of John), 202
  John, of Blackfriars, 107
  John, of Stratford, 108
  Richard, 6, 114, 125, 128, 224

Rodenhurste, William, 47–8
Roe, William, 109–10
Rogers, John, 66
　Justinian, 170
　Robert, 170
　Ruth, 198
Ropar, William, 42
Rosse, John, 67
Rosseter (Rossiter), Dudley, 124
　Elizabeth, 124
　Hugh, 124
　Philip, 119, **123–4**, 164, 232
Rowden, John, 86
Rowley, Alice, née Coley, 138–40
　Grace, 232
　Richard, 139
　Samuel, 18, 20, 88, 90, 132, **138–40**, 232
　Thomas, 139
　William, 26, 139–40, **232–3**
Rowpe, Thomas, 78
Rubbish (Rubbidge), Elizabeth, 120
　Rowland, 111–12, **120**
Russell, Elizabeth, 152
　John, 104–5
　Thomas, 7, 107–9
　William, Earl of Bedford, *see* Bedford

Sackville, Charles, Earl of Dorset, *see* Dorset
　Thomas, dramatist, ix
　Thomas, actor, 5, **236–7**
Sadler, Hamlett, 107–8
　Katharine, 195
Saers, *see* Seares
Sage, Jonas, 189
Saiers, *see* Seares
Sames (Sammes), William, 145, 168
Sancroft, William, abp. of Canterbury, *see* Canterbury
Sands (Sandes), Cicely Browne, née, later Robins, *see* Browne; Robins
　James, 73–75, 80–1
Sanford, John, 151

Thomas, 144–5
Saunders, Roger, 66
Saunderson, Mary Betterton, née, *see* Betterton
　Peter, 158
Savage (Savadge), Alice, 85–6
　Elizabeth, 86
　Frauncis, 87
　George, 86
　Jenet, 86
　John, 86
　Richard, 85–7
　Thomas, 14, 17–18, 20, 23, **85–8**, 121
　Thomas (s. of Thomas), 86
Savill, Arthur, 3, 169–70
Say (Saye), Edward, 64, 68
Scandret, William, 234
Scott (Scotte), . . ., b. of Bartholmewe, 39
　Bartholmewe, 39–40
　Eme, 59
　Harris, 59
　Robert, 56, 59–60
Seaman, Mrs . . ., widow of Thomas, 184
　Thomas, 182–5
Seares (Saers, Saiers), George, 63, 68
　Katheren, née Brend, 63, 67
　Mercy, 67
　Samuel, 67
Serle, Alexander, 228
Shaa, Robert, 142
　see also Shawe
Shakeshafte, William, 88
Shakespeare (Shackspeare, Shackspere, Shakspeare), [Anne] (w. of William), 14, 108
　Judith Quiney, née, *see* Quiney
　Susanna Hall, née, *see* Hall
　William, 1, 7–10, 12, 14, 17, 19, 21, 29, 64, 72–4, 87–8, 94, **105–9**, 114, 121, 123, 160, 168
Shanbrooke, John, 140
Shank (Shancke, Shanncke), James, 187–8

John, 3, 5, 8, 14, 22, 26, 29,
  112–13, 140, 169, **186–90**,
  196–7, 206, 209, 235
John (s. of John), 187–9, 195, 197,
  208–9
Winifred, later Fitch, 140,
  187–9; *see also* Fitch
Sharpe, Richard, 169
Sharpham (Sharpeham), Edward,
  77–9
Shatterell, Anne, 235
  Robert, 235
Shawe, Julius, 108
Sheffarde, William, 84
Sheffell (Sheeffell), Davyd, 136
Shepard (Sheparde, Sheppard,
  Shepheard, Shepherd), . . ., 51
  Amy, 140
  Margaret, 166
  Nicholas, 103–4
  Thomas, 166, 169, 192, 194
  William, 74–5
Sheppey (Shippey, Shepey), Thomas,
  220–1
Sherman, Thomas, 120
Sherrington, John, 147
Sherry (Sherrey), Margaret, later
  Wintershall, 202; *see also*
  Wintershall
Shippey, *see* Sheppey
Shirley, Christopher, 213
  Frances, 213–14
  George, alias Sachell, 213
  James, 1, 16–17, 212–15
  James (s. of James), 213
  Mary, alias Sachell, 213
  Mathias, 212
  Standerdine, alias Sachell, 213
Sidney, Sir Philip, 58
Simons, William, 88
Simpson (Sympson), . . ., brother-in-
  law of T. Giles, 54
  Elizabeth, 124
  William, 124
Sissers (Resert, Rissers), Abraham
  147

Skeate, John, 47
Skeath, William, 156
Skip, Mrs . . ., 121
Skoryer, Thomas, 142
Slighfelde, Edward, 39
Sly (Slye), William, 18, 21, 30, 74–5,
  80–1, 234
William (kinsman of William), 81
Smaley, Mother . . ., 51
Smart, Jasper, and mother, 184
  Joan, 184
Smith (Smithe, Smyth, Smythe),
  Anthony, 169
  Christopher, 58
  Edward, 104
  John, 68
  Mathew, 182
  Rebecca, 166
  Thomas, (i) 26; (ii) 144–5
  W., 123
  Wentworth, 75–6
  William, (i) 59–60; (ii) 223–4
  Capt. William, 166
Snowe, John, 207
  Raphe, 225
Sopor, Gilbert, 223–4
Sorell, John, 207
Southcott (Sowthcote),
  John, 50, 53
  . . . (w. of John, the younger), 51
  [Elizabeth], 51
Spencer, . . ., of Lincoln's Inn, 93
  Thomas, 86
Spittie, Elizabeth, 207–8
Stanley (Standley, Stanly), . . .,
  brewer, 91
  Isabell, 127–8
Starkey, Mary, and husband, 173
Stiles (Styles), Edward, 171–2, 174
  John, 171–2, 174
Stockwood, Thomas, 121
Stonehouse, James, 121
Stowers, Edward, 45–6
Strange, Elizabeth, 135
Strangwayes, Arthur, 86
Strawbridge, Nicholas, 224–5

Strelly, Margaret Brend, née, later Zinzan, *see* Brend
Stretch, Richard, 145
Strong, Ellinor, 218
Stubbes (Stubbs), Richard, 66, 228
Sturges, Robert, 213
Sturt, Edward, 195
    Ursula, 120
Styles, *see* Stiles
Sussex, Robert Radcliffe, Earl of, 149
Sutton, . . ., preacher, 100, 117, 119
Swainestone, Katherine, 129
Swanne, John, 121
Swanston (Swanstone), Elizabeth, 205
    Eyllaerdt, 169, 195–7, **205–6**, 235
    John, 206
    Sarah Wilson, née, *see* Wilson
Sweeteser, Mathew, 151, 153
Sweetman, Ellen Honyman, later, 190–1
    John, 191
Swinburne, Henry, 12, 15, 18, 21, 24, 28–30
Swinnerton (Swynnerton), John, 118–19
    Thomas, 119
Symonds, Thomas, 139
Sympson, *see* Simpson

Tailer, Tailor, *see* Taylor
Tallis, Thomas, 42–3
Tarlton (Tarleton), Helen Barnard, née, *see* Barnard
    Katherine, 9, 57
    Phillip, 57–8
    Richard, 3, 7, 9, 26, 28, **57–8**
Taylor (Tailer, Tailor, Tayllor, Taylour), Adam *or* John, 197
    Edward, 121
    George, 77
    John, 100
    John *or* Adam, 197
    John, tailor, 226
    Joseph, 125, 128, 169
    Margaret, 79
    Thomas, 103
Thompson (Tompson), Grace, 235
    John, 169
    Robert, 170
    Samuel, **235**
    Thomazin, 130
Thornley, Frances, 50
    John, 50
Throckmorton (Throkmorton), . . ., 102
    Arthur, 197
Thrope, Thomas, 54
Tilney, *see* Tylney
Tipsly, Anthony, 79
    Edward, 79
Tod, Camilla, 100
Tomlin, Mary, 118
Tompson, *see* Thompson
Tonson, Richard, 240–2, 244
Tooker, Charles, 194
Tooley, Nicholas, alias Wilkinson, 7, 17–18, 20, 22, 27, 73–4, 114, **124–8**, 145, 160, 234
Torperley, Nathanael, 140
Totnell, James, 203
Tourneur, Cyril, 6
Towne, Ann, 89–90
    John (b. of Thomas), 88
    John (cousin of Thomas), 88
    Thomas, 20, 24, **88–90**, 132, 140
Tracy, Dorothy, 218
Travers, Henry, 210
Treat (Treate), Robert, x, 97–8, 163–4
Treherne, William, 67
Tribbeck, William, 86
Trice, Thomas, 210
Trigg (Trige), William, 66–7, 188, 190–1
Trott (Trote), . . ., 54
    Raphe, 77
    Rosse, 77
Tucke, Margaret, and husband, 198
Tucker, John, 118
    Sara, 118
    Thomas, 118

Tufton (Tuffton), Sir Humfrey, 200
Tunstall, James, 64–5
 Jane, 64–5
Turner, Anthony, 6
 Drew, 6
 Edmund, 6
 Winifred Burbage, née, see
  Burbage
Tuttell, Richard, 181
Tyler, Richard, 107–8
Tylle, Edward, 39
Tylney, Edmund, 17–18, 20–1, 29,
 81–3
 Fredericke, 82
 Thomas, 82–3
Tyrry, . . ., widow, 137

Underwood, Burbage, 6, 142–4
 Elizabeth, 142–4
 Isabel, 142–5, 184, 186
 John, 6, 18, 24, 125, 128, 142–5,
 157, 160, 168, 186
 John (s. of John), 142–4
 Thomas, 142–4
Urrick, John, 200

Vaseley, Elizabeth, 205
Vaughan (Vawghan), Griffith, 82
 Katherine, 217
 Magdalene, 217
 Thomas, (i) 39–40; (ii) 192
 Walter, 217–18
Vavasour (Vavesour, Vavisour),
 Andrew, 44
Venge, Thomas, 50
Vincente, Thomas, 59–60

Wade, Mrs . . ., 40
Wagstaffe, Henry, 204
 Mary, 204
Waight, Richard, 147
Wainwright, Bridgett Cherson alias,
 see Cherson
Waldock, Jane, 152
Walker, Mother . . ., 51
 Alice, 125

Ann, 149
Robert, 45
Robert, of Bredsoe, 149
William, 107
Wall, Luce, 113
Waller, Dorothy, 169
 Elizabeth, 169
Walley (Wally), George, 177
 Henry, 177–8, 197–8
 James, 177
Wallis, Francis, 71
 Robert, 162
Walpole, Samuel, 176
Walsingham, Sir Francis, 7, 58
Walters, Marie, alias Adlington, 102
Walwyn (Walvyn), William, 202
Wanham, Frances, 164
 Francis, 164
Warde, Peter, 153
Warner (Warnar), Allice, 99
 John, 18, 97
Warren, Simon, 97
Warter, George, 213
 John, and wife, 213
Warwick, Eleanor Rich, Countess of,
 207
 Robert Rich, Earl of, 207–8
Waspe, William, 56
Wassell, Stephen, 58
Waterson, Simon, 116–17
Watkinson, Hugh, 86
Watson, Henry, 46–7
 Joan, 46
Webb (Web, Weebb), Agnis, 70, 75
 Anne, née Jones, 204
 James, 73, 75
 John, 204–5
 William, 73, 75
 William (s. in law of Arthur
  Wilson), and wife, 207
Weekes, Peter, 94
Weller, Daniel, 109
Welshe, . . ., mercer, 59
Wentworth, Thomas, 12
West, William, 12, 18–19, 24, 26,
 28–9

Westcott (Westcote), ..., 50
  Andrew, 50
  Elizabeth, 50–1
  Francis, 50
  George, 50
  Robert, 50, 52
  Roger, 50
  Sebastian, 20, 26, 29, 48–53, 55
  Sebastian (s. of William), 50
  William, 50
Whattcott, Robert, 108
Wheatley (Wheatlye), Andrew, 147
  William, 117
Wheaton, Elizabeth, and daughter, 159–60, 184, 186
White, ..., sister of Jane Poley, 66
  Bennet, 111
  Richard, 210
Whithorne, Tymothy, 73–4
Wibard, Edmond, 65
  Fabian, 65
  Frances, 65–6
  Henry, 65
  Jane, 65
Wiborow, see Wyborowe
Wicks, Henry, 204–5
Wiggan, Humphrey, 195
Wildey, Humfrey, 217
Wilkes, Mary, 193
Wilkins, Catherine, née Fowler or Fowles, 231
  George, 231
Wilkinson alias Tooley, see Tooley
Williams, Mary, 80
Willicke (Wyllike, Wylly), Otto, 39–40
Willingesun, Goodwife ..., 70
Wilson (Willson), **Arthur**, 17–18, **206–8**
  Joseph, 205–6
  Judeth, 207
  Katherine, 207
  Marie, 207
  Sarah, née Swanston, 205–6
  Thomas, 2, 26
  William, 100–1

Winchester, Thomas Bilson, bp of, 102, 104
Winge, John, 121
Wingfield (Winkefelde), Anthonye, 44
Wintershall, Margaret Sherry, later, 233
  William, 202
Witter, John, 75
Witton, Richard, 130
Wood (Woode), Marye, 155; see also Clarke alias Wood
  Richard, 54
  William, 118
Woodall, Mary, 209
Woodford, Abraham (or Woodfall or Woodhall), 122–3
  Robert, 195
  Stephen, 121
Woodgate alias Lee, Darkas, 163
Woodson, Ann, 173, 175
  Leonard, 175
Woodward, Joan Alleyn, née, see Alleyn
Woolwright, Agnes, 114, 116
  John, 116
Worsop (Worsopp, Worsoppe), Elizabeth, née Giles, 172–5
  John, (i) 147, (ii) 171, 173
Worth, Blandina, 209
  Elizeus, 209
  Ellis, 92, 164, 179, 182, **209–10**
  Frances, formerly Holcomb, 210
  Jane Alsop, née, formerly Ricroft, see Alsop
  Katheren (d. of Elizeus), 209
  Katheren (w. of Elizeus), 209
Wotton, Mrs ..., 87
  John, 86
Wrench (Wrinch), John, 70–2
Wright, John, 3
  Richard, 208–9
  Richard, carman, 65
Wyborowe (Wiborow), **Agnes**, 176
  Thomas, 176, 179
Wyllike, Wylly, see Willicke
Wythers, John, 121

Yardsley, Richard, 123
Yarington (Yarrington, Yarranton),
  Dorrotie, 145
  Robert, 145–6
  Thomas, 145

Young (Yonge), Darby, 162
  Robart, 160

Zinzan, Margaret Brend, née Strelly,
  later, *see* Brend
  Sir Sigismond, 64, 68